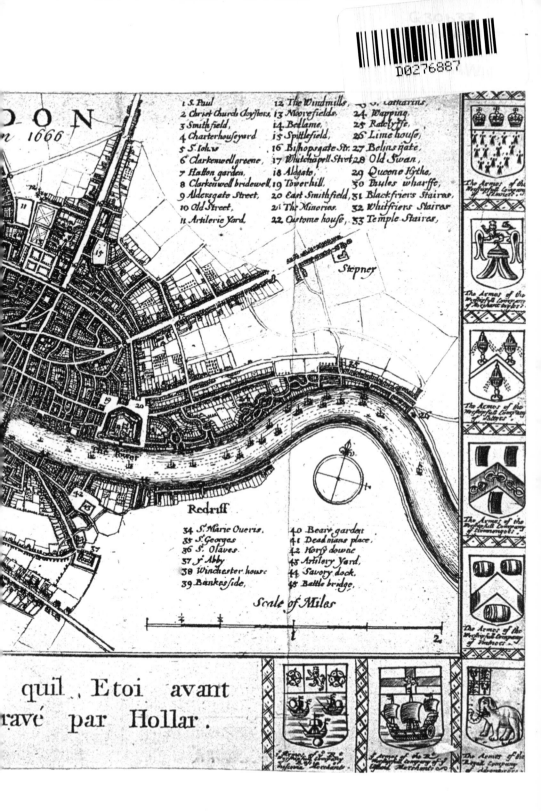

THE PHOENIX

THE PHOENIX

St Paul's Cathedral
and the Men Who
Made Modern London

LEO HOLLIS

Weidenfeld & Nicolson
LONDON

First published in Great Britain in 2008
by Weidenfeld & Nicolson
© Leo Hollis 2008

3 5 7 9 10 8 6 4 2

A CIP catalogue record for this book is
available from the British Library.

ISBN 9 780 297 85077 9

Typeset by Input Data Services Ltd, Frome

Printed and bound in the UK by CPI Mackays, Chatham ME5 8TD

The Orion Publishing Group's policy is to use papers that
are natural, renewable and recyclable products and made
from wood grown in sustainable forests. The logging and
manufacturing processes are expected to conform to the
environmental regulations of the country of origin.

Weidenfeld & Nicolson

An imprint of the Orion Publishing Group
Orion House, 5 Upper Saint Martin's Lane
London, WC2H 9EA

An Hachette Livre UK company

www.orionbooks.co.uk

Let us now praise famous Men, and our fathers that begat us; who were honoured in their generations, and were the glory of their Times. Of these let his Memorial be blessed, who builded the House and set up a holy Temple to the Lord: – who rais'd up our ruins again.

THE BOOK OF ECCLESIASTICUS

To Nigel and Michael

CONTENTS

PART FIVE
London Reborn

ILLUSTRATIONS

View of the fire from across the Thames © Museum of London /
   Bridgeman Art Library
John Locke, by Herman Verelst, 1689 © Wellcome Library
Nicholas Barbon insurance policy, 1682 © Bridgeman Art Library /
   Guildhall Library
View of the City of London from the north, *c.*1730 © Guildhall Library
Interior view of St Paul's by Jacobus van der Schley, 1736 © Guildhall
   Library
Sir Christopher Wren by Sir Godfrey Kneller, 1711 © National Portrait
   Gallery

While every effort has been made to trace copyright holders, if any have
inadvertently been overlooked, the publisher will be happy to acknowledge
them in future editions.

INTRODUCTION

A walk through London, its many streets and neighbourhoods, reveals an image of modernity and speed, of shining surfaces and traffic – the city presents itself as a vision of the future. London has many layers, however, and behind the steel and glass the past remains. In Leadenhall Market there is a barber's shop where, in the basement, the excavated stones of a first-century Roman forum are preserved. Beneath the courtyard in front of the Guildhall stand the remains of an amphitheatre which, once the Romans had left in the fifth century, became the location for the local council meeting place, the 'folksmoot' of the Anglo-Saxon tribes. The Guildhall that reigns above the surface has been the powerhouse of the City since the twelfth century. The history of the city is also preserved in its street names: medieval Cheapside, the central market within the city walls, is still fed today by Bread Street and Milk Street, and leads to Poultry, where chicken farmers and greengrocers sold their wares.

As the layers of the past are peeled away one by one, the city becomes plural. London is a city that has reinvented itself upon the remains of the past. In no time was this more spectacularly true than in the seventeenth century after the Great Fire of 1666, and nowhere was it more resplendent and emblematic than in the resurrection of St Paul's Cathedral. This extraordinary physical rebuilding of London went far beyond the stones of the city but encompassed its organisation and the layout of the streets, the bustle of the markets and the energy of the offices that still dominate in the financial centre of the Square Mile.

The seventeenth century marked not only the rebirth of London but also heralded the formation of the modern city, which has been replicated or translated in cities throughout the world. The questions that were first asked in this period are the problems we still deliberate today. What is government? How do we know whether something is true? Are there fundamental laws to the universe? How does one judge the morality of profit or the existence of God? *The Phoenix* is the story of how the seeds of this modern metropolis were first sown.

London in the middle of the seventeenth century was a paranoid city, gripped by anxiety and holy prediction. Visitors descending from a coach at one of the many inns that dotted the outskirts were thrust into the heart of the throng with their first step; arriving on the murky tidal waters of the Thames by boat, they would have passed the north bank, a huddle of medieval roofs and Gothic spires that rose up into the fog-filled air. On the waterfront, wooden houses clung to the riverbank, where sailors and merchants busied themselves among the wharfs and warehouses that stored the goods of the world. Disembarking before the elegant London Bridge, the travellers would have been be forced to jostle past the crowds waiting for passage, and found themselves assaulted by the maelstrom of city life.

Away from the riverbank and into the heart of the City, the streets were filled with carts and bodies; everything was in motion. The sky would have been almost masked by the eaves of the houses that bent over the street like praying monks. Smoke filled the air so that 'her inhabitants breathe nothing but an impure and thick mist, accompanied with a fuliginous and filthy vapour, which renders them obnoxious to a thousand inconveniences'.[1] Progress on foot was slow and precarious; some of the main streets had been paved but most were packed with sharp Kentish cobbles, the smaller routes lined with compact earth so that rain turned the road to a quagmire of greyish mud. The way was littered with refuse. During a rainless summer when the water had not rushed the waste down to the Thames the city stench was pervasive.

For the last half-century, London had been on the verge of collapse. The City had become so large that it could no longer be controlled by the medieval institutions of guilds, aldermen and the annually elected Lord Mayor. New neighbourhoods had sprung up outside the walls that circled the 'Square Mile', which had stood as both the defence and limits of the ancient city. By the 1640s over two-thirds of the population were outside in the burgeoning suburbs. The rise of the 'masterless men' – merchants who settled in the suburbs, and who did not wish to receive the privileges and obligations of the freedom of the City – was a hazard to the political economy of the capital.

Between 1642 and 1648, London became the focus of a civil war that tore the kingdoms of England, Ireland and Scotland apart. The capital had been the 'nursery of the present rebellion',[2] yet within a few years the city became the victim of its own creation: when the Crown was replaced by an uneasy republic, London lived in fear and trepidation. The revival of order, the Restoration, delivered a hope of return to the *status quo ante*, but such dreams were a chimera.

In 1665, five years after the Restoration, which had been welcomed with joy and hope, the capital was struck down by a plague that claimed nearly a hundred thousand lives. The following summer, England was hit by such a debilitating drought that the Oxford rivers ran dry. Apart from one freak hailstorm in July, there was no rain. By midsummer, London's wooden buildings were so dry that they were all but kindling. It would take only a spark to turn the city into a conflagration.

On the evening of Sunday, 2 September 1666, a fire had started in a baker's shop in Pudding Lane on the north side of the river, yet fires were an inevitable hazard in London's huddled streets. This time, however, something must have gone terribly wrong for on the following afternoon, as the diarist John Evelyn was leaving his home at Sayes Court in Deptford, the sailors in the King's Depot just across his garden wall were being mustered to fight the flames. Later that day, Evelyn travelled to the south shore of the Thames at Bankside and could not believe the scene in front of him. It was as if he was watching a terrible masque of destruction, and he searched for a way to explain what he had seen: 'The noise and cracking and thunder of the impetuous flames, the shrieking of women and children, the hurry of people, the fall of towers, houses, and churches, was like a hideous storm ... the ruins resembling the picture of Troy.'[3]

Earlier that day the smoke obscured the sun, making night of day, yet as dusk fell Evelyn recorded flames so high that night had been banished and the dusk turned 'light as day for ten miles round about, after a dreadful manner'. The sky was crimson, as if the air itself were alight, 'like the top of a burning oven'. But Evelyn could do nothing but mourn for his city: 'oh the miserable and calamitous spectacle, such as haply the world had not seen since the foundation of it, nor can be outdone till the universal conflagration thereof'. Before him the whole of London was ablaze, the flames leapt from street to street and house to house. The firestorm was indiscriminate, consuming everything in its path. As he looked helplessly on, he sighed, 'London was, but is no more.'[4]

In particular Evelyn watched the City's cathedral, St Paul's, which loomed over the capital from its summit on Ludgate Hill. At this point it still stood above the flames; but by Tuesday the cathedral's massive nave was packed with refugees who presumed that the sheer size of the structure of St Paul's, if not God himself, would protect those who sought sanctuary. The local merchants had rushed to store their goods under the walls while the printers whose shops clustered in the churchyard and the nearby Stationers' Hall had packed the crypt church, St Faith's, under the main cathedral with their paper, scripts and works.

By midday the fire encircled the churchyard. Within hours the cathedral was completely surrounded and almost everyone who had sought sanctuary within the stone walls was forced to take desperate flight. All except an old woman safely escaped; her charred remains were found three days later cowering against the Gothic bulk of the cathedral, alongside the burnt husks of dogs. The ancient site of St Paul's shared its fate with the city it had symbolised for a thousand years.

The inferno raged for four days, stoked by an easterly wind. The flames gutted 13,200 houses, eighty-seven parish churches and six consecrated chapels, and all the major sites of trade and government: the Guildhall, Royal Exchange, Customs House, Sessions House, fifty-two Company Halls, the prisons at Bridewell and Newgate, Wood Street and Poultry Compters, three city gates and four stone bridges. Fortunes were lost in an instant, plate melted into the earth and valuable spices vaporised with a heady odour. The printers of Stationers' Hall alone lost £2 million worth of books and paper in the burning crypt of St Paul's, and the wharves of Thames Street lost £1.5 million worth of wine, tobacco, sugar and plums.

London did, however, survive. Within sixty years the metropolis was transformed – for out of the ashes of the Great Fire a modern city was reborn. By 1708, within the span of a single lifetime, London was the largest city in Europe. The metropolis became the furnace of international trade and would launch the British Empire, establishing itself as the financial centre of the world, and also laying the foundations of the English Enlightenment.

Five men were at the heart of the metropolis's resurrection – Sir Christopher Wren, John Evelyn, Robert Hooke, John Locke and Nicholas Barbon. Their stories begin two decades before the Great Fire. Growing up during a time of upheaval and insecurity caused by the ruptures of the English Civil War left an indelible mark upon the rest of their lives. The war was a political and religious conflict that split the nation; its causes were varied but for the five men, their childhood experiences produced a shared determination to search for a new society.

John Evelyn was born the son of English gentry and as a child foresaw a life of leisured privilege underpinned by a firm belief in the established order of King, Church and duty. Christopher Wren grew up within the higher echelons of the Anglican Church. Robert Hooke's father was also a cleric, although at the opposite end of the religious hierarchy. As young boys Wren and Hooke imagined for themselves a traditional education and a lifetime in the service of the established Church. John Locke was the son of a rural lawyer in Somerset while Nicholas Barbon's father was a well-regarded London artisan as well as a preacher in a Puritan conventicle, forced to worship in secret, fearful of persecution.

For each of the five boys, the Civil War dismantled the stability of ordered life and replaced it with insecurity and uncertainty. During the turbulence Wren's and Hooke's fathers were deprived of their livings and named as 'delinquents'. John Evelyn sought solace away from England and set out on a voyage that would change his life for ever. Barbon's father became one of the leading rabble-rousers of the new regime; while Locke saw in the horrors of the conflict the seeds of the ideas that would inform the rest of his life. Although fighting between the Cavaliers and parliamentary forces ended in 1648, the struggle between the many factions that emerged in that time continued for over half a century, and in the attempts and failures to transform and heal the nation, modern Britain was born.

Yet the shock waves of the war and its aftermath were not just felt within the traditional orders of society but were also a cultural and intellectual turning point for the nation. The attacks of the Civil War called into question not just the person of the king but the whole structure of the hierarchy. On what was the king's authority based? As the Crown was attacked, so were the institutions that supported it – the church and universities – which had had a monopoly on truth. New notions and paths to knowledge were proposed and out of the cauldron of the Civil War a philosophy developed that heralded the birth of modern science. This pursuit of a new truth had ramifications in countless areas of the post-war society, and London became the principal crucible for all these many debates.

Unexpectedly, the devastating fire of 1666 proffered life-changing opportunities for each man. In the immediate aftermath, the very nature of the city was debated and planned. Was London to be rebuilt upon the foundations of the old or was a new urban model to rise up? For Robert Hooke, Nicholas Barbon, John Locke, John Evelyn and Christopher Wren, the fire offered a blank slate on which to recreate the modern city.

Robert Hooke was the man most responsible for the new shape of London immediately after the fire. As the exemplary man of ideas, he measured and recorded the extent of the burnt capital in a new way, reducing the medieval huddle to comprehensible science; the revived capital would thus be defined by mathematics. Hooke's work on the rebirth of the city went hand in hand with his own work as a New Philosopher at the heart of the recently established Royal Society, founded to promote the values of experimentation and data.

For men like Nicholas Barbon, the destruction of the city offered another form of opportunity: speculation, profit and the rise of the builder. Barbon began his business within the fabric of the metropolis, rebuilding burnt houses inside the city walls, yet as his ambitions grew he would espy new opportunities beyond the 'stones', developing the suburbs of Soho, Spitalfields and Holborn. Through his pursuit of profit Barbon set out the shape of the modern city and debated the emerging ideas of business and economics.

John Locke arrived in London after the conflagration and became embroiled in the political and intellectual upheavals of the day. Alongside his patron, Sir Anthony Ashley Cooper, he focused his mind on questions of trade and property, religious toleration, the foundations of government and the principles of knowledge. These ideas set Locke on a dangerous course that threatened sedition, persecution and exile, but his theories had a powerful impact on the intellectual formation of the capital.

For John Evelyn, the fire allowed a man of ideas and taste to expose his ideas to the most rigorous of proving grounds. Too often discounted as an ingenious dilettante, Evelyn gained a powerful role through his writing and his friendships with significant figures, as well as his own work at his home in Sayes Court, in questioning and debating the shape of the English imagination. What did it mean to be English? How did this express itself? What was the relationship between trade, religion, reason and culture?

This rise of London and the rise of the modern nation are best reflected, however, in the rebuilding of St Paul's Cathedral and Christopher Wren's own attempts to create a modern architecture. Wren first came to prominence as an astronomer at the forefront of a new view of the world that promoted reason, experiment and scientific method. When he became an architect, however, he redefined his discipline, adapting a modern approach that he had learnt in the laboratory to the traditional art of design. St Paul's Cathedral was a testament to this new method.

Throughout the seventeenth century the identity of St Paul's represented the fluid and volatile story of a nation as it came to grips with a period of immense transformation. Today, the cathedral remains an icon of London, the location of national celebration and solemn ceremony. As one stands under the dome of the cathedral of St Paul's, looking up into the hemisphere of stone that hangs above the silent halls and Whispering Gallery, the hush is broken by the cycle of daily worship and the shuffle of the 800,000 tourists that visit each year. The dome itself is perfectly proportioned; shafts of light flood the internal space from above; a single shard, like the eye of a telescope, is emitted from beneath the lantern at the apex of the cupola, the light almost becoming the building itself.

St Paul's is a complex mixture of ideas and moments frozen in stone. The cathedral stands at the centre of this narrative as an emblem and reflection of a period in the history of London, and Britain. By the beginning of the eighteenth century, only four decades after the Great Fire, St Paul's had been cast anew. In October 1708, Christopher Wren stood in the churchyard in front of the cathedral, looking up towards the summit of his creation, as the final stones of the cathedral were being laid. According to the family history, *Parentalia*: 'The Highest or last stone on the top of the lantern was laid by the hands of the Surveyor's son, Christopher Wren, deputed by his father.'[5]

It was the culmination of a lifetime's work and a permanent testament to the generation that had lived through civil war, plague, fire, revolution and political turmoil yet had been able to recast the surrounding metropolis as a modern capital.

PART ONE

Children of the Civil War

The Greatest Hazard that
Ever the Youth of England Saw

THE NURSERY OF OUR PRESENT REVOLUTION

On the wide open space in front of the Palace of Westminster, crowds began to gather, congregating in defiance and fear, in response to the gathering clouds of war. As December 1641 turned to January 1642, one Londoner observed: 'The war was begun in our streets before the King or the Parliament had any armies.'[1] Inside the city walls, the churches were being raided while rumours of revolution ran through the streets. The fear of Catholic plots bubbled below the surface and in the autumn of 1641 tales of Irish brutality against honest Protestants filled the citizenry with dangerous fears. Nobody knew what would happen next.

London was a dangerous place, particularly for the young. According to the writer Henry Peacham, in *The Art of Living in London*, written in 1642, as the tumult gathered outside, the metropolis was 'a vast sea, full of gusts, fearful-dangerous shelves and rocks, ready at every storm to sink and cast away the weak and inexperienced bark with her fresh water soldiers, as wanting her compass and her skilful pilot'.[2] The heralds of the wars were devastating and immediately struck at the heart of nine-year-old Christopher Wren's family life.

Wren was born in East Knoyles, Wiltshire, in October 1632, and was baptised, as was common in those uncertain times, with the name of his elder brother, who had died the previous year. His forty-three-year-old father was rector of the parish. When Christopher was six, his father was invited into the royal household as Chaplain in Ordinary to Charles I, a position of prestige that drew the family into the royal court and the Wrens to Windsor, where they took a house on the edge of the fortified walls of the ancient castle. Within the grounds of the palace, the family mixed with the grandest families of the nation. The Wren family typified the Establishment, secure in the knowledge that the world was ordered in a fixed hierarchy that placed God, king, bishops and nobles at the top of the social tree. This tree was about to be attacked root and branch.

In the autumn of 1641, the young boy made the short journey from Windsor to London, where he was to study at Westminster School. One of the most ancient and esteemed colleges in England, it had been formed in the early years of the Reformation by Henry VIII, as a bastion of English humanism. Under the stern headmaster, Dr Busby, the school was a forcing ground for some of the cleverest pupils in the land. Yet as young students pursued their education, events were roiling up on the open ground between the college and Westminster Hall, the home of Parliament.

Two days after Christmas 1641, there was a scuffle between the king's guards and men in the crowd who had hurled insults as the bishops had entered Parliament. The next night, under the cover of darkness, buoyed up by the aggressive war of words, the crowd took their aim at Westminster Abbey, a symbol of royal orthodoxy, at the western edge of the yard. The crowd first attacked the windows, then the doors, and soon violence erupted. The pupils of Westminster School were drawn into the maelstrom and, in preparation, muskets and 20 pounds of powder were stockpiled in the college grounds. As the more belligerent members of the crowd began to batter at the abbey door, pupils helped to defend the nearby ancient monument from the rabble.

Wren's family was synonymous with the Anglican Church that faced the brunt of the attacks: his uncle, Matthew Wren, was the Bishop of Ely, one of the leaders of the ecclesiastical hierarchy. The bishop was a target for pamphlet writers, his name ringing through the streets of London, demonised in numerous broadsides for waging a war against the godly and the subject of calls of condemnation within the Houses of Parliament. In August 1641, the month in which his nephew came to Westminster to study, the bishop was accused by Parliament of idolatry and superstition. The following year he was placed in the Tower of London, where he would remain for the next eighteen years.

Young Wren's stable world was shattered as the nation hurtled towards war. Three days after the assault on Westminster Yard he wrote a New Year's Day letter to his father, pledging: 'What in me lies I will perform as much as I am able, lest these gifts should be bestowed on a ungrateful soul. May the good God Almighty be with me in my undertakings and make

good to thee all thou most desirest in the tenderness of thy fatherly love.'[3]
What that future might be no longer seemed so secure or certain.

In the autumn of 1642, with Charles I's declaration of war, the Wren
family shared the deprivations and fears of the whole nation. In October
parliamentary forces, led by one Colonel Fogg, entered the castle at
Windsor. The Wrens lost everything, their possessions broken or stolen,
and they were evicted from the castle deanery, which was later ransacked.
To add insult, the soldiers also broke open the door of the chapel and
requisitioned all the plate. Only the jewels that had been buried by the
dean under the treasury were saved, hidden until 1660.

When the Wrens returned to the family home at East Knoyle they were
not welcomed by the parish. They were vilified by the local Puritans, who
smashed the decorations in the local church, paid for by the dean, and
reported the family as dangerous 'delinquents'. Eventually the dean was
deprived of his office and the family was sent packing again. They finally
found refuge in Bletchingdon, near Oxford, in the house of William
Holder, who had recently married Wren's sister, Susan.

During the first stirrings of the war, London embraced revolution. The
crowds that had gathered in Westminster Yard stoked the capital's passion
and paranoia as the streets filled with militia, and local wards and guilds
practised their drill. Inside the City the king's supporters wore red ribbons,
provoking brawls in the streets. Processions entered the capital from the
counties to add their support to Parliament's cause, while a ring of earthworks, the 'lines of communication', was dug that would unite and protect
the City and Westminster for the first time in London's history. The
construction was a communal activity, undertaken by the citizens themselves – women, children and even the Lady Mayoress. The trenches
encircled the capital, and were lined with forts that not only stood as
lookouts against advancing armies but also as surveillance 'against the
tumults of the citizens and to ensure a prompt obedience on all occasions'.[4]
No one was sure where the threat would come from. All buildings that
stood against the City walls were pulled down to act as a second line of
defence. The open streets leading to the suburbs were barricaded; batteries
of artillery were placed and regularly fired in anticipation.

In August, Charles I finally revealed his hand and declared war on his
subjects. From his camp in Nottingham he marched south, hoping to enter
London before winter. On 13 November 1642, the army reached within

five miles of the capital, and on the open ground of Turnham Green village the royalist forces faced the London militia, bolstered on all sides by citizens who had come to defend their homes; 24,000 men, women and children in all. Defences had been built overnight by anyone who could hold a shovel; they had been fed and told to pray devoutly as they clustered among the houses and alleys of the village, making any attack by royal cavalry impotent. Then Philip Skippon, commander of the London militia, rallied his men, the last line of defence before the City. In the face of the ragged opposition the king faltered, and called a retreat.

He would never get so close to London again. Charles had lost his capital, and among the most prized possessions that he was forced to abandon to his enemies was St Paul's Cathedral. The cathedral was the City's centre of worship, a mother to the citizenry in times of peril, once the second-largest church in the world, a font of London pride. It was also the most powerful symbol of royal rule, where the power of the Crown, through the ministry of the clergy and bishops, rose high above the diurnal jostle of urban life. Yet as the spectre of civil war descended upon London, all the sins of 'the Troubles' were writ large upon the City's church.

For a decade before the war the architect Inigo Jones had been working on the cathedral, transforming the Gothic bulk into a new vision of the king's power. It was unlike anything seen in England before. The Gothic body of the church built in the thirteenth century had been cut away and reclad in white Portland stone so that it shone in the daylight. The buttresses and chapter had been classicised, transforming the traditional form into an ancient basilica. From the west end of the churchyard, five vast black marble steps led up to a classical portico that appeared more Roman than English. On the rusticated western front, ten vast Corinthian columns, 4 feet wide and nearly 60 feet high, raised a long stone entablature high over the church doors, upon which stood two statues of James I and Charles I. In Jones's new temple the powers of God and kings were intertwined as sole guardians of the ancient powers of the capital.

The Puritan opposition that was emerging from secretive conventicles within the city thought otherwise. To them, the renovated cathedral was more proof that the king wished to crush their godly cause, and deliver England to Rome once again. They were swift to exact their retribution on the place that represented everything they had come to fear. In 1642, there were riots in the churchyard as the mob attempted to break the organ. From the small workshops of the printers that clustered around the

Inigo Jones's St Paul's Cathedral

cathedral over two thousand pamphlets were published from all perspectives of the conflict – royalist, Puritan, independent. The uncensored flood of newsprint directed, informed, damned and stirred the city in its escalating crisis. The metropolis began to rustle with handbills, broadsides, ballads and news. The streets of London became a Parliament of Paper in which every citizen had an opinion.

Following the first skirmishes of the Troubles in 1642, work on St Paul's was abandoned and Inigo Jones was forced to flee the city, his vision incomplete. St Paul's was left to the threats of the enemy, and pamphlets found in the churchyard fed rumours of the link between the royalist conspiracies and the 'vast useless pile'. The cathedral was systematically stripped, the scaffolding that Inigo Jones had hastily left around the central tower was torn down and sold to a Colonel Jephson, the removal of the supports causing part of the roof to collapse, while the classical west portico was vandalised. The marble flooring in the southern transept was pulled up and sold to wealthier citizens, before the area was turned into a sawmill, while the lead was stripped from the roofs. The grand temple had been reduced to a dilapidated barn. Such attacks were followed by questions as to whether the whole cathedral should be destroyed.

As the Puritans secured their grip upon the capital, the cathedral clergy was expelled and the organisation of the Anglican Church dismantled. The bishop's lands were sold to pay for the parliamentary army. By 1643, 80 per cent of the London clergy had been dragged from their pulpits and replaced by Puritan preachers. Briefly, the eastern end of St Paul's was used as a pulpit so that the nave echoed with Puritan harangues as various congregations were given free use of parts of the cathedral for their radical worship. On the outside, along the southern wall of the building, a series of lean-to houses were built that became a huddle of shops and stalls. The organ was finally destroyed in 1644 and all the treasures confiscated. The deanery was turned into a prison and its gold and plate melted down. The restoration fund to pay for Jones's renovations was used to pay the army's arrears.

For some, the insult to the cathedral was almost too much to bear. The symbol of hope for the nation had been desecrated: 'you would be amaz'd at the genius of this age', wrote John Evelyn later,

> that should suffer this goodly and venerable fabrick to be built about and converted into raskally warehouses, and so sordidly obscur'd and

defac'd that an argument of greater avarice, malice, meaness, and deformity of mind cannot possibly be expressed ... O! how loathsome a Golgotha is this Pauls! England is the sole spot in all the world where, amongst Christians, their churches are made jakes and stables, markets and tippling houses, and where there are more need of scorpions than thongs to drive the publicans and money changers.[5]

As the Troubles began, Westminster School gained a reputation as a dangerous refuge for royalists within London, and as one MP would later tell Oliver Cromwell, 'it would never be well with the nation until Westminster School was suppressed'.[6] There, Christopher Wren, the young son of a known royalist family, was no longer safe and joined the family in their retreat in Bletchingdon, Oxfordshire, which, for the time being, remained in royalist hands. The manor house was converted into a garrison for 200 soldiers until, on 24 April 1644, parliamentarian forces led by Oliver Cromwell arrived at the gates, and the local royalist commander, Sir Francis Windebanke, surrendered without a shot being fired.

Wren's future was precarious in an age of escalating insecurity; yet he was not alone. Throughout the nation a whole generation of children was faced with uncertainty, as the preacher Thomas Fuller warned: 'Many parents which other wise would have been pelicans, are by these unnatural wars forced to be ostriches to their own children, leaving them to the narrow mercy of the wide world.'[7] Ordinary men were forced away from their workshops, drilled and marched on to battlefields where artillery, the stampeding charge of the cavalry, musket shot or pike wreaked havoc. Women and children were not exempt from the violence. Many wives stood by their men, loading muskets, defending the walls or digging fortifications, and, on occasion, even leading companies into the field. Towns were garrisoned to the point of starvation before the troops moved on, then became victims of plundering, 'violence and rapine' by enemy soldiers; cattle was rustled; local churches broken and desecrated.

THE NARROW MERCY OF THE WIDE WORLD

Off the south coast of England, on the western tip of the Isle of Wight, lay the small fishing village of Freshwater where the curate of the parish, John Hooke, a lowly foot soldier in the Anglican hierarchy, made a humble living. The office included a small thatched cottage with a parlour, study, kitchen and three bedrooms, security enough to marry and grow a family. On 18 July 1635, Hooke's second son, Robert, was born. Robert's background could not have been more different from the young Christopher Wren's; both, however, would be transformed by the experience of war.

A sickly baby, young Hooke was not sent away to a wet nurse as was the custom but remained at home, and 'his chief food was milk, of things made thereof, and fruits, no flesh in the least agreeing with his weak constitution'.[8] Although he had an older brother, Robert was a solitary child. His lessons were abandoned by his father when the boy, tortured by headaches, was too weak to concentrate. John Hooke was initially hopeful that his second son would follow him into the Church, but when Robert was only seven years old, the Troubles arrived on the island almost as soon as they were born in London. For the Hooke family, these deprivations were sorely felt. The father lost his living, was banned from preaching the Anglican orthodoxy, and was fined, like Dean Wren, as a 'delinquent'. But under the control of the parliamentary army, life on the island may have been difficult but it was also relatively stable. For the young Robert, this became a time of solitude and exploration.

While Wren and Hooke were forced by their circumstances to face the vagaries of the wars at home, John Evelyn chose exile, escaping the dangers of the Troubles for the relative safety of the Continent. Born in 1620, the second son of a wealthy Surrey gentleman, he had had a coddled childhood, was put out to a wet nurse, pampered by his overprotective mother, and was then sent away to an indulgent step-grandmother in Lewes, Sussex. He endured an indifferent education, gaining the rudiments from a friar in the parish porch, Latin from a private French tutor, and then, at nine years old, he attended the local 'petit' school. When his father offered to send the boy to Eton, the fragile youth refused, fearing the brutal reputation of the school. He then went to Oxford, going up to Balliol College at seventeen, where he did not distinguish himself to any extent.

As a directionless, if rich young man, he was of 'a raw, vain, uncertain, and very unwary inclination'.[9] He made his way to London and failed to find his feet in law, and from his rooms at the Temple he watched as 'London, and especially the Court, were at this period in frequent disorders'.[10] At home, Evelyn faced another devastating prospect: his father was dying. After a long year of suffering from dropsy, Richard Evelyn passed away at Wotton on Christmas Eve, 1640.

At the dawn of the new year, after following his father's hearse to the burial ground, Evelyn would feel 'left to his own conduct in a conjuncture of the greatest and most prodigious hazard that ever the youth of England saw'.[11] In a portrait of the young lawyer, painted just before he left on his travels, he appeared haunted. Somewhat too uncomfortable in himself, he had inherited his mother's aquiline nose, and, by all accounts, her weakness for melancholy. For this fragile youth, mourning the loss of his father, appalled by events around him, there seemed only one course of action. He was fortunate to inherit some land in his father's will which would fund his travels, but as a recognised royalist his property was under the constant threat of confiscation. On 15 July 1641, he sailed to the Spanish Netherlands, taking his first, cautious step to 'see the world', partly to search for answers, partly to avoid the realities of life at home.

For Wren there was no escape from the insecurity of a life haunted by the devastations of the wars. Unlike Evelyn he was too young to take hold of his own future and had to rely on the protection of family. For Hooke, the attacks upon his home restricted his childhood to the small world of Freshwater. For all three young men, the present situation was dangerous, but more uncertain still was the future. Such threatening circumstances struck deep for all three, not just in terms of expectations, but also at the bedrock of their identity. Who were these young men, if not the sons of their fathers?

At the family home, far away from Westminster, Wren's education continued under the careful eye of his father – who had gained some minor renown as a virtuoso, interested in heraldry, astronomy and mathematics – as well as his brother-in-law, William Holder, a clergyman who had also lost his parish in the wars, and had a reputation as a modern thinker with a particular interest in medicine. In such informal circumstances Wren was instructed in reverence for the classic texts, the study of rhetoric and a powerful sense of public duty. In addition, Holder would lecture his charge on newer subjects that were only just emerging from the traditional scholastic curriculum – mathematics, physics and anatomy. It was these very lessons which would offer Wren a new path for the future.

When the young boy fell dangerously ill in 1646, Holder sought advice from a coterie of distinguished men who had gathered within the royalist camp stationed at nearby Oxford. The university had been commandeered by Charles I, who had temporarily set his court-in-exile among the colleges. Among the king's advisers and generals were a group of physicians and thinkers, including George Ent, Thomas Willis, Ralph Bathhurst and Charles Scarburgh. In times of war, a good doctor was always needed, and these men were the finest in London, leaders of the Royal College of Physicians. They were more than bone-crackers and bleeders, rather they were pioneers of a new frontier who congregated around the light of William Harvey, the king's physician.

In 1628 Harvey had discovered that blood, pumped by the heart, circulated around the body. This radical observation, the result of numerous experiments, seemed to go against all medical common sense, which still regarded as gospel the ancient humoural theory first promoted by the Greek Galen. At Oxford, Harvey and his disciples were able to continue their studies, exploring the new frontiers of anatomy and medicine while also patching up the wounded. The mass of cadavers slain on the field allowed for previously impossible experiments and explorations.

Holder was fortunate to be able to bring his sick brother-in-law, Wren, to the attention of Charles Scarburgh, who had arrived at Oxford as a member of the royalist army but had already gained a reputation as a mathematician and physician. He had become Harvey's pupil and, in 1645, had jointly written *De generatione animalium*, an early work in embryology that first suggested that all animals germinated from an egg. While looking after the sick Wren, Scarburgh was clearly impressed with his patient and when, in June 1646, Oxford fell to the parliamentary army, it was arranged that the youth accompany the physician to London. Wren would be safer in the capital under Scarburgh's patronage than he would remaining with the family in Oxfordshire.

For Wren, the meeting with Scarburgh offered a transformation of fortunes. Despite his being a royalist, the parliamentary powers seemed more than willing to forgive a physician who had skills that could be used in the capital, and Scarburgh was readmitted into the College of Physicians in 1648. At the physician's house in London the student Wren exchanged the role of patient for that of technical assistant and intellectual apprentice. Alongside Scarburgh, he would explore a panoply of ideas that offered hope in an age of anxiety.

Yet Wren was changed not only by his association with Scarburgh but also by the city itself. London, caught in the whirlwind of the Civil War, was the eye of the transformations that were sweeping the nation. From his house in Holborn, the poet and Puritan polemicist John Milton watched in wonder, and in his tract *Areopagitica* exhorted his readers to:

Behold now this Vast City; a city of refuge, the mansion house of liberty;
... the shop of warre hath not there more anvils and hammers waking,
to fashion out the plates and instruments of armed justice in defence of
Beleagur'd truth, then there be pens and heads there, sitting by their
studious lamps, musing, searching, revolving notions and ideas where-
with to present, as with their homage and their fealty the approaching
Reformation.[12]

London had become a forge of new ideas. The printing presses flooded
the city with notions and concepts while demands for revised ways of
looking at the world were preached from the city pulpits as the very basis
of civil society was put into question. The wars had destroyed the accepted
order of things – the king had been defeated on the battlefield, the established Church was broken, its ancient sites raided and smashed, and in the
enthusiasm of the conflict questions of politics, religion and knowledge,
the relationship between men and masters, were all being debated as if the
slate had been wiped clean.

Perhaps the most dangerous factor of all that rose from the battlefields
was Oliver Cromwell himself, a parliamentary MP who had campaigned
for the godly cause from the beginning of the conflict. Cromwell was a
Cambridgeshire gentleman who, during the 1630s, had had a religious
conversion; hearing the voice of God, he repented his sinful ways and
dedicated his life to the strict regimen of Puritanism. When he arrived in
London as a Member of Parliament in 1640 he found common ground
with the radical faction that were most critical of the king.

No mean orator, Cromwell made his true voice heard most clearly once
the war began in 1642. By 1644, the conflict was at a stalemate, both sides
inflicting wounds but no fatal blow. That winter Cromwell proposed
the nation's first professional army, the New Model Army. The newly
regimented forces, ruthlessly drilled on the battlefield, were a revolutionary
fighting corps consisting of 22,000 soldiers, provided with uniforms and a
soldier's catechism.

Cromwell recruited on merit, not status. Within these ranks he found
the zeal to fight for what became called the 'good old cause', which combined not just a determination to dominate on the battlefield but also to
fight for a new future. Cromwell allowed his men to follow their own
religious conscience and the ranks became a hotbed of independent thinkers who preached ideas of reforming society, demanding that the word of

the scriptures define the polity. The incautious whisperings of republicanism intertwined with ideas of a society preparing for Judgement Day. Nonconformist sects like the Ranters, who believed that God's grace was found in every creature, the Levellers, who fought for 'natural rights' for every man, and the Diggers, who wished to reclaim the land from private ownership, rose from within the army, and sought to recast the natural order of things, from the bottom of society to the top, in order to form a new paradise on English shores. Beyond the ranks Quakers began to enter the streets, naked, refusing to acknowledge any authority but the divine.

Radical visions of the shape of society, just as dangerous as Cromwell's sword, were also emerging from other quarters. The question of social order was not exclusive to debates on power – the role of the king, the legitimacy of government, the relationship between God and his people – but focused on the very fabric of society itself. The ancient hierarchical order was to be probed and re-examined, to determine not just what shape it should be, but what society's very origins were. The royalist mathematician, Thomas Hobbes, would spend the decade in exile constructing his philosophical reimagining of civilisation. In his disturbing vision of the world, *Leviathan* (published in 1651), Hobbes perceived man and society through the new-found laws of physics. He reduced man to his very basic needs: the individual was driven by appetites that were in constant conflict with others. Society without laws or authority was, he proposed, a vicious anarchy.

Hobbes's work was a damning interpretation of what the philosopher saw in front of him. Human nature was selfish and needed to be controlled, and his sole response to the rampant anarchy of the times was the licence to create strong government. The rule of law was the brutal barrier between peace and cataclysm. In his condemnation of society, he called for a new political philosophy based upon an unbreakable contract between subject and sovereign; subjects must give up their power to the sovereign or face destruction. His vision struck fear into all sides of the Troubles.

In contrast to Hobbes's harsh vision of authority, the émigré Samuel Hartlib had arrived in England in the 1630s with dreams of converting the nation to an alternative idea of community. Hartlib was an educationist with a 'pansophic' mission, and he campaigned for the power of universal learning to bring salvation to the present divisions. As the Civil War progressed, his aspirations combined with his Puritanism to form a millenarian forecast: the conflict would deliver a new society and a policy of nationwide education that would herald the Day of Reckoning. Thus he established his 'Office of Address', and in his 1641 book *Macaria* he envisaged a scientific society that would unite the people in knowledge, and bring forth paradise through learning.

The Civil War not only raised questions of political and social order, it laid siege to the very foundations of knowledge itself. The authority of ideas had thus far been intertwined with the institutions that governed and promoted them: the king, the Church, the universities. In addition, the printing presses had been heavily censored to ensure uniformity. But as these came into question, so too did the certainty of the truth they preserved: the great centres of learning were now seen as dangerous nurseries of Anglicanism, strictly regulated to promote the status quo. Until the onset of the wars, there had been only one opinion allowed, yet this was shattered as the nation splintered into a myriad of factions.

Knowledge was the study of God's creation on earth, but few could agree on how and what was permissible. For some Truth was to be rediscovered in the words of the Bible and the study of divine texts; for others, the physical world alone was the object of study without recourse to the sacred or ancient. This could only be understood by a new method of measurement, a certitude found outside the authority of Man and regulated by impersonal mathematics.

When Scarburgh and Christopher Wren arrived in London they entered into the heart of this debate, and at the physician's house the pair continued to explore their shared interests in the anatomical work of William Harvey. Together, they studied in preparation for a series of lectures at the Surgeons' Hall, developing Harvey's notion that the body was an organism that could be understood as a mechanical whole. Scarburgh was particularly interested in the way that muscles worked, and through a series of experiments and lectures attempted to discern their parts and functions. These early studies instilled in Wren a lifelong fascination with exploring the mysteries of the human body. In addition, Scarburgh introduced Wren to a system of thought that explored the whole world in the revolutionary light of a mechanistic philosophy. Out of the insecurities of the times Wren discovered an unexpected solace in the certitude of science.

In London, the two anatomists would also seek out fellow searchers of new knowledge. Every Thursday evening Wren, Scarburgh and a handful of others met and debated, hoping to uncover the rudiments of an English natural philosophy, a new way to observe and understand the world. As one of the principal members of the group, the mathematician John Wallis would remember: 'I had the opportunity of being acquainted with divers worthy person, inquisitive into Natural Philosophy and other parts of Humane Learning; and particularly of what hath been called the New Philosophy or Experimental Philosophy ... Our business was (precluding matters of theology and State Affairs) to discours and consider of Philosophical Enquiries, and such as related thereunto.'[13]

The informality of these meetings was crucial to the success of the project, for the participants ranged from medicine to the cloth, from professional scientists to virtuosi, Puritan and royalist. From the outset it was decided that no political and religious divisions should interfere with the dynamics of the group and that the pursuit of reason was above any personal or political animosity, just as the new ideas went in search of a method that objectively measured the world. In this aspiration lay the hope that Truth could be discovered beyond the violence that tore at the nation, beyond national boundaries or religious sentiment. Mathematics, the reduction of all things to height, weight, volume and velocity, was the universal measurement outside human influence, and would perhaps act as the oil to becalm the turbulent waters of the age, for was not a measure of wheat the same whether it was weighed by a Puritan, a Digger or a bishop?

As these ideas were debated within the group, Wren began to develop his own talents for mathematics, problem-solving and instrument-making. Up to this moment, the study of mathematics was seen to be beneath a gentleman, yet times were changing. Dean Wren and William Holder were more open than most to the benefits of scientific knowledge, but Christopher's talent for the subject was something unexpected. Previously a young man would have learnt the minimum of calculation in order to run his estate. The London merchant would undoubtedly have needed more in order to master navigation and accountancy. Yet what the young Wren was studying was on a different level, and even at an early age he acquired a remarkable talent for seeing the elegant certainty of the practical application of mathematics: the uses of geometry, trigonometry and the various rules of measurement.

He soon became an inventor of gadgets and machines that opened up the exploration of the world. At Surgeons' Hall, learning his lessons from Scarburgh as well as the debates at the club, Wren built a series of pasteboard models to express the functions of the muscles. The models were a stunning visual recreation of the discoveries that had been revealed on the dissector's table, and would be the first example of Wren's talent for discovering visual means to represent complex ideas. By the time he was sixteen, it was claimed that Wren had already 'enriched astronomy, gnomic, statics and mechanics with brilliant inventions, and from that time has continued to enrich them'.[14]

Within the group of London philosophers Wren was evolving into a practical, inventive young man, who had the potential to make new discoveries himself. He was soon encouraged by his new patrons to translate the mathematical tract *On Geometrical Time Measurement*, a treatise on sundials by William Oughtred, the leading English mathematician of the day, and inventor of the multiplication sign, 'x'. The exercise signalled his arrival among the small group of English philosophers. The master was complimentary to his junior, claiming in his preface: 'in truth [Wren] is one from whom, not vainly, to look for great things'.[15]

THE BEST OF EDUCATION

Wren had discovered an unexpected hope at the elbow of Charles Scarburgh and the informal group of New Philosophers. John Evelyn, however, sought 'the best of education, which everyone so decrying at home, made me conceive as a commodity only to be bought from a far countrie'.[16] He spent much of 1641 wandering through the Spanish Netherlands, adjusting his eye to the strangeness of Renaissance Europe, and soon fancied himself as something of a connoisseur.

He returned briefly to England in 1642, and this only convinced him further that it would be difficult to remain at home, so he sailed to France in November 1643. He made his way to Paris, found accommodation and, as a matter of courtesy, visited the King's Resident, Sir Richard Browne, in Paris, the nerve centre of the royalist community abroad. Paris was at that time the greatest city in Europe, larger even than London, with a population of nearly 400,000, and over the last fifty years it had begun a process that was transforming the medieval capital into a modern city.

Here, Evelyn, delighting in his first view of the city, commented on the elegance of the design, 'The confluence of the people and multitude of coaches passing every moment',[17] astounded by the theatre of the flow of goods and people that made up a thriving capital. At the beginning of the century Paris had been a decaying huddle unchanged for over a century, creaking under the pressures of degeneration. Following a vicious religious civil war, the new king, Henri IV, wanted a new capital at the centre of a modern nation to serve as an emblem for his progressive reign. He wanted to attract merchants and trade to enrich the nation, so he set about bringing order to the urban chaos and reignited the city with a series of projects. In the words of the poet Corneille, 'An entire city, built with Pomp, seems to have arisen miraculously from an old ditch.'[18] The new city would be brick or stone and would follow the strict classical orders of architecture, designed on principles of symmetry, proportion and geometry.

Henri introduced the clarity of the Italian piazza to Paris as the archetypal civic space. At the centre of the Pont Neuf, the finest bridge in Paris, which spanned the River Seine at its widest point and was completed by Henri in 1601, sat the Place Dauphin, a triangular geometric space lined with robust houses, an exquisite composition of open ground, architecture, perspectives and statuary. Ordered and elegant, Paris would claim the glories of ancient Rome as the capital of Europe.

The attempts to improve the city were combined with efforts to stimulate the economy. When Henri devised the Place Royale (later renamed Place des Vosges) in the Marais district beyond the medieval city walls, he also planned to encourage a domestic silk industry. The square, twice the size of Place Dauphin, was a perfectly ordered space lined with uniform housing, created to develop a home market in luxuries. Silk, gold and silver thread weavers were tempted to the square from Italy to launch Henri's new drive in technology and trade. By the time Evelyn had arrived the Place had become so popular that it attracted as many aristocrats as merchants.

Following the death of Henri IV in 1610, the transformation of Paris continued under his son, Louis XIII, and his chief minister, Cardinal Richelieu. Louis, easily distracted from issues of town planning by his love of the hunt, still encouraged the growth of the city. In 1614 the first steps were made in developing the Ile de Vache, later called the Ile Saint Louis, as a new suburb outside the city walls. It was the first Parisian project built on a geometric grid and was completed in the 1640s, just as Evelyn arrived. The scheme was controlled by the Crown but built with private investment and offered a new direction in urban design that created not just modern housing but new neighbourhoods. Five new bridges were built as testament to the Crown's desire for Paris to be a city in which trade and goods moved unimpeded.

The city was expanding: the urban growth was planned and ordered with the streets paved and the uniform façades of the houses adding grandeur and a sense of unity to the city. The new suburbs of St Germain on the left bank of the Seine had been converted from palace gardens into neat streets of housing and markets for the burgeoning labour market that flooded into the city. The rush to modernity encouraged Evelyn to write: 'Not only are there houses that are being built daily, but entire streets, so beautiful, so regular in form.'[19] To speed up the expansion of the city the architect Le Muet standardised design by composing a catalogue of house building, *Maniere de bien Bastir pour toutes sortes de personnes*, published in 1623, which reduced all vernacular architecture to four main types, advocating an accepted style that aided urban growth and elegant uniformity.

Evelyn also found that while Paris was slowly being classicised, a new style was being introduced into the city. The baroque, synonymous with Rome, was the signature style of the Counter-Reformation, and had been adapted and encouraged in Paris by the successive cardinals close to the throne – Richelieu, who had died in 1642, and his successor, Mazarin. In the first half of the seventeenth century, over seventy new institutions for sects such as the Jesuits, Oratarians and Sulpicians were built in this flamboyant style. Both cardinals wished to claim France as the dominant Catholic nation in Europe.

The finest example of the baroque, the Val de Grâce, was begun in 1645, the year after Evelyn's arrival, by the French architect, Mansart, imitating Michelangelo's dome of St Peter's. In the same style, the chapel at the Sorbonne University rose into the Parisian sky with its impressive dome. The two buildings did not just replicate the masterpieces of Rome but attempted to equal them with their own idiosyncratic French inter-pretation of the baroque, absorbing the 'frozen music' of the Italian style without abandoning national traditions. Paris was reinventing itself before Evelyn's eyes, and he would later record: 'I have seen Naples, Rome, Florence, Genoa, and Venice: all stately cities, and full of princely fabricks; but then I compare the extent, [Paris] infinitely excels any else in Europe.'[20]

In October 1644 Evelyn finally left Paris for the Mediterranean port of Marseilles, and began the second leg of his travels in Italy. Following the peace between France and Spain in 1630, the Giro d'Italia was emerging as the itinerary of the educated traveller south of the Alps, making Evelyn one of the pioneers of the 'Grand Tour'. At Genoa Evelyn had his first encounter with Italian architecture, particularly the rich merchant houses along the Strada Nuova, which had come to define this famous port. Guided by a merchant called Thomson around the port, with its impressive defensive wall circling the harbour, Evelyn sketched and took notes in his copy of Peter Paul Rubens's *Palazzi Antichi e Moderni di Genova*. After Genoa he travelled to Pisa, where he marvelled at the leaning campanile. And then finally to Leghorn (Livorno), with its notorious slave market in the piazza that had inspired Inigo Jones's Covent Garden in London, completed just before the wars.

Arriving in Florence, the cradle of the Renaissance in the fifteenth century, Evelyn was fixated on only the latest examples of the Medician splendour. By now the over-diligent student was behind schedule, and had time only to do the bare minimum with the promise to return later. He did manage, however, to go shopping, and purchased pieces for his own collection, a cabinet of wonders, which he had begun on his trip to the Netherlands. The nineteen pieces of inlaid marble would become the first in a large array that became a lifetime's obsession. It is also likely that he purchased his first cabinet in the same *pietra commissa* style (which is today in the Victorian and Albert Museum, London). The cabinet of wonders would be at the centre of Evelyn's emerging self-image as a virtuoso, the Renaissance man who sought to understand the world. Here he would place his collection – stones, medals, rare gems and folios. He soon developed a voracious eye for almost anything that could be studied or hoarded.

Rome was a revelation, and Evelyn hired a 'Sights-man' and 'began to be very pragmatical'.[21] For the first month of his visit he systematically rattled through every major site in all the quarters of the city, then spent a second month revisiting specific sites, seeing more in two months than any other Englishman of his day. Each afternoon he made his way to the Piazza Navona, graced by Bernini's newly completed fountains, where he would hunt down medals, pictures and curiosities from among the market stalls.

The young explorer was fortunate to be in Rome at the same time as Roger Pratt, a royalist exile who was also experiencing his own transformation. Pratt would return to England and become one of the finest architects of his generation. Thus far Evelyn had come to appreciate the marvels of the past and the Renaissance. On 19 November 1644, however, Evelyn and Pratt visited the cathedral of St Peter's within the Vatican. Here, the young travellers would appreciate the whole history of modern architecture in one building.

Michelangelo's powerful Basilica was beyond explanation: 'far surpassing any now extant in the world, and perhaps Solomon's Temple, excepted, any that was ever built'. Within a single building, the Italian maestro had 'restored the then lost art of architecture'. While the masters of the Renaissance had attempted to parallel the marvels of the ancients, Michelangelo aimed to surpass them. He seemed to be able to empower the very air that surrounded the building, manipulating the light within the church, turning the space of the building from a single harmonious chord into a polyphonic cascade of music. In particular, Michelangelo had revolutionised the cathedral's cupola. The dome now sat high upon a barrel of columns, a peristyle, which pushed the cathedral high into the Roman sky, forcing Evelyn to marvel: 'all of stone and of prodigious height is more in compass than that of the Pantheon (which was the largest amongst the old Romans, and is yet entire)'. The scholar who had been taught to revere the classical age now found himself standing in front of an idea that went beyond the imagination of the ancients, constructed in solid stone and of impossible scale.

Evelyn also discovered that Michelangelo's innovation had been developed further, and within Evelyn's own lifetime, in the work of the Italian architect Giovanni Bernini, the master of modern baroque. Inside the cathedral Evelyn and Pratt marvelled at Bernini's *baldacchino*, a twisting bronze canopy that stood above the central altar, which 'form a thing of that art, vastness, and magnificence, as is beyond all that man's industry has produced of the kind',[22] completed in 1633, as well as a number of exemplary statues, including the tomb of Pope Urban VIII in golden bronze and marble. Bernini had interpreted the classical rules of architecture in extraordinary new ways, for while Michelangelo's mannerist manipulations of classical form had adapted the sense of space within a building to give it a dynamic unity, Bernini further reconfigured the ancient grammar. As a sculptor, he had made the marble seem alive; in his architecture, he constructed the same vitality and movement on a vast scale to make it seem as if the building itself were breathing.

Now running out of money, Evelyn needed to reach Venice. Here he booked passage to the Levant to visit Jerusalem, but at the last minute his ship was requisitioned by the Venetian authorities. It was a stroke of good fortune for he then moved on to Padua, famed for its university, the most advanced intellectual institution in Europe. Evelyn planned to study there for a few months but gained a degree in a day, his honorary matriculation sealed with an invitation to lunch.

It was at Padua, two days later, that he was fortunate to meet Lord Thomas Howard, twenty-first Earl of Arundel, fourth Earl of Surrey and first Earl of Norfolk, England's most prominent Catholic nobleman, who had escaped the wars in 1642. The Howard estate, Albury, was close to Evelyn's family home in Surrey and the two had met before. Evelyn admired not just the aristocrat's power but also his role as the leading collector and patron of the arts in England. To Evelyn, Arundel personified the English virtuoso. From an early age the aristocrat had travelled abroad and he, alongside Inigo Jones, was responsible for the introduction of European arts into England. Acting as patron to the painters Rubens, Van Dyck and the Bohemian etcher Wenceslaus Hollar, he became the ideal on which Henry Peacham modelled *The Complete Gentleman*. His collection at Arundel House in the Strand, London, boasted ancient marbles, a magnificent library, numerous drawings by da Vinci, as well as work by Holbein, Titian, Dürer, Raphael and Bruegel. Arundel was the very essence of taste and learning.

In Padua, Arundel took Evelyn for an informal stroll around the city, visiting a number of famous sites, retracing the path that he had taken many years earlier. In 1614 Arundel had studied here with Inigo Jones and the aristocrat was now offering a lesson given to him by the finest English architect of the age. Staying with the Arundel group for a few days, Evelyn observed the life of a man of taste and his entourage, even if in the desperate straits of exile from the Civil Wars at home. This brief sojourn would fix Evelyn's mind on the life of a virtuoso, and it seemed that Arundel, the greatest living British aesthete, was passing his baton to his younger companion.

Evelyn took his leave from his mentor, requesting an itinerary for his journey, and made his way from Padua to Milan, across the Alps towards Geneva, and then once more to Paris. Once in Paris Evelyn would claim that 1647 was a time for relaxation and leisure. He learnt High Dutch, Spanish, brushed up his dancing, attended chemistry lectures with 'Monsieur Lefebure' and played the lute, while satisfying his bibliophilia in the many bookshops of the city. He also devised a scheme for a perpetual motion engine that, inevitably, came to nothing.

Yet it was not all leisure for Paris was beginning to fill with the Cavalier exiles who were fleeing England as the situation at home became increasingly hopeless. Inevitably Evelyn was drawn into the exiled community surrounding the King's Resident in Paris, Sir Richard Browne, whose home was at the heart of the desperate clique.

Amid the mayhem, however, Evelyn fell in love with Browne's daughter, Mary. She was only thirteen when she was betrothed to Evelyn, who perceived in her 'a Gravity I had not observ'd in so tender a bud'.[23] An English rose cultivated in French soil, the young girl spoke French and Italian, and studied mathematics and drawing. They married in a small ceremony in June 1647 at the Resident's Chapel in Faubourg St Germain, the only place in Paris that conducted the Anglican service. Marriage would force Evelyn to end his travels and focus his attention upon his own fortunes. It was time to return to England.

Throughout his voyages he had been able to keep abreast of news from home, but by 1647 the situation in England was looking dire and Evelyn was determined to protect his family affairs. He returned to London after four years' absence to find that the king was under armed guard at Hampton Court and that Cromwell's New Model Army, like an invading force, had entered London and turned the capital into a garrison. As the royalist cause faced defeat, Parliament was threatening loyal landowners with confiscation. Evelyn feared that he would lose his inheritance by remaining in Paris.

Once again the fate of London could be seen writ large in the suffering of its cathedral. At the centre of the city St Paul's, Inigo Jones's proud monument to the Stuart dynasty, had been requisitioned by the New Model Army. To add to the insult, the cathedral choir had been converted into a stable. One surprised visitor even witnessed a foal's birth; it was then promptly baptised in the font while complaints from locals in the church-yard did little to quell the boisterous behaviour of the militia.

On visiting his family at Wotton, Evelyn also took the opportunity to visit the imprisoned king, whom he found in unexpected good humour, at nearby Hampton Court. The king would not remain a prisoner for long, however, for in November 1647 a plot was hatched in which Charles escaped from the palace in disguise, slipping through the gardens to horses that would carry him to freedom. The escapade was a disaster. Even though the troop made good their flight, they had not decided on where to flee. In the end, they chose the Isle of Wight, which was still in the hands of the parliamentary army, and so it was that the king was soon recaptured.

Under arrest but not imprisoned, Charles was free to travel around the island and a court-in-exile soon evolved. The royal carriage was ferried to the island to help him explore his reduced dominion, and the king even had time to commission his royal portrait painter. At leisure in Carisbrooke

Castle he made overtures to Parliament for peace, while flirting with a local girl, Jane Whorwood. He was frequently visited by the local gentry and on occasion rode out in the royal coach. On such a trip he visited the estate of the landlord of Freshwater, Sir John Oglander, where he would undoubtedly have met the local curate, John Hooke. The king even found time to visit the local school where the young Robert studied.

In such unlikely circumstances he began to plot his last desperate attempt to regain the crown. While Charles gave the impression of leading a life of leisure, he was surreptitiously fanning the dying embers of war. Unlikely visitors, lords from Scotland, began to appear at the castle while secret negotiations were conducted behind closed doors. As a consequence, a second Civil War broke out during the summer of 1648. The conflict was short and bitter, rendering Charles powerless in the hands of his enemies. While still on the island, he was placed under strong guard and commanded to prepare to travel. On 1 December 1648, on its way to the port, Charles's retinue passed through the village of Freshwater as it began its fateful journey to London.

The final death knell of the royalist cause had been tolled. The king had been captured and the struggle lost. For Robert Hooke the defeat of the king was soon followed by a more personal blow when, in October, loyal John Hooke died – some suggested by his own hand. Like Wren, the young Robert Hooke would never speak of his childhood. At the age of thirteen, he was fatherless, and the cause that the curate had preached to the young boy was in tatters. The boy would have to make his own future, and learn to use his talents to survive in the wider world. That winter he sailed to London with an inheritance of £50 and the recommendations of family friends. But the capital in which Hooke arrived was in turmoil once more.

'FEAR AND TREMBLE AT IT, O, ENGLAND'

John Evelyn returned to London to protect the family property but he also travelled on more intellectual business, and arrived in the capital in search of a printer who would publish his first book, an exercise in French translation. Under the thinly disguised pseudonym Phileleutheros, he presented de la Mothe le Vayer's *Liberty and Servitude*, which demanded: 'If therefore we were once the most happy of subjects, why do we thus attempt to render our selves the most miserable of slaves?'[24] The book was published in January 1649 and placed Evelyn in danger, for he had added a preface for which he 'was severely threatened'.[25] That same month, his question gained a particular poignancy.

On the morning of 30 January, King Charles rose early. Outside St James's Palace the pale winter sun hung over the frozen city, which had been battered by harsh winds that winter. Attended by his courtier Thomas Herbert, he prepared himself for his execution. He asked for two shirts to guard against the cold; he did not want to be called a shivering coward by his enemies. For the next five hours he dressed himself, attended a service given by the devoted Bishop Juxon and took the holy sacrament. Outside, London was also in preparation: at Westminster School, Dr Busby locked the school gates and gathered his pupils in the school hall in prayer. In Whitehall, a crowd gathered in front of the Banqueting Hall. Before its plain classical façade a scaffold had been erected, and a block and a velvet-lined coffin lay in wait for the executioner and his victim.

At noon, a troop of guards arrived at St James's Palace to escort the king on his final journey. Before departure the king retired to his bedchamber for a last mouthful of rough bread and a glass of claret, sharing a few words with the bishop. He picked out a white satin nightcap with Thomas Herbert, who broke down and confessed he could go no farther. Herbert and Juxon then both knelt in tears and kissed the king's hand one last time. Charles then turned, ordered the door to be opened and commanded the guard to proceed to Whitehall. Just before three o'clock, as he crossed the grand room of the Banqueting Hall, a crowd gathered beyond. The mob that had jeered him following his trial now stood in hushed prayer.

He traversed the wide open space of the hall beneath the painted panels of the ceiling above, which had been commissioned from the painter Peter Paul Rubens. The panels displayed a series of images celebrating the monarchy of the Stuart dynasty, and there in the central panel, the 'Apotheosis of James I', Charles's father, who had spent his whole reign defending the Divine Right of Kings was shown ascending to heaven. Charles made his progress towards a window at the far end of the room, and then stepped out on to the scaffold beyond.

The King of England, Scotland and Ireland then addressed the crowd, gave instructions to the executioner, undressed, and handed his cloak to Bishop Juxon, with whom he exchanged final words. He placed his head on the block, said his prayers, then thrust out his hands as a signal for the axe to fall. His head fell with one swing of the executioner's weapon as the crowd let out a monstrous groan. The king was dead, a royal martyr was created and the whole nation was condemned to an uncertain future. As the Puritan preacher Ralph Josselin warned: *'fear and tremble at it, O, England'*.

The king's death was the final act in a most devastating drama. The Civil Wars of 1642–8 had torn the fabric of English society. Yet out of this turmoil, unexpected opportunities, and a new future, would emerge.

2

A Quiet Revolution

After Charles's execution Cromwell rose to power unimpeded and began to dismantle the established hierarchies of Church and state, declaring England a Commonwealth by abolishing the monarchy and the House of Lords. But breaking the ancient scaffolding of the old social order proved easier than constructing a new polity. In the first years of the interregnum the nation was victim to a series of unexpected hazards and political lurches as it groped in the constitutional darkness, searching for a new legislature, which Evelyn mournfully called the 'un-kingship'.

The destruction of power in the single person of the king caused the splintering of authority. The demolition of the single established Church – the hierarchy of Crown, bishops and ministers – was replaced by a rash of sects. When a single solution to the constitution was sought, multitudes were offered. The laws of censorship were abandoned and, once again, London was clogged with opinions and pamphlets. In a desperate attempt to refocus power, Cromwell himself flirted with the possibility of assuming the role of the monarch, taking the title Lord Protector, a king in all but name.

In such uncertainty, London was not the place for a known royalist to make his name. The doors to power had been firmly shut and there was to be no clemency for those who had stood on the wrong side of the conflict. For Christopher Wren and Robert Hooke, education, therefore, was the key to finding a role in the new regime. They would be joined by John Locke, who would be profoundly changed by his experiences at university. The lessons the three students received would form the keystone of their adult lives. John Evelyn returned to England from Europe, and, hoping to find a settlement with the new regime, chose internal exile, on the edge of London, far from the centres of power, excluded from participating in the political debates that were attempting to shape the nation. The experience would be transformative for all. For here a quiet revolution was evolving, waiting for the right opportunity to declare itself to the world beyond.

AN ASSEMBLY OF MEN

After the Roundhead army had sacked Oxford in 1646, the city had fallen victim to the changing fortunes of the war. Since the victory, the New Model Army had stamped hard on the institution that had supported the king and his Church, and the pulpits were filled with Presbyterian preachers. Punishment of the colleges followed, and 'within the compass of a few weeks an almost general riddance was made of the loyal University of Oxford', effecting a widespread purge of the schools, 'in whose room succeeded an illiterate rabble, swept up from the plough tail, from shops and grammar schools and the dregs of the neighbour university'.[1] The nursery of Anglicanism was converted into a forcing ground for the new Commonwealth.

Not all the new faculty members were Cambridge Puritans, however, and among the most prominent arrivals in April 1648 was John Wilkins, a clergyman, whom Christopher Wren knew from London. Wilkins was named warden of the recently established Wadham College, a handsome Jacobean house set around a courtyard with extensive gardens. Influenced in religious matters by his Puritan grandfather, Wilkins supported Parliament during the war but was content to associate with royalists, judging men more for their interest in natural philosophy than their religious leanings.

In 1649, other members of the informal group of London philosophers joined Wilkins at Oxford: the cleric Seth Ward, a friend of William Holder and Charles Scarburgh, was named as the Savilian Professor of Astronomy; the parliamentarian code-breaker John Wallis gained the Savilian Chair in Geometry; and in 1651 Cromwell's Physician in Chief, Dr Goddard, once of Gresham College, became master of Merton College. As a result Oxford began to attract a community of like-minded scholars that congregated around Wilkins, including Dr Thomas Willis, a chemist, who had been expelled from Christ Church in 1647 but remained in Oxford and offered his own laboratory for experiments. Dr William Petty, a royalist exile studying with Thomas Hobbes in Paris, managing to live off two pennies' worth of walnuts a week, returned from penury to throw in his lot with the Commonwealth. Together they would become 'an assembly of Men who are known both at home and abroad to be the most learned persons of this Age'.[2] A 'Philosophical Club' was set up, convening every Thursday afternoon, firstly in Dr Petty's lodgings at Buckley Hall, conveniently located above an apothecary, and then in Wilkins's rooms at Wadham.

Wren arrived at Wadham in 1649 to study for his Bachelor of Arts degree, which he completed in two years; he then commenced his master's degree in 1651. He continued to indulge his fascination with the workings of the human body, learnt from Charles Scarburgh, and grew close to the royalist Dr Thomas Willis, who, alongside William Petty, gained some renown in 1651 in the case of Anne Greene, a young woman hanged for murder yet who was revived on the laboratory table. At Willis's house, Beam Hall, Wren was able to conduct his own experiments and became skilled with the dissector's knife, probing for proofs of the functions of the body and creating experiments to discern the circulation of the blood. He experimented on a number of spaniels, injecting them with various substances, and became one of the innovators of intravenous injections.

Wren had little time for more regular student pastimes. He was neither athletic nor was he likely to be one of the university gallants who grew, as caricatured by Henry Peacham, 'perfect in Spanish, French and the Dutch, that is, sack, claret and Rhenish',[3] in the three hundred or so inns and taverns of the town. It was at Oxford, however, that Wren first encountered his sole vice – coffee. One of the first coffee houses, John's, was set up in Oxford in the 1650s, and here Wren would develop a taste for the Turkish liquor that would last a lifetime. For his soul he visited the secret Anglican congregation at Beam Hall in Thomas Willis's private rooms, a known plotting house for the king's cause, although there is no evidence that he was anything more than a diligent supplicant.

Instead, John Wilkins introduced the young experimenter to the wonders of mathematics and its applications – astronomy, geometry, architecture, navigation and mechanics. Mathematics offered not just the certitude of proof but also a toolbox. Wilkins was the ideal guide for Wren's explorations. In a series of books, the master of Wadham promoted the new ideas, many of them first discovered in Europe, that set the foundation for a mechanistic philosophy. *The Discovery of a World in the Moone* (1638) questioned the nature of Earth as distinct from the other planets, concluding that the laws that defined this planet worked for the whole universe, offering the possibility that proofs uncovered in the laboratory would be true everywhere and that one set of rules ran throughout the heavens. Wilkins's second work, *Discourse concerning a New Planet* (1641), defended Nicolaus Copernicus's observations of a heliocentric universe, in which the planets revolved around the sun. By accepting Copernicus's ideas, Wilkins was then able to defend later discoveries, including Johannes Kepler's elliptical path of the planets' motion, as well as the observations of the moon as a satellite around Earth conducted by the Italian Galileo Galilei.

Wren was also encouraged to turn his focus on numerous theoretical problems that evolved out of these conclusions. Following new Continental theories that had been popularised by Wilkins's *Mathematical Magick* (1648), Wren explored the ideas behind the emerging Mechanistic Philosophy. Thus far he had speculated on the possibility that the new discoveries that he made at the dissecting table might be connected to the laws that governed the whole universe. William Harvey's experiments on the circulation of the blood around the body suggested that the organism could be interpreted as a mechanism. Could the planets and stars also be read by the same method?

The Mechanistic Philosophy proposed that everything be reduced to the properties of physical matter – body – and the variety of forces that affect the substance's state – motion. Alongside Wilkins, Wren discovered that experiments could be created to measure weight, volume and geometric shape, as well as to define the laws of the forces that influenced them: acceleration, friction, gravity. If the philosophy was correct, Wren hoped to find that the whole universe could be commanded by the same laws of nature.

Wilkins's ideas posed vital questions for the foundations of a new system of knowledge: could the laws that underpinned the universe be discovered? What was the method that would allow such revelations? On what authority would this new knowledge rest? More importantly, these questions were asked by an author who was also a member of the Church. Wilkins passionately believed in the potential for modern astronomy to encourage new freedom of exploration beyond the narrow confines of received authority. Nonetheless, this new way of thinking was founded on the desire to uncover the ways of God and the belief that the New Philosophy would allow Man to see His purpose more clearly.

The young Wren, invigorated by this permission to seek out new territory, also found the means to put these lessons to the test, and he was a regular student at the lectures of astronomy professor Seth Ward. Under Ward, the Savilian lectures became the first forum in the university where the demonstration of experiments rather than the repetition of set texts became the norm. Wren soon learnt that truth was to be found by practical demonstrations, seen with his own eyes, rather than by accepting the second-hand authority of others.

Outside the laboratory and lecture halls, Wren began to have ambitions of his own, and after 1652, when an observatory was set up on the tower at Wadham, he began to view the heavens, focusing his lens upon the moon. From his desire to chart the stars he learnt the art of lens-grinding and the new technology of telescopes, that 'seems to be the only way to Penetrate into the most Hidden Parts of Nature'.[4] This passion was further fuelled when Wren happened upon the *Selenographia* by the Dutch star-gazer Hevelius, the last in a long tradition of scholars who measured the skies with the 'naked eye'. The young astronomer thought that he could do better and with his telescope began to collect data.

Thus, he absorbed the lesson that while mathematics could be used to discern the laws of nature it could also be applied to create technology to aid the search. At this early stage of exploration, the pursuit of new knowledge and the development of technology were inseparable, and Wren showed a preternatural instinct for this 'mixed mathematics', as his mind moved from astronomical instruments to all forms of gadgets and inventions. He devised a machine to write double, a weaving loom, studied ploughs and offered improvements to husbandry, proposed a new way of printing and even a compass that worked in a coach or the hand of a rider on horseback.

In the Wren family history, *Parentalia* (not always the most reliable source), a vast list of the young student's inventive achievements during this period highlighted his inexhaustible imagination. This early ingenuity is summed up by one of the most unlikely inventions by the young philosopher, a transparent beehive, which sat in the garden at Wadham College. The design would show the many sides to Wren's talents, including an early interest in model-making and architecture, the method of exploring mathematical principles in solid dimensions. There would be many other architectural experiments, including experiments on making: 'pavements harder and cheaper than marble; New designs tending to strength, convenience & Beauty in Building; Inventions for better making and Fortifying

Havens; for Clearing Sand; and to Sound at Sea; New Offensive & defensive engins; some inventions in Fortifications'.[5]

Experiments were nothing more than play without some form of philosophical framework, a method that gave meaning to the various pursuits. At that time many thinkers were reading René Descartes' *A Discourse on Method*, and adopting a 'deductive' model in which theories were proposed and then experiments were devised to confirm them. Descartes assumed that the hypothesis came before the experiments. Yet the Wadham group were not so convinced. Having only just experienced a war that highlighted the horrors of dogma and theory, Wren's companions desired a method that avoided all suppositions and held only to observable truth and objective data. They favoured the English philosopher Francis Bacon, who promoted an 'inductive' approach in which experiments took precedence over theory. Wren became a devoted Baconian, preaching a new gospel of 'natural Philosophy ... order'd in a geometrical way of Reasoning from Ocular Experiments, [so] that it might prove real science of Nature, not a Hypothesis of what Nature might be'.[6]

The 'Great Clubb' at Wadham was informed by the desperate need to find a revised future from the ruins of the past. This could be achieved only by a collaborative effort and the group first dedicated themselves to 'gather together such things as are already discovered and to make a booke with a general index of them' through a thorough survey of the university libraries. All knowledge was to be collected and examined; that which remained true was to be kept, and new areas of inquiry were to be marked for exploration. The rewriting of all the law books of nature would involve:

physic, anatomy, geometry, astronomy, navigation, statics, magnetics, chemics, mechanics and natural experiments; with the state of these studies, as then cultivated at home and abroad. We then discoursed of the circulation of the blood, the valves in the veins, the venae lactae, the lymphatic vessels, the Copernican hypothesis, the nature of comets, and new stars, the satellites of Saturn, the oval shape [as it then appeared] of Saturn, the spots in the sun, and its turning on its own axis, the inequalities and selenography of the moon, the several phases of Venus and Mercury, the improvement of telescopes, and the grinding of glass for that purpose, the weight of air, the possibility or impossibility of vacuities, and nature's abhorrence thereof, the Torricellian experiment in quicksilver, the descent of heavy bodies, and the degrees of acceleration therein.[7]

It was only then that the English explorers could set out the future established upon reason. Science and useful knowledge would be the path of the revived nation.

LITTLE BRITAINE

Elsewhere, the same hopes found a different expression, for while Wren and the Wadham group went in pursuit of the whole universe, John Evelyn would find the future in a small, unexpected corner of the capital. After the execution of the king, Evelyn briefly returned to Paris, but it soon became clear that the crown was not to be imminently returned to the sons of the executed king. Those exiles who wished to return began to trickle back, stomaching the dishonourable 'composition', hefty fines and a declaration of delinquency. In February 1652, Evelyn returned to London, travelling alone. He was now in charge of his father-in-law's estates, which had been threatened with confiscation, and after nearly ten years abroad, he desired 'a settled life, either in this or some other place, there being now so little appearance of any chance for the better, all being entirely in the rebels' hands, and this particular habitation and the estate contiguous to it (belonging to my father in law, actually in his Majesty's service)'.[8]

The family home, Sayes Court, in Deptford, stood on the south bank of the Thames, a short boat ride from the city's centre. The house had originally been leased by Elizabeth I to Mary Evelyn's grandparents, who had supervised the Royal Docks located on the eastern side of the garden wall. But in the new regime all Crown property was confiscated by the Commonwealth to be sold to the highest bidder. The house was further buffeted by a disastrous flood which had swept through Deptford the previous winter, the Thames breaking 7 feet above its banks. As Evelyn recorded in his diary, the house was 'very much suffering for want of some friend to rescue it out of the powers of the usurpers'.[9] Determined to reclaim ownership, Evelyn was finally able to purchase the lease for £3,500.

Evelyn devoted himself to making Sayes Court a family home for his new wife, who was to travel over from Paris, pregnant with their first child. He vowed to create a 'place of all terrestrial enjoyments the most ressembling Heaven'.[10] He was in love and Mary would be travelling to share exile in an alien place she probably had not visited since childhood. He was resigned to living out the adverse times in obscurity, solitary study and virtue. As Evelyn wrote to his friend William Prettyman, he had 'no ambitions at all to be a statesman, or meddle with the unlucky interests of Kingdomes, and shall contently submitts to the losse of my education by which I might have one day hoped for the future'.[11]

Instead Evelyn's attention focused on the fabric of the house; he hoped to convert the gabled Tudor manor, which had seen better days, into a 'villa' retreat, a respite from the city and the horrors of the new regime. The surrounding lands were flat and marshy. Across the garden wall, the noise and bustle of the docks, where a surge of building accompanied Cromwell's determination to expand the Commonwealth's navy, were a continual source of pollution and strife. Deptford was far from Evelyn's idea of paradise, but the young couple planned improvements together to modernise the house. The Tudor façade was replaced by a classical porch. On the roof a small cupola was designed to allow light into the interior of the house. Inside, they enlarged two parlours, increased the main staircase, built an extension and wood-panelled every room downstairs.

Mary gave birth to her first son, Richard, shortly after arriving at Sayes Court. Their second son, John Stansfield, was born nine months later, yet died within days. A year later another son was born, also called John. The Evelyns would have four more children. Becoming the head of a family had a profound effect on Evelyn, who found himself 'affected with a kind of tendernesse, such as I never perceived in myself before'.[12] He dedicated himself to the education of his children and took a particular delight in the early development of his first son, Richard. Over-earnestly he attached plaques and signs, painted with ornamental quotes and mottoes, through-out the house.

Although Sayes Court rested close to London, the house was developed as a critical response to the seething metropolis. On his return Evelyn had written a pamphlet, *The State of France*, as a rebuke to the English capital, and he mourned London as a poor reflection of Paris and commanded the educated traveller to visit the French capital to see its architectural and social advances. In contrast, his new home was a 'wooden, northern, and inartificial congestion of houses ... [in which] there was nothing here of ornament, nothing of magnificence, no publique and honourable works ... a very ugly town, pestred with hackney coaches, and insolent carre men, shops and taverns, noyse, and such a cloud of sea-coal, as if there be a ressemblence of hell upon earth'.[13]

Powerless to make any changes to the world around him, excluded from office and forced to live a retired life at Sayes Court, Evelyn still wished to develop his ideas of the life of virtue, and developed a motto that he held for the rest of his life: '*Omnia explorate, Meliore retinete*': Explore everything, keep only the best. In a series of commonplace books, he began to gather a compendium of knowledge that evolved into a verbose reflection of the virtuoso's mind. He also had time to consider his garden.

Throughout his travels Evelyn had been fascinated by the gardens of Europe, and there are signs that even at this early stage he was fixing his mind as a horticulturist. The Italian style of gardening was already the height of fashion in England and had come to replace the rigid forms of the Tudor knot in all the most fashionable gardens. The Renaissance garden was full of secrets and wonders, of shades and privacy in which the irregularity of nature was enhanced through art to entertain the senses. The organic intertwined with the architectural in the placing and building of grottoes, water features, mounts and temples to produce a dream of Prospero's island, the retreat of the shady cell and a place of contemplation. In his diaries Evelyn took particular delight in the devices and statuary that enhanced the natural landscape, such as the steep terraces of the Villa di Negro in Genoa that turned the garden into a theatre. Surrounded by high turreted walls and dotted with banqueting houses, the Villa Borghese in Rome similarly provided a vision of an enclosed 'elysium of delight'.[14] Water was the main element at the Villa d'Este, gurgling and spouting from urns, spraying from conches and settling in richly paved grottoes while a stream representing the Tiber flowed through a model of ancient Rome.

Yet the Renaissance garden was being replaced by newer forms and ideas that approached the manipulation of nature through reason rather than metaphysics. On his travels in the Spanish Netherlands Evelyn had noted the use of lime trees to form long avenues, bordered by flower beds, to encourage promenades, a public theatre of civilisation and motion, framing the impression of a culture boldly focused on the future. When Evelyn finally returned to Paris he found a more rhetorical style within the royal gardens which regimented nature along mathematical principles, strictly defining the boundaries between civilisation and the wilderness. Paris parks and gardens were intended to articulate political power rather than inspire contemplation.

In January 1653, as he began his projecting, Sayes Court was 'a rude orchard, and all the rest one entire field of 100 acres, without any hedge, except the hither holly hedge joining to the bank of the mount walk'.[15]

Over the next few years the scrubland was transformed into a garden of many parts. Close by the house, Evelyn indulged his interest in Italian style with a symbolic *giardino segreto*, an aviary and an 'elaboratory', where he performed botanical experiments. Here he placed the New Philosophy within an enclosed landscape, nature as both a subject of study and an object of art. There was also a kitchen garden and nursery near the house, which led to a grove, an organised wooded area dissected by walks and paths. And beyond stood a large orchard with apples, pears, cherries of every variety, gooseberries and raspberries, so that it became a compendium of horticulture as well as a working orchard. The various quarters of the garden were divided by hedges rather than walls, and Evelyn introduced the avenues of limes that he had seen in the Spanish Netherlands to link the sections.

At the heart of the garden, Evelyn designed a formal enclosure and chose to base his new creation on the plot of the Parisian nurseryman Pierre Morin, who happened to be his father-in-law's neighbour in St Germain. Morin had a small garden but had gained a wide reputation as a plantsman, introducing new flowers and sourcing new rare breeds of shrubs and evergreens. Evelyn had visited Morin on two occasions. What the French garden lacked in scale, it made up for in the balance between utility and elegance. It was a working garden that changed with the seasons and the introduction of new plants. At the centre of the space was a sundial surrounded by a wide oval parterre, with two rows of petal-shaped beds, hedged with box, radiating from it, enclosed by a 'palisade' of cypress trees, while around the edge were a variety of 'different kinds of rockwork niches, filled with plaster and stucco figures modelled on the antique and covered in ivy'.[16]

Sayes Court was an English garden that combined Italian, French and Dutch details, yet there were other layers of meaning, for Evelyn's idea of the garden would never be a fixed thing. Like a laboratory, it would be a place of experimentation in which notions and concerns of science and horticulture were exposed and observed, evolving into a multilayered discussion of the different ways art cultivated nature. In addition, the garden had religious overtones: Evelyn wished to create a place that became the 'best representation of our lost felicitie'.[17] The questions that Sayes Court raised would fascinate Evelyn for the rest of his life. It would be within this plot of land, cultivated in privacy, that his reputation would first germinate.

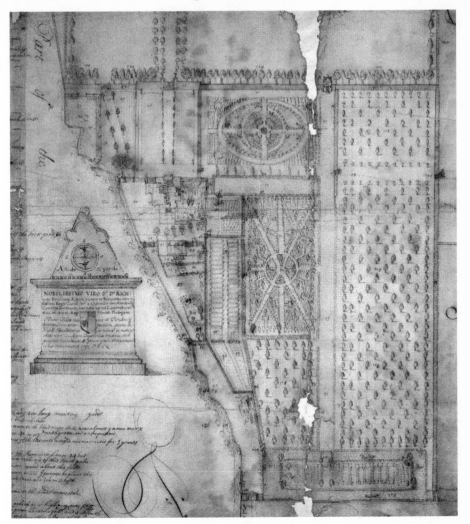

John Evelyn's plans for Sayes Court, a retreat as well as a proving ground
for Evelyn's ideas

NEW LESSONS

Robert Hooke arrived in London in 1648. By the beginning of the following
year he had already tried his hand at being an artist, working in the studio
of the portrait painter Peter Lely. Either because the thirteen-year-old
Hooke was allergic to the paints or because he quickly 'perceived what
was to be donne, so, thought he, why cannot I doe this by myself',[18] he left

his master and became a student at Dr Busby's Westminster School. The headmaster, who had probably been told of Hooke's plight by friends on the Isle of Wight, sympathised with the young royalist in jeopardy, and accepted him into his own house. Thus, on the day of the king's execution, Hooke and all the other pupils were locked in the school hall by Busby and commanded to pray for the soul of the Martyr King.

Another student who was shut in the Great Hall on that day was John Locke, three years older than Hooke. Locke's experience of the Civil Wars thus far contrasted with that of his contemporaries. He had been born into a Puritan family, far from the metropolis in the western county of Somerset. Like Hooke, the boy had a solitary childhood, but at the age of ten, Locke's quiet life was ruptured by the wars. In 1642, the father, a local county attorney, had ridden with the parliamentary army in the first months of the conflict and at the Battle of Devizes in July 1643 Captain Locke had faced the royalist forces after two days of fighting. The parliamentary troop were routed and the captain had returned to his village, Belluton, vowing to avoid the horrors of battle again.

Life was difficult for the next few years, and Captain Locke was forced to accept the unseemly role of county clerk for sewers. He was a diligent if strict father, in whom discipline and vigilance against the ungodly were encouraged, and from father to son the power of the word was passed on through books, sermons and lectures. In 1647, through the patronage of his father's senior cavalry officer, the MP Anthony Popham, young John was sent to London and a place at Westminster School.

Swiftly distinguishing himself within the demanding atmosphere of Busby's classroom, Locke was noted as a scholar, and excelled as a student of languages. Although the son of a Puritan, he was not perturbed by the openly Anglican atmosphere at Westminster, and by 1650 he had become a King's Scholar (only a few months after the king himself had been executed). He went up to Oxford in November 1652, where he took rooms at Christ Church, having gained a scholarship following a display of orations in Latin, Greek and Hebrew. Here, however, he found that university life was no less harsh than Busby's regime at Westminster. He would rise at five in the morning for prayers, eat breakfast at six and work in the hall for four hours with two more hours of study in the afternoon. Studying for his Bachelor of Arts degree, which was the traditional curriculum for all members of the nobility and those training for the clergy, Locke learnt the classical languages, logic and rhetoric in preparation for the art of disputation. Under the new Cromwellian regime, the students were also expected to sit through two sermons a day.

Like many humanities students over the ages, however, Locke spent his time doing as little as possible. He read romances (in particular he was a fan of Cervantes' *Don Quixote*), and contemplated a literary life, sketching a scenario for a play, *Orozco, King of Albania*, which never saw the light of day. He also spent a lot of his time courting the attentions of the fairer sex. He was a handsome man, and a deft flirt. In one letter to a mysterious correspondent he cooed: 'You cannot lose again what you have once made yours. Absence (the greatest destroyer of others' love) that could not hinder, will not be about to impair mine; nor will time ever be able to blot out the bright idea I have of you in my heart.'[19] It was also clear that his affections were not restricted to one target.

He would later complain, however, that he felt suffocated by the stuffy traditions of Oxford. Even in his first year, Locke baulked at the old-fashioned style of teaching, the scholastic method, which emphasised the art of discourse above all else. He grumbled years later that he 'lost a lot of time, when he first applied himself to study, because the only philosophy there known at Oxford was the peripatetick, perplexed with obscure terms and stuffed with useless questions'.[20]

To the young man, the conflict of the last decade seemed to have emerged from extremes – the emotional enthusiasm of religious fervour and the rigid traditions of the humanist curriculum, which praised a well-argued theory above reason. Unsatisfied with both doctrines, Locke went in search of new answers that would explain human understanding.

One of his friends within the college, another old boy of Westminster, was Richard Lower, who was becoming a minor member of the Wadham group. Through Lower, Locke began to keep a medical commonplace book in which he noted recipes for cures and curiosities of anatomy. Yet, for whatever reason, Locke would remain outside the group of New Philosophers who congregated only a few hundred yards from where he regularly studied. Instead, he preferred the more relaxing company of 'pleasant, and witty men',[21] and would not discover the works of René Descartes, which had been in the library since the 1640s, until 1659. And it was a few more years after that before he crossed from the book room into the laboratory.

Hooke arrived at Christ Church a year later. He had joined the same college as John Locke but their experiences of the first years of academic life were very different. Hooke, unlike his fellow student, did not have the luxury of leisurely moping, and instead went up as a chorister scholar and commoner servitor of a Mr Goodman, possibly a family connection from the island, on whom he was expected to attend. His initial appearance, 'low of stature, always very pale, his eyes grey and full . . . dark brown hair, very long and hung down over his face and lank', would have struck many as a disadvantage, but this belied a brilliant mind and a 'sharp ingenious look',[22] which served him well as he entered undergraduate life. In addition, he was also fortunate to take with him the recommendation of Dr Busby, who had contacted his old friend, Dr Thomas Willis. Through Willis the budding technician became acquainted with the Wadham group.

Hooke began his adventures in the New Philosophy as laboratory assistant to Willis, who, at that time, had a particular interest in the chemical functions of the human body. William Harvey's observations of the blood's circulation revealed the method behind the mechanism of the body, the *how*; yet nobody knew *why* – what was the function of blood? Chemistry, unlike astronomy or mathematics, was an emerging field of study, evolving from the metaphysical speculations of alchemy, and Willis was at the crossing point of the birth of the modern discipline. At the heart of this new chemical revolution was the revival of the ancient idea that everything was made of the same material. The French philosopher Pierre Gassendi had revived ideas that went as far back as ancient Greece, when he reignited the exploration of 'atoms', the smallest building blocks of all matter. Nobody knew what these atoms were, or how many varieties of atoms there were, but the idea was powerful enough to answer a number of vital questions.

Willis, with Hooke beside him, went in search of the materials of the human body. Hooke, already showing his talents as measurer and instrument-maker, would have been invaluable to the chemist's quest, but there was a problem: the assistant could not stand the sight of dissections. It swiftly became clear that Hooke would need to make his mark elsewhere. By coincidence, Willis would soon hire a new assistant, Locke's friend Richard Lower.

Wren and Hooke were similar in many ways. By 1653, however, Wren was a fellow of All Souls' College, and a leading light within the Wadham group, gaining a reputation in the many correspondences that passed between thinkers throughout Europe. Hooke, on the other hand, had not yet matriculated and was expected to adopt a junior role as laboratory technician, executing others' ideas and assisting in experiments and instrumentation. The two men would begin working together almost as soon as they met. Under the instruction of Wilkins, they devised new instruments – way wisers, weather clocks – made astronomical observations and refined their methods of how to collect data.

As philosophers, the two complemented each other. Even their flaws were symbiotic – for while Wren would often assault an idea with ingenuity only to give up enquiries halfway, Hooke could worry over questions for years. Together, they were bold enough to attack the biggest questions in New Philosophy. In particular they dreamt of finding a mechanical solution to the problem of longitude, the means of recording positions anywhere in the world upon the east/west axis. Both also became associated with developments in technology: the telescope had been developed in Europe at the beginning of the century and was commonly in use in England by the start of the Civil War, yet it was with the Wadham group that the science of lenses came to the fore. While the telescope probed and measured the night sky with a new-found accuracy, the microscope uncovered a universe on a miniature scale, revealing the smooth surface of objects to be pitted, the solidity of stone to be pocked and porous. Together Hooke and Wren began to investigate these hidden worlds and, as both were gifted draughtsmen, vividly sketch what they observed to show the world their new-found wonders.

The Oxford life, however, could not immunise the young philosophers against the realities of the world beyond the cloisters. In 1653, the regime commanded that a list of known Anglicans be drawn up and the named be expelled. Fortunately, Wren and Hooke found sympathetic protectors. In addition, the work at Wadham College had come under the scrutiny of the Commonwealth regime, who frowned upon their unorthodox ideas. Parliament attacked the universities as 'unrevolutionary', in their failure to uphold the theocratic aspirations of the times. In response, Wilkins and Ward wrote a pamphlet in Oxford's defence, highlighting Wren's and Hooke's exemplary work in the search for nature.

While Hooke studied as an undergraduate, Wren focused on making his name in astronomy, using his telescope to reveal new observations of the heavens, pointing his lens at the moon. At the turn of the century the Italian Galileo had been the first to realise that the moon was not a perfect sphere of untrammelled ground but pitted and cavernous, with seas and mountains. Wren was determined to go farther. Following an arduous series of observations, he was able to improve on the Italian's maps, recording all the data and then recreating a perfect model in plasterboard, bringing to life the whole lunar surface. The model was not just the result of a painstakingly thorough set of observations and data collection, but was one of the most visually striking promotional tools for the New Philosophy. Wren had not just measured the moon but had put it on display to the world.

In addition, Wren's telescope searched farther into the night sky, using improved lenses and longer telescope barrels of his own devising, to observe the planet Saturn. In 1655, while looking at the same planet, the British astronomer William Balle had discovered rings circling the celestial body. What were these unusual forms? What shape did they make? Wren would spend the next years exploring and examining these strange phenomena, which to the human eye were nothing more than a speck in the night sky. If Wren could observe the distant planet and collect enough evidence to prove the shape of the rings of Saturn, he would have achieved something that no one before had ever done and his name would remain for as long as man looked to the stars.

Hooke too was in pursuit of his own ambitions. In 1654 another scientist, Robert Boyle, the son of the Earl of Cork, was invited by Wilkins to join the Wadham group, bringing with him a considerable reputation as a brilliant experimenter as well as a lot of money. The aristocrat took rooms on the High Street, opposite All Souls' College, and fitted his own laboratory, employed glass-blowers and hired apothecaries, luring many admiring visitors. Hooke, on Wilkins's recommendation, was hired as Boyle's personal assistant and would provide the philosopher with the technical know-how to accomplish his great plans.

Like Willis, Boyle was fascinated by chemistry; unlike Willis, who delved into the viscera of the human body to find the answer, Boyle sought his revelations in the invisible matter around him, the air. For centuries, scientists had debated the existence of 'the void', the absence of matter in nature. Aristotle refused to accept the possibility that nature would allow such a lack, but in 1644 the Italian experimenter, Evangelista Torricelli, was able to create one by pouring mercury into a tube sealed at one end, and inverting it in a bowl of mercury, devising a barometer. Scientists were fascinated by the identity of the matter that filled the space between the meniscus of the mercury and the sealed end of the tube; it looked like air but could not be. Boyle wanted to recreate this 'vacuum' on a large scale to explore the properties of this absence, for if one could discern what 'nothingness' was, then one might be able to work out the chemical nature of its opposite, the air.

Boyle needed a machine that could mechanically produce such a vacuum. He also needed to observe experiments within his vacuum and demanded that his pump include a glass bowl robust enough to withstand the pressure. Hooke was perfectly placed to assist the inquisitive aristocrat and, following Boyle's particular requests, as well as improving them with a few suggestions of his own, he worked with the London instrumenter Ralph Greatorex, who had some knowledge of pumps from his experiences of irrigating the Cambridgeshire fenlands. The plans for the Pneumatick Air Pump were an extraordinary feat of engineering that fully illustrated Hooke's technical understanding of the needs of the experimenter: a glass hatch sat on top of the 15-inch glass bowl through which various objects could be placed – a lit candle that was extinguished on entry, a live bird that flapped in the absence of air and then died, a human arm that dilated on exposure to the vacuum. Boyle's pump would become the iconic image of the New Philosophy, and the chemist and his assistant began a series of groundbreaking experiments into the nature of the world.

OMNIA EXPLORATE, MELIORE RETINETE

But the search for a new future was not reserved to the library or laboratory. In 1654, from their garden at Deptford, John and Mary Evelyn set out to discover the country that they knew the least – England – taking a coach to visit the major towns and cities, surveying the most famous houses and gardens of the day. The tour began in the south-west of England then headed north as far as Worcester, then across the Midlands towards Yorkshire in the north-east and then, after four months of travelling and 700 miles of road, returned to London. Evelyn was struck by the variety and beauty of the pastoral scenery, which gave him a clear sense of the essence of the English landscape.

This discovery of England was reflected in Evelyn's increased interest in arboriculture. As the decade progressed, he planted fewer flowers and more trees at Sayes Court, in particular evergreens that he had seen on his travels in Europe. By integrating Continental evergreens among native groves, Evelyn was exploring a new vision for England's garden of paradise. His fascination with trees and shrubs would draw him into a wider political debate on the role of gardening in the new regime. Encouraged by Cromwell, the Puritan Commonwealth preached the spiritual value of sowing and reaping. In particular, the growing of fruit trees was seen as having both religious and economic significance. In numerous tracts of the day, such as *The Spiritual Use of Orchards* by the Calvinist preacher Richard Austen, the English Eden was pictured as an orchard. Evelyn was attracted by this spiritual interpretation of gardening, and at some point he grubbed up his orchard, dispensing the fruit trees throughout the main garden, while he converted the wider, old orchard space into a grove.

During their trip, Evelyn and his wife visited Oxford and the small community of New Philosophers there. He spent much time with Wilkins, and was given free access to the master's room at Wadham to examine the observatory and gardens. Here Evelyn saw the transparent beehive which Wilkins later donated to his visitor, and which would eventually find a home beside the laboratory at Sayes Court. Evelyn also had the opportunity to meet the apiary's designer, 'that miracle of a youth, Mr Christopher Wren', who dined with the Evelyns on their last night and presented the couple with 'a piece of white marble, which he had stained with a lively red, very deep, as beautiful as if it had been natural'.[23] The visit cemented the relationship between the virtuoso and the New Philosophers, and over the next few years Evelyn became close friends with many members of the Wadham group, visiting them when they travelled to London, showing them his garden and conducting experiments with them in his laboratory.

Another figure who came to feature in Evelyn's life at this time was Samuel Hartlib, the London philosopher and author of *Designe for Plentie by a Universall Planting of Fruit Trees*. Hartlib appealed to Evelyn both as a natural philosopher and a horticultural thinker. Through Hartlib, John Evelyn gained the confidence to begin his study of 'the history of trades', a compendium of universal industry. He kept a series of commonplace books that gathered his notes and ideas, as well as arcane readings and quotations, organised under a series of 'heads'. At some point, Evelyn began *A Booke of Promiscuous Notes and Observations concerning Husbandry, Building etc.*, which acted as a practical primer with observations, sketches and lore. *Trades, Secret & Receipts Mechanical, as they came casually to hand* attempted to bring together knowledge on every aspect of industry, including bell-founding, cabinet-making, lime-burning and shipwrighting, which he observed across his garden wall in the naval docks in Deptford.

Yet by 1657, Evelyn, who once suggested that he was near to completion, admitted that the project defeated him. He struggled to gain the confidence of the mechanics, who were uncertain about revealing their trade secrets, and the project seemed to grow beyond measure, and he did not get much farther than writing a series of heads dividing the trades into 'Frippery trades', 'Polite Arts', women's work and 'Liberal arts', as well as dividing work conducted on land and on sea. Instead, he concentrated on the translation of Lucretius's fiendishly difficult *De Rerum Natura*, and began a work on *Etching and ingraving: which treatise, together with five others (viz: Paynting in oyle, Miniature, Anealing in Glasse, Enamiling, and Marble Paper)*, a survey of the world of art, its traditions and crafts, as well as the latest innovations in technique.

He also returned to horticulture, encouraged by his friend Thomas Henshaw, to translate *The French Gardener* (1658), while at the same time began to think about a complete compendium of garden history, science, practice, husbandry and lore, which he would later call *Elysium Britannicum*. In a letter to the Norwich philosopher Sir Thomas Browne, he promised to address 'the many defects which I encounter'd in Bookes and in Gardens, wherein neither words nor cost had bin wanting, but judgement very much'. The book would be practical but also a work of philosophy, distilling all his knowledge, and 'show how the aire and genious of Gardens operat upon humane spirits towards virtue and sanctity ... How caves, grotts, Mounts, and irregular ornaments of Gardens do contribute to contemplative and philosophicall enthusiasms'.[24] The *Elysium Britannicum* would be a life's work, a perfect reflection of the author's mind.

By 1658, after six years of living at Sayes Court, both the garden and the cultivator had been transformed. Evelyn had hoped to create a haven away from the dangers of the Commonwealth, but as the decade came to a close and the republican regime appeared to be tottering, Evelyn's lonely aspirations for a life circumscribed by 'a Friend, a Booke and a Garden' seemed long gone. In his retreat Evelyn had developed a role for himself in the intellectual life of the nation. In developing his garden he had experimented with many forms, using nature as his laboratory, as he worried and refined his articulation of the English imagination. His answer combined politics, horticulture, philosophy and religion; it reflected his native home as well as what he had encountered abroad; it intertwined both the ancient and the most contemporary.

THE CAPITAL OF THE NEW PHILOSOPHY

While Evelyn wrote and dug his garden at Sayes Court, the New Philosophers at Oxford continued their experiments. In their discussions, many of his new circle of friends had harboured aspirations of a college to promote the New Philosophy. Samuel Hartlib had dreamt of a 'pansophic' academy since the 1640s, while John Wilkins had attempted to raise funding for a scientific college in Oxford, but failed. John Evelyn was enthusiastic about the idea of a monastery for the sages of the age (which, of course, included both him and Mary). Yet when Evelyn wrote in 1658 to Robert Boyle to discuss 'that Mathematico-Chymico-Mechanical School designed by our noble friend Dr Wilkins',[25] no definite plans had been laid. Thus far, the Wadham group had been able to flourish because it was so far away from the centre of power, but the time had arrived for the New Philosophers to establish themselves on the national stage.

Recent events all pointed to a base in London rather than in the quadrangles of Oxford: Wilkins had moved to Cambridge University, heralding the break-up of the Wadham group. In addition, on 7 August 1657, the twenty-four-year-old Christopher Wren made his entry into London life. It was to be a special day for the young philosopher for he was to be named Gresham Professor of Astronomy. Wren had become the pre-eminent stargazer in England, and through his brilliance would now be entrusted to promote the New Philosophy beyond the small community of like-minded scholars to the capital of the nation itself. Wren's inaugural speech would be the clearest presentation of his experimental philosophy and a challenge to the future.

The speech was a clarion appeal for the truth of the New Philosophy, in which Wren promised to promote the values of experiments and demonstration: 'Natural Philosophy having of late been order'd into a geometrical Way of reasoning from ocular Experiment, that it might prove a real Science of Nature, not a hypothesis of what Nature might be, the perfection of telescopes and Microscopes, by which our sense is so infinitely advanc'd seems to be the only Way to penetrate into the most hidden Parts of Nature, and to make the most of Creation.' Promoting the search for truth above discourse, Wren finished by linking the city of merchants with the fortunes of the New Philosophy. London would become the Capital of Reason: 'since navigation brings with it both Wealth, Splendour, Politeness and learning, what greater happiness can I wish to the Londoners? . . . that they always may be . . . "The Masters of the Sea" and that London may be an Alexandria, the established Residence of Mathematical Arts'.[26]

PART TWO

The Rise and Fall of Restoration London

3

Restoration and Renewal

In June 1658, following a bitter winter and a freak storm, a whale swam up the River Thames as far as Greenwich, and from his garden at Sayes Court, Evelyn was able to watch the leviathan, which soon attracted a large crowd. It was 'fifty eight feet [long], height sixteen; black skinned, like coach leather; very small eyes, great tail, only two small fins, a peaked snout, and a mouth so wide that divers men might stood upright in it'. As the tidal river started to ebb, the beast was caught in the shallow water and Evelyn was concerned that the nearby boats would be destroyed in the fury. He watched in horror as the mob attacked with a harpoon, and savagely killed it.

Such strange happenings would be taken by some as an omen of dangers to come, but Evelyn had already suffered a devastating catastrophe. On 27 January, his eldest son, five-year-old Richard, had died. Mary had plunged into deep mourning, weeping continuously, claiming to hear her son's voice in every corner of the house. Writing a year later, Evelyn confessed that the loss had turned his dark locks grey and, as he wrote, 'my tears mingle so far with my inke, that I must break off here, and be silent'.[1] Yet even in his private grief, there were pressing events in the capital that demanded his attention.

On 3 September, Protector Cromwell died, but on this occasion Evelyn revelled at the passing: 'the joyfullest funeral I ever saw; for there were none that cried but dogs, which the soldiers hooted away with a barbarous noise, drinking and taking tobacco in the streets as they went'.[2] The Protector's death, however, did not bring peace but rather the prospect of anarchy and confusion. By the end of his life Cromwell had ruled as a quasi-monarch yet had refused the crown, but history offered no precedent as to what should happen next. The title was passed to Cromwell's son,

Richard, but his failure to inspire loyalty only highlighted the fact that his power was based on the actions of men rather than divine ordination. The army, without the talismanic leadership of the Lord Protector to bind the many factions together, now held the city in its grip in desperation and was determined not to let go.

Despite the chaos in the city, Christopher Wren continued to make the day's ride from Oxford to the metropolis to deliver his weekly lectures at Gresham College, and by summer he was ready to present his observations of the planet Saturn. His English colleagues urged him to publish his observations to claim the discovery for himself, but Wren was cautious, planning to start a short thesis and follow it later with a more thorough discourse. His routine, however, was disturbed in October 1659 by the army's arrival at Gresham, making all progress impossible. The college was requisitioned and the professors ordered to leave as the building was converted into a garrison. Wren lost his laboratory and feared for his livelihood as the college was allowed to decline. He resolved to stay away from the dangers of the capital and spent more of his time in Oxford. Following the death of his father, he took up the official role as bursar at All Souls' College.

One other reason may also have encouraged this retreat. While he wrote up his notes for *De Corpore Saturni*, Wren heard from John Wallis that the renowned Dutch astronomer Christiaan Huygens had also aimed his tube at the far reaches of the universe and had proposed an alternative theory: the corona of Saturn was not an ellipse, as Wren had thought, but a uniform ring perfectly encircling the planet. The revelation came as a blow, for Huygens was a leading European philosopher with an international reputation. Wren, who had hoped to make his name with his discovery, immediately put *De Corpore* aside, hoping that in silence his failure would disappear. He was forced to think again about his future and resolved to seek new territory within the New Philosophy which he could call his own, rather than face the embarrassment of being trumped for a second time.

In London, winter was a time of riots and open protest by various factions within the city against the faltering army regime. There were reports that weapons and grenades were being stockpiled and that the army was prepared to enter the city, threatening to use St Paul's Cathedral as a final redoubt if it came to violence. On 5 December, 20,000 citizens signed a petition of complaint against their oppressors, which they attempted to deliver to the Lord Mayor. As they rallied towards the Guild-hall they were stopped by a troop on horseback commanded by a former London shoemaker, Captain Hewson. The crowd turned rowdy and began to pull up cobbles and pelted the cavalry with tiles, ice, turnips and even a frozen football. In response the soldiers fired into the crowd, killing seven and injuring others.

A few days later, 23,000 artisans, apprentices, tradesmen, seamen and watermen delivered another petition threatening that the city would 'rise up as one man' against the army, which remained confident in its might. To add oil to the flames, an official army investigation cleared Hewson of all wrongdoing, despite the city coroner's report that the deaths amounted to murder. The rebuke galvanised the city into opposition against the army and in a symbolic gesture of revenge they built a snowman with 'one eye in his heade and with an old face and haulter or rope about his neck, many old shewes lying around by him, a horne on his head',[3] which they placed at the centre of St Paul's churchyard for all to see.

But what would deliver a salve to the nation? Richard Cromwell appeared to be little more than a puppet controlled by the army generals, while some within Parliament began to speak out against the tyranny of 'the good old cause', and plot for a republic. John Evelyn was one of the first to press for the king's return, and two months before the deadly rally published anonymously *An Apology for the Royal Party*. In the pamphlet he mocked the reckless idealism of the Civil War in which the dreams of liberty had been usurped. The chaos of the world was thus the result of fanciful dreams, 'modells and childish chimaeras', which brought no peace 'but their coffine, guarded by the souldiers at Westminster'.[4] Evelyn then pronounced that the restoration of the king was the nation's best repentance. According to Evelyn, Charles was not only the anointed king but blessed with a personality that would unite the divided nation once more.

As the New Year approached the royalist party in London began to gain confidence. There was news that support was coming from the army in Scotland, whose leader, General Monck, threatened to march to London to restore order. There were also murmurs of an insurrection being launched from within Parliament, while others considered that stability could only be regained by negotiations with Charles. Evelyn put himself in danger when he visited his old school friend, Colonel Herbert Morley, in control of the army's stronghold, the Tower of London, and unsuccessfully attempted to persuade him to the cause. Beyond, London became clogged with plots and Evelyn risked censure when he concealed 'divers persons of quality in my house, when it had bin treason to have but conversed with them',[5] while also sending substantial sums of money to the king in Holland. By the beginning of 1660, nervous tension, exhaustion and perhaps overwhelming grief reduced Evelyn to his bed, where he remained, close to death, for two months.

The exiled Charles assumed the image of a monarch who promised everything to every man, a bandage to a splintered nation. During months of negotiations Charles was wary of creating enemies, knowing that his restoration was in the hands of others. Yet he was quietly determined to ensure that when he did finally assume power he would never let it out of his grasp. In an appeal from Holland, the Declaration of Breda, Charles presented himself as the man who offered amnesty to all during the Civil War, a religious settlement that gave hope to all 'tender consciences', accommodations with Parliament and the army and the promise to introduce senior members of the opposition into his closest confidence while also rewarding those who aided his return. He was generous when he had nothing to give; the test would come when he had regained everything that he hoped for.

Charles II eventually arrived on English shores on 20 May 1660. Nine days later, dressed in sober clothes, the blue sash of his Garter Star across his chest, and shunning a hat so that the crowds would recognise his face, he entered London from south of the river, where he was presented with the sword of the City by the Lord Mayor and entertained by a field of dancing girls who, dressed in white and blue, scattered flowers and herbs before his horse. The king then entered London to a clamorous welcome, crossing over London Bridge and proceeding past St Paul's, where the assembled remnants of the Anglican Church, who had been persecuted through the interregnum, gathered upon a dais. As the king rode past the symbol of his father's rule, the fabric of the church was as dilapidated as its personnel.

John Evelyn himself was swept up in the occasion and joined the crowds in the Strand:

the ways strewed with flowers, the bells ringing, the streets hung with tapestry, fountains running with wine; the Mayor, Aldermen, and all the companies, in their liveries, chains of gold, and banners; Lords and Nobles, clad in cloth of silver, gold, and velvet; the windows and balconies, all set with ladies; trumpets, music, and myriads of people flocking ... such a restoration was never mentioned in any history, ancient or modern, since the return of the Jews from the Babylonian captivity.[6]

After seven hours of parading the king finally arrived at his palace at Whitehall, where he took to his bed (with his mistress, Barbara Villiers), while on the streets the celebration and carousing would continue for three days and nights.

The Restoration of Charles II tolled the end of the 'English Revolution'. The years of constitutional experimentation following the execution of Charles I had been a disaster; Oliver Cromwell's death in 1658 proved that it was only the strength of his personality which had held the uneasy Commonwealth together. Without the firm grip of the Lord Protector, the many parts of the English Republic had splintered and the return of the king appeared the sole alternative for a nation that had run out of options. Charles II was welcomed because he offered the best chance of settlement after the anxieties of war, yet while the popular crowds had welcomed the king back with joy, it was not without a certain irony, as the poet John Dryden drily observed in 'Vox Populi':

> Crowds err not, though to both extremes they run;
> To kill the father, and recall the son.

THE SEARCH FOR A SETTLEMENT

In Oxford, John Locke was mystified by the events in London, which he only heard about by letter and reports. In the heat of the present events, he could not decide what to do next: 'I can not thinke to enter upon a steady course of life whilst the whole nation is reeling ... divisions are as wide, factions as violent and designes as pernicious as ever.'[7] His instincts told him to fight for what he believed, yet he confessed that he no longer knew which side to join. He had completed his MA and had been elected as a Senior Student, a fellow, at Christ Church, yet he remained uneasy about his future and spent a long time away from the university. This was exacerbated by events at his college, for just as London swung between extremes in the dying days of the Commonwealth, so was the university buffeted by dangerous and radical notions. In 1659, in the last months of the interregnum, the college master, John Owen, had been replaced by a

Quaker. To Locke, it seemed as if the bastion of reason was being overrun by fancy and enthusiasm.

Locke had come to fear the 'fanatick' extremism that had flourished during the Commonwealth and had become increasingly shocked by the constitutional experiments of the interregnum, in which the law was determined not by reason but by theology, 'kindled from the coals from the altars', and he placed the blame on the rise of the 'sectaries', because it allowed men to follow their own morality rather than put their faith in society: 'there is not a man but thinks he alone hath this light within and all besides stumbles in the dark'.[8]

The young philosopher's horror of the present decline of the nation forced him to re-examine all his childhood assumptions and by 1660 he had clearly decided to become an Anglican. The return of monarchy, Locke concluded, was the only reasonable solution to the present dilemma. As he wrote in a collection called *Britannia Rediviva* that the university published to celebrate Charles's return:

> Our Prayers are heard! nor have the fates in store
> An Equall blisse, for which we implore,
> Their Bounty, For in You, Great SIR's, the summe
> Of all our present joys, of all to come ...[9]

For the restored monarchy to find fertile ground, however, the theocratic foundations of the interregnum had to be dismantled. Among his friends in Oxford, John Locke got to grips with these ideas, debating the question of Natural Law, the study of the principles of law, and in particular the boundaries between the laws made by men and the rules ordained by God. In a series of pamphlets that he wrote but never published, he searched for a rational solution to the crisis and the role of the sovereign, asking whether his power came from God's ordination or man's, and on what aspects of everyday life the king could legislate. He concluded that Charles II should have 'an absolute and arbitrary power over all the indifferent actions of his people'.[10]

The people looked to Charles, himself a man shattered by his own experiences, to assuage the tempest, yet, in reality, the king knew that at the heart of the settlement was a compromise. He had been welcomed back not because of his own qualities, but because of the poverty of the alternative options. He had promised security and now he had to negotiate a new deal to unify the exhausted nation. Before he attempted to settle the present, however, he needed to rule over the memory of the last nineteen years. Charles wished to reconnect his reign with the past by dissolving the memory of the Civil Wars, and all legislation between 1641 and 1660 was repealed as it did not possess the king's imprimatur. As the pages were torn from council minute books, 1660 was declared Charles's eleventh year in office, banishing the constitution of the interregnum beyond memory. In the early years of the reign this manoeuvre attracted few opponents, yet it could not rub away the past completely.

Charles was also aware that he would never have returned without the support of many who had once been his sworn enemies, and he chose the role of the clement leader who forgave and understood the crimes of the past as unfortunate events in complicated times. In the 1660 Act of Oblivion, a general amnesty was declared to all but forty-one regicides and his father's two masked executioners. In a symbolic gesture, the bodies of Cromwell and his generals were disinterred, hung and decapitated. In addition, the army was dispersed and money found to pay arrears in the hope that the feeding ground of the republic would become neutralised as it scattered.

Locke remained in Oxford following the Restoration but kept a keen watch on the king's attempts to establish a new settlement. The new regime showed little interest in the university, and many of the scholars elevated during the Commonwealth remained in their positions, while only a few of the teachers purged in 1649 returned. Locke benefited from the reorganisation and was elected as Lecturer in Greek, while his college regained its role as the bastion of the Anglican establishment within the university. He became a tutor assigned to act *in loco parentis* for ten new students.

His interest in Natural Law led him to tackle another major issue of the times: religious toleration, in which the stability of the nation was in balance with the liberty of the individual. The return of the king did not just restore temporal power to the throne, for Charles II was also the divinely ordained head of the English Church, God's lieutenant on Earth. The Crown ruled the nation through the organisation of the Church, which had been the root cause of the Civil Wars. The Church itself needed to be addressed in order to find a true settlement.

Should Charles be understanding and allow the compliant non-conformist sects to continue their worship? Could the Anglican Church expand to include a diversity of congregations? Of particular importance to Locke as he pondered this question was the act of worship: was a prayer a personal or a political act? In the afterquakes of the interregnum, where the boundary between faith and politics had become indivisible, did the act of worship – the naked Quakers shouting in the streets, the Ranters who shook and screamed as they prayed, the Fifth Monarchists who demanded belief with the sword – need to be policed? Locke's fervent desire for order and strong government convinced him that the king should have total control of the religious practices of the nation.

Charles desired a new policy in which many of the compliant sects that had evolved from the Commonwealth would be tolerated, but he would not get his way. In the early months of 1661, a conference in London brought together the various congregations to debate the future of the English Church. There had been hopes that, while the more dangerous sects would be banned, a more tolerant atmosphere towards non-conformism would be promoted. It soon became clear, however, that the Anglican Church would be the only recognised orthodoxy. This was translated into law in a series of Acts passed by a rabidly Anglican parliament between 1661 and 1665, known as the Clarendon Code, named after Charles II's Chancellor, the ultra-conservative Lord Clarendon.

DISSENT AND EXILE

The Clarendon Code placed the nation in jeopardy, for under the new laws religious nonconformism was considered a political misdemeanour whether one was a fanatic or a compliant 'tender conscience'. Rather than uniting the nation, Charles II's settlement had cemented divisions, and Locke's call for strong government and a single official religion would criminalise many who wished to make their peace with the Crown. Others, who openly mourned the failures of the Commonwealth, were driven underground, hiding their faith in secret, hoping for the revival of the 'good old cause', or, as one old republican confessed in resignation: 'it was the King's time now to raigne ... it was upon sufferance for a little time, and it would be theirs agine before itt be long'.[11]

Even in its growing unpopularity, republicanism would not simply disappear, and among the grumbling and threats of determined malcontents, real dangers continued to erupt. In January 1661, fifty Fifth Monarchy Men, radical Puritans who wished to bring about salvation through holy war, stormed St Paul's churchyard and raided a nearby house belonging to a bookseller, Mr Johnson, who held the cathedral keys. When they were refused, the armed militants broke open the cathedral doors and stood guard, demanding allegiance from passers-by. Violence followed when one bystander was asked who he followed and replied the king. He was stabbed through the heart. The city militia were summoned but were repelled by the extremists, many of whom had served in the New Model Army. The Lord Mayor himself came with more troops and was able to drive the terrorists out of the city. Three days later the fanatics returned to St Paul's churchyard, where they fought with a whole regiment to the bitter end: twenty were shot in the yard, ten were captured, including the commander, Colonel Venner, and six who tried to escape were slaughtered.

This burning desire for the Puritan Revolution was kept alive in the hearts of people like PraiseGod Barbon. Through the years of the Civil Wars, Barbon had been a leading figure in London. He was a leather seller with a workshop under the sign of the Lock and Key on Fetter Lane, which wound off Fleet Street outside the city walls. He lived with his wife Sarah and their son, If-Jesus-Had-Not-Died-For-Thee-Thou-Wouldst-Be-Damned, born between 1637 and 1640. He was conscientious in his work, diligent towards his apprentices, who lived with the family, and participated within the the city hierarchy, the guilds. Literate – well versed in the English Bible, with a basic understanding of Latin and Greek – he was one of many in London who feared for his soul in the modern world. He was also a preacher, leader of a Baptist or Brownist congregation that would gather in his shop.

During the interregnum, Barbon had been chosen by Cromwell as one of the seven representatives for the City in the 1653 Parliament of Saints. The parliament had been at the heart of the new regime's attempts to establish a theocratic republic. It was PraiseGod's reputation as a radical, preparing the nation for Judgement Day, which gained the assembly the sobriquet 'Barebones Parliament', yet the experiment was halted by those who feared the extreme views of the members. Barbon nonetheless continued to pursue his millenarian vision and served within the City Common Council. Although he refused to sign a petition to call for the 'Fifth Monarchy' that heralded a New Jerusalem within London's walls, he was clearly one of its more vociferous supporters.

As the Commonwealth waned, he remained radically engaged and became a central figure at the republican meeting house in Bow Street, near Covent Garden. In 1660 he declared in a petition that the Restoration was illegal. Once the king had returned, he prepared a last-ditch attempt to overthrow the new regime, and in November 1661 was arrested for treason for his part in a plot to capture London and return a republican parliament. It was only ill health and the pleas of his wife, Sarah, that saved the preacher from the Tower.

The son of a dangerous radical, the boy baptised If-Jesus-Had-Not-Died-For-Thee-Thou-Wouldst-Be-Damned had grown up in London throughout the wars and Commonwealth, living with the family in Fetter Lane, and at the Restoration he faced persecution alongside his father. Like many young men, rather than accept the fears and limited existence of life under a distrusted monarchy, he fled. Many Puritans chose to rebuild their dreams of Jerusalem in the new colonies in America, while others, like Barbon, jumped the Channel and escaped to the Dutch Republic. Rather than remaining in the ports of The Hague or Rotterdam, the young Barbon looked for a future in the same place as Wren, Locke and Hook – education. He matriculated as a doctor of medicine in 1661 from the universities at Leiden and Utrecht.

Throughout the era of the Civil Wars it had been common for radicals to be rebaptised, and the ranks of the New Model Army were filled with soldiers with names such as Stand-fast-on-high Stringer, Fight-the-good-fight-of-faith White and even Kill-sin Pimple. At some point it was considered wise for If-Jesus-Had-Not-Died-For-Thee-Thou-Wouldst-Be-Damned to change his name to plain Nicholas.

In Europe, Barbon found himself surrounded by a society radically different to anything he had known in London. For in the mid-seventeenth century, the Republic, modern-day Holland, was a successful state held together by a convocation of Stadeholders, merchants and dominant nobles who saw religious toleration as the key to their nation's success. It was an urban society, dominated by the new bourgeoisie. The Republic offered a home for exiles fleeing the persecution of the Restoration, but also an alternative vision of what a modern Protestant nation could be – a true Commonwealth.

The Republic was a beacon of culture, a centre for art and architecture that far outstripped what was occurring elsewhere in Europe, especially England. The massive urbanisation that had followed the nation's rise as a seafaring power was reflected in the industrious bustle of the canalways and fine streets of Amsterdam, the leading city. Amsterdam defined what a financial capital should be, centred around its bourse, which dealt in every commodity from Baltic timber to Turkish tulips. The roads were paved and commodious while all around there were endless inventive works for drainage and the efficient transportation of goods and trade. Along the canals tall, elegant merchants' houses displayed the wealth that came from the busy port. These new houses displayed a proud national architecture, while in the major buildings of the capital the classical rules of the Renaissance had been adapted with Dutch flare. Symmetrical, tall and elegant, the houses were designed for modern living rather than gaudy display.

Barbon first studied medicine at the University of Leiden, where he learnt much more than the arts of diagnosis and cure. The university, set up in 1575, was the first in the country, and proud of its motto: *The Bastion of Liberty*. The institution encouraged freedom of speech and was the home of the exiled French philosopher René Descartes. The study of medicine was at the heart of the faculty, alongside theology, and it professed a revolutionary new curriculum that encouraged the practice of doctoring as well as study of ancient texts. John Evelyn had visited the school twenty years earlier and had noted the anatomy theatre that stood within a former Catholic church, which also housed a museum of rarities. Evelyn had matriculated from the university in one day but Barbon had to work much harder, and at St Cecilia's Hospital in the centre of town he was taught by Sylvius, the Professor of Applied Medicine, who was a leading light in new approaches to treating disease and bloodletting.

When Barbon went on to study at the newly established university at Utrecht he found a city that was home to Remonstrants, Lutherans, Mennonites, Collegiants, Jews and Catholics, who all got on with the business of business rather than tearing each other apart over questions of ritual. The young Barbon soaked up the atmosphere of a city dedicated to business, absorbing both the style and ambition of the Dutch city. The wealth that poured into the country's metropolitan areas brought with it a rapid urbanisation that in turn heralded a golden age of art, ideas and architecture. In the 1650s and '60s, Utrecht underwent a massive expansion, balancing the need for cheap housing to accommodate the rise of artisans and skilled immigrants with a sense of civic pride and grandeur that would beautify their city in comparison with other centres.

Watching Utrecht rise all around him, Barbon found himself greatly impressed by the scale of the building work and the wealth it generated. He would have noted the idiosyncratic Dutch style of housing that rose into the air to accommodate the rising population. Land was a rare commodity, but the Dutch builders had found an architecture that was both elegant and functional. It would be these lessons on the streets of Leiden and Utrecht rather than the techniques of bedside science which would have the most lingering influence on the young Puritan exile.

PREFERMENT

For those who welcomed the return of the king, the re-establishment of the royal court offered opportunity, while loyal members of the Establishment who had sat out the interregnum far from power dreamt of compensation and a return to favour. The royal palace of Whitehall became a hive of opportunists, the corridors bristling with petitioners hoping to jog the royal memory, or call in favours from one of the already anointed. 'I can't bussle,' John Evelyn admitted to his friend Samuel Pepys, and he failed to gain any rewards for his service during the Commonwealth. He soon realised that he would have to attract the king's attention some other way.

Evelyn's philosophical companions also sought to catch the royal eye, for the Restoration revived the dream of a college for Experimental Philosophy. Charles was known to be a keen experimenter, having passed some of his idle moments in exile in his laboratory. On 28 November 1660, after Christopher Wren had given his weekly Gresham lecture, a group of twelve men met to discuss the potential for setting up a new institution. In addition to a number of the leading names within the Wadham group, the meeting included a number of prominent royalists who had returned from exile alongside Charles: Sir Robert Moray, a talented amateur mathematician, and Viscount Brouncker, a royalist aristocrat whose father had been the king's childhood Vice Chamberlain. Sir Paul Neile, who had spent much time with Wren as they gazed at Saturn together, would be named Gentleman Usher of the Privy Chamber. From now on the progress in scientific knowledge that had once blossomed in the secluded academies of Oxford was forced to fend for itself in the commercial capital of the nation.

The location of the first meeting at Gresham College was a matter of circumstance, but soon after the group found that there was nowhere else to go. On 12 December, 1660, a committee was set up to approach the Royal College of Physicians, then considered a perfect match for the society, as 'the rendesvous of most of the learned Men about London, especially of those of the Royal Party'. It was more than a disappointment when the college turned them down and they were thus stuck at Gresham, 'weeke to weeke till further order',[12] sharing rooms with the permanent professors.

Next, the first members had to decide what kind of institution to be. They decided to follow the model of a debating society rather than an academic institution, based on the more informal European academies that a handful of the members had encountered on their travels. The new club, they claimed, had a role to play at the centre of culture and politics where 'reasonableness', and the avoidance of speculation, theory and dogmatism, could save the nation from the intellectual quagmire of the previous years. Wren, writing the draft Society Charter, attempted to announce this social agenda: 'the way to so happy a government we are sensible to is no manner more facilitated then by the Promoting of useful Arts and Sciences, which upon mature Inspection, are found to be the basis of Civil Community and free Governments'.[13]

In order to attract the attention of the powerful, however, the society also had to contain the influential. Thus the founders busied themselves with drawing up an ideal membership list in which prestige was as important as expertise, and it was clear from this list that the club looked west towards the court rather than seeking influence among the rich merchants of the City. At the first gathering the group had decided on an entry fee of 10 shillings, and a weekly subscription of 1 shilling. Hope of the king's favour came early when at the second meeting on 5 December 1660, Sir Robert Moray reported that 'the King had been acquainted with the designe of this meeting. And he did well approve of it, and would be ready to give encouragement to it.'[14] On 12 December 1660, forty prominent names were proposed, which read like a who's who of the new court. Early royal appreciation, however, took some time to turn into official approval.

Christopher Wren soon emerged as one of the most effective means of promoting the club. Following the Restoration, his uncle had been released from the Tower, having suffered eighteen years of imprisonment for his Laudian orthodoxy, and had returned to the see at Ely as a leading martyr of the Anglican cause. Christopher's cousin, also Matthew, had shot to the highest echelons of the new government as secretary to the first minister, Lord Clarendon. Wren, himself, was an early visitor to the court, returning to the king the papers that his father had held since being expelled from Windsor Castle in 1642.

The revived fortunes of the Wren family combined perfectly with the young philosopher's own ability to find favour with the king for his scientific prowess. He embodied the union between the Anglican orthodoxy and the potentially revolutionary notions of the New Philosophy, and was thus able to make the new system of knowledge look uncontroversial yet dynamic. His instinctive inclination to seek out practical and profitable experiments combined with his particular talent to construct visually exciting and entertaining results from experiments made the rarefied pursuits of the society look both brilliant and accessible.

Early in 1661, Wren showed the king his microscopical drawings devised under Wilkins's guiding hand in the 1650s. The studies included the image of a magnified louse in dreadful detail. In Wren's exquisite hand, the minutely small louse revealed its complex and sophisticated design. The picture had so impressed Charles II that Wren was then commanded to present more of his work, including a lunar globe that 'so accurately represents the Moon that on it are visible all the Moon's inequalities, heights, depths, seas, rivers, islands, continents etc.'[15] By August, Wren had completed his new version of the pasteboard model with the laudatory inscription 'To Charles the Second, King of Britain, France and Scotland, for whom Dr Christopher Wren has created the new world of this selenosphere, because, for one of his magnitude "one is not enough"'. Moray then arranged a meeting with the king at which the astronomer presented his gift in person.

Wren, however, was not the only member of the society working to gain the king's interest. John Evelyn first heard that he was invited into the society on 6 January 1661, recording: 'I was now chosen (and nominated by his Majesty for one of the Council), by the suffrage of the rest of the members, a Fellow of the Philosophic Society now meeting at Gresham College.'[16] From then on he worked tirelessly to raise the society's profile within the court. Although no more than a dabbler in chemistry in his laboratory at Sayes Court, Evelyn was integral to the society's commitment to 'useful knowledge', which, by its definition, could be turned to both cultural and financial capital.

In the first years of the Restoration he produced a rash of publications that promoted the club. In 1661 he translated Gabriel Naude's *Instructions Concerning the Erection of a Library* on how to catalogue and develop a library. In the preface, he twice used the name 'the Royal Society', the first instance of the official title in print. In a panegyric, a ceremonial oratory, read out before the king at his coronation in April 1661, Evelyn again made mention of the society. This was followed in 1662 by the translation of the French *Sculptura*, which surveyed the practice of the arts and included an appendix on the wildly fashionable new engraving method, *messo tinto*.

Later that year, Evelyn made a further contribution to the reputation of the society when he brought to bear his considerable experience and learning on the problem of London. *Fumifugium* presented a shocking portrait of the City. The pamphlet mixed erudition, social policy, environmentalism, town planning and architecture in one tract. The nation's capital stood in a sublime natural setting, he reported – 'the most considerable that the earth has standing on her bosome' – yet had been allowed to become a foul and stinking metropolis: 'the city of London resembles the face rather of Mount Etna, the court of Vulcan, Stromboli, or the suburbs of Hell'. In particular, the use of coal blighted and choked the city, ruined the elegance of the houses, caused fruit to wither on the trees and attacked the citizenry, so that they breathed 'nothing but an impure and thick mist, accompanied with a fuliginous and filthy vapour, which renders them obnoxious to a thousand inconveniences; corrupting the lungs, and disordering the entire habit of their bodies'.[17]

Evelyn's work attracted the attention of the king, who gave permission for the pamphlet to be published and began to use the author as a sounding board for his own concerns about the condition of London. In this role Evelyn, while developing his own reputation as a man of taste and distinction, was able to show that the New Philosophy was not just for the debating chamber or the laboratory but was capable of approaching the social issues of the day. Charles recruited Evelyn to sit on a number of official commissions under the Surveyor-General of the King's Works, the royal architect, who had been commanded to develop realistic solutions to the urban expansion. Evelyn became a mainstay in many of these protean quangos, shuffling through stuffy rooms discussing the problems of paving, sewerage and byways, the regulation of hackney carriages, as well as the role of the Royal Mint.

The society was finally granted its first charter on 15 July 1662. The charter not only gave the society a stamp of royal approval, the right to call itself 'Royal', but also the rights and privileges of a City Corporation. Two further charters were needed, however, to finalise the terms of the incorporation. In the second charter the king declared himself the Founder and Patron of the society and the name was changed to 'The Royal Society for the Promotion of Natural Knowledge by Experiment'. In addition, the society was given its own coat of arms and motto, *'Nullus in Verba'* (Take No Man's Word For It), both informed by Evelyn's antiquarian imagination. As a symbol of his patronage, the king also donated a royal mace, which would be present at every meeting.

UNEXPECTED OPPORTUNITIES

In February 1661, Wren was named Savilian Professor of Astronomy at Oxford. He gave up his professorship at Gresham College and left London, returning to Oxford. After the summer of 1661, therefore, he was in the capital less than before and attended fewer meetings at the society. Yet this did not stop the society from praising his name whenever it wished to promote itself. In the official *History of the Royal Society*, commissioned in 1663 and printed in 1667, the author, Thomas Sprat, was commanded to show how much the society had achieved in just under two years. The *History*, as much a marketing brochure as a historical record, placed Wren at the centre of the stage in order to bolster the club's reputation.

At Oxford, Wren continued his multifarious experiments in the company of others, in particular his colleague Robert Hooke. Oxford offered a small coterie of New Philosophers: Hooke continued to work with Boyle; John Wallis, the Savilian Professor of Mathematics, had held on to his post; Thomas Willis, the chemist of Beam Hall, had returned to the academy and took a prominent role at Christ Church as Professor of Natural Philosophy. Willis had hired Richard Lower, one of Busby's pupils from Westminster, as an assistant; he in turn brought into the group the lecturer in Greek at Christ Church, John Locke.

Locke had been introduced to the Wadham group only as it had begun to disintegrate. In 1659, he first read the philosophy of René Descartes and had soon become a regular attendee at Willis's lectures in the college. Eventually Locke met Boyle, and his old Westminster School fellow, Robert Hooke. Locke also attended the chemistry lectures by Boyle's protégé, Peter Stahl, and although there were complaints about his misbehaviour and his penchant for asking questions, his notes are the most thorough record of the lectures. The lessons had a powerful effect on the philosopher, for while his previous education had been dedicated to the study of books, he had now found a group of intellectuals who preferred the laboratory to the library, and he swiftly gained a passion for experimentation.

Wren was now at the pinnacle of the professional scientific community. In addition, he was getting new and unexpected offers for his talents which promised preferment and prestige beyond what the society or the university could promise. At a time when a professional scientist was a rarity, Wren's fascination with the New Philosophy did not offer the social status that a young Anglican grandee would have desired. Young, ambitious and burning with the desire to achieve something new, he could not ignore the opportunity of a court position.

He had already shown a practical interest in architecture. His glass apiary, which stood in Evelyn's garden at Sayes Court, was testament to the astronomer's interest in design, displaying his rare talent for ingenious and visually arresting solutions to complex problems. The list of his achievements also included the working out of numerous structural puzzles that were vital to the understanding of buildings. These had been small projects, dabbling in theories and experiments in model-making, beehives and sundials. Only the lack of opportunity, perhaps, had stopped him from building prior to this point.

His first chance at architecture arrived almost as soon as he gained the professorship. At the end of 1661 Wren was invited by the Crown to make a survey of Tangiers. The Mediterranean port had become English territory as part of the marriage dowry of Catherine of Braganza, who married Charles II in April 1662. The port had an unrivalled location at the mouth of the Mediterranean, where all trade could be monitored. The harbour, however, was considered vulnerable to attack. Matthew Wren, Lord Clarendon's secretary, had used his influence in putting the astronomer's name forward to conduct a report on the possibility of building a defensive 'mole' around the port. The role promised position, money and the prospect of future royal patronage. Wren seriously considered the job offer but, in the end, turned it down because of his weak constitution and poor health.

Yet Wren was soon being drawn away from his official role at Oxford by other projects. In a letter to Wren from Oxford at the end of 1661, Thomas Spratt reported that the vice-chancellor of the university was asking after the whereabouts of the Savilian Professor. If Wren was neither at the society nor at Oxford, where was he? Spratt's improvised excuse to Richard Baylie is tantalising: 'I used the arguments I could for yr. defence. I told him that Charles the Second was King of England, Scotland, France and Ireland; that he was by the late Act of Parliament declar'd absolute Monarch in these Dominions; and that it was this Mighty Prince who had confin'd you to London."[18] Charles II was already talking to Wren about Tangiers and, quite possibly, other architectural schemes.

For Robert Hooke, unexpected opportunities were also on the horizon, and he soon returned to London after almost a decade in Oxford. Hooke had won no favours in the Restoration and he would have to find his own position through his talents alone, but in the city his ascent was rapid. At the height of his inventive powers, Hooke came to represent the 'Baconian' man in action and would define the ambitions of the Royal Society, as it attempted to make a place for itself at the heart of the new regime.

The first note of Hooke's participation at the Royal Society was in April 1661 with the announcement of 'An Attempt for the Explanation of the Phaenomena, Observable in an Experiment Published by the Honorable Robert Boyle Esq; in the XXXV. Experiment of his Epistolical Discourse touching the Aire. In Confirmation of a former Conjecture made by R.H'. The original experiment had in fact been devised by Hooke in 1660 in Boyle's laboratory, but at the moment of announcement it was the patron who gained credit for the assistant's work.

By 1662 Hooke had become familiar with the newly chartered society, accompanying Boyle to meetings and making his own demonstrations with the Pneumatick Pump. When Hooke constructed a second pump, improving on the first, the original model was donated to the society at Gresham College, but as he was the only person who could operate the pump without embarrassing glitches, Hooke became a regular figure in the debating chamber. His timing could not have been better planned, for having received royal approval the society was attempting to settle down into some form of permanency. So far its main concerns had been gaining patronage and prestige; now it had to make good on its claims as a scientific institution, and one of the rights of the corporation was the ability to hire employees.

Henry Oldenburg was offered the post of secretary. In its desire to 'the settling of an universal, constant, and impartial survey of the whole creation',[19] a systematic library of materials, findings, reports and minutes had to be undertaken. Oldenburg thus conducted over three hundred correspondences a year with philosophers throughout Europe, spreading the name and deeds of the society as well as accumulating news of other discoveries conducted beyond London. He also oversaw the management of information within the society itself, devising and maintaining the *Philosophical Transactions*, a minute book of meetings and demonstrations held within the society. Oldenburg's role allowed the society to consider itself to be a unique information centre, but it did not help the club to fulfil its aspirations as a major research institution.

From the first meetings, the Royal Society was considered a place for experimentation. Each week particular members were asked to bring a demonstration to entertain and educate the meeting. Over the course of the first year, the informal position of curator was created and members were encouraged to bring their ideas and experiments to be displayed. It soon became apparent, however, that the society was split between a core of experimenters, members of the Wadham group and active virtuosi like Evelyn, and a wider audience of grandees and the fashionable, who came to be entertained. In addition, this haphazard approach to experiments did little to promote the long-term aspirations of the society; as Oldenburg would write to Boyle: 'we grow more remiss and careless ... our meetings are very thin'.[20]

Almost as soon as it was incorporated, therefore, the society had to re-examine its priorities. What good was the society without a systematic agenda of experiments and demonstrations? In November 1662, Sir Robert Moray proposed establishing a permanent position of curator, 'to furnish them every day when they met, with three or four considerable experiments'.[21] The meeting was unanimous in its approval, and only one name was put on the list of candidates: Robert Hooke.

Within the week, Moray reported back that he had gained Boyle's permission to release his assistant and Hooke was free to start work. From such easy initial negotiations it is an indictment of the society's precarious financial position that it took two years for Hooke's wages to be resolved. The society's offer stipulated an income of £80 a year, a sum which it could hardly afford on the uncertain flow of subscriptions. Instead they went in search of ways to supplement their offer with other sources to cover the difference, and in June 1663 Hooke was made a fellow of the society, which placed him in the inner circle of the club and exempted him from paying the usual membership fees. Six months later rooms were found at Gresham College for the curator, not only so that he might be close to where the society met but also to reduce his living costs. It was hoped that Hooke would soon gain a formal position within the college, and when Isaac

Barrow resigned as Professor of Geometry in May 1664 the society backed Hooke as their candidate against a London physician, Arthur Dacre, but was outvoted. Hooke was devastated and was certain he had been the victim of a conspiracy.

In the meantime, Hooke had been introduced to a wealthy merchant, John Cutler, who proposed to establish a new professorship at Gresham for Hooke to promote the History of Trades, offering an annual income of £50. As the society negotiated with Cutler it became clear that this £50 would be used to contribute to Hooke's £80 curatorship income rather than constituting a separate gift. Hooke was now expected to do two jobs for the price of one. In addition, in March 1665, having contested the election of Dacre, which turned out to have been rigged, Hooke gained a third role, committed to lecturing at Gresham twice a week on geometry. He took up permanent rooms within the quadrangle of the college, which would be his home for the rest of his life.

The curator must have struck a strange figure in front of the worthies and virtuosi of London. Only twenty-seven years old, Hooke, as described by John Aubrey, was 'of middling stature, something crooked, pale faced', yet his impact on the running of the society was almost immediate. By 1665, he had made such a name for himself he even deserved his own satirical portrait from the barbed pen of Samuel Butler:

> A Learned man, who once a week
> A hundred virtuosos seek,
> and like an oracle apply to
> T'ask questions, and admire and lie to.[22]

Hooke was to be the world's first professional research scientist commanded to conduct a systematic exploration of the New Philosophy. He was the right man for the job. His arrival allowed the society to rethink its priorities. In 1663, he offered a mission statement: *A Proposal for the Good of the Royal Society*, and in another document stated the aims of the club: 'To improve the knowledge of naturall things, and all useful Arts, Mechanick practise, Engynes and Inventions by Experiments – (not meddling with Divinity, Metaphysics, Moralls, Politicks, grammar, Rhetorick or Logick).'[23]

One particular area of investigation that the whole society was keen to explore was marine science and navigation, the space race of its day, and a supremely English subject. It was also well known that Charles II had a passion for sailing and placed the navy at the heart of his foreign policy. England's fortunes were to be made upon the oceans, and understanding the laws of the sea and marine inventions would be not only useful but profitable. In his first years as curator, Hooke, who had grown up by the shore and studied it as a child, concocted a series of instruments and experiments that attempted to reveal the mysteries of the deep and produce valuable patents for the society. There were inventions to check water depth, as well as engines to collect water from different depths to discover temperature and salinity, as well as to define the science of tides.

In a series of diving-bell experiments conducted in 1664, Hooke worked from his initial experiments on the weight of air within the pneumatic pump. He knew that one could extract air from a solid as easily as pumping it in. Thus, after initially devising a bell, bellows and goggles, John Evelyn was sent to the King's Docks at Deptford to find a foolhardy sailor willing to partake in a diving experiment on the Thames. By 4 June, after a few false starts, a diver was able to last four minutes underwater. The experiment was hailed a success, but the invention, like so many of the ideas that were generated by the society at the time, was too impractical and unwieldy to use day to day.

He had more practical success in discovering 'the History of Weather'. The original idea had come from Wren, who invented a rain gauge in 1661, and Hooke took the project over as his friend's attention waned. The curator could not stop himself making improvements: he perfected the thermometer to establish the freezing point of distilled water at the 'o degree' mark and contrived a hygroscope after ingeniously observing that an ear of oats bends in relation to the levels of atmospheric humidity.

Hooke's inventiveness was unbounded, and from his rooms at Gresham College he served the society with enthusiasm. At this most creative time in his life Hooke also had a determined appetite for the greatest challenge in the New Philosophy: gravity. René Descartes had proposed that the whole universe could be reduced to motion and weight, and that the motion of the planets was created out of the relationship between gravity and a centrifugal force; but he had offered no conclusive experiments to prove his hypothesis. Hooke therefore went in search of demonstrations that could build on Galileo's assumptions that there was some constant force that drew objects towards the Earth regardless of mass. But how did this force work upon the differing objects? Was it a magnetic attraction, its force decreasing the farther the object was away from the source? Could this attractive force influence the weight of an object in relation to its position vis-à-vis the Earth? Did an object lose weight as it travelled away from the world's surface?

In August 1664, Hooke took his experiments to the tower of St Paul's Cathedral. The tower, struck by lightning a century before, was precariously pinned together with scaffolding and iron bolts, yet at 204 feet high was the tallest structure in England. Here, throughout the summer, Hooke conducted a series of experiments recording the speed of objects dropping to the Earth and the changes in air pressure, as well as attempting to weigh objects at different heights. The calculation of the speed of the acceleration of objects was a painfully difficult operation: the pendulum was not an accurate enough instrument to record time and few man-made objects were tall enough to facilitate the calculation of the changes in an object's weight.

In order to measure the height, time and weight of things, Hooke devised a series of ingenious tools and instruments, including an 180-foot pendulum, to help him discern the minute differences, despite the inconveniences of the situation. By the end of 1664 he felt he had enough evidence to present his first ideas to the society. 'All bodies and motions in the world to be subject to change,'[24] he reported; gravity was variable according to height and location.

The terms of the Royal Society charter meant that they were also permitted to produce books under their own imprimatur without official censorship. The first title to be produced by the society was John Evelyn's *Sylva*, in 1664. Five years before, he had wondered whether to write a book on trees, and in a letter to John Wilkins he offered to contribute his own thoughts on arboriculture to the meeting, perhaps as an ongoing project from his *Elysium Britannicum*. The resulting book was an instant bestseller and reflected how the society went about its projects, for the production of the title owed as much to the society's system of investigation as it did to what Oldenburg described as Evelyn's 'exquisite pen'.

Since the end of the Civil Wars, the state of English forests had declined precipitously. Extensive logging had decimated tracts of woodland as a result of the slow supply of coal, and the need for aristocrats to sell their assets to keep afloat during the interregnum. The original discussion on forestry had begun at the society in 1662, requested by the Commissioners of the Navy on behalf of Charles II, who needed to rebuild his fleet. But it was Evelyn's virtuosity which transformed the book from a dry survey concerning supply and demand into one of the greatest volumes in English gardening history. The book brought John Evelyn the fame that he desired and confirmed his reputation as the leading horticultural commentator of the day. It also promoted the name of the Royal Society in all the best circles, not just as a centre for weighing air but as an organisation of real practical importance.

The second notable title to come from the society's printing press was Robert Hooke's *Micrographia* (1665). It was the culmination of his microscopical studies and brilliantly highlighted the society's commitment to seeing and promoting a new vision of the world. *Micrographia* was a very different book from *Sylva*, and with visual splendour promoted the Baconian experimental philosophy at the heart of the New Philosophy. The book set out Hooke's own creed: technology was vital in the discovery of truth and knowledge. The microscope or telescope, for example, improved man's defective vision, enabling mankind to examine the mysteries of the universe: 'By the addition of such artificial instruments and methods, there may be, in some manner, a reparation made for the mischiefs, and imperfection mankind has drawn upon itself.' Yet technology was nothing without method, and Hooke made a clear defence of the Baconian model: 'The science of Nature has already too long made only a work of the Brain and the Fancy'; it needed to be replaced by 'the real, the mechanical, the experimental philosophy'.[25]

Hooke started his investigations into the nature of things with man-made objects: under magnification a sharp needle point was shown to be blunt and ragged, a printed full stop was blurred, revealing 'so many marks of the rudeness and bungling of Art'.[26] Man's craft and industry were revealed to be imprecise compared with the complex beauty of nature. The book then turned its attention towards the living: the texture of moss, the pitted surface of sliced cork, the inexplicable beauty of seed pods. As the survey gathered speed, Hooke focused on the intricately small designs within fish scales, the sting of a bee, the shape of a louse and the multi-lensed eye of a fly. Hooke's illustrations revealed a new world to a general reading public; Samuel Pepys claimed that he had sat up in bed all night reading, transfixed by the curator's illustrations. Hooke's skilled hand as a draughtsman became a powerful rhetorical weapon in promoting his belief that the exploration of the mysteries of the unknown would not only reveal the infinite beauty of God's design, but would also show that these inventions reflected the same hidden laws that controlled the universe.

Hooke then ventured beyond the microscopist's bench and recounted his many investigations, including his observations of the moon, studies in combustion, refraction and optics, his rudimentary findings in gravity, pendulum and barometer experiments. His searches were so wide ranging that for many years after, when new discoveries were raised within the society, more often than not Hooke would be forced to declare that the subject had already been charted and recorded in *Micrographia*.

As winter turned to spring, following the publication of *Micrographia* in April, Hooke was finally to gain the recognition that he deserved – not just as a servant to the society but its most iridescent light. He had seized the opportunities – like his contemporaries Wren, Locke and Evelyn – that the Restoration had offered and found a role within the new era. Transformations, opportunities and preferment would be found throughout the new capital, not just among the courtiers and philosophers who celebrated Charles II's return. But despite the desire for change, the hopes of the new reign failed to hide the dangers that lurked beneath London's surface.

4

The Two Cities

In the first years of the reign of Charles II, London became the crucible for the transformation of the nation. It was here the first explosion of new ideas was felt and yet, while the revival of old institutions and the creation of new clubs and societies heralded the many notions that would hope to define the age, the city at large remained in a desperate situation.

The capital had burst from the city walls and everywhere one looked were people. The population of Westminster was eight times what it had been fifty years before, yet this hazardous expansion had been allowed without any official controls. Elegant Gothic spires rose out of the quagmire of slums; sturdy stone buildings – a livery hall, the house of a grandee – were surrounded by low tenements. The streets were crammed with pedestrians, horse riders and carts. It was quicker and safer to go by boat – even risking the perilous flows under London Bridge – than chance the streets and byways.

Descending from St Paul's churchyard on the summit of Ludgate Hill, the seventeenth-century traveller would exit the walls through Ludgate, the west entrance to the City that also doubled as a debtors' prison, and approach the fetid Fleet Ditch, once a defensive limit of clear spring water running from northerly Highgate Hill but now frequently choked with mud and filth – later described by the poet Alexander Pope as:

> Fleet Ditch, with disemboguing streams,
> Rolls the large tribute of dead dogs to Thames.[1]

Beyond the ditch, the road then led to Fleet Street, which ran parallel to the River Thames and westwards towards Westminster. As the city grew in size the outlying regions of Holborn, St Giles-in-the-Fields, Clerkenwell and Covent Garden had become the natural places for the first overspills of new immigrants to settle on land once owned by the monasteries and holy houses dissolved during the Reformation. Every attempt to curb this growth of the city had failed as the metropolis – a word first used to describe London in the 1650s – became too strong a magnet. The population explosion tipped the balance of power towards the areas outside the city walls.

Up Fleet Street were the warrens and forbidding houses of Bridewell, St Bride's Church and Salisbury Court. Farther to the north stood Fetter Lane, where, under the sign of the Lock and Key, stood the home of PraiseGod Barbon and his son, Nicholas, who had returned to the capital before 1664. Yards from Barbon's house stood the Temple Bar, an ornate stone gateway that acted as the ceremonial limit of the City, where, on official occasions, the king waited to be invited into the City by the Lord Mayor. To the west lay the aristocratic palaces of the Strand and the court and Palace of Whitehall, a region of royal land that had only recently begun to be developed outside the jurisdiction of the city authorities. London was in fact two cities that were merging together: the royal capital of Westminster to the west had become interwoven with the ancient City of London.

One generation before, the Strand had been the home of the finest aristocratic houses, such as Arundel House, the residence of Evelyn's hero Thomas Arundel and his fine collection of European art and marbles. This exclusive enclave had, however, lost some of its glamour; the neighbourhood had been swamped by new housing, so that the 'mansions of the nobles and courtiers rubbed shoulders with blind alleys, sheds and penthouses, springing up around, behind and against them'.[2] For the grandees returning from the capitals of Europe, the ramshackle Tudor palaces of the Strand only highlighted London's failure to present itself as a modern metropolis.

Signs of improvement could be seen to the north on open ground that until the 1630s had been farmland. Lincoln's Inn Fields had been two pastures on the edge of the lawyers' inns of court. The entrepreneur William Newton purchased the site and in 1639 persuaded Charles I to grant a building licence for thirty-two houses. In an attempt to develop a Continental square, plots on three sides were sold to builders. Close by, on the land of the Duke of Bedford granted to the family in the 1550s, more ambitious plans were afoot. Covent Garden, the city's first piazza, was being developed by Inigo Jones, inspired by the Piazza in Leghorn. Both

Lincoln's Inn Fields and Covent Garden were a signal for a new type of urban planning, but the wars had halted all attempts to glorify the capital with architecture. At the Restoration, London was in desperate need of attention.

The return of Charles II demanded not only changes in the religious, political and intellectual compass of the nation but also a transformation of the capital itself. In Louis XIV's Paris, architectural innovation emanated from the Crown; the king was the principal patron of the arts and set the fashion that everyone else followed. In England, however, Charles's forebears had rarely showered themselves in architectural glory. Charles, after years in the courts of Europe, had grander aspirations, and wished to present himself as a Baroque Prince. Nonetheless, his dreams of setting his reign in glorious stone soon turned to disappointment.

In May 1661, John Webb presented the king with initial designs for a new palace at Whitehall, placing Inigo Jones's Banqueting Hall at the centre of his plans. Webb was the most qualified architect in England and a nephew by marriage of Jones. His selection of the Banqueting Hall as the fulcrum of his projections was not happenstance. Jones's hall had already become one of the iconic buildings of the nation; built in 1619, it was the most classically perfect building in England. It was there that Charles's grandfather, James I, had entertained foreign dignitaries. The room, draped in rich tapestries, epitomised the grandiose (and aspirational) self-image of the king, while on the ceiling the finest artist in northern Europe, Peter Paul Rubens, had depicted the Stuart dynasty as God's lieutenants on earth. In addition, the site had gained symbolic resonance in 1649 as the stage for Charles I's execution. Through design and accident, Jones's masterpiece would become a symbol of the many different ways in which the new era wished to express itself: a modern building heralding what was to come; the signature of royal architecture expressing the absolutism of the Stuart dynasty; the memorial of an Anglican martyr that would resonate in church-building for a generation.

Beyond the hall, Whitehall was, as the French visitor Samuel Sorbiere noted, 'nothing but a heap of houses erected at divers times'.[3] Circumstances and the limits of the royal purse, however, distracted the king from a wholesale conversion of the palace, and while he wished to adopt the French style of kingship, he only added to the clutter. A new bedroom was built where Charles conducted the public ritual of falling asleep every

Inigo Jones's Banqueting Hall, one of the first modern buildings in Britain

night, and a privy bedchamber where the king finally slumbered. A new bathroom was attached to the apartment and, near by, a laboratory for the royal dabbling in chemistry. When the new queen, Catherine of Braganza, arrived in 1662, her apartments were also improved.

After 1663 Webb began to focus on plans for a palace at Greenwich, on the south bank of the Thames, which was begun in 1664. The King's Palace at Greenwich would be Charles II's first attempt to set his modern reign in stone. Ever jealous of his cousin, Louis XIV, in Paris, Charles allowed Webb to draw up plans for England's first baroque palace to rival Versailles. André le Nôtre, the designer of Louis XIV's palace gardens, was contracted to develop the landscape. The designer sent plans but never visited the site. Marble was ordered from Italy in preparation.

If the king could ill afford to enhance his monarchy with stone he was still determined to pose as the modern prince, seen and admired at a distance. The garden rather than the palace was the ideal setting for such promenades, and the Privy Gardens at Whitehall were improved, as was St James's Park, the royal hunting lands that stretched from Whitehall towards Westminster. The park was designed in the French style for the public display of business: avenues of trees to produce shaded promenades for the protection of the king as he strolled with his advisers. Here Charles would introduce the 'power walk' as he galloped up Constitution Hill, his attendants desperately trying to keep up. In addition, it was a place of leisure. The Earl of Rochester, the archetypal libertine, would rhapsodise about what he could get away with among the bushes, while a playing area was constructed for the new fashion for Pelle Melle, a French ball game that would later give the avenue its name, Pall Mall.

Yet Charles knew that he did not have the power to transform the nation through his own patronage alone, and in October 1661, aboard the royal yacht, he shared with Evelyn his concern that modern architecture was 'now very rare in England comparatively to other countries'.[4] London, unlike Paris, he feared, would rise through private commissions, not royal fancy. The king's ability to control this revival was cursory at best, for while all new commissions were legally expected to have their intentions approved by the Surveyor-General's office, the 'police architectonical',[5] yet this process was more to do with the purpose and practical aspects of the new project rather than its design or style. The renewal of London as a classically designed, modern city would therefore have to be won by argument and influence rather than by edict.

Advising the Surveyor-General on urban issues was not the most glamorous of roles but Evelyn accepted it and investigated the crisis in sewerage and byways with verve. Nonetheless, he kept in mind the image of the exemplary capitals he had encountered in Europe, and hoped to bring some of their learning to London. In the 1650s, as he set about the renovations at Sayes Court, he had begun a translation of a work on French architecture by the leading Parisian theorist, Roland Fréart de Chambray, but had set it aside. In the light of the emerging building boom, he returned to his desk with the hope that introducing the best Continental arguments for the modern style would have some influence on the development of taste in England. *Parallel* was finally published in the same year as his work on arboriculture, *Sylva*, and was an instant success.

Fréart's argument re-examined the classical orders derived from ancient Rome and revived during the Renaissance. He suggested that the new generation of architects should go back to the received assumptions and look again with new eyes, and learn new lessons. Their Renaissance forebears, such as Inigo Jones, saw proportion, the balance and relation between things, as the template for all architectural correctness. As a contemporary of Descartes and the first New Philosophers, Fréart proposed that perfection was to be found not in the relationship between things but in their exact measurement and dimensions. The ideal architects would therefore be New Philosophers who had 'their first studies well founded on the principles of geometry before they ventur'd to work, [and thus] do afterwards easily, and with assurance, arrive to the knowledge of the perfection of the Art'.[6]

Yet within Evelyn's translation was a warning. *Parallel* offered a scheme of looking at buildings in a modern way but it did not tell people what to build. Evelyn had noted that modern architecture was flexible enough to embody national sentiment and ideas: in Paris he had noted how the open spaces of the Place Royale had been inspired by the piazza at Leghorn but it was not an exact copy; in Holland he had seen that local traditions had manipulated and enhanced the universal standards set by the ancients; even in Rome itself he had marvelled at how Michelangelo and Bernini had been able to transform St Peter's from a traditional basilica into a modern masterpiece. He believed that England too could find its own style rather than slavishly aping the manners of others. If Evelyn was right, what did this 'Englishness' of English architecture look like?

In the first years of the 1660s, Restoration London became a laboratory of architectures as new buildings rose incorporating Roman, French, Dutch, Renaissance, baroque and traditional English styles, each chosen to visually signify status and taste in the new society. Out of these many experiments a modern national style would emerge, for as Evelyn would comment: 'we have as good right to invent, and follow our own genius, as the Ancients, without rendering our selves their slaves; since Art is an infinite thing, growing every day to more perfection, and suiting it self to the humour of several ages, and nations, who judge it differently, and define what is agreeable, everyone according to his own mode'.[7]

The first group of patrons who would explore the new frontiers of taste were the returning grandees, rich from the favours given to them following the Restoration, full of ideas they had picked up from their exile abroad. The most prized lands were no longer on the clogged Strand but close to the palace, in Piccadilly, far enough way from the urban squalor

Roger Pratt's design for Clarendon House, a revolutionary design
following the Restoration

without being in the countryside. The enclave would become an experiment in the articulation of aristocratic power, expressed as a modern European elite; the new houses, modelled on the Parisian *hôtels*, offered a bold vision for the future.

Lord Clarendon, Charles II's first minister, built Clarendon House to reflect his new-found position. Designed by Roger Pratt, Evelyn's travelling partner in Rome, the house was the epitome of English classicism. During his travels in Europe Pratt had experienced the many lessons of classical architecture, and he later wrote his own 'History of Architecture'. He had returned to England claiming the mantle of Inigo Jones, and thus displaying little interest in the new theories. In a series of ideas, *Certain Heads to be Largely Treated of Concerning the Undertaking of Any Building*, penned in June 1660, he defined his traditional classicism, which he brought to bear on Piccadilly.

At Clarendon House, Pratt was free to intermingle French, Italian and English motifs that he had absorbed from his travels, causing Evelyn to call it 'without hyperbolies, the best contriv'd, the most useful, gracefull, and magnificent house in England'.[8] In the early 1660s Pratt, more than any other architect, promised a powerful classical restraint to English architecture, a continuation of Jones's project. Unfortunately, the house was destroyed in the 1670s, following the fall from grace of Lord Clarendon, robbing the city of one of its finest buildings.

Next door to Clarendon House, Berkeley House rose from the fields of Westminster, designed by Hugh May, who had spent the interregnum as an exile in Holland. His travels had a profound effect on his designs, making him the leading exponent of Dutch Palladianism espoused by the new generation of Dutch architects, such as Jacob van Campen and Pieter Post, which attempted to classicise the traditional Flemish style. Like their French counterparts, the Dutch had absorbed the classical templates of Palladio without losing their own national sensibilities, transposing Dutch motifs, such as using brick with only a minimal amount of stone in the portico and pilasters. In Piccadilly May offered a new interpretation of the classical house which expressed a distinctive national style, avoiding all forms of rhetorical bombast, eschewing the ornate or florid.

The rise of new buildings in Piccadilly designed by Pratt and May set the tone for the first years of Restoration London, and while there were differences between the two, the similarities were more telling. Both attempted to revive the classical model in homage to Jones, yet were flexible in decorative effect. The importance of foreign travel to the taste of these two architects was paramount. Both designers had been influenced by their experiences abroad, and were willing to bring the lessons learnt to London. In addition, both highlighted the rise of the professional architect – for where houses had once been designed by experienced artisans, architecture was now a matter of taste and experience, devised by a gentleman who rarely got his hands dirty, and who took on the role of artist.

Just south of Clarendon House, between Piccadilly and Whitehall, another development was rising that would have a lasting effect on the shape of the city. Henry Jermyn, Lord St Albans, had served (some would say over-diligently) the king's mother in Paris during the 1650s, and while many cavaliers starved in exile, Jermyn had a full table and guarded it jealously. On his return, he insinuated himself into the court and began negotiating with the king for a plot of land to build a housing scheme, 'fit for the dwelling of noble men and other persons of quality'.[9] He had his eye on St James's Field, which had already become attractive to the well-to-do with a number of aristocratic dwellings. In gratitude for Jermyn's services, the aristocrat was granted a large parcel of land that stretched towards Bloomsbury, but only on a sixty-year lease. Jermyn's first project in 1662 was to build an *hôtel* for himself. He had greater ambitions, however, and the rise of St James's Square over the next thirty years would be a template of how the West End of London evolved, creating what the historian Roy Porter called a new class of 'aristocratic capitalists' who initiated the 'leasehold' revolution.

This new development of the suburbs not only heralded a new era in urban planning but also a change in architectural fashion and the adoption of Henri IV's Place Royale in Paris as the model for the London square. In the first years of the development Jermyn needed to find a balance between taste and economy. Matters of leases and freeholds were as important as the eventual designs for his square, and the aristocrat was forced to waste five years obtaining the freehold of the land before his plans could work, for as he explained in a petition to the king: 'men will not build palaces upon any terms but that of inheritance'. As other great houses for rich nobles went up along Piccadilly, Jermyn was forced to wait, for he was not building for his own glory but for profit.

The landowner sought advantage from the exploitation of his lands through building, and by parcelling out the land with a long lease to the finest builders Jermyn could guarantee the best fabric and the most elegant town houses on his land. The aristocrat's schemes went beyond the square: he envisioned a whole community, what Evelyn would call 'a small town': a number of principal dwellings around the square, with mews for trades-men and secondary streets for middling sorts. He even planned a market, and a parish church.

The scheme was simple. The individual plots of land were leased to speculators who were obliged to follow the directives of the landowner. The builders themselves were businessmen and in search of profit. After first contracts with the speculators, a seed rent was paid while the 'carcass' of the building was being constructed. As soon as the bare shell was finished, the builders then attempted to sell the property on to prospective owners while also subcontracting down the chain to painters and dec-orators who could finish the building to the new owner's specifications. The aristocratic capitalists made money on the long-term guarantee of ground rents under the terms of the lease, while the speculator could make a fortune on the short-term sale price of the house.

A PLACE FOR THANKSGIVING

Yet not all the rebuilding schemes were begun with the hope of noble splendour or profit. The revival of the Anglican hierarchy in 1660 brought with it a renewed interest in the power of ritual and liturgy as expressed in the return to power of the bishops. The established Church had been devastated during the interregnum, and at its centre St Paul's Cathedral was the most visual symbol of the crisis. The sacred space had been abandoned during the Commonwealth, and as was reported in the House of Commons in February 1659: 'all the workmen in the world will tell you the foundation is rotten'.[10] This was hardly the image of the divine king's return that Charles wanted.

Nonetheless, the king could not immediately turn his attention to the cathedral and as a temporary half-measure, space was cleared inside the east end of the nave for a small auditory. In the meantime Charles was forced to restore London's clergy, which had been scattered and persecuted during the interregnum. A new generation of ministers needed to be found, and it was difficult to promote from within the shattered hierarchy. Dr Gilbert Sheldon, a forceful and devout man who had clandestinely kept the Anglican flame alive in London during the 1650s, was named bishop to replace Juxon, who had died in August 1660. Once elevated to the see of London, Sheldon gathered around him a chapter of hard-line conservatives and focused the energies of the cathedral on ridding the city of its Puritan past, weeding out nonconformist clerics from the pulpits.

The fabric of the cathedral soon asserted itself as a priority, however, when masonry was found to be peeling off the building. In April 1663, Charles set up a commission to assess the damage to 'that magnificent structure ... which hath so much suffered by the iniquity of the late times'. The commission comprised bishop, dean and six others, including Lord Clarendon, and the Surveyor-General, Sir John Denham, and was set the task of preparing the ground for rebuilding and to 'search, discover, try, and find out the true state of the said church and the particular decays thereof'[11] and start fund-raising, while also assessing the stone quarries that would provide the new material for the building.

The first priority of the group was to collect money, which was slow in coming. The cathedral belonged to the king and the Church, and neither institution was in a ready position to fund a major renovation. Parliament had more pressing issues to discuss than architecture, and while many Londoners had lined the streets to celebrate the king's return, they were not yet ready to open their purses to fund the cathedral, which had recently symbolised the dangers of absolute monarchy. By the end of the first year, the commission had raised only £3,000; by 1666, just over £6,000.

The commission then had to decide how best to restore the cathedral. In acknowledgement of the severity of the problem the committee did not fall under the sole architectural guidance of the Surveyor-General but, for the first time in the Church's history, was free to seek advice from 'other persons of known ability and integrity'.[12] The first person to report on the condition of the church, however, was Sir John Denham, alongside John Webb and the Royal Mason, Edward Marshall. The Surveyor made the mistake of assuming that his royal position gave him precedence over the commission, and before delivering his report he began ordering supplies in order to commence the work, importing timber from Norway for the scaffolding.

When the report did arrive in July 1664, it sent a shiver through the committee. The tower, ruined by lightning a century before, was 'much decayed and anciently settled & badly cracked', which placed an impossible burden on the rest of the structure. Serious recovery work was prescribed: taking down all the roofs and removing the spire; the vaults needed rebuilding as a result, yet 'the Work can not be done without great danger and Hazard of the workmen's lives'.[13] The commission had only just begun their fund-raising efforts so the scale of work proposed in the report made the group pause. To stall the work, the commission requested that Webb focus on the repair of the west portico rather than begin dismantling the heart of the structure.

In the meantime, the commission went in search of more palatable recommendations, requesting Roger Pratt to make a full survey of the nave and tower, while Hugh May reported on the state of the vaults and pillars. Pratt's January 1665 report outlined how the building could be patched up for as little cost as possible. There was no need for wide-scale alterations; a structural survey was needed for the roof to see how it was standing, but most repairs could be completed in brick or stones that lay round about and then covered in mortar to hide the work. Pratt's penny-pinching recommendations were appealing to the commission but not absolutely convincing, particularly as they seemed to suggest another round of surveys rather than a definite solution.

The commissioners now had two contrasting reports on the state of the cathedral, yet they still could not make a final decision. There was not enough money in the coffers to start work, and in addition there was a series of changes within the cathedral hierarchy to add to the delay. One other reason for pause, however, was prominent: the problems with the cathedral were more than just a question of orders and ornaments, but also of science and engineering. The size of the structure was awesome. The solution to St Paul's revival would demand not just the experience of a brilliant designer but also someone with the skills of a supreme engineer.

In the past few years, far from London, Christopher Wren had begun to express his New Philosophy in stone. In 1662, after his release from the Tower of London, Wren's uncle, the reinstated Bishop Matthew Wren, fulfilling a promise he had made in jail, donated money for a chapel to be built at his old alma mater, Pembroke College, Cambridge. The commission was a private project, wholly funded by the bishop, who had the freedom to choose any design or architect that he wished. He selected, somewhat surprisingly, his nephew, Christopher, as architect. At a time when the architect's primary concern was to develop plans and elevations rather than oversee the building work, Wren had gained enough of the theory to be able to complete the job. In addition, he was commissioned to develop the structure of the building and its façade while other designers devised the interior. His initial plans were drawn up in the winter of 1662 and approved by both the bishop and the college the following spring.

Wren made a wooden model as a means of exploring and explaining his architectural ideas. The building itself was conventional, but where he was able to express his first ideas of composition was on the façade, looking out on to busy Trumpington Street. Wren sought inspiration from the classical masters, borrowing a design from Sebastiano Serlio's influential book *On Architecture*. But while Wren adopted Serlio's orthodox design he also adapted it: two bold pilasters, columns embedded in the flat face of the building, rose from the ground and encased a central rounded window. The classical form was manipulated to give the temple façade the appearance of a triumphal arch, alluding to both the revival of the bishop's fortunes and the restoration of the king. This playfulness in expressing a dual meaning would never have been accepted by the stricter classical architects, such as Jones or Pratt, but from the very start Wren was expressing a flexibility of effect, infused with the baroque's sense of the modern.

In the same year, through family contacts and as a high-profile Oxford professor, Wren gained a second commission from another leading member of the Anglican hierarchy, Bishop Gilbert Sheldon, an Oxford man to the core. Since the days of Archbishop Laud there had been hopes that a new place could be found for the annual graduation ceremonies that had traditionally taken place in the university church of St Mary's in the High Street. It was considered tasteless that the potentially rowdy, secular event should happen in a house of God. Sheldon wanted to gift a new building to his beloved academy and donated £1,000 in the hope that others would add to the pot; no one else came forward. In the end Sheldon was forced to pay for the whole building, donating £25,000 of his own money.

The new building was to be a secular space, so Wren returned to his books of classical templates and began designs modelled on the Theatre of Marcellus in Rome. The design and size of the building were far more ambitious than those of the small chapel in Cambridge and brought with them a number of challenges. In April 1663, Henry Oldenburg reported to John Evelyn that Wren had brought his model for the theatre into the Royal Society for approval but had been sent back to the drawing board, his first designs deemed too expensive. The first stone was not laid until July 1664. In the intervening year, Wren worked on his design, thinking through the implications and structural issues as an experimenter works through his method. He also sought advice from John Evelyn, who introduced his friend to his own ideas on the formation of modern English architecture. Not surprisingly, therefore, as Evelyn's translation of Fréart's *Parallel* was completed, the virtuoso made sure that Wren was one of the first people to receive a copy.

The interior of the theatre was a vast open space, modelled on a recognised classical theatre. Built in a D shape, the room curved around a central focal point where the vice-chancellor would speak on official occasions. At the flat end of the room large windows flooded the space with light, as did windows around the sides that focused on the centre of the space. At the same time Wren was thinking about a double reflecting telescope that also focused light on to the image of a distant star in the same manner. High-banked tiered seating ran up the walls and a higher gallery reached to the roof. The galleries were supported by pillars, thin enough not to obscure sight lines.

Wren's most inspired innovation was the construction of the roof. The

Roman theatre, designed for the southern Continental summer, had been open to the sky but could be covered with a cloth awning when necessary. Wren needed to find a way to construct a covering with a span of 70 feet, far wider that any single plank of timber. The roof, in effect, had to keep itself up, and here Wren's skill as a problem solver came to the fore. At Wadham College, John Wallis had worked out a way to lattice planks together to make a self-supporting 'geometric flat floor'.[14] The rigid right-angled web of timbers spread the pressure throughout the whole structure and could withstand great weights.

Having consulted his old Wadham colleague, Wren turned this floor design upside down with a series of beams that held the structure up. The ceiling was then decorated by a *trompe l'oeil*, the first of its kind to be designed by an Englishman, the king's painter, Robert Streater. When Evelyn saw the room on the inaugural opening in 1669, he remarked on the creation of his friend: 'It is, in truth, a fabric comparable to any of this kind of former ages, and doubtless exceeding any of the present.'[15] The ceiling was so strong that centuries later the attic was used by the University Press as their warehouse.

Wren was learning architecture through practice, just as he had uncovered the laws of nature through experiment. Even at this early stage of his new career he absorbed and studied the works of the ancients but never accepted their authority as received wisdom. He was developing an eloquent, flexible means of expression, even if he had not yet found his architectural voice. That would find its true expression as he turned his focus towards London's cathedral.

It is unclear exactly when Wren was first consulted on the condition of St Paul's. There are some suggestions that the king privately requested his counsel in 1661, but he was not one of the original commissioners. In 1663 William Sancroft, who was close to the Wren family and in the same year had requested designs from the architect for a new chapel at Emmanuel College, Cambridge, was named dean of the cathedral. Some time afterwards Wren was asked to make his judgement as one of the 'other persons of known ability and integrity'. Unexpectedly, he did nothing.

At the same time Wren was also becoming increasingly central in Charles II's plans for Whitehall, an opportunity that came about as much from his emerging talents as from the unusual circumstances. Sir John Denham, the Surveyor-General, was gravely ill that summer, suffering from smallpox so severe that his face had turned into a mass of ulcers. He was old and showing signs of physical and mental collapse, exacerbated by the embarrassing spectacle of his young wife being brazenly courted by James, Duke of York. Dishonoured and disheartened, Denham flew into a fit of despair, acting erratically. It was even claimed that he visited the king, announcing he was the Holy Ghost. In the interim Hugh May was hurriedly named to execute the role of Surveyor, while Wren was commanded to focus his attentions on Whitehall. In 1664 John Evelyn came across the king in the Privy Garden at Whitehall, who then sketched a new plan of the whole palace for Evelyn's approval. As described by Evelyn, the king's designs were very similar to Wren's own plans. Wren was clearly beginning to make a name for himself in London not just as a leading astronomer but also as an architect.

THE VISITATION

While pockets of London began to show signs of modern building, and the talents of architects such as Pratt, May and Wren were bringing new lessons to the capital, the city itself was a medieval jam of alleys and back streets. In 1665, John Graunt, a member of the Royal Society, conducted a survey of the rise of the burgeoning population, concluding: 'London, the Metropolis of England, is perhaps a head too big for the body ... our parishes are now grown madly disproportionate ... the old streets are unfit for the present frequency of coaches.'[16] Amid this bustle, a general fear began to spread that something terrible was about to occur.

The seeds of London's demise were sown in astrologers' books, almanacs, the pamphlets from firebrand preachers and the rantings of deluded fools. In the winter of 1664, a comet passed over the city and Wren and Hooke were charged by the Royal Society to chart its path. Others did not see it so objectively – the astrologer George Thomson warned, 'Blazing stars, do portend some Evil to come upon Mortals.'[17] Yet it was not just the arrival of the comet which brought bad news, for the planets were lined up against London, and William Lilly saw in a lunar eclipse in January the herald of 'the sword, famine, pestilence and mortality or plague'.[18]

Closer to home, London was suffering its second bad winter in a row. It had not rained since October and a heavy snowfall in January with frost, wind and ice brought the metropolis to a halt. Coal prices were at a peak and conditions became so harsh that the city was forced to regulate the price of bread. As the stores of grain decreased, the weight of a penny loaf was reduced from 11.5 ounces to 9.5 ounces. This was a surer sign that the city was in danger of a deathly visitation.

At Christmas 1664, in the parish of St Giles-in-the-Fields, a few hundred yards north of Covent Garden, the first recording of a plague death was written into the parish register. Some accounts of how this occurred claimed the plague had arrived from abroad, bundled in a pack of cloth from Holland. The Dutch had fallen to the 'distemper' the year before, and all ports had been boycotted by the English fleet. Yet greed always found a way through the barricade, and in autumn 1664 signs of the plague had reached Yarmouth on the east coast, a frequent trading port. Somehow death made its way to London.

Two medical accounts, written by the physician Nathaniel Hodges and the apothecary William Boghurst during that 'dreadful visitation', had different theories. Hodges was a local physician who was called out to attend to a patient during the Christmas holidays: 'to a young man in a fever, who after two days course of alexiterial Medicines, had two risings about the bigness of a nutmeg broke out, one on each thigh';[19] the fortunate man survived. In Hodges' opinion the disease had travelled to London from Holland and was abroad within the parish of St Giles by Christmas. Boghurst, the apothecary, however, thought that these early deaths showed that the plague was ever present within the city, latent in the soil: 'the earth the seminary and seedplott of these venomous vapours'.[20] In his view, the decay of the overburdened city presented the right conditions for death to settle and begin its work, while the bitter winter pummelled the weak in anticipation of the epidemic.

Another death was announced on 14 February 1665, in St Giles parish, but it did not cause a stir. In April there was a single rainstorm and it remained cold until the end of that month. During the calm, the Bills of Mortality, the weekly parish register of deaths, reported a dramatic rise in death from 'spotted fever' (smallpox), and 'gripes of the stomach', perhaps a misdiagnosis of the plague 'tokens' that mimicked the appearance of many other afflictions. It was only at the end of April, when two more deaths were announced in Drury Lane, that panic began to filter through the city. On 27 April, news reached the King's Council at Whitehall, which immediately ordered that the family of the dead be locked in the contaminated house for forty days. This rash edict ignited a 'ryett'. Local friends and family overpowered the guards: 'the door opened in a vicious manner and the people of the house permitted to go abroad into the streets promiscuously with others'.[21]

In response the council commanded watchmen to stand on parish boundaries and to make sure that no affected persons moved from one neighbourhood to another. But this was a measure too little, too late, and due preparations were made for an epidemic: three justices of the peace were given money to purchase land on the outskirts of the city for a series of new pest houses, rudimentary hospitals to combat the infestation, to be built at Marylebone, Soho in the west and Stepney in the east. Roads and fords were prepared to deliver the sick without having to transport them through populous neighbourhoods. By the end of that month, the plague was claiming over one hundred deaths a week and was swiftly making its way from the West End into the heart of the City.

In the first weeks of May, as the weather turned from the dead of winter to a hot and humid summer, a death was reported in the parish of St Mary, Woolchurch, causing a wave of fear as the official newssheet, Roger L'Estrange's *Intelligencer*, attempted to downplay the extent of the disease. Nonetheless, the Earl of Clarendon noted that experience was the best part of valour: 'ancient men, who well remember'd in what manner the last great plague first broke out, and the progress it afterwards made, foretold a terrible summer'.[22] Anyone who could leave the city prepared their departure and the streets began to clog up as the better sorts took to their country houses, following the axiom 'go early, stay long, return late'. Charles II prorogued Parliament until the following September so that the members could scamper away to the country. By July, Whitehall was almost empty; the 25,000 people who lived and worked around the court had departed. As the Puritan divine Thomas Vincent drily observed: 'The great orbs begin first to move; the Lord and gentry retire into their countries; their remote houses are prepared, goods removed, and London is quickly upon their backs'.[23]

Clerics, doctors and city elders were the next to go, leaving 'their debts as well as their charity'. As the Puritan Edward Cotes later mourned: 'may neither the physicians of our souls or bodies hereafter in such numbers forsake us'.[24] The lawyers left the Temple and Inns to guards and the courts were closed. After setting up a relief fund for the parishioners within the cathedral parish, Dean Sancroft was one of the first to flee, retiring to the spa town of Tunbridge Wells, Kent. Before the Royal College of Surgeons was officially shut, the president announced that an official apothecary, William Johnson, on Amen Corner, would dispense 'a peculiar and proper medicine' for free. The Royal College of Physicians also made their recommendations before leaving, producing *Directions for Cure of the Plague*. These worthies were soon followed by the tradesmen, faced with the dilemma of leaving their workshops and risking financial ruin or staying only to encounter death.

The last meeting of the Royal Society was held at Gresham College on 28 June before the fellows scattered. Robert Hooke left his rooms at Gresham and travelled with John Wilkins and William Petty to the country estate of Sir Charles Berkeley at Durdans, near Epsom. Here, the New Philosophers continued their experiments and were visited in August by John Evelyn, who found them 'contriving chariots, new rigging for ships, a wheel for one to run races in, and other mechanical inventions'.[25] Hooke in particular found the retreat highly productive, for while he had struggled devising experiments to determine gravity among the rafters of St Paul's, he was fortunate to find a series of deep caves on nearby Banstead Downs. His preliminary experiments in London had shown that weight and pressure varied as a body was lifted away from the earth; he could now test whether the reverse was true as he experimented in the wells and crevasses that reached deep into the ground.

In London, measures were taken in hand to control the spread of disease and anarchy. The king had left the city in the hands of his generals, Lord Albemarle and Lord Craven. In fear that the plague might encourage insurrection, a repressive campaign was initiated to banish all old soldiers from Cromwell's army, and arrest hundreds of suspects. The Tower was reinforced to hold those presumed guilty without trial. Hooke's friend, Sir John Lawrence, the Lord Mayor, remained at the Guildhall and on 1 July published his *Orders*, which outlined the city's response to the plague, which was soon claiming over a thousand deaths a week. All entertainments were banned, fairs were cancelled, theatres shut up and tippling houses were closed at nine every night. A wholesale slaughter of 'hogs, dogs or cats, or tame pigeons, or conies' was ordered and catchers paid twice the daily wage for each carcass, culling over forty thousand pets in total. Begging was forbidden while steps were taken to clean up the parishes. Municipal rakers and scavengers visited daily to collect refuse and made sure that 'no stinking fish, or unwholesome flesh, or musty corn, or other corrupt fruits'[26] were held or sold.

The *Orders* commanded the shutting up of contaminated houses as the sole prevention of the spread of disease. When a person fell sick it was the obligation of the master of the house to inform the authorities. The patient was then searched by an examiner together with a surgeon. If found to possess the plague, the patient was either transported to one of the pest houses or the house was shut up and placed under quarantine with all the members of the family inside. A watchman was to stand guard outdoors while a nurse tended the sick inside. On the doors of such houses a red cross was drawn, often with the exhortation 'Lord Have Mercy on Us'. For many this preventive measure was nothing short of barbarous, condemning a whole family to certain death. Some families tried to escape this fate, tunnelling through the back of the house, or exploding gunpowder in the face of the watchman, rather than wait for death.

The mayor also attempted to set up an official commission of physicians, surgeons and apothecaries to oversee the care of the sick. Only four physicians, including Nathaniel Hodges, remained in the city. They were promised £30 and a further wage at Christmas, if they survived that long. Nicholas Barbon, recently admitted as an honorary fellow of the College of Physicians after his years of study in Holland, wrote to the Guildhall to offer his help but was rejected as a dissenter and presumed foreigner; his presence in the city was considered too dangerous. Even in such desperate conditions, being the son of PraiseGod Barbon was an unwashable stain.

Instead, Barbon was sent to work in one of the pest houses that ringed the city. The ramshackle barns, with room for less than a hundred patients, were crammed with the beds of the dying. The floor had become so fetid with vomit and waste that it was safer and easier to climb over the packed beds. Patients came here to die rather than find cures. A pit was built yards from the house in which the bodies were flung, their still-warm beds soon to be filled by new victims. In a later petition from Charles Wilcox, the doctor in charge of the pest house near the Tower, the picture of life inside the hospital was grim. There was no medicine; most of what there was was paid for by Wilcox, who never received compensation. The cycle of contagion was merciless: 'many of the sick persons were unruly in their distempers, which necessitated more servants and nurses to attend them, and they also falling sick at times did increase the number of sick'.[27]

By August all attempts to combat the epidemic were failing and the city fell silent as the death toll reached over eight thousand a week at its peak. The streets were empty: 'few ruffling gallants walk the streets; few spotted ladies to be seen at windows'. Gardens were left to ruin so that 'Roses and other sweet flowers wither in the Gardens, [and] are disregarded in the Markets'.[28] The disease had infected every street, so it soon became 'impossible, and indeed to no purpose, to go about to inquire who was sick and who was well'.[29]

Hodges and Boghurst continued their visits and doctoring, with little hope of success. Boghurst reported that he 'drest forty soares in a day, held their pulse sweating in the bed half a quarter of an hour together to give judgement and informe myself in the various tricks of it. I lett one blood, gave glisters, though but to a few, held them up in their beds to keep them from strangling and choking half an houre together', and more often than not 'stayd by them to see the manner of their death, and closed up their mouth and eyes'.[30]

Where once the parish church bells rang out announcing every death, filling the air from dawn until dusk, now they fell silent. At Cripplegate, the bells broke with overuse, while elsewhere there was no one left to toll the dead. Instead, the streets were quiet, except for the cries from inside the locked houses, where 'in one room might be heard dying groaning, in another the Ravings of a delirium, and not far off Relations and Friends bewailing both their loss and the dismal prospect of their own sudden departure'. Desperation gripped the city and, walking one day, the Puritan Thomas Vincent watched as an infected man ran himself against a wall, dashing his head open, 'hanging with his bloody face over the rails, and bleeding upon the ground', only to die half an hour later.[31]

John Evelyn remained in the city on business, tearfully sending away his wife and family to a safe distance. In February, Charles II had declared war on Holland and Evelyn had been named as a prestigious commissioner to care for the sick and prisoners of the war. Throughout the summer he was busy as he managed the care and incarceration of thousands of sailors. As the British navy began to engage their Dutch enemy, he was sent around the ports of the south coast to collect prisoners and set up field hospitals. Initially the war went well with a victory led by the Duke of York, but soon the plague was found among sailors in Portsmouth and a pest ship had to be arranged. The numerous tasks forced Evelyn to ride to London often (usually to ask for more money, which was slow to arrive), and in August he was dismayed to see 'so many coffins exposed in the streets, now thin of people; the shops shut up, and all in mournful silence, not knowing whose turn it might be next'.[32]

Another group that remained in the city were the Puritans and fanatics who had been forced underground in the first years of the Restoration by the machinations of the Clarendon Code. The plague brought the dissenters back into the streets, provoking fear in the authorities. Pamphlets such as *Golgotha* and *God's Terrible Voice in the City of London* began to appear, calling the plague a message from God to punish the luxury and sin of the citizenry. As the plague entered every parish the unguarded pulpits soon filled with Puritans haranguing the city, the services becoming so popular that the preacher 'could not come near the pulpit door for the press [of the congregation], but are forced to climb over the pews to them'.[33] Quakers too took to the streets, visited and nursed their own, undaunted by the doors daubed with red crosses, willing to accept the judgement of God as they continued in their charity.

This soul-searching combined with a desperate need for mourning and by August, against the commands of the Lord Mayor, funeral processions began to snake through the city as the living felt an unbearable urge to mark the passing of their kin. Nearly 100,000 bodies went to the grave by the end of that year. It is impossible to say how many were natural deaths and how many caused by the plague, but with the estimate that nearly 100,000 citizens had fled the city during that period, it is apparent that one in three who remained did not survive to see the end of the year.

Corpses began to pile up in the houses as the carters were overwhelmed by their task. The parish burial grounds were soon full and began to swell and move as the corpses decomposed in their shallow graves. There remained few sextons to dig the graves; instead new pits were dug into which hundreds of bodies were thrown and covered in lime. When the timber yards had no more wood to make coffins, the dead were wrapped in shrouds, the sheets they died in, yet as their bodies were so roughly manhandled they often slipped into the clay naked and exposed. Puritan preachers stood vigil by the pits while, according to the novelist Daniel Defoe, men ran and threw themselves on to the rising pile of bodies to hasten their deaths, while others scavenged among the corpses for jewellery.

Winter saw the slow decline of the death toll. On 31 December, John Evelyn wrote in his diary: 'Now blessed be God for His extraordinary mercies and preservation of me this year, when thousands, and ten thousands, perished, and were swept away on each side of me.'[34] Reports of deaths continued into the New Year and the court did not return to London until February, when things began to return to normal within the city and the shops tentatively reopened. Yet for some this return was a cruel moment of peace before the return of God's wrath. The Puritan preacher Thomas Vincent watched his city with exasperation and warned: 'when they apprehended the danger to be over, they dropt asleep faster than before; still they are the same or worse than formerly; they that were drunken, are drunken still; and they that were filthy, are filthy still'.[35]

LESSONS FROM ABROAD

The responses to the plague had been varied: Robert Hooke had sought an escape to continue his work in the countryside, while Barbon and Evelyn had remained. Barbon exposed himself to the dangers of the disease, working in the pest houses; Evelyn had dedicated himself to service of the Crown in his role as the commissioner for the sick in the war against the Dutch. As the capital suffered, however, others chose to leave the country. During this period Wren and Locke, for the first time, set out on journeys to the Continent.

In Oxford, John Locke had risen within the college faculty and in 1664 was elected Censor of Moral Philosophy, a position that lasted only a year. If he wanted to continue the academic life his best chance of preferment would come if he joined the Anglican Church. Instinctively he knew that a clerical life was not for him. His investigations into the New Philosophy alongside Boyle, Hooke and Willis had instilled within him a passion for science, and he contemplated becoming a doctor. He sought advice from his friends; John Strachey feared that he was already having independent ideas that would not fit comfortably with the restraints of the Anglican hegemony, and the role would 'meddle with your owne genius and inclination'.[36]

Instead, he travelled to Germany, joining the diplomatic team of Sir Henry Vane, who had been commanded by the king to visit the Elector of Brandenburg in Cleves, Germany, to negotiate allegiance in the war against the Dutch. The mission was a failure; the elector was happy to remain neutral, but at a cost that Charles II could ill afford. The delay in negotiations, however, allowed Locke to explore his surroundings, and like Evelyn and Barbon before him he was struck by his first visit to the Continent. He also had plenty of time to write to friends at home, while the mysterious lady 'Scribelia' kept him abreast of all the news in London and Oxford.

In one letter to his friend Robert Boyle it became clear that the foreign city was having an unexpected impact upon the young philosopher. He was particularly impressed by the policy of religious toleration, writing, 'they quietly permit one another to choose their way to heaven; and I cannot observe any quarrels or animosities amongst them on account of religion. This good correspondence is owing partly to the prudence and good nature of the people, who, as I find by enquiry, entertain different opinions without any secret hatred or rancour'.[37] The experience of Cleves inspired him not to take holy orders and to find a new course. He was offered another diplomatic brief, but decided against going on his travels again and returned to Oxford, determined to become a doctor. Locke's brief travels to the Continent while the plague ravaged London would signal the philosopher's first steps towards formulating a new philosophy of liberalism.

Wren's travels would also have a transforming effect. In April 1665, Evelyn wrote to Wren: 'I am told by Sr Jo Denham that you looke towards France this somer.'[38] Wren was to go to Paris on official architectural business and see the glories of the Bourbon monarchs with his own eyes. In July, as the plague swept through London, Wren set out for Europe alongside Lord St Albans. By August word had already returned to London that Wren was 'well received in Paris'[39] and had ingratiated himself with the best society.

Paris in 1665 was at a turning point in its fortunes and Wren was able to observe a capital city at the high-water mark of a 'Golden Century'. Louis XIII had died in 1643 and the crown had passed to the five-year-old Dauphin, Louis, who was governed by his mother, Anne of Austria, as regent and her own first minister, the Italian Cardinal Mazarin. In 1661, when Mazarin finally died, Louis XIV was determined to rule alone, without first ministers or powerful aristocrats. His was to be an absolute crown, his authority stamped on every level of the state hierarchy.

The success of Louis XIV depended as much on victories on the battlefield as on moulding a new modern society. To oversee this task the king had the ideal instrument, the clinical mind of Jean-Baptiste Colbert, who had risen under the strong guidance of Mazarin. Colbert was the right man to articulate Louis' grand vision of the new France. The nation would be rich again in order to fund its wars in Europe; it also needed large amounts of money to support Colbert's aims to establish the *gloire* of France itself, the person of the king. Paris was to become a new Rome by the Seine: 'Paris being the capital of the Kingdom and the abode of Kings, it directly affects the rest of the country, and all business begins in Paris.'[40] To do this Colbert had to make the capital city the world centre for arts and culture to reflect the king's iridescent rule.

Wren's passion for the New Philosophy bridged the national divide and the savants were keen to pick his brain about the Royal Society, as they deliberated on how to set up a similar club in Paris. He found fellows in a wide variety of thinkers, such as Adrien Auzout, a polymath with interests that included architecture, who was currently conducting a dispute with Robert Hooke concerning comments the Englishman had made in *Micrographia* about lens-grinding; the astronomer Pierre Petit, who had been watching the recent comets above Paris and London; and the King's librarian, Henri Justel, who introduced his English friend to salons such as at Abbé Burdelo's Monday soirée. Wren also visited laboratories where he saw numerous new inventions, such as Pascal's instrument, which could calculate to six digits, and numerous demonstrations such as a deaf boy who could dance to music. Wren was so busy among the savants that, ever the Baconian man, he privately admitted that he longed to return to the laboratory to conduct experiments.

Wren was not in Paris on society business, however, but had been sent by Sir John Denham to take stock of the changes in French architecture. In a letter he wrote to a friend, probably Evelyn, Wren catalogued the varied architectures that he encountered as he 'busied [him]self in surveying the most esteemed fabricks of Paris', agreeing that one city could 'altogether make a school of architecture, the best probably, at this day in Europe'. In particular he highlighted the wonders of the French baroque churches at the Sorbonne, Val de Grâce and Ste Marie de la Visitation, where he noted how the centre of the church, at the crossing of the nave and transept, rose into the air under the tremendous arc of a dome. The abundance of styles and new building would have given Wren a lifetime's study, and he collected many studies, folios and prints, so 'that I might not lose the impression of them', claiming he had collected 'all France' for his library.[41]

Wren had arrived at a key moment in the evolution of French architecture, for on the left bank of the Seine, opposite the Louvre palace, Le Vau, the most Italian of the French architects, had begun work on the

Collège de Quatre Nations, bequeathed to the nation by Mazarin. The building was to celebrate in eternity the contribution the Italian cardinal had made to France and to house the many new academies that brought glory to the Crown. In the spring of 1665, however, work was unexpectedly halted; Le Vau was dissatisfied and was dithering over details. The reason for this delay may have had its source in the news concerning the palace across the river, the Louvre.

Since the sixteenth century the Louvre had been a continual building site for royal dreams, but by the 1660s work on Henri IV's *Grand Plan* had ground to a halt and lay incomplete. To reflect the new *gloire* of Louis XIV, Colbert was determined to reimagine the palace, and in 1664 he was named Superintendent des Bâtiments. Yet while he was an accountant of genius, Colbert was less sure on matters of architecture. Lacking the courage to commission a local architect, he went abroad for a solution. A competition was set up in Rome, and it soon became clear that Colbert's target was the man considered the greatest sculptor and architect of the age, Bernini. The Italian produced designs which were scrutinised and accepted. He arrived in Paris in April 1665, a few weeks before Wren, with an entourage of nine to manage his immense arrogance.

Bernini had every right to be proud of his achievements. There were few architects who had been visited at home by more than one pope. For the last forty years he had been the creative director of the Vatican, first as a sculptor, then later as an architect. Beyond the Holy City, where he was transforming the piazza in front of St Peter's with a bold curved colonnade, Rome had been forever changed by his hand. In Paris, the Italian would bring his art, which had so successfully been used to praise God's representative on earth, the pope, to elevate the glory of the Sun King.

The presence of the Italian master would put the whole of French architecture to the test. He did not think much of his hosts' efforts. He criticised the dome of Val de Grâce as a skullcap on an over-large head; he considered the new generation of designers minnows and browbeat the king, insisting that he wanted total control and that Louis should commission nothing small, gaining the assurance 'as far as money is concerned, there need be no restriction'.[42]

By August, however, Bernini and Colbert had fallen out on questions of design. Colbert, the arch-auditor, wanted precise plans, while Bernini was interested only in discussing grand gestures. The Italian sensed this decline of favour and rather than focusing his attentions on the Louvre he spent most of his time completing a marble bust of Louis XIV. Besieged by bad press and cautious of spies, Bernini became suspicious of all visitors, so that when Wren came to the Palais Mazarin, the young Englishman was given short shrift: 'Bernini's design of the Louvre I would have given my skin for, but the old reserv'd Italian gave me but a few minutes View; it was five little designs in Paper, for which he hath received as many thousand Pistoles; I had only time to copy it in my Fancy and Memory; I shall be able by Discourse, and a crayon, to give you a tolerable Account of it.'[43]

Wren's tantalising sight of Bernini's inner sanctum and snatched glances at his designs were an epiphany. He had come face to face with one of the great artists of the world, and he was struck as much by the art as by its creator. Bernini embodied the role of the professional architect arrogant enough to command kings. He laid his philosophy of the baroque in the monumental and eternal stones of the city; his creations formed and reflected a new society on a grand scale. Wren thus saw in living flesh what Evelyn had written in *Parallel*: 'we have as good right to invent, and follow our own genius, as the Ancients'.

Wren also learnt another lesson from his brief encounter – architecture was politics in stone, a subtle expansion of the domain of power which commanded space and demanded awe. This was driven home to him after 17 October, when Louis XIV laid the foundation stone to Bernini's designs at the Louvre. Wren then became a fervent observer of the daily progress on the building site, 'where no less than a thousand hands are constantly employ'd in the works; some in laying mighty Foundations, some in raising the Stories, Columns, Entablements &c, with vast stones, by great and useful engines; others in carving, inlaying of marbles, plais-tering, painting, gilding &c.'[44]

In his letter home, Wren formed his thesis: 'Building certainly ought to have the attribute of eternal, and therefore the only thing uncapable of new Fashions,'[45] yet what he omitted to say was that architecture, while possessing universal aims, was also national. This was made clear in the glaring disparity between Bernini and the French community of architects. The Cavalière would later claim that he had been defeated by public opinion, but what his visit really showed was how distinct French and Italian architecture had become. The traditional assumption of a single definition of beauty or order was thrown into question when

Bernini placed his Italian baroque alongside the French. Feeling under-appreciated, the Italian left Paris in October 1665, at which point building on the Louvre was halted. The young French architects, such as Le Vau, were liberated from the hegemony of the Roman masters and felt free to explore their own national genius. When work recommenced at the Louvre a new French baroque would emerge to the glory of Louis XIV.

When Wren returned to England in March 1666 he was a changed man. The shy, collaborative nature of the New Philosopher had been transformed by the image of the genius artist and the wonders of Paris. In a letter to William Sancroft, who was finally back in his parish after the plague, Wren revealed that, since his return to Oxford, the cathedral had been on his mind: 'I am glad Mr [Hugh] May hath given in his judgement, I am preparing for you too.'[46] He feigned caution and wrote as a friend rather than an architect, but he could not help laying the foundations of his own argument. Sniping at Roger Pratt's economical survey, he warned, 'thrift proves often more expensefull than the better, and remains an eyesore at last'.[47] Yet the speed with which he developed his ideas and plans was astounding. Within five weeks of his return, Wren presented his survey of the cathedral to the commission in London.

Wren's report arrived at St Paul's on 1 May 1666. It was an incendiary and revolutionary document. He first attacked the Denham report, 'some may possibly aim at too great magnificence, wch neither ye Disposition nor the Extent of this Age will probably bring to a period', while extending his attack on Pratt's penny-pinching: 'others again may fall so low, as to think of piecing up the old fabrick, here with a stone. There with Brick and covering all faults with a coat of plaster leaving it still to ye next Posterity as a further object of charity'. Having softened the opposition, Wren did not rein in his appetite for attack and without hesitation sent a warning to the commissioners themselves: 'I suppose your [Lordships] may think fitt to take ye middle way & to neglect nothing yt may answer to decent uniform beauty or durable firmness in ye fabrick & suitable to ye expense.'[48] To pull the strings of the purse too tightly would be to diminish the cathedral, yet ornament for its own sake was worthless.

Even before he laid out his own solutions, Wren was laying claim to his skill as an engineer who understood building better than an architect and in a one-line manifesto encapsulated all the lessons he had absorbed in Paris: 'This also may safely be affirmed not only by an architect taking his measure from the precepts & examples of the Ancients, but by a

Geometrician.' Where Roger Pratt, the gentleman architect, had signalled that structural surveys were necessary, Wren pointed out exactly where the building had failed – the roof had been poorly made in the first place and was forcing out the side walls, opening ruinous cracks. This stress placed too much pressure on the pillars that held up the nave, which were themselves poorly constructed. The stone itself was showing signs of decay: 'there are few stones to be found yt are not mouldered and flawed away with saltpetre [pollution]. Yt is in them an incurable disease which perpetually throws what ever coat is laid on it'.[49] Any attempts to patch the roof up again would bring further stress and damage to the other parts of the building.

Wren then treated the building as a whole in his search for a solution. His proposal was confident, persuasive, passionate and perfectly calibrated to both impress and reassure the commissioner, who had one eye on their legacy and the other on the failures of their fund-raising efforts. He introduced a scheme that had never been seen in an English church before:

> to reduce the middle part into a spacious dome or rotunda with a cupolo or hemispherical Roof & upon ye cupolo for ye outward Ornament, a lantern with a spire to rise proportionally ... By this means ye difformities of ye Unequall Intercolumnations will be taken away. Ye church which is much too narrow for its height rendered spacious in ye middle wch may be a proper place for a Vast Auditory. The outward appearance of ye church will seem to swell in ye middle by degrees to a large basis rising into a rotundo.[50]

Wren hoped to raise a dome above London. It would symbolise all that he had learnt from his explorations as a scientist and express his hopes as an architect. Yet the reality of bringing his vision to the capital was distant. Despite the hopes of the Restoration settlement and the scattered attempts to bring new architectural ideas to the capital, the London that lay beneath the cathedral was still a wretched city, a huddled, wooden, medieval jumble that was barely raising itself after the tortures of the plague. Worse was to come.

5

London Was, But Is No More

'Certainly this year of 1666 will be a great year of action, but what the consequence of it will be God Knows,'¹ Samuel Pepys wrote in his diary at the beginning of the year. The astrologers had long been predicting 1666 as a year of cataclysm, yet there was no need to look to the Bible or the motion of the stars to recognise that the city was suffering. The scars of the plague year were slow to heal and the contagion was now spreading out to the rest of the nation. Drought gripped the city during the summer, and by August St Mary's on Fish Street was taking donations for prayers for rain.

By that summer, the hopes that the return of the king would deliver security began to appear a chimera. The Clarendon Code, which for the last six years had attempted to force the nation into Anglican conformity, had done nothing of the sort. The king, who had wished to forgive and unite the nation, had done the complete opposite. And the fortunes of the monument to the revived Anglican Church, St Paul's Cathedral, were looking decidedly dim. By the end of the summer, the commission had still not decided on how to progress the restoration of the city's most glorious monument.

Christopher Wren had delivered his report on St Paul's in May, yet over the summer the commission had asked for surveys and responses from the other architects. Roger Pratt, the more senior architect who benefited from the patronage of the Chancellor, the Earl of Clarendon, was given the opportunity to criticise Wren's conclusions, and defend his reputation. His letter to the commission complained about plans for a thorough survey of the cathedral as a waste of money that could be spent on other things. He then attacked Wren's assertion that the outward thrust of the roof was pushing the walls and pillars off line. He resurrected the image of his great mentor, Inigo Jones, who had not seen it necessary to make alterations to the steeple or pillars in the 1630s. Pratt's final rebuttal was piquantly counterpoised against Wren's self-promotion as an architect-geometrician, and in one line he displayed the contested landscape of the future of English national architecture: 'I should endeavour to shew myself an artist.'[2]

It was decided that a grand meeting was to be convened outside St Paul's itself, where the commissioners, architects and advisers came together to see for themselves the state of the cathedral and finally fix the next course of action. The meeting was called for 27 August. On that morning, Wren, Pratt, Hugh May and John Evelyn (called at the last moment to bring his considerable taste to bear on the matter), as well as a number of commissioners, including Bishop Henchman and William Sancroft, technical experts such as Edward Marshall, master mason, and his son Joshua, met at the churchyard. The assembly entered the cavernous nave of the cathedral. The ceiling was vaulted like medieval palms above their heads, but the object of the learned group's study was the walls, which Wren had suggested were leaning perilously outwards owing to the weight of the roof. The masons checked the slant with their plumb lines. When it was discovered that Wren was correct, Pratt excused the fault as the intention of the original builders to aid the perspective of the whole body.

The group then proceeded to the centre of the cathedral at the crossing where the nave and transepts met, under the dilapidated tower that still reached askew into the London sky. Pratt, again, insisted that it could be repaired and a few in the group agreed, but Evelyn and Wren concurred that it would be better to start again. Evelyn, although he had travelled with Pratt and they had visited St Peter's in Rome together, sided with his young, inexperienced companion from the Royal Society. In his diary, he recorded his support for Wren in the hopes for a 'noble cupola, a form of church-building not as yet known in England but of wonderful grace'.[3] Rather than stick with the certitude of experience and art, Evelyn placed his confidence in the untested talents of a geometrician. The disagreement split the group and the dispute was resolved only by the prospect of more deliberation. Wren was to produce more plans and come up with a financial estimate for the costs of giving London its dome. In order to win the ultimate prize, he had to learn to act both as Bernini and Colbert, combining his passion for the grand gesture with an eye for detail in order that every aspect of his plans obtained approval.

ALL IN ONE FLAME!

In the early hours of Sunday, 2 September, six days after that meeting in the churchyard, news reached England of another battle out at sea between the English navy and the Dutch. The impetuous British admiral, the King's cousin, Prince Rupert, had attempted to engage the enemy off the French coast, but as the Dutch ships hugged the coastline outside the port of Boulogne, a gust of wind attacked the British sails, cutting their lines and sending the fleet into disorder. The storm then continued eastwards, hitting the coast of Kent and travelling up the Thames estuary until it arrived in London that evening.

That same night, while 'most persons, especially the poorer sort, were newly in bed and in the first dead sleep',[4] a fire began in Pudding Lane. The street was renowned for its bakers and pie makers and the previous day had been market day, 'the day of receipts and payment, the markets last not then only all day but some part of the night'. Here Thomas Farriner, a baker of tack biscuits for the King's Navy, raked the coals of the bakery oven before he went to bed, laying a few flitches of bacon to smoke 'leaving his providence with his slippers'.[5]

During the dark morning hours the bakery began to fill with smoke. Within a few hours, sparks had risen on the wind from the flames and travelled to nearby plots. Another house was set alight, and hay lying in the yard of the nearby Star Inn became a nursery for the growing inferno. On such occasions, the local community customarily followed an established fire drill that had been laid out in numerous proclamations, and while still only a common house fire, Farriner's flames should have been stamped out; tragically this did not happen.

When the family awoke with the fumes, finding their way through the ground floor barred, they scrambled over the leaning jutties of the house to the neighbour's; only the maid refused to escape and became the first victim of the flames. After the alarm had been raised, the nearby houses were evacuated and the local authorities called; the constable was dragged from his bed, the church bells rung '*backwards*' to call for help and the street was blocked off. A chain of firefighters was formed carrying buckets of Thames water to douse the flames while a number of engines, squirts and scoops were stationed in the nearby parish church to control the outburst. Yet, on this occasion, something went wrong.

As the fire strengthened it became imperative to stop its spread by

bringing down the surrounding houses. The Lord Mayor, Thomas Bludworth, was called from the comfort of his home and escorted by coach to
the top of Pudding Lane to survey the crisis and give the City's permission
to commence the destruction of private property. On arrival, the mayor
refused to descend from his carriage, batting away concerns that the fire
was spreading, claiming that a woman could piss it out.

The Lord Mayor did not want to bring down the surrounding houses
because of the cost of rebuilding them, and, at this stage, the flames on
Pudding Lane seemed little more than a local fire. Thus, according to Rege
Sincera, the Great Fire began not with a single cause but multiple accidents:
'the carelessness of a baker, the solitariness and darkness of the night, the
disposition of the old ruinous buildings, the narrowness of the streets, the
abundance of combustible and bituminous matter, the foregoing summer
extraordinarily hot and dry, a violent easterly wind, and the waste of
engines and water'.[6]

As dawn broke on Sunday, 2 September, the extent of the fire was first
understood. Samuel Pepys, who lived eight streets to the east, had been
woken in the early hours to assess the crisis but had returned unconcerned
to bed. In the morning, however, from the top of the Tower of London, he
was struck with fear as he watched the fire crawl beyond Pudding Lane
and begin to attack the surrounding streets. Pepys took a boat upriver to
Westminster to inform the king at Whitehall. When Charles II heard his
report he immediately organised his barge to take him to the crisis.

Beyond the city walls, news of the fire arrived slowly. At ten in the
morning the young scholar William Taswell was standing by the abbey in
Westminster Yard when he 'perceived some people below me running to
and fro in a seeming disquietude and consternation; immediately almost a
report reached my ears that London was in conflagration'. Moving down
to the Thames to catch more news, Taswell came in contact with the first
victims coming up the river: 'four boats crowded with objects of distress
... scarce under any other covering except that of a blanket'.[7]

Throughout the day, the fire gained power. From the epicentre at
Pudding Lane, the outburst split into two arcs. Travelling northwards up
Fish Street Hill towards the centre of the City, the flames rose into the air,
a burning brand finding a home in the spire of St Laurence Pountney, 'as
if taking a view from that lofty place of what it intended to devour'.[8] Then
it set about the church, working its way under the lead of the steeple, which
so many had hoped was a barrier against the advancing flames. The

second arc worked its way downwards towards the Thames until it hit the riverbanks, where citizens were already clambering at the steps, heaving their goods into boats or throwing them into the water so that soon the river became 'covered with goods floating, all the barges and boats laden with what some had time and courage to save'.[9] The fire made a steady path along the waterfront, attacking the mighty St Magnus Martyr's which stood at the mouth of London Bridge, incinerating the church plate and pewter before the clerk had time to remove them.

The flames began to spread on to the bridge, cutting off the only means to cross the river for the fleeing crowd. London Bridge had stood here since the twelfth century and was considered one of the finest monuments of the city, with its houses resting on the bridge's edge and the covered thoroughfare that ran through the centre offering rowdy inns, chapels and market stalls. Advancing from Bridge Foot the fire made its way towards the southern banks, where only a break in the houses near the centre of the bridge halted its progress. A single spark made its way to the southern bank at Rotherhithe, where it found fuel in a stable yard. The locals were swift to quash the flames and pulled down three surrounding houses to ensure that they were quenched.

By this time the flames had attacked the *forcier*, a vast wooden water-wheel that sat under the last 'starling' arch on the northern side of the bridge. The wheel had been a wonder of the city, invented by the Dutch engineer Pieter Morrice, who had shown off his noisy contraption in 1581 by pumping a spurt of water over the steeple of St Laurence Pountney. The wheel was vital in supplying water from the river's edge to the heart of the city. As it slipped from its axle and ran into the mud flats that ribboned the river at low tide, the hopes for much-needed water to defend the city were dashed. The flames continued their progress westwards along the riverbank until they reached Thames Street, the heart of the maritime city, where the warehouses held the wealth of the merchants. Within the dry wood buildings all the paraphernalia of a maritime nation stood in stock – hemp, tar, coal, straw, pitch, resin, oil – and fed the hunger of the flames. In the nearby breweries, the beer boiled in the barrels, then burst out, running down the streets.

Corn and timber from the Baltic, luxury goods from the Mediterranean, the spices from the East, all the merchant goods from their voyages overseas were consumed and turned to ash. The flames became indiscriminate in their frenzy and began to attack the impressive stone houses of the City guilds, the ancient centres of trade and tradition that stood on the water-front. Ornate Fishmongers' Hall, set around an elegant courtyard facing out to the river, was the first to succumb, the flames leaving no evidence of the guild's proud history behind.

That night, Pepys sat on board a ship on the Thames, watching the strange glow of the conflagration. He had seen many things that would haunt his dreams for days to come. Having left Whitehall, he had taken a message to the Lord Mayor, who had broken down in exhaustion like a 'fainting woman',[10] yet refused royal help. Above the flames he had watched as a pigeon, too scared to flee its perch, waited too long until its wings singed and it plunged dead to the ground. From the boat Pepys could see that the flames had lost none of their appetite. He wept for his city.

The next morning, the fire continued its route to the heart of the metropolis. From Fish Street Hill it moved north along Gracechurch Street towards Leadenhall Market, where it was halted by the determination of one alderman, John Rushworth, who rallied those around him with a hatful of coins. At St Dunstan-in-the-East, a group of Westminster School scholars attempted to bat the flames away from the church doors. The students, including William Taswell, had been marched through the city by their master, John Dolben, and spent the day carting buckets of water to fend away the flames. The fire even gained as far as the corner of Gresham College on Cornhill.

Yet, as Thomas Vincent observed, 'if [the fire] be a little allayed, or beaten down, or put to a stand in some places, it is but a very little while; it quickly recruits, and recovers its force; it leaps and mounts, and takes more furious onset, drives back its oppressors, snatcheth their weapons out of their hands'.[11] In one street to the west, Lombard Street, where the leading banks and moneylenders had made their home since the twelfth century, the fire crept without obstacle. The banker Sir Robert Vyner had just enough time to collect his papers, detailing the vast debt owed to him by the Crown, and plate, and thus protected his fortune. As the fire ran up the streets, the elegant three- and four-storey houses collapsed, 'tumble, tumble, tumble, from one end of the street to the other with a great crash'.[12] The flames now moved westwards towards Threadneedle Street, where the great thoroughfares of the city converged.

As the city turned into a furnace, the citizens began to fear for their own safety: 'for the first rank they minded only for their own preservation; the middle sort so distracted and amazed, that they did not know what they did; the poorer, they minded nothing but pilfering'.[13] Even in the early darkness, thoughts of fighting the fire had turned to desperate flight, and by four o'clock in the morning Pepys was observing, 'the streets and highways are crowded with people, running and riding and getting carts at any rate to fetch away things'.[14]

Soon the streets were crammed with desperate refugees, as they all headed for the city gates. The merchant Nicholas Corsellis wrote: 'the goods [were] thrown into the street and ye crowds of people so that ye carts could not possible bee brought into ye lane, that little which here be saved was carried on men's backs to London Wall and then thrown over and taken up by country carts and carried away, ye citty gattes being too much obstructed that there was no passage to bee gott'.[15] The narrow streets became clogged with carts, whose owners took the opportunity to charge whatever price they could get to pull the citizens' goods to safety. Those who could not afford the ever-escalating price became, in Vincent's words: 'a porter to himself and scarcely a back either of man or woman that hath strength but had a burden on it in the streets'.[16]

While the citizenry thought only of its own safety, attempts continued to combat the conflagration. On Monday, the king and James, Duke of York, decided to ignore the Lord Mayor's refusal of help inside the walls and began to muster their troops. Even in such dire straits, it was a bold move that went against all traditions. The trained militia from the surrounding counties were commanded to wait for instructions just outside the city. As Evelyn observed over the wall of Sayes Court on the south bank of the Thames, sailors were mustered at the Royal Docks and moved to the Tower with supplies of grappling rope and gunpowder, and put under the command of Lord Berkeley.

Closer to the action, both Charles and James stepped down from their royal barge on the Thames and rode on horseback into the thick of the action. To the west, in the eye of the easterly wind that was driving the flames closer, the Duke of York set two rings of watching posts around the city. The outer ring of five posts had a local constable, a city authority and a division of the London trained militia; there were also a number of courtiers who could overrule the caution of the aldermen and demand the pulling down of houses in the king's name.

At Temple Bar, the architect Hugh May and others stood ready to stop the progress up Fleet Street, while at nearby Fetter Lane, James forced the locals to aid his efforts in preparation for the arrival of the fire, 'up to the ankles in water, and playing the engines for many hours'.[17] At Cowgate, near Smithfield, John Evelyn's father-in-law, Sir Richard Browne, stood to repel the flames from the market spaces just beyond the city walls. There was also an inner ring of fire stations just outside the walls. At Aldersgate, Sir Anthony Ashley Cooper organised the evacuation of the hordes that flooded through the city gate. James then rode towards the fire to rally efforts inside the walls and put himself in great danger for his efforts.

Yet still the fire continued its relentless path: the Royal Exchange, the financial centre of the merchant city, was next, attacked by the flames that bellowed through the streets. The Exchange had been built by Sir Thomas Gresham as the beating heart of the trading nation. There was a magnificent open courtyard surrounded by a four-storey quadrangle of wainscotted and glass-covered walkways, lined with niches and galleries of small stalls that purveyed luxury goods from around the world. On the west side a tall bell tower rose into the city sky, topped with Gresham's insignia, the grasshopper, and was so impressive that when Elizabeth I first saw the completed building she demanded that it be proclaimed 'Royal'. On Monday, 3 September 1666, 'the fire ran around the galleries, filling them with flames, then descending the stairs ... giving forth flaming vollies, and filling the courts with sheets of fire'.[18] The spices held in the cellars let out a pungent stink that hung over the broken building long after the flames had done their worst, and only the statue of Thomas Gresham remained standing.

By the end of the second day of the fire the people of London were set adrift before the inferno. Their helplessness led to anger and, soon, madness. As the populace began to huddle in safety outside the walls, leaving behind their homes and goods to the will of the flames, rumours began to circulate that the fire was no accident but had been started by England's enemies.

Throughout Monday, Londoners, having lost everything, began to attack foreigners, looting their shops and razing their houses to the ground. The young Taswell watched as a blacksmith, 'meeting an innocent Frenchman walking along the street, felled him instantly to the ground with an iron bar'.[19] Elsewhere there were accusations of foreign fire-starters. In Newgate Market a member of the Portuguese embassy was accused of throwing a fireball when he had only bent down to pick up a crust of bread. As the citizens gathered to shelter on Moorfields a Frenchman was lynched for carrying a case of incendiaries that turned out to be a box of tennis balls. A fury of women, 'some of them armed with spits, some with bread staffs',[20] set upon the ex-Capuchin friar Denis de Repas. The king's French firework maker was forced to seek refuge in the palace when rumours circulated that he was the master arsonist. For their own good 'strangers' were placed in the secure jails at Newgate and Bridewell, but as the fires approached the western walls of the city not even these unlikely havens were safe.

By the end of Monday, when John Evelyn had made his journey from Sayes Court to see with his own eyes the devastation from the safety of the south bank of the Thames, the fire had taken a grip of the walled city. The virtuoso stood powerless before the inferno: 'God grant mine eyes never behold the like, who now saw above 10,000 houses all in one flame! The noise and cracking and thunder of the impetuous flames, the shrieking of women and children, the hurry of people, the fall of towers, houses, and churches, was like a hideous storm.'[21]

Throughout the night the inferno kept up its terrible pace, generating its own vortex of heat and wind that 'blew equally to the right and to the left, and caused the fire to burn on all sides'.[22] Far away from the city, news of the fire and its effects was spreading. In Kensington one writer claimed: 'you would have thought ... it had been Doomsday ... My walks and gardens are almost covered with the ashes of paper, linen etc. and pieces of ceiling and plasterwork blow thither by the tempest'.[23] In Windsor, 30 miles to the west, reports were seen of charred paper and silks floating in the wind, while in Oxford Locke recorded in his meteorological diary: 'this unusual colour of the air, which without a cloud appearing made the sunbeams a strange red, dim light'.[24]

Within the City the fire had formed into three burning arcs: the flames that had run along the Thames now charred the city walls and attacked the redoubtable fortress of Baynard's Castle under cover of darkness. The castle, built by William the Conqueror in the eleventh century, had stood as a resolute defence against attack from the west but was overcome by the easterly flames in ten hours of relentless assault; by dawn, only two broken-toothed turrets remained. One arc of flames then leapt westwards towards the Fleet river. The second arc was funnelled by the city walls and made its way northwards, encircling the base of Ludgate Hill and working its way along the east side of the Fleet Ditch towards 'the shambles' of Ludgate and Aldersgate, slowly rising up to the summit where St Paul's Cathedral stood untouched above the smoke. The third arc moved through the city from the east.

The Fleet Ditch curled along the western reaches of the walled city from the north through Clerkenwell, entering the Thames at Blackfriars. A single bridge spanned the stream, leading to the suburbs that grew from the western approaches of Fleet Street. The fire leapt over the water and made a new home in the fetid slum housing on its west bank, breaking into the two prisons that clung to the banks. Once on the western shore the fire seemed to regain its force and began its ascent of Fleet Street, devouring the buildings on either side of the thoroughfare, creeping ever closer to the hurriedly prepared fire stations set by James, Duke of York.

In the centre of the City, the wind was now driving the third arc of fire from the Royal Exchange to the grand market thoroughfare, Cheapside, that ran westwards towards St Paul's Cathedral. Along the route an exhausted team of ten firefighters had attempted to bring down houses in the path of the flames, but the fire had moved so fast that as soon as the houses had been razed the fearful citizens had to flee, leaving the debris as kindling in the conflagration's path.

The stone church of St Mary-le-Bow, halfway along Cheapside, failed to act as a break to the flames; the famous Bow bell, which called the curfew every night before the city gates were closed, came crashing down from its tower. Next the flames took hold of the ancient gothic Guildhall, the powerhouse of the civic authorities. The stained glass windows of the medieval hall began to melt, and once the flames had entered the building the ancient oak beams glowed in the heat 'in a bright shining coal, as if it had been a palace of gold, or a great building of burnished brass'.[25] The fire continued westwards, making small meat of Goldsmiths' Row, the splendid collection of Tudor houses described by John Stow as 'the most beautiful frame of fair houses and shops that be within the walls of London, or elsewhere in England',[26] before moving up the slight incline towards the summit of Ludgate Hill. Elsewhere the flames were encircling the promontory and slowly making progress towards the huge building on its peak, St Paul's Cathedral.

The previous day, William Taswell, travelling across the city, had noted that 'the people who lived contiguous to St Paul's church raised their expectations greatly concerning the absolute security of that place upon account of the immense thickness of its walls and situation; built in a large piece of ground, on every side remote from houses. Upon this account they filled it with all sorts of goods'.[27] The local merchants had rushed to store their goods under the walls or inside the building itself. The printers whose shops cluttered the churchyard had packed the crypt church, St Faith's, under the main cathedral with their papers, scripts and works – including the complete print run of John Wilkins's magnum opus on the universal language of New Philosophy – sealing the door to prevent air feeding the flames.

As the fire approached, first from the east, where it consumed St Paul's School, then from the west, a single brand rose from the cluster of houses to the south and landed on the roof of the cathedral, where the lead had been removed during the interregnum to expose the wooden beams below. As Martin, a local bookseller, later reported to Pepys, 'it took fire first upon the end of a board that, among others, was laid upon the roof instead of lead, the lead being broken off'.[28] Fire began to creep along the roof. The bare wood beneath had been dried to tinder in the summer's drought, and so the fire moved unchecked along the roof supports, smouldering on under the areas that were still covered with lead and giving off an unearthly hissing. As the jackdaws circled the cathedral's Gothic spire, the nave below began to fill with smoke while the remaining roof, a solid area of almost six acres of hard metal, liquefied and began to drip into the body of the church, running down the walls and flowing out of the rain spouts on to the stones of the yard and down Ludgate Hill.

The crowd gathered inside the cathedral succumbed to panic and were forced to dart to safety through the flames as the heat burned through the wooden scaffolding above. Soon the melted lead of the roof dripped into the cracks of the cathedral's fabric and the very stones began to explode in the heat, 'like grenadoes'.[29] The walls sheared and plummeted to the ground below. Gaping holes opened up in the structure which allowed air to rush in and stoke the flames further. The east window, a rose of stained glass, turned to liquid and, finally, the crumbling masonry of the vaulted roof crashed down and broke through the marble flooring, exposing the crypt beneath like a disinterred tomb. The flames did not take long to follow, and the precious works of the printers, neatly stacked and protected, caught fire. They would burn for a full week. The falling masonry broke open the long-forgotten tombs within the nave. The cadaver of Robert Braybrooke, lain to rest 250 years before, was exposed intact, his skin hard and brittle but his hair still red.

The next day, the winds began to subside. In Fleet Street, the change in fortunes slowed the progress of the fire. That morning John Evelyn made his way to man the fire station at Fetter Lane, where he found other courtiers preparing, with a group of sailors from Deptford docks, to blow up houses before the inferno reached their position, 'to make a wider gap than any had yet been made by the ordinary method of pulling them down with engines'. The houses, workshops and inns of Fetter Lane were razed to the ground, including the workshop belonging to PraiseGod Barbon at the sign of the Lock and Key.

The operation was a success and, beyond a single fire that rose within the Temple, the progress of the flames was halted. Elsewhere in the city, as the wind began to dissipate, the fire came under control. Although coals within the cellars of houses would burn for the next two months and the remains of houses, broken, solitary chimney stacks and rubble would smoke and smoulder for weeks, the worst of the fire was over by the end of the day. To count the cost at such an early stage was impossible, but as Thomas Vincent noted:

> The Glory of London is now fled away like a Bird, The Trade of London is shattered and broken to pieces, her delights have also vanished, and pleasant things laid aside; now no chaunting to the sound of the Viol, and dancing to the sweet musick of the other instruments; now no drinking Wine in Bowls, and stretching upon the beds of lust; now no excess of wine and banquetting; no feasts in Halls and curious Dishes; no amorous looks, and wanton dalliances; no ruffling silks, and costly dresses; these things in that place are at an end.[30]

On Thursday, 6 September, John Evelyn took a boat from Sayes Court to Whitehall, and after visiting the court walked within the city. Stumbling up from his boat by London Bridge, he could feel the heat of the ground rise through his shoes as he clambered over 'heaps of yet smoking rubbish'. It had become impossible to recognise a street or where a house had once stood, let alone which parish he was in. He mourned the passing of the many great buildings that had once glorified London: 'the exquisitely wrought Mercers' Chapel, the sumptuous Exchange, the august fabric of Christ Church, all the rest of the Companies' Halls, splendid buildings, arches, entries, all in dust; the fountains dried up and ruined, whilst the very waters remained boiling; the voragos of subterranean cellars, wells, and dungeons'. Evelyn watched as fellow citizens went in search of their homes, 'like men in some dismal desert'.[31]

From the west, near Fetter Lane, where the flames finally subsided, Edward Atkyns reported, 'there is nothing but stones and rubbish, all exposed to the open air so that you can see from one end of the city to another'.[32] To another viewer, the scene resembled a wind-blasted moor rather than a thriving city. The flames had not only gutted eighty-seven parish churches and six consecrated chapels but all the major sites of trade and government: the Guildhall, Royal Exchange, Customs House, Sessions House, fifty-two company halls, the prisons at Bridewell and Newgate, Wood Street and Poultry Compter, three city gates and four stone bridges.

Nearly one hundred thousand citizens were homeless. In all, over thirteen thousand houses were destroyed, covering a ground area of 436 acres, comprising 400 streets and 80 per cent of the land inside the walls, as well as large regions within the liberties beyond. Fortunes were lost in an instant, plate melted into the earth and valuable spices vaporised with a heady odour. Of human losses, the record is even less exact; according to anecdotal evidence, from the death of Farriner's maid to the final quenching of the flames, less that twenty people fell before the inferno.

In particular Evelyn was struck by the damaged St Paul's Cathedral, which still stood high above the city like some torn and discarded shroud. 'Now a sad ruin,' he recorded,

> and that beautiful portico (for structure comparable to any in Europe, as not long before repaired by the late King) now rent in pieces, flakes of large stones split asunder ... It was astonishing to see what immense stones the heat had in a manner calcined, so that all the ornaments, columns, friezes, capitals and projectures of massy Portland stone, flew off, even to the very roof where a sheet of lead covering a great space (no less than six acres by measure) was totally melted ... Thus lay in ashes that most venerable church, one of the most ancient pieces of early piety in the Christian world.[33]

William Taswell also wandered towards the cathedral, the 'ground so hot as almost to scorch my shoes; and the air so intensely warm that unless I had stopped some time upon Fleet Bridge to rest myself I must have fainted'. Around the churchyard he found melted globs of bell metal, the carcasses of dogs 'stiff as a plank, the skin being tough like leather'. He was also shocked to uncover a burned woman who had hidden by the walls but failed to escape the flames, 'every limb reduced to a coal'.

Evelyn then walked up to the fields beyond the city walls, where the thousands of refugees (he overestimated at 200,000) had spent the last night, clinging on to their possessions, hungry and destitute. The thronging crowds had nothing with which to protect or support themselves, 'some under tents, some under miserable huts and hovels, many without a rag, or any necessary utensils, bed or board'.[34] The previous night rumours of a foreign invasion had spread through the throng. Some heard that 'the French were coming armed against them to cut their throats and spoil them of what they have saved out of the fire.'[35] The night was broken with calls of 'Arms!' which made panic ripple through the groggy hordes as they searched for weapons at hand to defend the devastated City to the last.

The king became so concerned by these fears that the next day he rode with his council to the fields and addressed the refugees himself to soothe their panic, as reported in the *Gazette*: 'He told them it was immediate from the hand of God, and no plot; assured them he had examined several himself which were spoken of under suspicion, and found no reason to suspect anything of that nature'. He then promised food, '£500 worth of bread he intends to send them tomorrow, and next day intends to send them as much more'.[36] Yet these emergency measures would work only for a short time. While the City still smouldered, plans for the restoration of London needed to be put in place.

The City's first reaction was despondency and mourning. The streets became a dangerous place at night, and to wander alone was to risk one's life. There were reports of bodies left in cellars and gruesome murders. Yet while the timbers of the houses were still smouldering steps were being taken to restore order. On Thursday, 6 September, the king produced a proclamation to allay the initial fears of the crowds that remained in the fields and to initiate the restoration process. London had to get back to order; by calling on the trained militia that had mustered around the outskirts of the City to stand down, Charles gave the power of the City back to the Lord Mayor and his aldermen.

Many of the burnt-out guilds began to pick up the pieces and found new temporary homes from where they could coordinate the revival of the City's trades. The post office was temporarily stationed in a tavern in Covent Garden. The Customs House was removed to an undamaged building near to the Tower. The city authorities moved their offices from the Guildhall to Gresham College. The college also took on the role of an ad hoc exchange and a hundred stalls and tents were crammed into the quadrangle. The Gresham professors were forced out of their lodges as their homes were turned into the centre of emergency administration. Only Robert Hooke was allowed to remain at the college, and in the very first days of the aftermath of the fire he observed the early attempts to revive the capital.

Food needed to be distributed and a series of temporary markets were established at London Bridge, Smithfield and the Artillery Ground; business was to return to normal and no exceptions to the normal way of supply and payment were accepted. On Moorfields the crowds of refugees still clung to their possessions, waiting for the supply of tents, fearful of any rumour or attack. Once again in his proclamation Charles II made it clear that no foreign invasion was imminent: 'to prevent all tumults and disorders which may thereof or otherwise arise, it is our will and pleasure, that upon any alarm raised or taken, no man stir or disquiet himself by reason thereof, but only attend the business of quenching the fire'.[37]

The crowds that lingered in the fields were slow to come to their senses. To comfort them while they assessed their losses, public buildings outside the walls were opened to secure their goods. Others who tried to move their possessions elsewhere had to be careful of thieves. Charles hoped to clear the refugees from the surrounding fields within four days and return them to their houses, and so ordered that each household clear away the rubbish from their own plot. Yet many saw the wreck of the city and turned away, forcing Charles to command the surrounding suburbs and towns to welcome the refugees. The rich who could afford the ballooning rents from avaricious landlords found new homes in the suburbs.

On Sunday, 9 September, the city crammed into the nearby parish churches, where the whole populace prayed for London and the pardon of their own sins. A few weeks later, William Sancroft, dean of St Paul's, preached his own sermon, *Lex Ignea*, in front of the king on a day of solemn fasting. The dean saw echoes of the destruction of Jerusalem within the wasteland of London, not as a punishment but a test of the nation.

THE PHOENIX STIRS

Mourning was swiftly replaced by a spirit of revival: London was to arise again, and now more resplendent than ever. To begin with, however, the city needed to assess what had been lost and a rudimentary logbook was opened at Gresham College where householders came to record their title deeds. No rebuilding was allowed until a thorough examination of the burnt neighbourhoods had been conducted. As the necessary administrative groundwork was being organised, new ideas for the city were evolving, inspired by the hopes that London would be reborn as, in the words of Evelyn, a 'more glorious phoenix' from the flames. But who was to bring this new life to the City? The New Philosophers had failed to devise a prevention, but could they invent the cure? London needed a plan of a modern city. The Great Fire demanded a bold response and offered an extraordinary opportunity for change.

There were few in the country more versed in the grammar of contemporary urban theory than John Evelyn. In his work of the last decade he had continuously returned to the question of making London modern. In *The Character of England* (1659) he shamed his home capital in comparison to Paris. *Fumifugium* (1661) forcefully attacked the decline of London and the failures of the City to deal with the hazards of pollution. In 1664, his translation of Fréart de Chambray's *Parallel* praised the early improvements to the metropolis that he had seen while a commissioner for the king and he offered his volume as a template for the Restoration building boom. He had explored and thought about his city without ever thinking that an opportunity would arise when he could fully bring his ideas to bear. As he clambered over the burning rubble of the city, Evelyn was thinking of his 'phoenix' London, and within days had written a discourse, *Londinium Redivivum*, and developed an accompanying map to express his plans for the City.

Evelyn's baroque capital was an improved and regimented version of the old capital. As he worked over the ground plan of the old metropolis he realised that there would need to be changes to the layout and communication network. The city plan should be governed by reason and geometry so that it 'might doubtless be rendered as far superior to any other city in the habitable world for beauty, commodiousness and magnificence'.[38] As a result, it was to be measured and calculated, both in terms of space as well as topography, so that hill gradients, the decline of river fronts and the shape of the streams could be mapped.

Once the City was measured, and parts of it levelled off to reduce 'the deepest valleys, holes, and more sudden declivities, within the city, for the more ease of commerce, carriages, coaches, and people in the streets',[39] a street plan and grid could be imposed from which the modern capital would rise. There would be new roads of impressive width: Evelyn

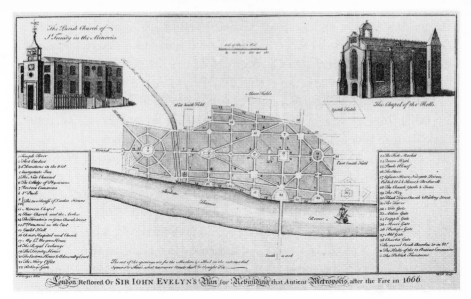

John Evelyn's plans for a 'more glorious phoenix', 1666

imagined grand boulevards, just as Louis XIV was devising at the same time in Paris. The new streets would be places for the traffic and transport of goods, bodies and money in and out of the City; they would also be places of grandeur and display. As Evelyn was devising this street plan he was undoubtedly thinking of Bernini's Rome. During the reign of Sixtus V at the end of the last century, the pope had transformed the eternal city with a series of straight, paved roads linking a geometric plan of piazzas, churches and monuments. Evelyn's main thoroughfares would be no less than 'an hundred foot in breadth, nor any of the narrowest than thirty, their openings, and heights proportionate'.[40] The street's width would itself be an indication of the importance of the location. From these routes the greater buildings of the city and the parish churches would radiate.

Evelyn would also reorder parish boundaries and resite the local churches to reflect the redistribution of population in each district, which had become woefully unbalanced. Each new church would be rebuilt in the modern style. The other major buildings, stationers' shops and ministers' houses would line the new piazzas. The livery halls and the Royal Exchange would move to suit the new order of the city, 'fronted at least with stone, adorned with statues, and other ornaments',[41] to display the power of the capital, and room would be found for a grand house for the

Lord Mayor and a new Guildhall. In Evelyn's London, the new piazzas would be of various shapes and be home to 'the several markets, in others the coaches may wait etc. and in some should be public fountains placed'.[42] Here the business of the City would be conducted, the power allowed to circulate through it via a radiating grid of streets. To Evelyn the new city would be like a human body, with the lifeblood of money, goods and trade freely circulating out from the heart to refresh the organism.

He also put a strong emphasis on the role of the Thames. As part of a trading city that welcomed in the raw materials of the world, the port was given new prominence. The new Royal Exchange, 'where the traffic, and business is most vigourous',[43] would stand at the centre of the riverbank and along the front the old wooden warehouses and stores, unruly steps and haphazard machines that acted as docks would be replaced by an impressive quay to aid the swift transport of the nation's wealth ashore.

Evelyn's plan was an amalgam of modern styles taken from Rome and Paris, yet his ideas also took into account the formation of the destroyed foundation of the old city. On Tuesday, 11 September, only one week after St Paul's Cathedral had crashed to the ground, he shared his ideas with Christopher Wren, who had returned from Oxford at the news of the fire. There is some evidence of revisions to Evelyn's plans following the meeting, and two days later Evelyn presented his discourse to the king at Whitehall.

He was not the only person who was thinking about the future of the City. As Henry Oldenburg, secretary of the Royal Society, wrote to Robert Boyle, many of the leading men of the City 'discoursed of almost nothing but of a survey of London and a dessein for rebuilding, and that in such a manner (with bricks, and large Streets, leaving great Intervalls and partitions in severall places) that for the future they may not be so easily subject to the like destruction'.[44] Numerous plans arrived at Whitehall over the coming weeks, each with a new idea of the City. The most powerful proposals came from the generation of New Philosophers and three leading members of the Royal Society – in addition to Evelyn – who put forward the most effective designs.

William Petty, a founder member of the society, who had spent the previous summer out of reach of the plague at Durdans with Robert Hooke, was a man of many talents. He was no architect but a brilliant thinker and statistician, an urban philosopher, who offered no drawings but a new idea for the city. Instead of re-establishing the old boundaries of the City and liberties with Westminster beyond, he created a new greater

London, turning the City into a county with broad administrative powers. Petty's London would be modern in organisation, yet unfortunately he never completed his presentation and it was never presented to the king.

The second New Philosopher to give consideration to the shape of London was Robert Hooke, who had remained close to the city grandees at Gresham College. Almost immediately after the fire, he had turned his mind to the capital's improvement. In the first meeting of the society in September, when he and Wren had hoped to present their new ideas in telescopy, Hooke offered some experiments in brick-making. He also was thinking about how to change the whole city and began to draw up plans for replacing the huddled medieval streets and alleys with a geometrical grid plan, with the main streets 'as from Leaden-Hall corner to Newgate, and the like, [lying] in an exact strait line, and all other cross streets turning out of them at right angles, all the churches, publick buildings, Market places, and the like, in proper and convenient places'.[45] When he showed this initial design to the aldermen who now packed the college they responded with interest, claiming it better than the plan they had commissioned from their official surveyor, Peter Mills. Soon, Hooke's plans were adopted by the city authorities, and it was with this validation that, on 19 September, he presented his drawings to the Royal Society for their approval. Hooke's designs therefore arrived before the king with both the city's and the society's blessing.

Yet all these plans had been trumped by Christopher Wren. When John Evelyn arrived at Whitehall on 13 September, he found that his plan was the second proposal to arrive, and that 'Dr Wren had got the start of me'.[46] Wren had delivered his own ideas about the city on the day he and Evelyn had discussed their designs. Two days later, Henry Oldenburg moaned that Wren had not sought the approval of the Royal Society for his designs. Wren's only excuse was that he was in a rush to be first to present his ideas. Where Evelyn's baroque city had been bold and adventurous, seeking to improve and regularise the old city, Wren's imagined London completely remodelled the metropolis.

London was to be a new city. Ignoring all implications of cost, practicality, tradition and means, Wren's design, with Bernini's grand gestures still fresh in mind, was the essence of what the English baroque city could be. There was no mistaking how similar Wren's designs were to Evelyn's, but Wren had gone farther in his conception. Buoyed up by the meeting only two weeks previously at St Paul's, when his plans for the rebuilding

Christopher Wren's reimagining of what London could be, 1666

of the cathedral had been given a reserved approval by the commissioners, Wren's imagination filled with bold, perhaps even arrogant, thoughts of what the new metropolis should look like.

Wren's scheme was unashamedly European. The design, like Evelyn's, was a linked network of wide open streets leading to grand piazzas and monumental circuses, the City divided by a variety of grid systems and octagonal piazzas from which streets radiated like spokes. Many commentators, acknowledging Wren's later work on St Paul's Cathedral, claim that the architect placed his church at the centre of the designs; in fact he placed the Royal Exchange at the heart of the City, from where emanated the lifeblood of the metropolis – money. The Exchange was placed in the middle of a business zone that linked the Customs House on the Thames with the other major urban institutions. The powerhouses of the City, the guilds, would line a splendid 'grand terrace' along the river front, where Wren devised a straight wharf. At the mouth of London Bridge, he placed a piazza similar to Henri IV's Place Dauphin on the Pont Neuf. He also proposed to renovate and enlarge the Fleet river to improve the sanitation of the stinking ditch, with two strong stone quays as a docking bay for barges.

He had split the metropolis into parts that worked independently but were brought together with a communication network of roads and vistas. The city had been rationalised and broken down into sectors, reconfigured and made whole again, just as an experimenter reduces his observations to data and then builds up his conclusions. The centrality of trade and business in Wren's new London was obvious, but he also rationalised the religious life of the City. St Paul's Cathedral was reduced in size and given a dome but made prominent through the sight lines and street plans to the west beyond the city walls, visible in the London sky from as far as Whitehall. The front portico of the church jutted out towards a triangular split in the approaching thoroughfare, which divided into two major streets, one leading towards the Royal Exchange, the other connecting to the streets radiating from the wharfs. The city churches would be reduced in number and ordered within the scheme.

The vision of the new London that was to rise from the ashes of the Great Fire was in the hands of the New Philosophers. The new metropolis would be commanded by reason and geometry, informed by the best examples of the modern European styles, observed in Paris and Rome. Hooke, Evelyn and Wren had all produced a new version for how London lived and worked and moved. Only time, however, would determine what shape this 'more glorious phoenix' would eventually take.

PART THREE

Resurgam

6

Measuring the City

In the week after the fire, new plans and ideas for the metropolis filled the city, while rumours circulated that the king would purchase the land in order that a grand scheme could be commissioned for his own glory. When Evelyn delivered his draft on 13 September, he was invited into the king's bedchamber and asked to discuss the plans with the enthusiastic Charles, James, Duke of York, and the queen.

It was too early for the king to outline what was to be built but he did make certain that no rash pre-emptive rebuilding was started. While many were calling for the rapid return of London the king made his first proclamation on the course of rebuilding the city. The proclamation demanded delay and the threat of punishment hung over any hasty projects. Personal property was to be respected and only once a land register had been composed to ascertain the extent of the damaged area, establish who owned what and where, who was the landlord and who the tenant, and on what terms, could the authorities then decide the next step.

The announcement also included a number of initial decisions that would thereafter set the foundations of the new city. Brick or stone was to be the new material for London. The overhanging jetties of the wood-framed houses were to become a thing of the past; houses would have perpendicular walls and hold the line of the street rather than overshadow the thoroughfares below. This would make the streets outside more commodious to trade and traffic. Second, the proclamation promoted a broad scheme of road-widening to ensure that the city would no longer be a den of warrens and alleys. Which roads and how wide was to be decided later. The plan would set a new grid for the city, either laid over the old road system or completely reinvented; the roads would be paved and made useful to all traffic, reviving civic pride in all citizens: 'convenient and noble for the advancement of trade of any city in Europe ... both for use and beauty'.[1]

The king did, however, indicate his personal taste for the plans and ideas of Wren and Evelyn without endorsing any particular project: 'we shall cause a plot or model to be made for the whole building through those ruined places; which being well examined by all those people who have most concernment as well as experience, we make no question but all men will be pleased with it'. The model imagined a 'Key or wharf on all the riverside; that no houses shall be erected within so many feet of the river'; this would be lined with the most elegant houses in the city, making modern London a trading capital that received the wealth of the world by ship. This wealth would then be distributed to the City through the king's Customs House, which he promised to resurrect as soon as possible, enlarged 'with the most conveniences for the merchants that can be devised'.[2] In addition, as Evelyn had demanded in *Fumifugium*, the proclamation called for the expulsion of the noxious trades outside the city walls.

The proclamation was a revolutionary document, the very first of its type, setting out the ground rules of redevelopment. But in the meantime it acted as no more than a holding order. The king could only prescribe so much; he recognised that to demand more was to appear arbitrary or absolute. Thus the proclamation was littered with referrals to 'the assistance and advise of the lord mayor and court of aldermen',[3] and the final shape of the city would result not from monarchical caprice but from negotiation and due diligence between court, City and Parliament.

Elsewhere, haste was everything. In order for a thorough survey of the burnt region to be conducted the administration needed to clear the whole area of the charred debris that in parts was piled over four feet high. On 22 September, a series of booths was set up throughout the outlying neighbourhoods for landlords and tenants to lay claim to their legal rights. This was to be the first land register of the city and was conducted under the most difficult circumstances, and when the response was found to be less than forthcoming – in some parishes fewer than 10 per cent filed claims – the citizenry was bustled along, first by appeals to reason, and then by threats.

The capital, however, had been brought to a standstill and the population scattered. The wealthy, who could afford the rising rents in the suburbs, had already left the remnants of the walled city, and houses in Westminster and beyond were going for ten times their usual rates. Those who could not afford the escalating rents were forced to make do, setting up booths in the outlying fields to continue their trade. The poor were in even more dire straits and had to learn how to survive, setting up 'little sheds of brick upon the ruins of their own Houses'.[4] Many more left the city altogether, migrating away from the ashes to family or surrounding towns, some never to return. There were fears that this exodus would ruin the chances of revival.

Despite the hiatus, no building was allowed until the survey was completed. In addition the king desired to consult Parliament and set out the first steps towards legislation. Parliament, however, was less keen to debate the crisis in London than the war against the Dutch, which was still raging and needed funding. But the two problems were linked, for London was the nation's major source of revenue and the English navy floated on taxes collected through the Port of London, as well as loans on excise from the metropolitan goldsmiths such as Robert Vyner, who continued to charge 10 per cent interest on outstanding government debts. The capital contributed at least one fourteenth of all direct tax revenue and a lion's share of indirect tax to the Treasury. Yet how could the Treasury continue to raise chimney tax where no hearths existed?

The MPs knew that the markets of London and the port needed to be working, but in the heat of a cash crisis there was little chance of finding a consensus on questions of urban planning, for as the MP John Milward noted: 'It was the general opinion of the whole House that if some speedy way of rebuilding the City was not agreed upon that the City would be in danger never to be built.'[5] But they were less successful in finding a solution. Without concrete proposals they could pass no laws. In the interim, a parliamentary committee was set up and Wren's plans for London were placed in front of them. The MPs had neither the means nor enough information to make any new laws or even give useful advice. The debate was brought to the Commons, which was able to focus on the issue only for two days in which the MPs proved themselves the least qualified group to discuss issues of architecture.

Nobody wanted to see the city resurrected completely as it had been before but, as Oldenburg informed Robert Boyle, the debate on Wren's model provided few answers: 'Some are for a quite new model, according to Dr Wren's draught; some are for the old, yet to build with brick; others for a middle way, by building a Key, and enlarging some streets, but keeping the old foundation and vaults.'⁶ Wren's plans offered beauty but delay and expense; they also revived the ghost of absolutism. Time, money and the extension of the power of the Crown were the bugbears that agitated Parliament, yet it could offer no alternatives. The politicians returned the problem to the King's Privy Council and the Lord Mayor, advising that they would consider the matter further when there were some concrete legislative proposals on the table.

PUBLIC EMPLOYMENT

Five months after the fire, John Evelyn completed a nine-page pamphlet, *Public Employment, and an active Life with its Appanages, preferred to Solitude*. The publication was hardly groundbreaking news and the tract was, in Evelyn's own opinion, a trifling amusement. The previous year Sir George MacKenzie, an Edinburgh advocate, had penned a 'moral essay' promoting the benefits of solitude for the man of ideas, proposing that retirement suited the life of the mind, while employment in the courts or public sphere was anathema to the virtuous pursuit of truth. Evelyn, who had professed the exact same philosophy during the Commonwealth, concluded that the philosopher was a man of action as much as a man of solitary contemplation. The fire demanded the active participation of virtuous public men who, in Evelyn's words, 'continue humble and govern their passions, amidst the temptations of Pride and Insolence; if they remain generous, chast and patient amongst all assaults of avarice, dissolution and importunity of Clients'.⁷

By the beginning of October 1666, the king and the Lord Mayor had decided to form a committee of experts to set out the ground rules for the rebuilding. Of the committee of six, the king nominated three commissioners who met weekly with three city surveyors to formulate the new shape of London, complete the survey and deliver proposals to the court and Common Council, before the whole city population had migrated beyond the walls for good. The complexion of this Rebuilding Commission would determine the final shape of London far more than any previous proclamation or design, yet nothing would define the procedures of the commission more than the pressures of time. The building season had already ended by October. Everything had to be prepared by spring the next year.

The king, still hoping for a thoroughly modern capital as he had experienced in Europe, chose his three commissioners wisely. Rather than resort to his own personal designers within the Surveyor-General's Office of Works, Charles selected his commissioners from among the most exciting names in contemporary design. Roger Pratt was the most senior architect in England, and as designer of Clarendon House in Piccadilly the leading modernist of the day. Hugh May had been instrumental in the work on Whitehall Palace and as Comptroller of the Office of Works was ideally equipped to oversee the financial aspects of rebuilding; at Berkeley House in Piccadilly, he had already shown himself to be a designer who pushed the boundaries of English style. The last commissioner was Christopher Wren, whose designs for the metropolis had so enthralled Charles II. Wren's inclusion was a stroke of good fortune and must have been influenced by the recommendation of others, such as Evelyn, rather than resulting from his achievements thus far, making him the junior partner in the group.

The City nominated their own men to the commission and selected from the pool of leading artisans and masters of the guilds who had learnt their trade within the city walls. Peter Mills was the City's General Surveyor while Edward Jerman was a carpenter and 'an experienced man in building';[8] both men had worked on large-scale projects within the city and had learnt their trade through the traditional system of apprenticeship and masters. Neither had spent much time abroad, but both knew how to get a job completed. The third city commissioner was Robert Hooke, who had little experience of any building. Hooke's plans for the City had impressed the council billeted at Gresham College, and he had ingratiated himself with his new neighbours; and as the City's professor of geometry at Gresham College he would bring a scientific understanding to the practical task of the surveyors. The known relationship between Wren and Hooke was also an advantage in the make-up of the commission, and one that was quickly noticed in October when Henry Oldenburg was already yoking the two New Philosophers together in their joint task of conducting the survey of the city.

The first meeting took place on 4 October. Pratt, as the most senior commissioner, took control of the committee, and the accounts of the meetings over the next months come from his notes (thus undermining the myth promoted by *Parentalia* and repeated by historians that Wren was named 'Surveyor general and Principal architect for rebuilding the Whole City'[9]). The meeting focused on moving the survey forward so that all property rights could be ascertained in the event of street-widening, and the question of compensation. In the second meeting, on 8 October, the commissioners devised ways to accelerate the clearance of the debris so that the survey could take place by appointing contractors to clean the area and surveyors to oversee each city ward. By the third meeting, on 11 October, the commissioners, unable to devise any concrete plans owing to the slowness of the survey, were searching for more abstract improvements to the still-cluttered streets.

Everyone could agree that the old London streets were too narrow, but what should the new byways of the city look like? Wren's plans had promoted grand promenades 90 feet wide, secondary thoroughfares of 60 feet and then smaller ways of 30 feet, but this was now considered unfeasible. Instead the team devised an ad hoc rule of thumb concerning street widths:

the breadth of the severall future streets to be as followeth:

That of the Key 100 foot
That of the High Streete 70f
That of other streetes 50f
That of some others 42f
That of the least 30 or 25f
that of alleys, if any, 16f [10]

In the next meeting, on 18 October, they determined how this was going to work on the ground, even without the survey in front of them. These results were then passed on to the Common Council of the civic administration. This was, for all involved, a sign of progress.

Without the results of the survey, the commission could not focus on the actual layout of the City on the ground and instead turned its attention to minutiae. If London was to be built anew, it needed supplies, and fast. The commissioners discussed the questions of the quality and supply of brick and the material form of the City, for the supply of materials would determine the scale of London and the speed of the revival. The transition from questions of 'what' to build to 'how' offered vast riches, and would be a catalyst to the transformation of London as an economic capital.

This entrepreneurial spirit, however, tolled the death knell of Wren's grand project, and by November bad luck, poor weather, the failure to clear the city, the cooling of passions and the return of common sense had caused the hopes for a new baroque city to fade away. On reflection, however, Wren may never have expected his designs to become real. The plans were the rushed sketches of a heated dreamer which suited the feelings of desperation in the days following the fire. The beauty of Wren's designs was not in the possibility that they could ever be realised but in the bold display of his powerful imagination, arrogant enough to dream of the new city.

The end of October also brought another layer of confusion to the rebuilding effort, for on the 31st, the Frenchman Robert Hubert was brought to Tyburn. A deranged simpleton, Hubert had confessed to starting the fire, even though he was both physically and mentally incapable. At London's most infamous execution ground, a baying crowd revelled as it watched his swinging body kick on the rope. Once he was cut down, his body was ripped from the hands of the apothecaries who had planned to use his corpse for dissection and was torn limb from limb until nothing was left.

Hubert's death was not just a travesty of justice but also raised a sticky point of law that had far-reaching ramifications for the rebuilding plans. If the fire was proved to be started by an enemy of the state, the financial burden for the rebuilding fell to the landlords rather than the tenants of each property. Hubert's death had thus placed the responsibility for rebuilding upon the rich owners. Were they likely to rebuild their properties at the same speed as the desperately homeless tenants? Would they want to spend extra to build in costly brick and stone? In response to this conundrum a parliamentary committee was set up to prove that the fire was not started by the feeble-minded Frenchman. They were forced to work fast and issued their report in January 1667; predictably, it confirmed that the fire had been an accident.

London was also hit by another terrible winter which hindered all hopes of progress. Evelyn recorded in his diary on 21 October: 'This season, after so long and extraordinary a drought in August and September, as if preparing for the dreadful fire, was so very wet and rainy as many feared an ensuing famine'.[11] Food, donated by outlying towns, had to be delivered by boat to the city to feed the poor and homeless. On Guy Fawkes' Night, 5 November, the metropolis, usually ablaze with bonfires, remained quiet and dark. To so many the brief flicker of hope, the image of London rising from the flames, must have been a trick of the light in the dying embers of the city.

Throughout the winter, the commissioners, Common Council and Privy Council worked to gather together all their findings and directives to present to Parliament. In the bitter cold, Hooke, alongside six other surveyors, drew up a basic survey of the burnt neighbourhoods. It was a simplified street survey rather than a registry of all property rights, useful enough for the rough sketching of various street-widening schemes. Markings on the map show that the document was used to test out new streets and plans, such as extending a quay along the Thames. In the meantime, the city authorities worked tirelessly to get a Bill prepared and met 'weekly on Mundays Wednesdays & Fridays at Eight of the clock in the fore Noone and [were] constantly warned by Ticketts and attended by officers thereupon appointed'.[12] In the first weeks of the new year all these preparations were then sent to Parliament to formulate a Bill.

Yet once Parliament had received all they needed in order to legislate, progress was slow. Rather than focus on the issues of rebuilding, the two houses were distracted by a scandal involving one of the peers. Lord Mordaunt had been accused of reckless behaviour and was to stand trial. Debate raged on where the defendant should sit during his trial, and if he should be allowed to wear his hat. Hours were wasted as Parliament examined its own navel rather than debate the fate of the City a mile down the river. Charles II tried his best to place the rebuilding Bill in front of the distracted MPs, but the process was painfully lethargic. Once a debate was arranged there were legal quibbles on terms and arguments about how many parish churches London needed, but in the end the Bill gained royal approval on 8 February. The next day, Charles closed both houses and sent the MPs back to their constituencies. The rebuilding of London could finally begin.

The First Rebuilding Act of February 1667 encapsulated the many decisions, intentions and resolutions of the past months into a single document. The Act defined the shape and form of the metropolis, deciding where streets should be widened for the improvement of traffic and circulation of goods, formalising a civic structure of regulated order, while leaving the responsibility for rebuilding in the hands of private individuals.

The first significant directive to the City was a policy of street-widening. The new London would be like a human body in which the unhindered circulation of people, money and goods would nourish and bring life to all corners of the capital. Main streets and highways were identified and a process of staking out the new streets was planned. No byway was to be less than 16 feet wide, allowing a cart or carriage to pass throughout the whole city. Any dwelling that was compromised by the new street width was to be compensated and a new court would be set up to cope with this process of arbitration. Compensation was to be paid by a new tax of 12 pence for every ton of coal brought into the city ports, and would be collected by the city administration until June 1677.

The Act also defined the design of all houses to be rebuilt. These would be uniform and ordered, facing out on to the newly widened streets, while brick or stone were the only materials prescribed, with oak to be used for door cases and window frames. All overhangings such as 'bulks, jetties, windows, posts, seats or anything of any sort' were banned and every dwelling was standardised to fit one of four types that were defined by location and importance: 'the first or least sort of houses fronting by lanes; the second sort of houses fronting streets and lanes of note; the third sort of houses fronting high and principal streets; the fourth and largest sort, of mansion houses, for citizens, or other persons of extraordinary quality, not fronting either of the three former ways; the roofs of each of the said first sorts of houses respectively, shall be uniform'.[13] Each house would have its own regular dimensions: the first sort would have two storeys and a garret; the second, three; the third, four; and the fourth – being the houses of the rich, who obviously were above standardisation – were 'left to the discretion of the builder'. For houses that looked out on to a high street, balconies were mandatory.

Yet the process of raising the city also had to be managed. The City Surveyors would begin staking out the new street grid in a matter of weeks, yet how were the private citizens to go about rebuilding their own homes? Once ownership had been established, a builder was contracted. To ensure that no one profited too greatly from the deal, both the price of materials and the rate of wages were to be monitored. In addition, to ensure that there were enough builders, London needed to attract a new army of labourers to the city. In a radical move that threatened the long-established guild system, foreign labour was welcomed into London and promised the right of free practice:

all carpenters, bricklayers, masons, plaisterers, joiners and other artificers, workmen or labourers to be imployed in the said buildings, who
are not freemen of the said City, shall for the space of seven years, next
ensuing, and for so long time after as until the said buildings shall be

fully finished, have and enjoy such and the same liberty of working, and being set to work in the same building, as the freemen of the city of the same trades and professions have and ought to enjoy.[14]

St Paul's Cathedral was the one site within the city that was exempt from the Act. As royal land, it stood outside the concerns of Parliament. If the cathedral was to rise up once more it would have to be by the will of Charles II and his Church.

MEASURING THE CITY

The First Rebuilding Act was still a vague document that outlined the course of the new city in general while avoiding the responsibility of articulating the exact form of the revived metropolis. The number of parish churches was reduced to thirty-nine but their sites were to be settled later. To commemorate the fire an annual day of remembrance was named and a monument planned – 'a column or pillar of brass or stone, be erected on, or as near unto, the place where the said fire so unhappily began'.[15] Thames Street overlooking the river was to be raised 3 feet to prevent flooding. All final responsibility for the layout and manner of the rebuilding of London was placed on the shoulders of the city authorities and, in particular, the City Surveyors – Mills, Jerman and Hooke. Throughout March and April 1667, the Lord Mayor, Common Council and surveyors were tasked with defining the actual form of the new phoenix city.

Despite the bitter weather, 'Great frosts, snow and winds', so that even by April Evelyn recorded 'The cold so intense, that there was hardly a leaf on a tree,'[16] the authorities had to make a final decision on which streets needed to be widened in compliance with the Act. On 12 March, the City placed a map of London before the king. The new map showed the widening of streets as highlighted in the Rebuilding Act with added recommendations. The land in front of St Paul's was to be cleared to open up the churchyard, and a system of main roads was newly laid out to drive traffic across the whole city. The event was intended to rubber-stamp the City's plans rather than act as a formal consultation, yet the king was allowed to peruse the plans for a week and then return his positive verdict.

The next day, in anticipation of the building season and the king's approval, the Common Council elected that: 'Mr Peter Mills Mr Edward Jarman Mr Robert Hooke & Mr John Oliver are chosen to be surveyors and supervisors of the houses to be built in this citty & destroyed by the late fire according to the late Act of Parliament in that behalf. And it is ordered that the said surveyors doe forthwith proceed to the staking out the streets as is ordered & directed by this Court in pursuance of the said Act.'[17]

Hooke and Mills were sworn in the next day. Jerman was absent, already thinking about the projects that he could gain as a private contractor, while the glazier John Oliver, although named, had requested that he act only as deputy to Mills, who, at sixty-nine years old, was possibly too old for the task.

To show willingness, the king offered the services of his three commissioners, Pratt, May and Wren, whose main task had ended with the Act of Parliament. They were, however, less than keen to participate in the actual process of staking out the new street grid. All three men were architects rather than master builders and the hands-on practice of building was not in their ken, nor a suitable role for men of their status. Wren remained in London on and off throughout 1667, while Pratt returned his focus to completing Clarendon House in Piccadilly.

The City Surveyors were left to conduct the measuring of the city on their own. On 27 March, Hooke and Mills began staking out Fleet Street, at the western limit of the fire's devastation. Within nine weeks nearly the whole 436 acres of devastated ground of the burnt city were charted. It was an extraordinary feat of work in terms of speed but also of accuracy. According to the historian Michael Cooper, Hooke and Mills, using stakes of about five feet long, posted every 100 feet, worked with a team of carpenters and labourers for seven days a week, charting over eleven miles of street. Although there is no indication that Hooke and Mills used any new instruments beyond the traditional surveying tools, their achievement was a testament to common sense, experience and the utility of the New Philosophy. Hooke rationalised London, reducing the once incomprehensible warrens and byways into an ordered plan.

The process of staking out the new plan also highlighted where private land was to be used to accommodate the newly widened streets. In January 1668 the City Lands Committee was set up to adjudicate in such cases and, on occasion, Hooke was placed at the forefront of such disputes. For a claim to be valid, a surveyor had to be employed (for a small fee) to make a viewing of the property and draw up a certificate specifying how the new street width infringed property rights. The claim was then taken to the City Lands Committee and a hearing arranged, where compensation or redress was negotiated and then finally paid by the City Chamberlain six months later. Such confrontations could potentially be contentious, and Hooke had to use all his charms and sense of fairness to achieve the best possible outcome. He would be involved in such disputes long after the rebuilding, his final certificate dated 11 March 1687.

In addition to questions of compensation, the City Surveyors were involved in the issue of rebuilding and defining the extent and rights of individual private plots. Having charted the new city street grids, Hooke and Mills were then tasked with the massive operation of setting out the boundaries of every house to be rebuilt from the ashes. This was a survey not just of the dimensions of any given plot but also the relationship between the builder, the tenant and the landlord. On 29 April 1667, the City published the Act of Common Council which set out the procedure.

A builder had to first claim his foundations and pay a certain sum to the chamberlain, which was recorded in the day book. The builder was then issued with a receipt and the name of the surveyor who would visit the plot. A surveyor's fee was negotiated and a viewing arranged to gather information on the location, dimensions and situation of the plot, and the names of the neighbours, while a sketch of the ground plan was entered into the surveyor's book. The builder was subsequently issued with a certificate (in exchange for another small fee for the surveyor) which outlined all the information. Only then could building begin. As a result, Hooke soon became a recognised face throughout the streets of London, satchel and instruments under his arm, always heading to a new viewing, or conducting a survey with builders, client and local ward officials at hand. The demand for rebuilding was so great that soon Mills became ill and exhausted, while Hooke continued at his relentless pace.

Between May 1667 and December 1671, 8,394 foundations were viewed and recorded in the chamberlain's day books, set ready for rebuilding. Hooke undertook the majority of these tasks, working every morning of the week for the commission. Michael Cooper has calculated that the day book assigned over 1,582 to Hooke and of the four thousand or so viewings unallocated Hooke staked out at least 1,400. It is, however, impossible to know the exact final tally as the surveyor's book that Hooke carried around with him every day between 1667 and 1672 has been lost. This loss meant that for a long time it was only Mills' and his replacement John Oliver's books which recorded the progress of events. For this reason alone, Hooke's central role in rebuilding the City has only recently been acknowledged.

Hooke was tireless in his measurement of the City. In staking out the street plan, he set out the basic form of the new metropolis, its foundations firmly based in the New Philosophy. In addition, he was well paid for his work. He was paid £150 a year by the city authorities but also collected a small fee with every viewing and certificate that he authenticated. His contemporary biographer, Richard Waller, would note how he was rewarded and how he stored his money in 'a large Iron chest of Money found after his death, which had been lock'd down with a key in it, with a date and the time, by which it appear'd to have been so shut up for above thirty years – many thousands in Gold and Silver, a due recompense in so fatiguing an employ'.[18]

The surveyorship offered Hooke something that the Royal Society never had: status and financial security. Nonetheless, throughout the period Hooke was dedicated to the society, where he remained curator, and was expected to deliver weekly experiments and demonstrations. As a small concession to Hooke's workload, two new curators were appointed, Dr Walter Needham and Dr Richard Lower, John Locke's school friend. Later in 1668 Hooke was allowed to hire a boy to assist him in his experiments.

Hooke's dual role as City Surveyor and curator of the Royal Society was an ideal example of the New Philosophy at work in the real world. Upon the streets, the experimental method and the hopes of the city combined. As he performed his tasks, his mind was rarely far away from a novel demonstration: on cold days he complained when the fog made it impossible for him to observe the stars. While staking out the streets, he considered whether it was possible to test the curvature of the earth by recording the relative difference in heights between stakes, driven into the ground 100 yards apart. The possibilities of uncovering knowledge were never distant from the surveyor's mind.

THE PHILOSOPHER ARRIVES

John Locke also felt drawn to the ideas that were so powerfully displayed in the first years of rebuilding. Since returning from his travels he had decided to become a doctor. At Oxford, he continued to experiment alongside Boyle and began to write on scientific matters: a short post-mortem essay on a child with rickets and a study on respiration. In the summer before the fire this led to an important meeting of minds which would change the course of his life. The scholar received a letter from a friend in London, Dr David Thomas, who was attached to the household of Sir Anthony Ashley Cooper, the Chancellor of the Exchequer: 'I request one favour from you, which is to send mee word by the next opportunity, whether you can procure 12 bottle of water for my Lord Ashly, to drink in Oxford sunday and munday morneing; if you possibly doe it, you will be very much oblidge him and mee.'[19]

The Chancellor was suffering from a liver abscess and had come to Oxford that weekend to visit his son at the university, and wished to drink the local Astrop spa water. Locke was invited to drink with the grandee and they struck up a rapport, and over the course of the summer a friendship evolved. Although Ashley Cooper was in need of a doctor, Locke had much more in common with the leading politician than appeared on the surface. In the spring of 1667, Ashley Cooper invited Locke to live with and work for him at his home, Exeter House, on the Strand, a few hundred yards from the edge of the burnt limits of the city.

Far away from the cloistered halls of Oxford, John Locke was transformed over the following years from an academic to a political philosopher, and from a laboratory-bound physician into a practical man of medicine. London made the man of books and experiments into a man of ideas and action. His friendship with Ashley Cooper would become the most influential relationship in Locke's life.

At Exeter House, Locke continued to develop his medical skills. In his notebooks there are numerous incidents of domestic concerns, such as treating 'Lucy, a Kitchen maid', who suffered from the dropsy. Soon he was so busy that he found little time for chemistry and letter writing as he became increasingly absorbed in metropolitan life. He was fortunate enough to meet Thomas Sydenham, a radical physician. Sydenham claimed that nature rather than ancient theory was the best way to treat a patient. Rather than examining a patient and diagnosing according to some form of theory, he preferred to observe the disease and register its symptoms.

Sydenham rarely gained the appreciation of his peers. He was particularly interested in epidemics and fevers that seemed to fester in the darkest corners of the city, where poor housing and sanitation incubated the disease. In 1666 he had published *The Method of Curing Fevers*, which was dedicated to Robert Boyle. Locke soon became a keen student of this new method and worked with Sydenham on the treatment of smallpox, which was so prevalent in London – in 1667, only two years after the plague, 1,196 died of the disease alone. Alongside his new mentor, Locke made numerous visits throughout the city and began to gather copious clinical notes as he jotted down all aspects of symptoms, prognosis and cure.

In Sydenham's opinion, the physician's skill lay in aiding the body to cure itself rather than imposing a medical regime upon an already damaged body. Thus, rather than overheating the feverish patient, he prescribed a cooling regime, with the patient allowed to stay on his feet rather than being banished to his bed. The patient was also encouraged to drink plenty of fluids. On numerous occasions he, as later reported: 'consulted my patients' safety and my own reputation most effectually by doing nothing at all'.[20]

Locke was influenced not just by Sydenham's practice but also by his method. The physician was putting the New Philosophy into practice within the new capital, and in 1668 Locke acted as Sydenham's secretary when he began to collate his ideas together into *De Arte Medica*, in which the author emphasised the importance of experience over received wisdom: 'True knowledge grew first in the world by experience and rational observation.'[21]

This journey from the university library to bedside doctoring bore fruit in May 1668. That month, Ashley Cooper fell ill and was prescribed a purgative by Charles II's Physician in Ordinary, Francis Glisson. Glisson's medicine only worsened the situation; the pain increased and a tumour the size of a newborn's head appeared on his belly. Locke was placed in charge, and through his meticulous notes he recorded the painful progress of the illness. He wanted to operate on the tumour and asked the advice of a number of leading physicians, who approved. On 12 June, a surgeon cauterised the tumour, which appeared to have grown from the liver.

As Locke reported: 'a large quantity of purulent matter many bags and skins came away',[22] but the wound continued to issue pus and matter, and in order to make sure that all the poison was expelled, the surgeon's hole was kept open with a wax candle and was cleaned daily for six weeks. As the wound was allowed to heal, Locke devised a silver drain that funnelled the fluid from the wound. After some months it was decided that the drain should stay in place for as long as the abscess continued to discharge. Ashley Cooper thus returned to work, albeit to the mirth of his detractors, who called him 'Tapski', and Locke's contraption became the inspiration for the renaming of a wine barrel operated by a turncock, a 'Shaftesbury'.

The power of these new ideas would be felt in other areas of Locke's first years in London. The work with Sydenham struck deep into his concerns about the foundations of knowledge. Sydenham denied all authority except that which could be gained by the bedside in the treatment of patients. At the same time as curing patients, Locke began to question the role of experience in the formation of human understanding, asking: how do we know anything?

In the winter of 1670, Locke and a few friends gathered at Exeter House to form an informal speculative club. Unlike the Royal Society, which Locke had joined in 1668, this group was not involved in experiments and demonstrations upon the laboratory bench but used the same method to dissect and measure ideas, as he later recorded:

> five or six friends, meeting at my chamber and discoursing on a subject very remote to this, found themselves quickly at a stand by the difficulties that rose on every side. After we had awhile puzzled ourselves, without coming nearer to a conclusion of those doubts which perplexed us, it came into my thoughts, that we took a wrong course; and that before we set ourselves upon inquiries of that nature, it was necessary to examine our own abilities, and see what objects our understandings were or were not fitted to dealing with.[23]

As one of those companions, James Tyrrell, would later record, the subject of this discussion was not just how one measures the world, but the origins of morality.

Locke began writing down his ideas, and in one excerpt from the document (later called Draft A) he noted: 'for having seen water yesterday I shal always know and it will be always an unquestionable true proposition to me that water did exist 10 Jul. 71'.[24] He had a further attempt on the problem that winter when he rewrote his original manuscript (now called Draft B). Locke was hoping to find a system of thought, derived from the New Philosophy, that offered an alternative bedrock to understanding: knowledge did not come from the divine revelation or the commentaries of the established Church nor the proclamations of kings but from experience and reason. As Locke would later claim, it was this search for the foundations of human understanding which would sweep away the debris of the past and set a new keystone for the rebuilding of the modern society, just as a few hundred yards beyond the confines of Exeter House, a new modern city was emerging from the ashes of the inferno.

SPECULATION

In 1667, an advertisement was placed on the front wall of the Temple Exchange Coffee House, at the western end of Fleet Street:

> You see before You
> The Last House of the city in flames
> The first of the City to be restored: May this be favourable and fortunate
> For both city and house
> Especially for those who are auspiciously building.
> Elizabeth Moore Owner of the site,
> and
> Thomas Tuckey, tenant.[25]

Since the City would be rebuilt by private money, each tenant looking after their own plot, the project rose and fell in waves: between 1667 and 1669, it began in haphazard fits and starts, dependent on the flow of supplies, money and labour. The cold winter and the continuing conflict with the Dutch navy, who blocked the channel and attacked every type of English ship, meant that supplies arrived sporadically up the Thames. This damaged the delivery of building stock and coal from the north, reducing the coffers that the Lord Mayor used to pay compensation.

In June 1667, this became particularly dangerous when the Dutch fleet sailed up the undefended Thames and raided Chatham, thirty miles from London, where the Royal Navy had their main base. From his garden in Sayes Court, John Evelyn had heard the rout as the Dutch navy, 'doing us not only disgrace, but incredible mischief in burning several of our best men-of-war lying at anchor and moored there ... the alarm was so great that it put both country and City into fear, a panic and consternation, such I hope I shall never see more'.[26] The blockade was ended the following month with the hastily negotiated Treaty of Breda, but this was nonetheless too late to reignite the building season for that year. By December only 150 houses had been completed. Samuel Rolle, a preacher, worried by the chaotic state of the rebuilding, feared that the city was returning to life not street by street but house by house. Would the metropolis ever be completed?

Progress was necessarily slow, as shown in the work of the surveyors. The revival of the City was to be paid for by the private citizen; it also had to follow the dictates of the Rebuilding Act. Each plot had to be viewed before rebuilding began. As the dimensions of the houses were recorded in the surveyors' books, so too were the names of neighbouring plots. This was essential, for the measurement of each plot was defined by shared party walls, 'set out equally on each builders' ground',[27] and the rebuilding process depended on such small neighbourly considerations. The Act set out the means for one builder to commence rebuilding without having to wait for the neighbour to start.

The party wall that divided two dwellings was 'built by the first beginner of such building; and that convenient toothing be left in the front wall by the first builder, for the better joining of the next house that shall be built to the same.'[28] Suitable compensation for the first builder's work was paid later when the second house was complete. In addition, there was little debate on the type and scale of each new house, as all were forced to conform to the four types expressed in the Act, defined by their location and the type of street they faced. Thus the surveyors were able to define in their books the shape of a particular plot, as detailed in one example in Oliver's book: 'according to the Act of rebuild: of the Second Sort of building'.

For example, on 19 March 1668, Mills visited the foundations of a house 'in fleet street neer fetter lane belonging to Nicholas Barebones, Doctor of Phisick'. The surveyor duly measured the property, noting the dimensions and names of the neighbours on both sides of the dwelling: 'containing upon the front east and west 12 foot 9 inches from the middle of each party wall (and in breadth at the back house 12 ft 11 inches from the middle of each party wall) and in depth from the front north and south with the ground that is taken into the street 49 ft 5 inches to the middle of the party wall north. Mr Wheeley on the West side Mr Feadson on the East Side and North'.[29] Barbon was then issued with a certificate and allowed to commence rebuilding on the land that had once been his father's workshop. Later in Mills's book, there is even a drawing of the Fetter Lane plot (see overleaf).

As the tenant, Barbon was obliged to pay for the costs of rebuilding, yet he wished to contest the lease with his landlady in light of the costly undertaking. In January 1667, in expectation of such disputes, Parliament passed the 'Act for erecting a judicature for determination of differences

A plan of the Barbon family plot in Mills's book. The whole of the burnt regions of London were measured and plotted in this way.

touching houses burned or demolished by reason of the late fire which happened in London', setting up a series of Fire Courts in Clifford's Inn, Holborn, to adjudicate over any contests that might arise over property rights. It was one of the few instances of Stuart jurisprudence that actually helped rather than hindered the progress of justice. The Fire Courts were set up to arbitrate between disputing sides, find a compromise and get the City back to work. If a tenant was willing to rebuild, a reduction in rent and an extension of the lease was encouraged. If the lessee did not want to rebuild, then the lease was terminated and the landlord free to do whatever he wanted. If the landlord wanted to develop the site himself, then a price to buy back the lease was arranged.

At Fetter Lane, Barbon was willing to rebuild at his own expense, yet he wished this to be acknowledged by the landlord and requested that the lease be extended. The judgement of the Fire Court was delivered on 10 March 1668. Barbon's request was considered not unreasonable, and he negotiated a new lease with the landlady, 'Elizabeth Speght, widow and James Speght, an infant':

Upon summons Elizabeth appeared personally, James by Matthew Pindar, admitted by the Court as his guardian, and the petitioner with Mr Sturges his counsel. The petitioner asked for 40 years to be added to his term and his rent reduced to £15 p.a. The Court considered the terms reasonable and the defendants consented . . . first payment at Lady Day 1669, and that the petitioner might require the said James Speght to execute new lease for so many years of the extended term as are to come and surrender the old lease.[30]

By the spring of 1668, the City was more prepared than the previous year, although there were still fears that the process of rebuilding would itself be the City's downfall. The deregulation of labour laws stirred worries that work would fall into the hands of unscrupulous speculators. A worker in London could earn more than in the provinces, and work sites became filled with 'foreign' builders and artificers despite the guilds' best attempts to restrict their practice. The gates had been opened for a new labour force to rebuild the City, and it was impossible to shut them again. A new type of labour market emerged in which the builders themselves became entrepreneurs for hire rather than members of a strict hierarchy, and where supply and demand regulated prices.

The loss of the guilds' power to regulate prices also created a sense of concern about the rising costs of building. From his pulpit, Rolle preached about the morality of a fair price. Stephen Primatt, a lawyer, and the scientist William Leybourn both published pamphlets that attempted to set a standard for the rebuilding effort, introducing the reader to the science of measuring and construction as well as the rational pricing of labour and materials.

The burden of finding supplies was a second major concern. When the Port of London finally reopened, supplies arrived from all over the nation and abroad: wood came from Scandinavia and, it was said: 'The Norwegians warmed themselves comfortable by the Fire of London,' but competition between suppliers soon established a fair price for most materials. Most houses were built of brick rather than stone, and around London new kilns and lime burners were established. In Moorfields, a mile north of the city walls, one Henry Tindall was able to secure a licence for £20 a year to produce bricks from his land, and between 1667 and 1670 he baked over 5.5 million bricks. Others were not so lucky: John Evelyn invested in an escapade with a Dutchman, John Kivet, to make bricks from the Thames mud but he lost £500, a small fortune, after tests proved that the river clay was unusable.

There were other schemes that were emerging from the attempts to rebuild London. The surveyor's book of 1668, in addition to Nicholas Barbon's family home in Fetter Lane, also revealed more facts about the young speculator's business. Since the fire the physician had begun to buy up or lease plots within the burnt streets of the City, for in the aftermath, as many citizens fled the capital, house prices plummeted. Some more wily speculators had looked into the future and predicted that the value of land within the walls would one day rise again. In Mills's and Oliver's books Barbon appeared to have gained two properties in a court off Newgate Market as well as a dwelling in Cheapside.

In January 1668 he mortgaged the family house in Fetter Lane for £300 from Thomas Fountain of Lincoln's Inn and spent £400 in total on the rebuilding of the new house. Rather than keeping this as his family home, he developed his father's workshop into Crane Court – a series of dwellings around a courtyard, which he then leased out. He took the largest house as his own, planning to live in some luxury. The upstairs room gave the impression of a well-to-do businessman to all creditors and petitioners who visited. The courtyard outside was paved with black marble and white polished Purbeck stone. Even with interest and mortgage payments, his income on this property was substantial. Barbon was making his first steps as a property speculator.

Barbon was also developing his role as an entrepreneur when he created the Insurance Office, the first fire insurance company in the world. The precise dating of the opening of the office is uncertain, but by 1681 the company had been renamed the Fire Office, and was located at the back of the Royal Exchange. His scheme was brilliantly simple: it offered a defence against the risks of living in the city while also making him a healthy profit. For a premium of 2.5 per cent of the yearly rent for brick buildings and 5 per cent for wooden-frame structures he offered insurance against fire for terms of seven, eleven, twenty-one and thirty-one years. By the 1680s he would have over four thousand subscribers.

The problem with innovation is that it is often copied, and Barbon's ideas were swiftly replicated. In 1670 the City Corporation set up its own scheme, offering terms for life. Barbon had to work hard to sell his services before the opposition stole his market. The Corporation soon found that it was offering too much in order to get customers and wound down the operation, only to revive the idea in the 1680s. In response Barbon developed a firefighting service to combat the flames rather than subscribers having to pay out insurance. In 1667 he advertised the Cohortes Vigilum, or fire-watchers, 'a company of men versed and experienced in extinguishing and preventing of fire'.[31] Of course, the brigade was formed only to protect the houses of those who displayed the Insurance Office's mark, a lead plate featuring a phoenix rising from the flames.

By the end of 1668, London had begun to look like a city again. Rolle estimated that 800 buildings had been completed and 1,200 foundations had been staked out. Houses were emerging from the street fronts but the shops had not returned. Many of the families that rebuilt the first houses did not return to live in them but instead converted them into taverns for the immigrant builders. The new marketplaces, as devised by Charles II, had been staked out but were slow to regain their popularity. While the domestic lives of the city were slowly reviving, the same could not be said for its major institutions.

The Surveyor-General

By 1669, London was slowly getting back to work. By the end of that summer, Samuel Rolle estimated that over 1,600 private houses had been completed; yet something was missing. Despite the progress in reviving the private fortunes of the citizens, the City still lacked its major institutions – its offices and courts, the individual livery halls, the Royal Exchange and the Guildhall, where the civic administration negotiated, dealt and governed. The capital also lacked its spiritual centre, St Paul's Cathedral.

As the embers of the fire died down, the city fathers had demanded immediate action to be taken on the restoration of the Royal Exchange. Here the world had congregated twice a day to haggle and deal, but now the walls stood broken, the cellars burnt, with all the stored goods destroyed. London needed to trade again in order for the City to revive and the Exchange needed a permanent base instead of its temporary home in the quadrangle at Gresham College.

In November 1666, Hooke, Jerman and Mills were commanded to visit the Exchange to offer recommendations. Hooke was the first to respond and delivered an estimated price for rebuilding, but he was not awarded the job – his calculations were underestimates and he made the economical, but unflattering, suggestion that much of the building could be remade with the old stone. The two other surveyors, more experienced in how to clinch a contract, held off on submitting their advice.

While plans for the Exchange were up in the air, Christopher Wren went to survey the broken hulk of St Paul's in December at the request of his friend William Sancroft. Thus far no efforts had been made to repair the site or to assess whether it would be possible to recover some space for the City's worship. Wren recorded his dismal conclusions in a letter: 'it now appears like some antique ruin of 2000 years standing, and to repair it sufficiently will be like the minding of the argo navis, scarce any thing will at last be left of the old'.[1] Was the site that had stood so long at the centre of London's history to be left behind by the modern city?

Sancroft, however, did not have time to consider the complete rebuilding of the cathedral and was searching for a temporary measure. Although the hulk of the building had been destroyed and the marble floor of the choir ravaged to expose the crypt of St Faith's below, the role of the church within the city needed to continue, and the dean wanted to know whether any part of the ruins could be saved for temporary use. Wren was not convinced; he approached the wreck like a physician before a terminal patient: 'Having shewn in part the deplorable condition of our patient we are to consult of the cure if possibly art may affect it, and heerin we must imitate the Physician who when he finds a totall decay of Nature bends his skill to a palliation, to give respite for a better settlement of the estate of the patient.'[2]

Wren concluded that if a choir was needed, the 'least worst' place was at the west end of the nave, where Inigo Jones's grand portico still stood. This was confirmed in a survey by four builders that repeated Wren's fears but suggested temporary repairs. It was undoubtedly an ugly solution, and Wren was keen to stress that this form of medicine could be palliative at best. Thus a temporary choir was constructed in the west end of the cathedral, covered by a new system of roofing, 'composed of boards only', while Wren continued to complain that this was hardly a scheme 'fit for Paules'.[3]

While Wren was left to plead with the Anglican authorities, at the Exchange, although there was no budget or plan in place, the City commissioned Mills and Jerman to begin reconstruction in March 1667, not wishing to miss the building season. Both Mills and Jerman were named as 'surveyor', even though neither man had produced a survey or report. Yet Jerman demurred; he was holding out for a promotion, expecting to be busy with profitable, private projects. By the end of April, his stubbornness had worked and he was named as sole designer and was commanded to start immediately.

Edward Jerman was an architect of note and an experienced city builder, a third-generation master carpenter who had worked within the walls all his life. Before the fire he had worked for individual guilds – he was the surveyor for Fishmongers' Hall, carpenter to the goldsmiths – as well as taking on civic roles such as City Viewer (a structural surveyor for the Lord Mayor), City Carpenter and designer of the city pageants. In the 1650s he had branched out into a few development projects of his own where he had acted as designer. Jerman was an example of the city artificer who had more than a passing knowledge of the most recent styles and possibly had even worked with Inigo Jones himself.

As a City Surveyor after the fire he had declined to work alongside Hooke and Mills staking out the streets, as wealthy private clients were already requesting his services. Over the next four years he would work on no less that eight livery halls: Drapers' Hall, Vintners' Hall, the façade and chapel of the Mercers' Company on Cheapside, Apothecaries' Hall, Haberdashers' Company and Fishmongers' Hall. In addition, he was commissioned to draw up designs for St Paul's School, owned by the Mercers' Company, which stood at the east end of the burnt cathedral. Indeed, by 1669 it appeared that Jerman was rebuilding the City by himself.

At St Paul's, repairs to the west end of the nave were under way. Wren feared, however, that this would act as an excuse for the commission not to build a new cathedral. In October 1667, an Acquittance Book was begun by the Clerk of Works for the cathedral, John Tillison, which accounted for all the work that was conducted in the cathedral church-yard. In the first few months, in preparation for the renovation of the choir, workmen were hired to start clearing away the rubbish while a wall was built around the whole cathedral. Wood was purchased to prepare for scaffolding.

The cathedral was to be repaired but no further plans for its rebuilding had yet been discussed. In a desperate letter in November 1667, Wren urged Sancroft to consider the future: 'Having with this ease obtained a present cathedral, there will be time to consider of a more durable and noble fabrick to be made in the place of the Tower and eastern parts of the Church.' He was even willing to reduce his ambitions for a grand edifice: 'I hope whatever you do of this nature is but in order to something of a better mould. For though I despair this age should erect any more such huge piles, yet I believe the reputation of Paul's and the compassion men have for its ruins may at least produce some neat fabrick, wch shall recompence in Art and beauty what it wants in bulke.'[4]

In January 1668, a meeting at Whitehall was called, involving the Anglican hierarchy – Gilbert Sheldon, Archbishop of Canterbury, Bishop

Henchman of London and Sancroft – which approved Wren's proposal for a temporary choir, but it was clear that there were no further plans for the rebuilding effort. Although it was not the response that Wren would have wanted from the commission, it confirmed that he was the primary architect on the cathedral project.

Wren had gained the role that he had long desired yet his hopes to recast a new cathedral seemed even more distant than they had been before the fire. But three months later, in a letter to Wren, Sancroft recounted that he had been inside the cathedral when a piece of masonry fell from the ceiling, exposing Inigo Jones's own work to be faulty. The dean was now ready to eat humble pie: 'what you whispered in my Ear, at your last coming hither, is now come to pass. Our work at the West end of St Paul's is fallen about our ears. Your quick eye discern'd the Walls and Pillars gone off from their perpendicular, and I believe other defects too, which are now expos'd to every common observer'.[5] Sancroft pleaded with Wren to come to London as soon as he could and to bring with him his previous designs, which he had drafted before the fire.

Once again, Wren could dream of building a new Temple in London, yet he did nothing. Perhaps conscious of the pressures of 'tyme and treasure' that had so diverted the commission away from contemplating grand schemes at the beginning of the year, he feigned caution, writing to his friend on 24 May: 'I am very unwilling to give hasty resolutions in thinges for perpetuity, nor will the end of a letter in wch I am already troublesome afford you satisfaction, to design such things for you that will not be suitable to our age and readily practicable is to build only on paper.'[6] The architect had gained enough experience to know that only a fool would rush in so quickly in response to the present disasters.

While Wren was learning to navigate the chicanery of Church bureaucracy, Jerman worked at raising the Exchange. In 1668, as the project was nearing completion, however, Jerman died and the work was passed over to the master mason Thomas Cartwright. The building was completed in 1669 and trading began on 28 September. It swiftly became a source of celebration within the city. Samuel Rolle called it 'one of the greatest glories and Ornaments of London',[7] while the poets also made their voices heard:

> In all thy travels, thou didn'st ne'er perceive
> A Place like this. And herein thou may'st say

> To all the rest, that they must now give way
> We have the Phoenix in our English nation.[8]

It did not seem to matter to the poets that the building had suffered from a lack of financial preparation and had nearly bankrupted the Mercers' Company, which shared the building with the City. Hooke's cautious survey in 1667 had stated that with the reuse of some of the old stones and metal the cost of rebuilding would be £4,500; in the end it had cost just over £58,000. The lessons were plain: there had been too much haste in getting the Exchange back to work, but once complete it swiftly became the symbol of the reborn capital.

Meanwhile, St Paul's still languished in disrepair, suffering from too little attention. Nonetheless, as Wren had learnt from Paris, it was not designs and ideas alone which changed the fate of cities. He wrote to Sancroft, observing: 'I think it is silver upon which the foundation of any worke must be first layd, least it sinke while it is yet rising,' and before he even contemplated designs for the new cathedral, he wanted to know 'the largenesse and security of this sort of foundation [before] I shall presently resolve you what fabrick it will beare'.[9] If Wren's hopes for St Paul's were to be realised, he would need to establish what he could afford.

THE KING'S ARCHITECT

In March 1669, however, Wren's fortunes changed. The Surveyor-General, Sir John Denham, was near to death and, in a canny political move, recommended Wren to succeed him. The machinations behind this nomination are a portrait in miniature of the convoluted politics of the Stuart court. Charles's favourite, the Duke of Buckingham, had told Denham to push for Wren, knowing that this was what the king wanted, and Wren was the person the king had most likely promised the job to years earlier. The courtier wanted to be seen to support Wren's promotion, safe in the knowledge that it was a *fait accompli*.

Wren was duly appointed the Surveyor-General, the king's architect, on 29 March; yet not to universal approval. Hugh May had no conflict with Wren but was annoyed that his patron, Buckingham, had betrayed him, and his silence had to be bought with a series of pensions and sinecures that made him a very rich man (far richer than he would have been in the surveyor's post). John Webb, on the other hand, could not understand why they had chosen the astronomer, 'who in whatever respects is [Denham's] inferior by farr', and in a moment of folly even offered to share the post 'whereof [Wren] professeth to bee wholly ignorant'.[10] Pratt, it appears, kept his opinions to himself.

The role of Surveyor-General, however, was something of a poisoned chalice. It was first and foremost a grace-and-favour position that came with a respectable pension of around £380 a year (including Christmas bonus and expenses), a free house in Scotland Yard within Whitehall and a country residence in the grounds at Hampton Court. These perks had most suited Sir John Denham, who had been named surveyor following the Restoration in acknowledgement of his royalist sympathies and a particular act of bravery during the Civil Wars, rather than for his reputation as an architect. As Evelyn drily noted, he was a 'better poet than architect'.[11]

Second, it was an administrative post: the Surveyor-General was head of a board that oversaw the upkeep of the royal palaces. The board, which comprised surveyor, comptroller, master mason, master carpenter and almost every other trade within the royal household, met 'in the office every morning between 8 and 9 to consider the business which is incident that day.'[12] This chiefly entailed checking the accounts of the five clerks in charge of the palaces at Whitehall, Westminster and St James, Somerset House and the Tower of London, Hampton Court, Greenwich and Windsor.

Much of the office's work was the day-to-day running of the palaces, paid for by an annual income from the king's private treasury, currently run by Locke's patron, the Chancellor, Ashley Cooper. As a result the most important man on the board was not the Surveyor-General but the Paymaster, Hugh May, however thankless a task it may have been. Cash was always late and the balancing act between the demands for repairs and the funds to pay for the work was precarious. In addition, the office of the Surveyor-General was endlessly the focus of efficiency drives and cutbacks, and in the year before Wren arrived it suffered a severe belt-tightening exercise when Ashley Cooper reduced the income from £10,000 to £8,000 a year.

The Surveyor-General had a third role as the king's premier designer, and there was always the possibility that the king might build great palaces. Thus far Wren had worked within the universities and primarily for the established – and conservative – Church. As surveyor, Wren could become Charles II's Vitruvius, and set about establishing the glory of the Stuarts in stone. In accepting the appointment, therefore, Wren had agreed to a dangerous bargain: he was to ally himself to the pitching fortunes of the Crown, but in return he might have the opportunity to build grand designs. The new role would finally draw Wren away from Oxford to London, but there was still doubt as to whether the Crown would be able to restore its monuments.

Wren had finally gained a role that suited his ambitions. Since the Restoration he had been developing his architectural reputation and had also established himself as one of the leading New Philosophers within the Royal Society. In the aftermath of the fire, he had gained promotion as one of the commissioners, determining the shape of the new London on paper. Now he had gained the prize of the surveyorship he might actually see his architectural experiments and dreams set in London stone.

The sense of celebration is revealed in one of the rare insights into Wren's private life. He would spend most of his life as a public man and few fragments remain that peel away the layers of his persona to reveal the private soul underneath. He seemed to have lived his early years dedicated to the New Philosophy and architecture to the exclusion of all vices, excepting perhaps coffee. On gaining his new role, however, the Surveyor-General considered himself to have finally arrived, and as a result he did something unexpected – at the age of thirty-seven, he married.

Up to this moment there had been few hints of sex or relationships within his busy schedule, but on moving into his new home in Scotland Yard at Whitehall, Wren married Faith Coghill, the thirty-three-year-old daughter of the local landowner in Bletchingdon, Oxfordshire, where Wren's family had fled in the Civil War. For the romantically minded, Wren's choice of bride may have been the result of a lifetime's affection, first formed in the heat of the dangerous Troubles. Faith certainly did not come from the court, nor were her family rich, so a love match seems plausible. The record, however, is too brief to be conclusive, apart from a single letter that the architect wrote, in the summer of 1669, returning to his betrothed a pocket watch that he had repaired: 'I have sent the watch at last & envie the felicity of it, that it should be soe neer your side & soe often enjoy your eye ... But have a care for it, for I have put such a Spell into it; that every beating of the ballance will tell you 'tis the pulse of my heart, which labours as much to serve you and more trewly than the Watch.'[13]

They married on 7 December 1669 at the Temple church of St Mary's.

Marriage, however, did not seem to affect Wren's day-to-day lifestyle. He continued to spend much of the day in business, or in the coffee houses, rather than in domestic bliss. In 1672, a son, Gilbert, was born, named after Archbishop Sheldon, but he died at seventeen months old. A second son, Christopher, was born in 1675.

Once settled in Whitehall, Wren inherited a curious situation within the Office of Works, for at that time the Crown could afford only one new project, Greenwich Palace, which had been under way since 1664. John Webb, the architect and on-site surveyor, was hoping to build a palace that would have made even his kinsman, Inigo Jones, jealous. Progress was slow, however, owing partly to the sluggish supply of money, which was provided by an 'extraordinary' income paid directly from the Treasury. When Webb took the opportunity to criticise the appointment of Wren, he also claimed that the Crown owed him money, he unwittingly insulted both his new boss and his patron in one go. By 1672 Wren had cancelled the whole project with only one wing of the palace complete, standing blankly besides the Thames. Webb was driven into retirement in Somerset.

Wren focused the office on the rebuilding of London and the royal projects that had been allowed to stand since the fire. His arrival announced the second wave of rebuilding in the city, for while the first had seen the restoration of private property so that the citizens could return to their neighbourhoods, and the revival of the civic institutions that regulated and governed trade, the second wave would be dominated by a different form of architecture. Before Wren could start building, however, there was the small matter of money. He now knew that the question of funding would define the final form of London as deeply as any architectural philosophy, but the king was too broke to commission grand gestures. As the Anglo-Dutch wars had already crippled the royal treasury, how could the king's architect expect to shower the Crown in glory without a budget? Wren, therefore, started his new role determined to revive the one place that generated revenue for the Crown.

In 1667, Charles II had promised to rebuild the Customs House as soon as he could. That same year Sir John Denham had surveyed the ground but the land had become tied up in the proceedings of the Fire Courts, where the examination of the convoluted proprietary rights and responsibilities took all of 1667. By 1668 there were designs for a new structure but no money to fund the rebuilding. Inevitably, as Jerman's Royal

Exchange was nearing completion in 1669, nothing had been accomplished at the Customs House. At the start of the rebuilding season, a loan had been raised and work was about to start. Wren, however, Surveyor-General for only a month, called a halt to the plans and trashed the designs. He demanded alterations and forced the Treasury to advance a funding increase of 50 per cent to the project.

Completed in 1671, the building was Wren's first assault on reshaping the new capital. The long, elegant structure, flanked by two wings, faced out across a broad courtyard towards the Thames. As the gateway into the City for all seaborne traffic, the Customs House was both elegant and functional. Built of a mixture of red brick and white Portland stone, warehouses stretched along the ground floor, where the goods brought ashore from the newly arrived ships were stored. Above, the 'Great Room' filled the entire span of the first floor, studded by eleven tall round-headed windows. Wren's first venture into the rebuilding of the City was a triumph.

Wren soon became involved in all the royal schemes within London, yet there was little progress at St Paul's Cathedral, where work was continuing on the clearance of the rubble. While there were still no calls for new designs, Wren was able to offer his invaluable judgement to the job of demolition. He demanded that Inigo Jones's west front, the simple Tuscan façade with the Corinthian portico and black marble steps, be preserved while everything else was to be dismantled. In 1668 workmen had begun to break up the east end of the structure. The task was dangerous and laborious; the broken-toothed walls of the cathedral that had stood for over three hundred years needed to be taken down bit by bit.

The tower was particularly dangerous, and Wren attempted to dynamite the structure with mixed results. On his first attempt he used the right amount of charge to lift the tower 'about nine inches, which suddenly jumping down, made a great heap of ruin in the Place without scattering'. On the second attempt, while Wren was away, his assistant (thought to be Hooke) used too much dynamite and caused a disaster: 'yet one stone shot out to the opposite side of the Church-yard through an open window into a room of a private house, where some women were sitting at work.'[14] Following the debacle, the workmen were forced to continue their task by hand, and the demolition would continue until 1674.

Wren refused to work on designs for a new cathedral, however, for, as he had written to Dean Sancroft the previous year, without money the dreams to revive the capital were paper fantasies. Since the king's purse could not afford to rebuild royal London, some new way to pay for the cathedral needed to be found. A return to Parliament was the only hope for the restoration of St Paul's.

On 1 May 1670, Parliament passed a Second Rebuilding Act, which included important innovations. In the first Act, 12 pence (1 shilling) had been levied for every ton, or cauldron, of coal that arrived through the Port of London; in the new Act, this was to be raised to 3 shillings. The first shilling would continue to pay for compensation for land loss due to the street-widening scheme. Another tranche was allocated 'for and towards the building, erecting and repairing of the said parish churches', of which some was set aside for the express purpose of 'making of wharves, keys, public market places and other publick uses'. Four and a half pence was to go to rebuilding St Paul's.

The Act then named fifty-one Anglican parish churches to be built to replace the eighty-seven churches and six chapels that had been lost in the fire. The Act also set out where the churches were to be placed: seventeen were to remain as they were before the fire, while most of the remainder combined two neighbouring congregations into a single parish. In addition, the Second Rebuilding Act outlined a list of new civic projects to be completed: a memorial to the Great Fire, promised in the first Act, had not yet commenced; a quay should be built along the Thames front 'all along from London Bridge to The Temple, of breadth of 40 foot'; while the Fleet river was to be developed into a 100-foot-wide navigable canal 'from the chanel of the river Thames to Holbourn Bridge'.[15]

The second wave of rebuilding therefore combined royal projects with new innovations to enhance the revived city. The Act bound together the king, the city, Parliament and the established Church in a single law and the shared hope for the future of London, but it was by no means a comfortable fit. Within recent memory the failures of these four corners of power had fuelled the Civil Wars and distrust still remained. The need to see the city restored, however, drove them together with a common purpose. Only time would tell whether this was a rash and desperate measure.

The Second Rebuilding Act would place St Paul's Cathedral at the crossroads of the capital. The king's cathedral, the symbol of his role as God's lieutenant within the city, would no longer be the sole property of the Crown and funded from the royal purse. Although the Act did not question Charles's role as the Defender of the Faith, the Anglican Church was to be reborn with money raised from a tax on imports coming into the Port of London. The rebuilding fund would be managed from the Guildhall, not Whitehall or the Bishop's Palace. It would be Parliament's decision whether the funding should continue or be cut off. All these issues would become vital, raising the difficult question: who owned St Paul's?

CITY PROJECTS

The Surveyor-General could now make plans that he would never have been able to imagine if he had been bound by the royal purse strings alone. Yet the funding came with conditions, for although he would finally be able to build his monuments, the architect became the servant of many masters. Many of the rebuilding projects were overseen by a commission, and thus Wren was obliged to pay service to the Crown, the city and, when necessary, the Anglican Church. Another obligation was more significant: on many of the projects Wren had to work alongside his opposite number, the City Surveyor, none other than Robert Hooke. The coming together of the two New Philosophers would announce one of the most significant collaborations in London's history.

Since becoming the City Surveyor, Hooke had balanced his roles as city man with the curatorship at the Royal Society. While staking out the streets, he was also involved in a series of new schemes to improve the restored city: the clearing away of waste, a system to convey clean water throughout the city and to plot the new marketplaces as set out at the king's request. In addition, he began to show an interest in architectural problems beyond the technical concerns of a surveyor, and by 1669 was already capable of aiding Wren with the new designs for the Customs House.

By 1670 Hooke had declared himself an architect. His first commission came that year from the Royal College of Physicians, who asked him to rebuild their hall on Warwick Lane. He was able to keep costs low while displaying a modicum of flair in the ornamentation. The complex, centred around a quadrangle, was a building of many parts that needed to satisfy the numerous functions of the college – a dining room, the Great Hall and houses for the fellows. At the front of the building, facing on to the lane, Hooke displayed his most cunning architectural invention: an octagonal gatehouse that rose on the first floor into a dome, under which was placed an anatomy theatre. As the college poet Sir Samuel Garth wrote:

A dome majestic to the sight
And sumptuous arches bear its oval height;
A golden globe plac'd high with artful skill
Seems, to the distant sight, a gilded pill.[16]

In addition, the college saw one of the first examples of sash windows, a signature of London houses, invented either by Hooke, Wren or the master joiner Thomas Kinward. The sash window itself was a beguilingly simple innovation that highlighted the symbiosis of architecture and the New Philosophy, for it allowed large windows to slide up and down, rather than using latches to open outwards into the street. This was not only safer but allowed for more light to enter the anatomy theatre, enabling students to observe clearly the dissections and demonstrations.

In these first years of Hooke's experimentation with architecture he was the ideal ally for the new Surveyor-General as they tackled the difficult technical issues of designing a quay along the Thames river front. The hope for a 40-foot quay that would run from the Tower of London to the Temple was, however, less a question of design and more an issue of compensation. Who was to pay for the compulsory purchase of land along the waterfront? How could the scheme be made to turn a profit? In the end, no one wanted to put up the cash, and while Hooke was compelled to make a thorough survey of the area and attempts were made to clear the sites, the project soon lost steam and ground to a halt.

The project to build the Fleet Canal appeared more probable and a task perfectly suited to both Wren's and Hooke's interests; unfortunately the venture was an untimely and expensive money pit. A joint report, delivered in May 1671, proposed a 100-foot-wide canal with wooden wharfs on either bank. In order to achieve this the fetid Fleet Ditch had to be drained and cleared, which was not an easy proposition, involving: '14 lighters to attend the digging, 7 to goe off every tide & 7 to lye till the next tide to be filled at Ebbe & during the tyde to carry on the dry digging'.[17] While the mud was cut away from the dry banks of the canal and packed into solid walls, the wet mud along the river bed was scooped out and carried off in wheelbarrows and baskets. Three and a half years later, the workers were still digging out the mud. The steep sides of the canal banks were never dry but seeped groundwater, making it difficult to support the wooden wharfs.

Even worse, the river itself continued to deliver heaps of rubbish that had been dumped further upstream. The residents in Clerkenwell, which stood outside the city jurisdiction, continued to use the water as a refuse pipe for their slaughterhouses. As costs spiralled, Wren and Hooke's venture was looking like an expensive embarrassment, yet the New Philosophers could not come up with a solution. By the autumn of 1674 the canal was completed at a staggering cost of £51,000. A small corner of London briefly appeared Venetian, and the City hoped that the canal would eventually pay for itself in docking fees when boats tied up alongside the wharf, but it never became popular.

The third project devised by the Surveyor-General and the City Surveyor was more of a success. The king had long desired a column or pillar to commemorate the fire, to be placed near the site of Farriner's house in Pudding Lane. In 1670 a plot halfway down Fish Street Hill, a few hundred yards to the west of the bakery, was found and Hooke drew up some designs, which were first approved by the Lord Mayor and then signed by Wren on behalf of the king. The single Doric pillar, 120 feet tall, rose high into the London sky and dwarfed the many new houses around its base. It stood on a pedestal 40 feet high and 21 feet wide, a design carved upon each of the four sides to commemorate the dreadful events of September 1666.

The pillar combined the twin passions of Christopher Wren and Robert Hooke – science and architecture – for the Monument was both a memorial and a scientific instrument. Hooke had already tried to build a zenith telescope, a fixed tube that pointed into the sky to record the motion of the stars, at his lodgings at Gresham, but had found that the vibrations of nearby traffic made accurate data collection impossible. The pillar, on the other hand, was 160 feet high, hollow with a spiralling staircase curling around the inside of the wall. At the base a room was built so that an astronomer could watch the night sky, and by marking the motion of the stars could calculate the parallax of the celestial bodies. The hollow shaft was also ideal for conducting experiments with pendulums and trials of gravity.

By 1675 the pillar was almost complete; only the top of the memorial and the decorations at the base of the pedestal were missing. There was much debate on what to place at the summit: the king had requested 'a large ball of gilt', while Wren's first designs were for a phoenix rising from the flames, which he later dismissed as 'costly, not easily understood at that highth and worst understood at a distance & lastly dangerous by reason of the sayle the spread winges will carry in the winde'.[18] In the end the committee decided on an urn of flames, and Hooke, with his knowledge of the craftsmen of the city, set about commissioning the wooden urn, chased in copper, brass and gilt. Hooke also ensured that the decoration was light enough to be moved on a hinge so that experiments could continue in the pillar.

The king's favourite carver, Caius Cibber, made drafts for the stone reliefs around the pedestal which told the story of the fire and the revival of the city. On the western panel he carved a classical scene in which Charles II in toga and emperor's laurels leads a troop of scantily clad figures – personifying Science, Liberty, Architecture, Victory, Justice and Fortitude – to save the fainting figure of London, held up by the winged but aged Time. Up above the smoke, surveying the scene, sat Plenty and Peace.

By the time the Fish Street pillar had been completed the collaboration between Hooke and Wren had begun to alter the landscape of London. Throughout the period, while overseeing the quay, the Fleet Canal and the pillar, Wren and Hooke had also been collaborating on one major project that would be a lifetime's work. On this occasion, the patron was not the City but the Anglican Church, funding supplied by the coal tax set out in the Second Rebuilding Act. The complete rebuilding of fifty-one parish churches within the burnt metropolis would be the largest public building scheme following the fire.

Following the Second Rebuilding Act in May 1670, Wren was named by a commission led by the Archbishop of Canterbury, Gilbert Sheldon, who had just seen his completed theatre open the previous year in Oxford. On Wren's recommendation the commission also nominated two further members of the team, Robert Hooke and Edward Woodroffe. Together they were commanded 'to repair forthwith the aforesaid churches and take an account of the extent of the parishes, the sites of the churches, the state and conditions of the ruins and accordingly prepare fit models and draughts to be presented for his majesty's approbation and also estimates proper to inform us what share and proportion of the money out of the imposition upon coals may be requisite to allow for the fabric of each church'.[19]

The three men would form the core of the Architect's Office, an extraordinary feat in design, building and management that stands as a turning point in the history of architecture. The office operated a new type of organisation, set up to deal with its enormous task. Its efficiency was as important as the resulting designs or work on the sites. It was a 'modern' operation which redefined the division of labour, the process of manufacture from first designs to final building, as well as offering a new means of payment and measurement of work.

Christopher Wren was the figurehead for the project, the signature designer of all materials that left the office, and all drawings possessed his imprimatur, even if they were not his own designs. He was also in charge of the money and the distribution to the parishes of the coal tax fund held by the Lord Mayor. He first ran his team from the Office of Works in Scotland Yard, Whitehall, but later moved it to a purpose-built block in St Paul's churchyard. There he met with Hooke and Woodroffe every Thursday and Saturday morning to discuss plans, money and schedules. It was also here that Wren met petitioners from the various parishes who wanted to berate or cajole the Surveyor-General on behalf of their interests.

Hooke was employed as Wren's deputy, and while he was paid £800 a year (half the amount of Wren's income) by the commission, his boss also gave him a stipend to cover his costs as the office manager. In this role he was in charge of the permanent business of the office – supervising the team of draughtsmen who devised and drew up the plans for the churches as well as negotiating and subcontracting all the building agreements and supplies. He also took on the new role of quantity surveyor and acted as Wren's representative on the street. He had already gained a reputation as a fair and diligent man, and he was known by all the city authorities as one of their own. As he had spent the last four years drawing up plans and working with builders on over three thousand plots throughout the city there was no one more qualified to know the price of brick or lime, the going rate for land compensation, or where to get timber quickly.

This was a vital skill, for the fire had changed the definition of work. Within the closed shop of the guilds, building was assessed by the skill and position of the craftsman contracted and payment set by the masons and carpenters themselves. With the influx of multitasking foreigners, there was no means to assess quality or control prices. Instead, work was increasingly paid for by the measure, a sure and scientific approach. A builder would be paid by the yardage of work completed rather than by the time he took to accomplish the job. With this method Hooke could get the best prices but also ensure that each job cost the correct amount.

The third member of the office, Edward Woodroffe, played another crucial role. Born a Londoner in 1622, he worked as a draughtsman within the office of John Webb of the Office of Works in the 1650s. In 1662, however, he was named Assistant Surveyor of Westminster Abbey, a royal appointment, and by 1669 was a senior and experienced operator with a hands-on knowledge of building – the kind of experience that Wren lacked. Woodroffe was ideally placed to translate Wren's ideas into stone, deal with the builders and work through the on-site issues that emerged.

While Wren remained in the office and Woodroffe spent much of his time on-site, the role of architectural drawings and models became increasingly important within the design process. As the office institutionalised the divide between the designer and the builder, Wren needed somehow to express his thinking to the workers who would convert his ideas into stone. While drawings and models had always been an important part of the task, Wren placed them at the centre of his practice. Within the office the designer's book became a laboratory in which the philosophers explored the many possibilities of architecture. The office would be filled with paper, plans and experiments, some drawn up by Wren, others by Hooke with Wren's signature. In time, Wren hired a team of copyists to help with the project.

It is this confusion of paper which makes attribution of individual churches so difficult. This may have been intentional as the name of the Architect's Office was more important than any individual designer, yet it has done everyone but Wren a disservice, in particular Robert Hooke. Recent studies have shown that Hooke was more than just the office deputy and surveyor and had a hand in the design of many of the churches – both sharing credit with Wren on some buildings and taking full responsibility for others. He undoubtedly designed St Edmund the King, Lombard Street. There is also good evidence that he oversaw the designs of St Benet Paul's Wharf, and St Martin's, Ludgate.

On the ground Woodroffe negotiated with a small group of experienced contractors who, in turn, managed their own teams. Each contract was on a freelance basis to keep costs as low as possible. Some of the teams came from respected City guilds, others were foreign labour who had entered London after the fire: Thomas Wise, for example, came to London from the quarries at Portland, Dorset, where much of the stone for the new churches was to be sourced. Similarly, Wren had worked with Thomas Strong on the Sheldonian Theatre at Oxford and brought him to London. In addition new partnerships were formed, such as the carpenter Wilcox, 'partners with Christopher Russell, bricklayer', and there were even some female workers: 'Sarah Freeman, plumber', 'Widdow Pearce, Painter', Ann Brooks, Smith'.[20] Many of the names that appeared in the office accounts would be those of workmen soon to appear at St Paul's Cathedral.

The commission presented Wren with a staggered building schedule: fifteen churches needed to begin rebuilding straight away, with a timetable for the other projects to be completed. This schedule was devised not just to balance the workload but also in expectation of the steady trickle of coal tax into the City's coffers. In the meantime, Wren was to construct wooden tabernacles for the parishes that had to wait for their new place of worship. This all seemed a very sensible plan on paper but ignored the unpredictability of human nature, and assumed that the coal tax would arrive on time and in bountiful amounts. Neither proved to be the case.

The fifteen churches named on the first list were those of the major parishes of the city, including the rich St Bride's outside the city walls, and the Archbishop of Canterbury's own St Mary-le-Bow. Four churches had already begun their own rebuilding or repairs and were looking to Wren's office for cash rather than architectural advice. One church, St Mary Aldermary, had raised enough money from its own parishioners to go ahead without the coal levy altogether. While the most prominent parishes expected to be completed first, the remaining thirty-six were vexed by the question of who was next on the list. Leading city grandees were unlikely to wait patiently for their parish churches to be rebuilt.

It soon became clear that money was short and the coal tax was not coming in as expected. The commission therefore encouraged parishes to start their own fund-raising efforts and promised that they would match every £500 raised with £1,500 from the coal tax. This proved to be almost too successful: the parishes that provided the most funds began to demand that they jump the list. Other parishes were not above promoting their cause with gifts: Wren and his employees become the subject of bribes (when things were going well) followed by protest (when not). In no time at all there was no way to control the poorly thought-out schedule. By 1671 it was commanded that 'no more churches be begun until a competent [number] of those that are in hand be finished and paid off'.[21]

Nevertheless, Wren's city churches are one of the finest achievements in any era of the city's history. The variety and diversity of church designs that passed through the office in the following years are stunning. Although some of the original sites were demolished in the nineteenth century or bombed during the 1940s, the palette of styles, the variety of stone and materials, and the unique detailing still stand as testament to Wren's extraordinary imagination. Of fifty-one churches completed no two are alike; each building is the creation of the unique set of its circumstances as well as being a wider exploration of Wren's architectural ideas.

The new churches were formulated to articulate the soul of the reborn Anglican Church within the capital. London had been the nursery of the 1640s rebellion and remained predominantly nonconformist even when it welcomed back Charles II. The forceful condemnation of Presbyterianism following the Restoration was resented within the city and nonconformist congregations continued to worship within the walls. Would Wren's new churches impose an unloved doctrine upon the city? Was the Office an aggressive attempt to stamp orthodoxy within the walls?

In addition, Wren had few precedents for what a modern 'Anglican' church should look like. Inigo Jones's St Paul's Church in Covent Garden was one of the few examples of establishment Laudian church building. There had also been a few smaller projects in the suburbs before the Civil Wars in Southwark, Westminster, Shadwell and Whitechapel which experimented with a 'Calvinist churchman' style that sought a 'Low Church' nonconformism. Wren would need to reimagine the style of his city church between these two divergent fashions.

According to a famous quote of Wren's of years later, the most important element in a new church was: 'that all who are present can both hear and see. The Romanists, indeed, may build larger Churches, it is enough if they hear the murmur of the Mass, and see the elevation of the host, but ours are to be fitted for auditories'.[22] This demand for audibility and visibility, the preacher as instructor teaching the congregation rather than superior intermediary, allowed Wren to reconfigure the interiors in a way that satisfied the two sides of the religious divide: all the churches faced east to west, with the door at the west end and a tower or spire, leading to a central nave or space with the altar at the east end. The new designs, therefore, would answer both the Anglican desire for ceremony and the Calvinist demands for the preacher to be close to his congregation.

In addition to these theological issues, Wren had a number of practical hurdles to overcome. Many of the new churches would have to be built on top of the older walls that had survived the inferno, as it was cheaper to keep the existing foundations rather than build anew and risk having to pay compensation. As a result Wren was forced to work upon the most unprepossessing shapes – polygons and quadrilaterals with uneven walls that met far from the perpendicular – rather than a pure symmetrical or geometric form. Never wedded to one set of standards, Wren remained flexible and practical in his designs, and this pragmatic approach became a philosophy for him.

Despite these many problems on the ground Wren attempted to find a theoretical uniformity to put into practice. He reduced all fifty-one city churches to three templates of a modern temple. The most common example involved replacing the original Gothic design – a high central nave with two lower aisles – with a Latin basilica. This new interior space had many advantages: the lack of stone pillars lining the aisles improved visibility while both side walls could be studded with round-headed windows that flooded the central space with light. Also, Wren, using his experience of building the tiered seating at the Sheldonian Theatre, created a series of banked galleries on either side of the nave to hold more worshippers. This style of church can still be seen in many of Wren's most famous designs such as St Bride's, Fleet Street, and St James's, Piccadilly.

The second type of design was the open box space, a single irregular room, with the altar at the east end, which was particularly useful in the smaller churches. In some cases an aisle was placed down one side – Wren seemed to revel in the asymmetry of the space and the mathematical conundrum of such a room. This produced the ovoid space of St Benet Fink, and the bottle-like St Olave Old Jewry, with the tower rising above the tapered neck. On a few occasions Wren had just enough space to place an aisle down one side of the nave, such as at St Vedast-alias-Foster.

The third type of interior space was the centrally organised square room. There are only five examples of this type but they were influential, most famously St Stephen Walbrook. This parish church has often been connected with the development of Wren's ideas on St Paul's Cathedral, which he was planning at the same time. The rectangular interior space is divided into a cross with an arrangement of columns, but above that stands a central dome, the first in London.

Within the restraints of these three templates there was infinite opportunity for invention and variety. Wren experimented with different treatments for the ceiling and interiors: flat roofs, with or without coves; semicircular, segmental or elliptical barrel vaults; groined vaults and domes. In addition, once the office had completed the structure of the building, the parish was free to decorate the interior at its own expense. Many parishes followed Wren's advice, subcontracting his workmen or encouraging him to design some of the features. Pews were of crucial importance to all churches but attention was also given to carved communion tables, altar rails, a chandelier or 'branch', a sword-rest for the Lord Mayor and a staff with a silver top for the beadle, a royal coat of arms, a baptismal font carved in stone and even an organ.

On the exterior walls of the church Wren used an array of designs and templates that highlighted his own philosophy of architecture and the demands of the Anglican orthodoxy. Light was an important aspect of his architecture and his churches displayed a variety of clear glass windows that illuminated the internal space. The exteriors, plain in detail, followed the classical 'better Style', with a series of pilasters, columns embedded in the side walls. He favoured a portico at the west end of the building and was determined that every new church be crowned with 'handsome Spires, or lanterns rising in good Proportion about the neighbouring Houses'.[23] As the medieval churches had pinpricked the London skyline, so Wren's revived churches would punctuate the air of the phoenix city.

LUDGATE HILL

While Wren was exploring his philosophy in stone, he also sat down with pen and ink and attempted to define the laws and history of architecture in the *Architectural Tracts*. The *Tracts* treated buildings like scientific data to create a 'natural history', and offer a rare insight into the mind of Wren as he attempted to solve the ultimate conundrum: what is the purpose of architecture?

Wren attacked the question as if it were an equation, opening with a supposition: 'Architecture has its political Use: Publick Buildings being the Ornament of a Country; it establishes a Nation, Draws People and Commerce; makes the People love their native country, which Passion is the Original of all great Actions in a Common-Wealth ... Architecture aims at Eternity.'[24] Thus he set up a paradox between the artistic act of designing and the political reasons for building – architecture aspired to be eternal but was always of its time. The New Philosopher hoped to wipe the slate clean and planned to rethink both the history and the function of building.

Upon this *tabula rasa*, Wren went in search of the first principles within architecture. The classical master, Vitruvius, demanded that design should follow the mantra of '*Firmitas, utilitas, venustas*' (strength, utility and grace). Wren turned this received wisdom on its head and replaced it with 'beauty, firmness and convenience'; the difference was subtle but radical. 'Beauty' could be studied as a subset of optics; 'firmness' could be understood through a knowledge of statics; geometry was at the heart of both: 'Geometrical Figures are naturally more beautiful than other irregular; in this all consents to a Law of Nature ... the Square and the Circle are the most beautiful, next, the parallelogram and the oval. Strait lines are more beautiful than curve.'[25] 'Convenience', the very last term, was custom and convention and was to be approached with caution.

As his mind turned to St Paul's, Wren focused his thoughts on the relationship between the pillar and the arch, the base of the cupola and the dome. In a number of succinct diagrams he showed the value of mathematical calculation and geometric simplicity, for 'the generality of our late Architects dwell so much on this ornamental, and so slightly pass over the geometrical, which is the most essential Part of Architecture.'[26] While previous generations had been content to see that such things stood up, both Hooke and Wren as modern architects needed to understand how the arch worked. Through the following decade the *Philosophical Transactions* of the Royal Society are sprinkled with insights and the testing of various stones and materials.

While 'firmness' was a scientific proof, Wren knew that 'beauty' was not constant but changed with time and location, was 'convenient' or 'customary'. Each era had its own idea of beauty, each nation promoted its own aesthetic above its neighbours'. Architecture, Wren proposed, was philosophy *and* politics made stone. To prove this he wrote one of the very first 'histories' of architecture. If beauty was not a fixed natural law, one needed to observe the subject and assess the data. Only by looking again at the achievements of the ancients was Wren able to see that the past was a master that commanded 'laws, too strict and pedantick, and so as not too be transgressed without the Crime of Barbarity',[27] and that all previous works of art were 'but the Modes and fashions of those Ages wherein they were used; but because they were found in the great Structures ... we think ourselves strictly obliged to follow the fashion'.[28]

Thus, while architecture aspires to immortality, no single style was more perfect than another; the story of building was the history of fashions. In addition, buildings and building types were generated for specific regional and temporal functions. The first porticos were invented 'with walks of trees ... these avenues afterwards, as Cities grew more wealthy, reformed into Porticoes of marble'.[29] The pillar was shaped, not by the perfect proportions of the human body, but by the trunk of a tree, while the first temple was a wooden glade. Thus Wren shows that many of the most hallowed classical templates derived not from transcendental laws of aesthetics but from particular historical necessities and conventions.

This realisation allowed Wren to unshackle his theory of architecture from the weight of authority that had passed down the Western tradition from Ancient Rome to the Renaissance. If all buildings were an expression of fashion and function, each should be approached and studied equally without the burden of tradition. Wren's fourth *Tract* therefore explored classical, Gothic, Byzantine, Greek, Alexandrian, Tyrian and even the mythic buildings of the ancient world to show that the modern architect could take his influences from where he liked rather than being restricted to the limited range of Greece, Rome and Renaissance Italy.

The *Tracts* were the laboratory of Wren's ideas as well as the justification of his ambitions. The same flexibility of approach, the desire for effect, the understanding of statics and the political nature of architecture would inform and instruct Wren's single most important commission on Ludgate Hill – St Paul's. From 1669 to 1675 he produced four different models for the cathedral which he expectantly showed to the commission and the king for their approval. The pursuit of the perfect form for St Paul's was a battle of wills as Wren searched for a design that would balance his own desire for a new plan with the more traditional aspirations of his varied clients.

In 1669, Wren's first ideas for the cathedral were placed in front of a committee of Anglican bishops and courtiers. Only fragments of this first assault remain – a wooden model, an awkward and incomplete design – and on such meagre evidence it is hard to imagine the architect's intentions. The structure contained a portico, a cupola and an auditorium, and it is presumed that Inigo Jones's portico would have stood at the west end while the long nave receded towards the east. Wren had imagined a Romanesque basilica to replace the Gothic bulk, the open auditory with two rows of aisles either side derived from the earliest forms of worship. As he had shown in his *Tracts*, he had adopted the model of the Temple of Peace in the Forum of Rome as the archetypal religious space, promoting unity after the religious devastation of the Civil Wars. Wren wrote of the Temple, 'no language, no poetry can so describe Peace, and the effect of it in Men's minds, as the Design of the Temple naturally paints it'.[30]

The design baffled the committee. Wren had failed to find a satisfying compromise between the customary high Gothic interior of the old St Paul's as it was remembered and his new ideas of what an Anglican cathedral should be. He had heeded the original brief demanding 'a Fabrick of Moderate Bulk, but of Good Proportion; a convenient Quire, with a Vestibule, and Portico's and a Dome conspicuous above the houses,'[31] but the results were mixed. Wren had been conscious of the burden of cost and had deliberately designed the cathedral with that in mind, commenting, 'it seemed in vain in any new designs, to propose an edifice too large and costly'.[32] Ironically, the committee found Wren's first attempt too modest.

Wren went back to the drawing board, hoping to find a model that might 'gratify the tast of the connoisseurs, and criticks with something Beautiful, with a design Antique and well-studied, comparable to the best stile of the Greek and Roman Architecture.'[33] The second design promised a cathedral governed by geometry and reason, a perfect symmetry of space and stone, and high above the metropolis a dome that crowned the London sky. The Temple of Peace had become a Temple to Reason. Exacting in its symmetry, it was a Greek cross with four equal, perpendicular arms emerging from a central domed crossing. It was unlike anything seen in England before. Wren was so pleased with his design that he showed it to the king, who gave his approval in the winter of 1672, as well as 'Some persons of Distinction, Skill'd in Antiquity and Architecture [who] express'd themselves much pleas'd with the Design and wish'd to see it in a model'.[34]

Unfortunately it was not understood by everyone, not least by the conservative Anglican grandees, 'who thought it deviated too much from the old Gothick form of Cathedral Churches, which they had been used to'.[35] The surveyor was paid £100 for his designs, and sent back to reconsider his plans. Yet he was unwilling to let the whole design go, and he continued to make alterations and changes to it, to satisfy the demands for Gothic space within a classical form.

As Wren worked over his designs, activity on the building site at St Paul's continued, although there was a shift in the organisation of the project. In September 1673, three years after the Second Rebuilding Act had prepared for the revival of the cathedral with the promise of coal tax revenue, a Royal Commission for the Rebuilding of the Cathedral Church of St Paul's was finally instituted. The official commission brought together the great and the good on a panel of churchmen, Privy Councillors and city officials, and replaced the more informal Anglican outfit that had stood so far. The new committee would reflect the changing position of the cathedral in the relationship between Church, Crown, Parliament and City. Each element would have its say on all matters from the hiring of workmen to the final design.

In 1673 Wren presented his third set of plans, later called the Great Model, to the new commission. Charles II again gave his full support to his surveyor, writing, 'we do more especially approve and have commanded a model thereof to be made after so large and exact a manner as it may remain as perpetual and unchangeable rule and direction for the conduction of the whole work'.[36] The Great Model, once it had been intricately carved in wood, showed the original Greek cross design but with a long nave added to the west end, leading to Jones's western portico. It was a glorious compromise between Wren's modern geometric form and the traditional Gothic cruciform.

But Wren was once again caught between the various demands within the commission. Despite the king's approval the Anglican hierarchy did not consider the Great Model to their taste; even worse, the new designs looked suspiciously like something found in Rome. In addition, the commission was concerned about the costs of such a structure. If the cathedral was to be paid for by the coal tax it needed to be built in stages, so that if anything went wrong, ambitions could be managed rather than the cathedral left unfinished. No one wanted a half-completed eyesore at the centre of the city.

It is said that Wren wept when he heard that his Great Model had been rejected, and for a brief moment fell out with the king, who he thought had betrayed him, yet as he had to admit to himself in his *Tracts*: 'Whatever a man's sentiments are upon mature deliberation, it will be still necessary for him in a conspicuous Work to preserve his Undertaking from general censure, and so for him to accommodate his Designs to the Gust of the Age he lives, tho it appears to him less rational.'[37] Wren would have to compromise once more if he was to finally gain the prize of rebuilding St Paul's.

Although he lost his design, in recompense he was rewarded by other means. On 11 November 1673, Hooke reported that 'Dr Wren knighted

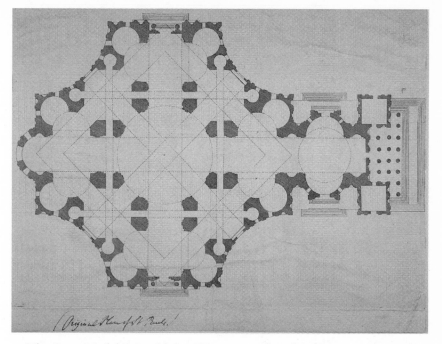

The Great Model. It is said that Wren wept when this design was rejected
by the commission

and gone to Oxford,'[38] where he resigned his position as Savilian Professor
of Astronomy. From now on Sir Christopher Wren would be an architect.
In addition to this momentous career change, and perhaps in a moment of
understandable vanity, he commissioned a bust of himself in his new
role, from the sculptor Edward Pearce, which bears more than a striking
resemblance to Bernini's bust of Louis XIV which Wren would have seen
in Paris in 1665. He appears young (although he was now forty-one years
old) and heroic. His face is modern, alive and vibrant, the eyes bulging
slightly as he looks into the future.

Wren continued with his attempts to find a new form for St Paul's. As
the official architect he also had to take an interest in the work on-site, and
both he and Edward Woodroffe moved into permanent offices in the
Convocation House in St Paul's Courtyard to observe the clearing-up
operation. In 1675 he produced what became known as the Warrant
Design, a bizarre mixture of styles and design solutions that fitted no age
or philosophy yet looked sufficiently similar to designs by Inigo Jones from

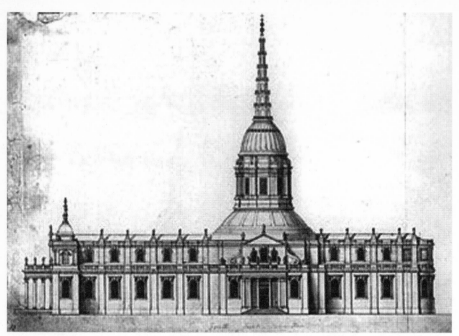

The Warrant Design, approved by the commission, but never to see the light of day

the 1630s, and which in his words 'reconcile[d], as near as possible, the Gothick to a Better Model of Architecture'.[39] The commission gave it their full approval, adding that 'we found it very artificial, proper, and useful; as because it was so ordered as it might be built in parts.'[40] The king gave his warrant on 14 May 1675 and Wren was to start straight away on the building.

From the moment of the royal warrant, Wren fixed to 'make no more Models, or publickly expose his drawings, which, (as he found by experience,) did but lose time, and subjected his Business many times, to incompetent Judges'.[41] This may have been a moment's exasperation at the arduous process of the last six years, but more likely it was a cover for a most extraordinary act of legerdemain.

Following the approval of the Warrant Design, Charles II was noted as telling his surveyor that he could 'make some variations, rather ornamental, than essential, as from time to time he sees proper'.[42] Wren took this royal aside as permission to go farther and immediately began to tinker with his plans. The Surveyor-General had finally gained approval and the rebuild-

A portrait of John Evelyn, composed just before the virtuoso set off to Europe. Attempting to strike a romantic pose, Evelyn's eye can not help revealing the wary concerns of the Children of the Civil War.

THE OXFORD ALMANACK
For the Year of our Lord God
MDCCXXXVIII

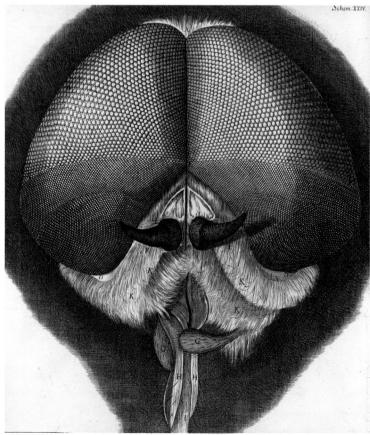

Schem: XXIV.

Wadham College and the New Philosophers, including John Wilkins and the young Christopher Wren (second from right). Far from the corridors of power in London, the Oxford group were able to lay the foundations for a new age in knowledge.

Robert Hooke's fly. Technology and the Baconian method revealing the wonders of nature in *Micrographia*.

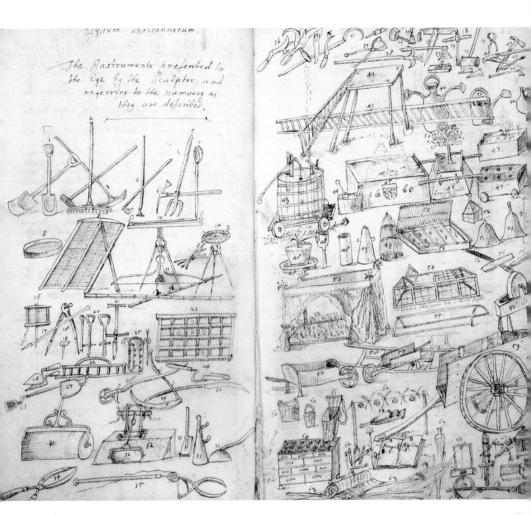

A page from John Evelyn's unfinished and unpublished *Elysium Britannicum*, showing the many gardening tools a horticulturalist should use. The work was a perfect reflection of the virtuoso's mind.

The City beset by fire. 'London was, but is no more,' observed John Evelyn.

John Locke in 1689. Finally embraced by the new regime but still hiding his authorship of his major works until after his death, he assumes the image of the rational philosopher.

An insurance policy from Nicholas Barbon's Insurance Office, one of the first examples of fire insurance following the fire.

Number 1405

This present Instrument or Policy of Insurance, witnesseth, That

in Consideration of the Sume of

in hand paid by

for the Insuring of an House Scituate on

for the Term of   yeares from the Date hereof, Do desire, direct, and appoint, That the Trustees, for the time being, for Houses, and Lands settled for the Insuring of Houses against Fire shall pay or satisfy unto the said   Executors or Administrators, [or their Assigns, by Endorsement on this present Policy] the Sume of   Pounds at the end of Two Months, after the said House shall be Burnt down, Demolished, or Damnifyed, by, or by Reason or Means of Fire; and so often as any New House, to be Built in the place thereof, shall be Burnt down, Demolished, or Damnifyed, by, or by Reason or Means of Fire, within the said Term of   Years the like Sume of   Pounds. If the said

and their Participants, or some, or one of them, his or their Heirs, Executors, Administrators, Agents, or Assigns, shall not within the said Two Months, pay unto the said   Executors, or Administrators [or such his or their Assigns] the said Sume of   Pounds. Or in case the said House, or such New House, be only Damnifyed: Then, if such House be not Repaired, and put in so good Condition, as the same was before, at the Charge of the said

and their Participants, or some, or one of them, his or their Heirs, Executors, Administrators, Agents, or Assigns, within Two Months next, after such Damnification shall happen. Witness our Hands and Seals, the
— Anno Dom 1682 Annoqz Regni Regis
quarto.

Nicolas Barbon

Sealed and Delivered
in the Presence of

St Paul's dominating the London skyline in a painting taken from the north of the city near Islington in the early 1700s. London spreads out towards the east and west as the new suburbs come to dominate the capital.

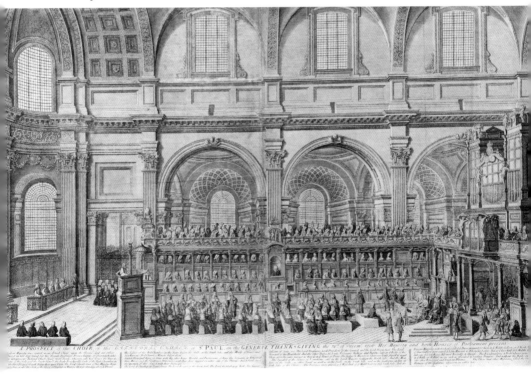

The Choir at the east end of St Paul's Cathedral in all its pomp. The moveable pulpit can be seen on the left of the stalls.

The most recognisable portrait of Sir Christopher Wren, painted three years after the completion of St Paul's by Sir Godfrey Kneller. The plans of the cathedral unfurl from the table while he holds the tools of the New Philosophy in his right hand.

ing of the cathedral could start immediately, but as he began secretly to redraft his schemes he hoped he could find a new design that would reflect the reborn modern London that was beginning to emerge from around the broken hulk of St Paul's.

PART FOUR

The Making of
Modern London

8

The City of Speculation

It was no accident that the birth of the English Empire coincided with the changing fortunes of London. The traditional city of trade was becoming a modern marketplace in which commodities were exchanged and manufactured using materials shipped from the far corners of the world, as well as delivering new ideas on the foundations of economics and colonisation. While the fire had transformed London with devastating resolution from within, the impact of ideas and adventures from abroad would have an equal and lasting effect. John Locke, as he worked alongside his patron, Anthony Ashley Cooper, was at the heart of this revolution in speculation.

In August 1669, three boats, the *Carolina*, the *Port Royal* and the *Albemarle*, sailed from The Downs on the Thames estuary and moved along the southern coast of England, stopping briefly in Ireland. The ships then crossed the Atlantic and arrived in Barbados in October. The three ships had been stocked and funded by some of the richest and most powerful men in London and contained over one hundred passengers, including gentlemen, servants and freemen. At Barbados, the ships were delayed as they were wracked by storms until 2 November, when the *Albemarle* was sunk. Fortunately the passengers were able to escape to shore and from the small community of Barbadians the traders were able to lease a new ship, the *Three Brothers*, to continue their journey.

Storms again cursed the voyage towards the American mainland, and the *Port Royal* was lost, drifting towards the Bahamas, where only forty-four passengers made it back ashore. Only the *Carolina* made it to the mainland. A temporary colony, Port Royal, was set up where they were greeted by friendly Indians, but it was soon considered wise to sail farther up the newly named Ashley river where it met the Cooper river at

Albemarle Point, where a more permanent settlement, first named Charles Towne, later Charleston, was formed. Almost immediately they faced hostility from local tribes, influenced by the Spanish missionaries from Florida to the south. It was the unimpressive beginning of the new colony, Carolina.

Before the Civil Wars, England had few colonies or international interests. In 1642 there were, for example, only 15,000 British settlers in New England. During the interregnum, however, Oliver Cromwell launched his Protectorate with an aggressive move against his foreign rivals to control the wealth of the Atlantic. In a series of Navigation Acts all foreign trade was excluded from British outposts so that only English ships could trade with the British settlements. In addition, all goods were to be sold through Britain's ports; London, in particular. The Restoration of 1660 saw no pause in pursuit of the Protectorate's foreign policy. The king reaffirmed the Navigation Acts and kept the policy as well as the personalities who had overseen Cromwell's expansion, including Anthony Ashley Cooper. As his reign progressed, the development of international trade became central to the settlement of England.

In 1663, Charles II had donated a slice of the New World to eight of his favourites, including Ashley Cooper. In that year a Royal Charter was drawn up to establish a colony on the south-eastern seaboard of the new continent; it was named in the king's honour Carolina, founded on land belonging to the Indian tribes of the Yamasee, among others. The land was seen as perfect territory for the expansion of the English colony based in Virginia, as well as for those who had not struck it lucky on the Caribbean island of Barbados, where an English community quickly flourished.

Charles II was more interested in profit than politics in Carolina, and allowed the new owners legal and political power to set up whatever kind of society they wanted. Carolina was thus a blank slate on which a new society could be written, and the eight proprietors set about envisioning the perfect community, drawing up the 'Fundamental Constitutions' which were approved in March 1669. As secretary to the committee of the Proprietary Lords, John Locke drew up this important document. Carolina would be an ordered and peaceful society founded with the primary aim of creating wealth for the principal owners. It also attempted to attract settlers who were seduced by the liberal constitution, and the potential fortunes to be made from working the land.

The new territories had been settled for one purpose: the enrichment of the home nation, and particularly its capital. The drive towards expansion in the years following the Restoration provided previously uncontemplated opportunities for investment. While the greatest rewards were to be found in the formation of the Atlantic Empire, English ships had become experienced in sailing across the globe in search of goods. The East India Company had been founded in 1600 to share in some of the trade the Portuguese and Dutch had established in the previous century, such as cotton, silk, indigo dye, saltpetre and tea. Following the marriage of Charles II to the Portuguese princess Catherine of Braganza, the exploitation of Mughal India was advanced, and in 1670 Charles granted the company exclusive rights to territories and autonomy on governance. In the 1660s, the company imported £82,475 into England. By the end of the 1670s this had risen to £269,748 and would double again the following decade. In 1670, Charles II also granted an exclusive right to trade to the company of adventurers trading into Hudson Bay in Canada, in an attempt to gain a share in the fur trade. Similarly, the Levant Company, controlled from London but with factories in Aleppo and Constantinople, was given a new charter to expand its interests in the Middle East.

The Port of London soon became the destination of ships from around the world delivering calico from India, sugar from the West Indies, gold from West Africa, tobacco from Virginia. The increase in trade and goods brought money to the City, where there was a discernible difference on the streets of the metropolis itself. The vast amounts of goods that were being offloaded on to the quays of the capital would have been beyond belief a few decades before. More quays and wharfs were built within the port to cope with the rise in traffic; the ship tonnage of the English fleet more than doubled between 1660 and 1686. At the same time, Hooke and Wren were designing the Customs House, Fleet Ditch and New Thames Quay to accommodate this new influx.

The availability of new materials and goods also changed the taste and spending patterns of the metropolis. As imports increased, prices fell, and it soon became common for every person to use sugar to sweeten their coffee, to take a saucer of chocolate, or to cook sweet puddings. Smoking, using the finest Virginian tobacco, became commonplace. Indian calico threatened the wool market as the height of fashion. This commercial transformation in the very first decades of the post-Civil War era sowed the seeds for mass consumer society.

While the exploitation of Carolina took longer than desired to show a profit it still raised the question of colonialism itself. What right did England have to take foreign soil and claim it as its own? What constituted ownership? Did settlement have a long-term benefit to England or would the settlements become a burden on the British economy? Locke's Fundamental Constitution was an important investigation into all these questions, as well as a revolutionary proposal of the rights of colonialism.

In previous eras, the earliest settlements had found legitimacy in establishing colonies not only to trade but also with the expressed desire to convert the natives. Locke did not see religious difference as a basis for claiming ownership, and he proposed a very different definition of property: the right of 'ownership' was not a governance of people but of the land.

Locke proposed that in the beginning God gave the Earth to mankind in common, yet this did not constitute ownership. Property rights were available only to those who worked the earth and gained possession in exchange for their labour. The Native Americans, therefore, did not own the land because they were hunter-gatherers rather than farmers and, as he would write in 1671 to the governor of Carolina, William Sallie, they should be treated fairly:

> suffer not the people out of greediness to molest either the Spaniards on that side or any of our neighbour Indians in their quiet possessions ... the people may go noe farther up into the country than what shall be necessary to their planting ... Neither do we thinke it advantageous for our people to live by rapin and plunder ... therefore I must presse it upon you that you bind the people's mind wholy to planting and trade, wherein if they will with industry and honestly imploy themselves they will not only answer his Majesty's and our ends of sending them thither but finde themselves with great safety and ease become masters of all that is desirable in those places.[1]

Locke's argument would establish the philosophical foundations of English expansionism for the next century.

'NOT WORTH HIS WHILE TO DEAL LITTLE ...'

While trade brought new wealth from abroad, London itself was aiding its own revival. The speed of recovery within the city walls had been impressive, and by 1673 over eight thousand plots had been redeveloped and plans were afoot to develop five hundred more. The economy was almost completely revived and the urban infrastructure – city gates, jails, warehouses and Guildhall – had been restored. Yet there was a disturbing silence at the centre of this rapid recovery: of the 8,000 redeveloped plots over 3,500 new houses stood empty. In addition, there was enough unclaimed ground to build another 1,000 homes, which no one was willing to claim or develop.

Since the fire, however, the expansion of the suburbs had accelerated exponentially. The Lord Mayor and city authorities complained about the rash of speculative building beyond the walls, campaigning against 'Great mischief and Inconveniences dayle arising to the citty from ye multitude of New Building arected in the outparts thereof by which means the citty is deprived of many thousands of her inhabitants and a vast number of new built houses with the same stand empty and unemployed'.[2] The complaints fell on deaf ears.

Charles II also made some efforts to reduce the suburban sprawl. In 1671 he released a proclamation – as hollow as every similar proclamation in the previous 150 years – concerned with the growth of development between the City and Westminster. Charles's plea, however, was less an attack on development than a means to control the type of development that was rising up around his palace. The proclamation attempted to place control of the development of the 'West End' in the hands of his Surveyor-General, Christopher Wren, who would now have a say in granting permission for building development. Yet officialdom was always one step behind the rampant pursuit of profit.

A new breed of builder-speculator was beginning to emerge among the building sites of the West End. Pre-eminent among them was Dr Nicholas Barbon, who would transform the business of building and the manner in which London property was traded and developed. He began within the city walls, building up from the ashes of the fire. In 1670, Barbon drew up plans to develop a plot that was close to the proposed site of the Monument, at that time being designed by Hooke and Wren. In November the City Commission had to decide whether to allow Barbon to continue or whether to purchase the plot from the developer. His first brush with officialdom was a mild one for, after Hooke had surveyed the site, Barbon was allowed to proceed.

His next scheme within the walls was completed in 1674 when he developed 'a good estate' he had bought on Mincing Lane. It was perhaps the profits from the first development which funded the building of seven houses on the site, one of which sold for £2,650. Mincing Lane was a straightforward rebuilding project, under the strict control of the surveyors and the Second Rebuilding Act, but Barbon would be found out for shoddy workmanship, the vaults collapsing 'most scandalously'[3] soon after completion.

Barbon was soon making a healthy profit from his speculations and started to look to the rapid rise of Westminster as the ideal site to feed his ambitions. Building in the suburbs was different from working within the regulated confines of the City – there were fewer restrictions (one only had to get around the Surveyor-General's office) – but demanded larger investment and risk. New money pouring into the ports raised the spirit of speculation in all forms, and Barbon found little difficulty in prising investment from the new classes of professionals. He was clearly keen on the challenge, as he would tell the lawyer Roger North, who recorded with a certain admiration: 'it was not worth his while to deal little; that a bricklayer could do'. To function on a large scale, however, he needed cash, and throughout his career he would 'compass his designs either by borrowed money or by credit with those he dealt with, either by fair means or foul'.[4]

The building trade was a precarious one, which entailed heavy investments, tying up cash in long-term projects, and banking on the stability of the market. Barbon was a master manipulator of cash flow and creditors; he was brilliant at gaining investors and found a multitude of ways to avoid paying for anything. He preferred credit as it was easier to postpone paying a debt than to pay interest on a loan. He would often wait for the claimant to take him to court, which he knew many would not do as they depended on him for work. To keep him out of hot water, he gathered a 'gang of clerks, attorneys, scriveners, and lawyers'[5] to run his commercial office, deal with the large sums of money, complex contracts and leases, and keep his creditors at bay.

Barbon's investors were varied, as the market in speculative building was being invented by a new breed of businessmen, an emerging class of self-made Londoners who understood business, either as merchants or city tradesmen, and invested their surplus in the speculator's promise of profits. Barbon, however, was rarely less than cunning in gaining their confidence, developing a number of strategies to turn a profit. When buying the freehold of a number of sites, he encouraged fellow investors in the deal, managed the redevelopment and turned a profit on the quick resale of the plot.

The first spectacular example of Barbon at work occurred in 1674, when he purchased Essex House, on the Strand, near Ashley Cooper's Exeter House. It was also an occasion when Barbon showed his full powers of persuasion and ingenuity. Essex House had seen better days and was now a neighbour to slums and workshops. In addition, in the first years of the Restoration the once aristocratic enclave had been superseded by fashionable Piccadilly, where the grandees who had gained something from the wars were erecting their baroque palaces in the new European styles.

Soon after the Restoration, therefore, the Strand palaces started to be put up for sale. Some were sold as houses: Ashley Cooper was pleased to buy Exeter House, once home to the Bishops of Exeter, and he remained there (somewhat uncomfortably) until 1676. Others were sold to speculators, who within weeks had demolished the old buildings and had plans to redevelop the site as housing and retail space for the rising middling sort. In 1673, the Earl of Salisbury gained permission to redevelop his land, and in 1674, for between £13,000 and £15,000, sold the freehold to Barbon. Within a year he had pulled the palace down, built a number of new dwellings and sold them off at a profit of between £5,000 and £6,000, an extraordinary sum for twelve months' work.

When Barbon first made the purchase, however, there were attempts to stop the transaction from both the Crown, who wanted the land for the Earl of Essex, and the neighbouring Temple, whose lawyers were nervous about what Barbon was to build on their front doorstep. The Privy Council summoned Barbon to the court, and he even received a request from the king himself, but he refused to budge. Instead, his solution was simple: divide and rule; as recounted by Roger North: 'lure them singly by some advantage above the rest, and if he could not gain all, divide them, for which purpose he had a ready wit'.[6]

Barbon ignored the king but offered to build new lodgings, New Court, for the lawyers in the Temple; unsurprisingly their objections became increasingly muted. The speculator also faced opposition from existing tenants but he ground them down, and when the only possible solution was to take the case to court, Barbon made his appeals and waited for the judgement. In the meantime, he demolished all the houses and began building. The judgement took so long to be delivered that by the time the court demanded he pay compensation, Barbon had already sold the project

The Strand, redeveloped by speculators like Nicholas Barbon,
transformed from an aristocratic enclave

and so, rather than pay the compensation, Barbon was able to pass the bill to the new owner and wash his hands of the whole affair, his profits intact.

Barbon had converted the traditional Tudor Essex House from a single dilapidated dwelling into a series of streets and houses, leading to a wharf on the Thames edge. To its detractors, a grand palace had been replaced by 'houses and tenements for taverns, alehouses, cookshoppes and vaulting schools, and the garden adjoining the river into wharves for brewers and woodmongers',[7] yet the new designs were, in their way, revolutionary. The land had been cleverly planned to mix business and domestic use, offering a new style of urban living. The proof could be swiftly gauged as the project attracted many noblemen, gentry and wealthy tradesmen, who enjoyed the convenience of living and working between Whitehall and the City. The success of the project could further be estimated by the reaction of the City, which feared 'if permitted, [the new projects] will tend to the ruine of the said citty already languishing under great decay of the Retayle Trade'.[8]

Barbon was quick to funnel the profits from Essex House into newer and bigger projects. In 1675 he invested in a property on Henry Jermyn's grand project at St James's Square. Since the 1660s, the nobleman's plans for a 'Place Royale' in London had been slow, hindered by plague and the fire. The first house, the aristocrat's own, was occupied by 1667, but he had failed to sell any of the plots surrounding it until 1669/70. The first three plots were taken by distinguished grandees, but the landlord had difficulty moving the rest, and he was then forced to deal with builder-speculators. Barbon himself gained number 4 in the north-east corner of the square.

Each builder had to make his designs conform to the general scheme of the square, which was to be approved by the Surveyor-General. On this occasion at least Barbon had to toe the line. He began building as soon as he had purchased the plot, paying a ground rent of £28 12s 8d a year in the meantime. By 1677, the new house was ready to sell and was bought by the Earl of Kent, who paid £6,600. As with so many of Barbon's dealings, however, there was controversy. Negotiations for the sale began in November 1677 and a certain 'William Coombes, gentleman, who was then a servant to the said earle' offered Barbon 'considerable Kindness and service in relacion to the dispatch and compleating of the bargaine'.[9] When all was done, Coombes came to Barbon for his payment; Barbon refused. A suit for damages was followed by counterclaims. Barbon played innocent to

Coombes's version of the story. There appears to be no records of the resolution of the dispute.

After these initial successes Barbon began to broaden his 'portfolio'. To do this he needed to ensure that large amounts of cash were not tied up in individual projects. Rather than continuing to purchase freeholds, Barbon began to develop an adept skill in manipulating the leasehold system to his advantage. This method became so associated with Barbon that Roger North would claim that the speculator actually invented it. Barbon would buy the rights to build on certain plots of land from the freeholder and arrange a timed lease. He would pay a small annual ground rent as he developed the site and then sell the property and obligation to pay the rent on to the new owner. He made a profit on the sale value of the fully developed site which was calculated as an escalation of the value of ground rent. In 1677, he was back in the Strand, redeveloping York House, as well as seeking out new opportunity in the unbuilt regions of Soho, to the north of Westminster.

The leasehold arrangement allowed him to invest in projects with a wider array of investors. While this method offered less profit than the development of freehold properties it ensured a quicker recouping of funds. It also gave him new assets that he could gain cheaply and sell or pass on, for 'he hated to make up accounts with anyone, and seldom failed to sink in his profits a considerable balance'.[10] In lieu of payment to his workmen or associates he often drew them into a project with payment of land rather than cash. As a result, the workmen were obliged to build the plots for themselves in order to gain any recompense, while Barbon kept his overheads to a minimum. He was also not above using the leased plots to raise more cash by mortgage. To do this he had to find a dummy investor or associate who claimed to have bought the land so the plot would begin to accrue ground rent and an income. Barbon then mortgaged the future revenue to other lenders. Inevitably, when the lender came visiting, he soon found that his money had been spent elsewhere and the mortgage was worthless.

In most cases, he subcontracted out all tasks to an army of craftsmen who oversaw the work for him. Yet even this relationship was remanaged to Barbon's advantage. Where the craftsman had previously been protected by the guilds and payment judged by level of skill and seniority, Barbon's builders were paid by measured work while the price was overseen by a separate quantity surveyor. Unlike with the similar method devised by

Wren and Hooke in the Architect's Office for the city church project, however, Barbon encouraged many of his master builders to invest in the project by offering plots of land rather than wages.

More importantly, the designs of many houses were uniform. The First Rebuilding Act of 1667 had set down the new criteria for London housing: brick and stone rather than wood and strict rules on the four types of houses allowed. In addition, the emerging leasehold system had an unexpected influence on the shape of new designs. Under the new system speculators made their money from ground rents calculated by the size of the house as it fronted out towards the street. It is no wonder, therefore, that the London house became so tall and thin. As Roger North reported, Barbon squeezed as many houses into his plots as possible: 'by casting of grounds into streets and small houses, and to augment their number with as little front as possible'.[11]

This uniformity was also established by an increased standardisation of production. The use of bricks, uniformly manufactured and standard in shape, dictated a regularity to the shape of most houses. In addition, the increased import of timber from Scandinavia dictated that wood arrived on the work site already cut in standardised planks. Barbon, more than most, saw in this increased uniformity of materials a means to speed up the process of building. For a man like Barbon, whose interest was in profit rather than architecture, there seemed little reason to redesign a house on every occasion. This had, in consequence, an effect on the quality of the houses themselves. As two disgruntled purchasers would comment, having moved into a house built by Barbon, their new homes were 'very incomplete, imperfect and unfinished, and such works as were done were so ill ... several of the piers being cracked, the floor shrunk, and the house in some places in danger of falling'.[12]

The standardisation of all processes of rebuilding further increased the alarming growth rate of the London suburbs. The next major area of development was in the former hunting grounds of Soho on the edge of Westminster. In 1676, Charles II granted St Albans a series of fields north of St James's, which were immediately passed over to the speculators. Barbon began the construction of Rupert Street, a mixed residential and working environment similar to the design he had completed at Essex House. The following year he also leased another stretch of land which would become Coventry Street.

In the same year Barbon had dreams of a grander scheme for the

Devonshire Square, a new form of urban planning, designed and built
on the eastern fringes of the City by Nicholas Barbon

whole of Soho Fields. The land, currently pastures leased to two farmers,
belonged to Jermyn, who had already leased it to a brewer from St Marylebone. The brewer had no intention of building himself but saw that the
plot would soon become prime real estate for development. Soho Fields
would be a rich prize for the speculator who was able to do business with
the brewer, but Barbon, not through want of trying, failed. His rival,
Richard Frith, gained the contract and set out a design for a grand square
and surrounding streets of elegant housing.[13]

Barbon was never one to lick his wounds and find new ventures. If
he could not have the Soho Fields contract he would do the next best
thing and hinder Frith's plans as much as possible. As Frith was
beginning his scheme Barbon subleased ground from two farmers who
still owned pasture leases, even though building rights had been sold to
Frith that year. Barbon refused to sell the land and – because he did not
have the rights to build – let it stand as fields. This chicanery meant
that neither speculator could build but forced Frith to 'alter all the said

streets and trench and mark them to be placed in the other part of the sayd field'.[14]

Barbon was in a more speculative mode, however, in 1677 when he purchased the lease on the Military Ground, a small plot of 2 acres uncomfortably squashed between Soho Fields to the north and Leicester Fields (which was in development) to the south, and pressed against the garden wall of Newport House to the east. The ground had previously been an exercise field for the local militia, but as the land prices in the neighbourhood began to rise, the land was bought by retired soldier Baron Gerard of Brandon. Gerard had been keen to develop his plot since the 1660s. He had expelled the militia yet the sole leaseholder, Browne the gardener, had refused to move until 1677. In July of that year, Barbon bought the leasehold and set about building a main orderly street, Gerard Street, with alleys leading to the already developed Hedge Lane (later Wardour Street) and King Street (Shaftesbury Avenue).

As London revived, it grew to accommodate a transformation in taste, and new money. This emerging professional class demanded a type of housing that defined their aspirations. A speculator like Nicholas Barbon was able to provide them with exactly what they wanted. In 1678, Barbon set out his vision for the city in an anonymous pamphlet, *A Discourse shewing the great Advantages that New Buildings, and the Enlarging of Towns and Cities Do Bring to a Nation*, which struck at the heart of the debate on what the new capital should be.

One house – 21 Gerard Street – showed Barbon's eye for detail. As he developed his role he learnt that his houses should contain all the latest innovations and utilities that any house buyer might want: the interiors were 'wainscotted and painted ... All the fireplaces had painted chimneypieces, firestone and marble hearths, and were set with "galley" tiles. At the rear of the house was the kitchen and a "Lardery", the former fitted with a buttery and supplied by a pump with New River water'.[15]

The archetypal London terrace house therefore evolved out of the restrictions of the First Rebuilding Act, the desire of the speculator to cram as many houses upon a street frontage as possible and the standardisation of every aspect of design for convenience. This would be the home for the new 'emulators', where 'All men by a perpetual industry are struggling to mend their former condition: and thus the people grow rich, which is the great advantage of a nation.'[16] Barbon had not only identified the motivation of the new commercial city but also its form: the London terraced house, modelled perhaps on the Dutch houses that Barbon had seen while a student in Leiden in the 1660s, would remain a template for bourgeois living for nearly three hundred years.

TRADE WARS

The rise of London as a commercial capital placed the city upon the international stage. The Port of London began to fill once again with ships from the far-flung corners of the world, while the metropolis went in search of a new identity. It was no surprise that it looked to its two nearest neighbours – Paris and Amsterdam – for inspiration. On the streets of London, examples of French architecture and town planning – Clarendon House, St James's Square, Charles's dreams for a baroque palace beside the Thames – sat next to buildings that looked to Holland – Barbon's terraced housing, the Customs House, Hooke's city churches. This search for a model encompassed every aspect of urban and political life.

France under Louis XIV was the dominant country in Europe. To many, French absolutism, the manipulation and control of the whole nation to the *gloire* of the king, was the perfect model of power – one that clearly appealed to Charles II. For others, the economic might of Holland, a republic in the midst of a golden age of trade and culture, was to be emulated. Rather than being a monarchy the nation was governed as a collection of seven provinces, each with their own estates and a Stadtholder who sat in the States-General. Which model would England follow?

The issues of the debate gained particular emphasis in discussions on international trade. If England was to prosper it needed to manage colonial expansion and the policing of the Navigation Acts, and there were many who believed that the development and protection of settlements abroad should become the concern of the government in London. In 1660 Charles maintained Cromwell's Council of Trade alongside a Council of Plantations. Here, for the first time, the issues of shipping and settlement were handled as a single area of government. By 1670, Ashley Cooper, in his role as Chancellor, was a leading member of both. Ashley Cooper saw England as a world centre of trade, in emulation of the Dutch republic. In 1673 Locke was elevated to the role of secretary of the council.

Yet the pursuit of such aggressive foreign policy soon prompted anger from abroad. This situation put England in inevitable opposition to its rivals, who aspired equally to the claim. The Anglo-Dutch Wars would be the first conflicts that dealt not with religion or claims of kingship but with trade. They were the first modern conflicts in which men went to their deaths defending their nation's rights to control the seas. Yet the costs of war, and the maintenance of the Royal Navy in particular, were not the responsibility of speculators or virtuosi, but the king.

It was the Crown and not the merchants who decided where the fleet should sail and who it should attack, and on numerous counts the two factions did not agree. There were many within the city who feared the rise of France more than Holland, and saw a war with Louis XIV as a religious as well as an economic imperative. Thus far, Charles's attempts to add glory to his reign on the battlefield had been stillborn. The second Anglo-Dutch War had ended inconclusively with the memory of the Dutch fleet sailing up the Thames to Chatham and Britain conceding land in the East Indies; it was only by good fortune that Charles gained the American port of New Amsterdam, renamed New York. Britain's hopes of ruling the waves were hampered by a rudimentary navy and poor leadership. Rather than achieving glory and the foundation of a new power, conflict had placed the king's reputation in a delicate balance. His failure to gain victory on any front ensured animosity from the City.

But wars cost money and one of the great ironies of the times was that by the 1670s, despite the nation growing in wealth, the king was in financial crisis. The Restoration settlement of 1660 now looked less than generous; the two previous wars, the loss of customs and excise due to the plague and fire in London, and the cost of rebuilding, had crippled the Treasury. To cap this, Charles was also at loggerheads with the very institution that could relieve his embarrassment: Parliament.

While Parliament was keen to pursue a trade war against the Dutch, it had become suspicious of Charles's ambitions. The king would find that, as he attempted to conduct a new war, the questions that had haunted the Troubles re-emerged, and brought into stark light the relationship between England, Holland and France. To Ashley Cooper and Locke the debate was clear: should England emulate France and be ruled with an absolute and intolerant iron fist, or should the king follow the Dutch, a tolerant people who ruled by liberty and conscience, a Protestant nation governed by reason? As with so many of these questions, the dispute came to the fore over the small issue of money.

Rather than deal with a recalcitrant Parliament that wished to clip his aspirations, Charles was forced to sell his future on the London market, taking on loans in exchange for tallies or receipts of incoming excise duties. Without the structures of a modern banking system the Exchequer went out and got what funds it could, from rich merchants, guilds, religious associations and trading companies, at any negotiable rate. By mortgaging off the future, Charles was able to survive the present without calling another parliament. Soon enough, however, the Crown found itself in hock to the London gold merchants. By 1672 the Crown was £1.4 million in debt and concerned that it could not even afford the interest payments.

The desperate need for cash drove the king to unexpected sources. In 1670 Charles began negotiations with his cousin, Louis XIV of France, to gain support and funds for a renewed attack on the Dutch. The two Treaties of Dover of 1670 were the most dangerous, and unlikely, diplomatic ventures that Charles could have conducted. In the first treaty, which remained a secret beyond the king and only a very select number of courtiers, Charles promised support to Louis XIV in his battle for the Spanish throne. In exchange, England was promised money and troops. In addition, Charles had to promise to secretly convert to Catholicism. This was a ridiculously risky agreement for a sum of money, no more than a year's income, that would never cover Charles's expenses.

The secret was kept hidden. The second Treaty of Dover, a cover-up for the first, was signed on 21 December 1670, in the presence of all members of his council, including Ashley Cooper (who would never discover the truth). The same details were rubber-stamped, except the Catholic clause, which was nowhere to be found. The treaty gave Charles the money he needed but he was bound to spend that money on waging war upon a fellow Protestant nation on behalf of a hated Catholic one. The cat's cradle of intrigue would be enough to tie the king up for the rest of his reign.

Yet Charles was not out of the financial conundrum quite yet. In the hope of conducting a short, decisive war against the Dutch, the king played a lethal gambit. In January 1672, he 'stopped' the Exchequer, calling a halt on interest payments to all loans for twelve months while the war was conducted. The gamble was a disaster: fortunes were lost by anyone who had trusted the Crown with their money, bankers missed their payments to their clients, merchants could not meet their bills. In all, over ten thousand investors were damaged and, as Evelyn angrily observed, the ploy 'ruined many widows and orphans, whose stocks were lent him'.[17] The king would never recover his position with the City again.

To oversee this mess, Charles promoted Ashley Cooper, as the most vociferous campaigner for the Dutch wars, to first minister. The lord had initially led the call for war, seeing the defeat of Holland as the only route to trade dominance, and the king was willing to give him what he wanted as long as he could deliver support. In an attempt to assuage the protests, Ashley Cooper, who was given the new title of the Earl of Shaftesbury, persuaded Charles to adopt one of his favourite policies and deliver a Declaration of Indulgence, a proclamation that allowed limited religious toleration to nonconformists.

For Charles II, the proclamation would act as a bandage to cover the wounds of the 'stop' and to calm the forthcoming conflict. For Shaftesbury and Locke, it was long-overdue political justice for 'tender consciences'. Charles, however, was determined that if Shaftesbury allowed liberty for dissenting Protestants, the Declaration should also offer toleration to Catholics. Locke had expressly omitted papism from his ideas on toleration, yet he had to accept the king's conditions if the Declaration was to be made. On behalf of Shaftesbury, Locke ensured that the declaration was legal, even though it had not passed through Parliament.

The third Anglo-Dutch War was a catastrophe. The first battle in open waters, on 7 June, caused huge casualties on both sides. From then on, the depleted Dutch fleet refused to engage on the seas and conducted an effective guerrilla campaign among the sands and coves off Holland's shores. On land, flooding the dykes and ditches made the progress of the superior French forces slow and burdensome. By the summer, the English forces had lost all desire to attack the enemy.

As the conflict dragged on, Charles was forced to stop the Exchequer for the second time and recall Parliament in February 1673; it assembled in Westminster itching for a fight. On 5 February, Shaftesbury stood up before the new members, and was forced to defend the king's policies, claiming that the king went to war on Parliament's behalf. He gamely attempted to defend the expediency of the stop on the Exchequer and dramatically found support for the war on Holland.

He was less successful in defending the Declaration of Indulgence. Parliament saw Charles's proclamation as an attack on its right to create laws and, once it was in session, the controversy would not ebb. As long as the Crown asked for money, Parliament demanded to debate the Declaration. In the end, Charles gained his money, £70,000 a month for three years, but only at the expense of the document, which was cancelled. To rub salt in the wound, Parliament also devised the Second Test Act, which demanded that all officials in positions of responsibility, from Privy Councillors to clerks, take an oath of Anglican orthodoxy.

That Easter, all officers were expected to take communion. At St Clement Danes church on the Strand, John Locke stood and recorded as Shaftesbury took the eucharist. Elsewhere, the Lord Treasurer, Thomas Clifford, refused and was forced to step down, his Catholicism exposed. To the shock of the nation, the Lord High Admiral, none other than the king's brother, James, Duke of York, also declared his conversion to Rome and was relieved of his job. The Test Act had revealed that the natural successor to Charles II was a Catholic.

It was a devastating blow made all the more dangerous in September when James married his second wife, Mary of Modena, a Catholic princess. The fear of a papist heir gripped the nation, no more so than within Shaftesbury's coterie of friends. While Shaftesbury had always promoted the tolerant and liberal model of Holland as the new political identity for England, it was becoming clear that the Stuarts looked instead to France and Catholic absolutism. Thus the king and his first minister found themselves irrevocably in opposition.

Shaftesbury attempted to use Parliament to stop James's marriage but Charles II would not tolerate these attacks on his family. Within months, Charles had had enough and Shaftesbury was sacked. In response, the minister returned his seals of office and vowed revenge. He was removed from the Privy Council in May 1674 and commanded to leave London. Shaftesbury would from now on use his power outside government to be a stone in the Crown's shoe, a champion against the prerogatives of the king.

Inevitably, John Locke also lost his position. He retreated to Oxford to complete his medical training, only returning to London during the university holidays, where he remained involved in Shaftesbury's household. Together they fomented an opposition to the Crown. In 1675 they produced *A Letter from a Person of Quality to his Friend in the Countryside*, which reported,

after fifteen years of the highest Peace, Quiet, and Obedience, that ever was in any country, that there should be a pretence taken up, and a reviving of former miscarriages, especially after so many promises and declarations, as well as Acts of Oblivion, and so much merit of the

Offending Party, in being the instruments of the King's happy return.
... [The king now planned] to declare us first into another government
more Absolute and arbitrary than the Oath of Allegiance or old Law
knew.[18]

Eventually the strain of events became too much for Locke. His health was
declining and Shaftesbury allowed him to leave his service. In November
1675, as *A Letter from a Person of Quality* ... was being distributed upon
the streets of London, causing a stir to the point that copies were being sold
for twenty times their original price, Locke left for France, where he would
remain for four years.

Ancient and Modern

The first stone of the new St Paul's was laid on 21 June 1675, almost nine years after the fire. On that day, Wren, alongside his master mason, Thomas Strong, began to set out the new cathedral's dimensions on the ground. Needing a centre point around which Wren's design would rise, they made a rough cast of the shape of the building. As Wren reported, even on this first day of rebuilding the church at the heart of the city there were good omens, for: 'a common labourer was ordered to bring a flat stone from the heaps of rubbish (such as should first come to hand) to be laid for a mark and direction to the masons; the stone was immediately brought down for the purpose, happened to be a piece of a grave stone, with nothing remaining of the inscription but this single word in large capitals RESURGAM – I will arise.'[1]

The cathedral was finally to be rebuilt anew, but from the very first attempts to set the foundations the plans for the cathedral were not drawn upon a clean slate – the hopes for the future were dictated by a dialogue between the old city and the new. In the schemes for street-widening and house building and in every area of intellectual life, there was conflict between those who wished to keep to the old traditional ways of thinking and the promoters of an improving modernity. The work on Ludgate Hill would be no different.

The king was appreciative of Wren's designs but did not have the power to protect his architect, while the Church hierarchy mistrusted many of the new gestures, and were concerned that the classical cathedral diverged from the traditional Gothic form. From the beginning, therefore, Wren was forced to keep a flexible plan of the cathedral in his head, and throughout the next thirty-three years of building he would have to be alert to the changing circumstances in the city that surrounded the cathedral as well as the day-to-day trials on-site.

The cathedral was a puzzle in stone, and Wren would need all his experience and charm, as well as the lessons of the New Philosophy, to solve the conundrum. He was now the servant of a complex web of clients – the king, the city, Parliament and the Church – and would still hope to find a single architectural voice that absorbed these many different factions and fused them into one project. Thus Wren gathered around him a team that he trusted, many of whom had worked with the surveyor in the office of the city church projects. Edward Woodroffe was named assistant surveyor, as was John Oliver, the City Surveyor who had worked with Wren on the rebuilding commission in 1667. John Tillison and Thomas Bateman were both master masons who oversaw the building on-site. While Hooke was never given an official position, his constant friendship with Wren meant that he was often called on to give his opinion on the thorny issues of design and engineering. Once a team had been gathered and approved by the commission, Wren's first task was to set out the foundations.

Wren knew that his modern plans would have to rest upon the legacy of over a millennium of development. The new structure would be smaller than the thirteenth-century Gothic fabric and the earth below the surface needed to be excavated. Wren's curiosity, however, encouraged him to investigate further. As the foundations were set he dug deeper to discover what was below: '[he] accordingly dug wells in several places and discerned that this pot-earth to be on the north side of the Churchyard about six feet deep ... still he searched lower, and found nothing but dry sand, mix'd sometimes unequally, but loose ... He went on until he came to water and sand mixed with periwinkles and other seashells'.[2] Wren's exploration of the layers of London beneath the cathedral presented a new 'natural history' of the city – the Thames had once been a broad estuary and Ludgate Hill had once been underwater. Over the past few thousand years, the mound had grown from the river silt.

Yet these excavations also revealed problems, for as workers dug through the soil on the north-eastern corner of the summit they found something very unexpected: a Roman clay kiln with 'quantities of urns, broken vessels, and Pottery ware of divers Sorts and Shapes'.[3] It would be impossible to use this unstable site as a foundation. Wren would therefore have to find a solution to this legacy of the past or change his plans completely. He dug a 40-foot hole that reached down to the hard clay at Thames river level and filled it with rubble and masonry and then constructed an arch that spanned from the new pit to the old foundations.

The discovery of the Roman kiln would not be the only surprise in the first years of work. Even at this early stage it was clear to anyone who understood such things that the designs for the cathedral had been altered: the dimensions of the building had changed from those outlined in the approved Warrant Design. The king had whispered to his architect that he could make minor alterations to his plans, but Wren had taken this liberty as permission to redesign the whole building. As soon as he had gained the warrant, he had returned to the drawing board and created the 'Definitive' plans, which had been neither seen nor approved by anyone within the commission.

The Definitive Design was a wholly new plan for St Paul's. The projection held to the same pattern as the Warrant plan – a traditional cruciform structure with a long nave and transepts meeting at a crossing – yet the new scheme was bolder. In particular, Wren had revived his idea for a grand dome to reign over London. Such a cupola would require walls that were very different from those proposed in his Warrant Design. The new designs also responded to another problem. Wren refused to contemplate that his masterpiece should be stymied by quarrels over cash and he had ignored the directive and begun laying foundations for the whole building – the new cathedral would need to be built as a single piece. By July 1677, the churchyard had been transformed from a demolition zone into a building site. Amid the rubble only Inigo Jones's classical façade remained from the original cathedral, while below workmen swarmed in the yard, which was filling up with piles of stone and timber.

More than anything else, the supply of stone would dictate the pace of rebuilding, in particular the royal stone used by Inigo Jones at Whitehall and on the cathedral portico. The distinctive white stone had to be delivered to London from the royal quarry on the island of Portland, Dorset, on the south-west coast. Before the stone could be moved, however, Wren had to repair the damage to the quarry, roads, pier and cranes. Because the condition of the roads was so poor, it was decided to transport the stone by sailing boat, each carrying a maximum of 150 tons. This method presented hazards: bad weather and the threat of Dutch warships jeopardised delivery; in addition, once the boats arrived in London, the blocks had to be transferred on to barges to negotiate the low arches of London Bridge and proceed the short distance to St Paul's Wharf. On land, a route needed to be found that weaved through the city traffic to deliver the stones up Ludgate Hill. For the larger stones a pulley system turned by horses or men was contrived, some blocks taking up to a fortnight to reach the churchyard.

By July 1677, the commission calculated that 3,500 tons of Portland and other stone had been delivered to the yard; this was in addition to all the other stones: the 37,000 'sup feet and upwards of old stone' that had been collected for the outside of the building as well as 20,600 tons of rubble that had been used to fill the foundations that were between 22 and, in some places, 35 feet deep. In addition there were accounts made for '7500 hundreds of lime, 400 thousands of bricks, 440 tunnes of sand and upwards, besides three times the quantity of old sand sifted out of the rubbish'.[4] Loose stone was also used to build a makeshift wall around the site to ward off intruders and night thieves. Spikes and tenterhooks were placed above the gateways to stop pilfering of supplies.

The building was slowly beginning to emerge from the earth. Foundation stones had been laid along all the edges, except at the western end, giving London the first impression of the dimensions of the new cathedral: 'the [choir] being 170 ft long and 121 Broad, with great vaults underneath, and is raised 24 ft above the ground: the greatest part of the Foundation of the Cross Isles are laid, and the dome, which is 108 ft diameter within the walls, is carried to the same height with the chore … so that the whole Fabrick of the Church, so far as it is now begun extends from east to West 320 feet and from North to South 310 ft'.[5]

As Wren began to lay the first stones, St Paul's was a study in statics, weights and loads. Hooke, more than anyone, had helped Wren understand the technical issues, and in 1675 he presented to the Royal Society his ideas on 'the true Mathematical and Mechanical Form of all manner of arches for Building, with the true abutment necessary to each of them'.[6] In his talk he proposed ideas on how an arch could evenly balance its weight. If St Paul's was to stand up, it would be by careful calculation and measurement, as much an essay in geometry as a discourse on the history of architecture. Both of these concerns found their focus in the first preparations for the dome, which began as soon as the foundations were set.

Since his visit to Paris in 1665, Wren had fixed the cupola at the centre of his every conception of the cathedral. As St Paul's would be the first cathedral in England with such a dome, it would also link London to the distinguished tradition begun with the Pantheon in Rome, built by the

Emperor Hadrian in the second century. The Pantheon was a masterpiece of proportion and symmetry for, from the dome's summit to the temple floor, a perfect sphere can be drawn in a pure demonstration of geometry and order. The Ancient Romans had constructed the building in concrete made from volcanic ash and the dome rose 143 feet into the air, seemingly without support. Although the original temple had been built for pagan worship, it had been converted into a Christian church, Santa Maria Rotunda, and since the dawn of the Renaissance had been studied and measured by every generation in search of classical perfection.

Although Wren had absorbed the many examples of Ancient Rome he was not solely interested in the achievements of the West. Hagia Sophia, or the Great Church, built in the sixth century in Constantinople by the Emperor Justinian, was considered by many the eighth wonder of the ancient world. Designed by the mathematician and astronomer Isidore of Miletus and Anthemius of Tralles, it offered an alternative template for the dome. The dome of Hagia Sophia was an innovation, standing at the centre of the square crossing of the basilica, supported by pendentives, triangular segments of a sphere that sat upon four large piers which allowed the cupola to be raised high for the first time.

Following centuries of Romanesque temples and Gothic towers and spires, the cupola was rediscovered by the West during the fifteenth-century Renaissance, symbolising the heavens and the proportional perfection of God's power. The Pantheon's ideal structure would become the model for the architect Filippo Brunelleschi as he built the Duomo of Santa Maria Fiore in Florence, high above the Florentine skyline, a symbol of the heavens on earth.

Brunelleschi began his masterpiece in the 1430s and it took over a decade to complete. The cupola was built in brick, laid in herringbone fashion, 91 feet above the ground. It was a deft piece of mathematical engineering as it was intended to support itself and was constructed without scaffolding. Each row of bricks was arduously laid, the mortar mixed perfectly to fix the structure, while five marble ribs ran from base to lantern above. Most ingeniously Brunelleschi had devised a double dome with a thick inner shell, a brick skeleton between 5 and 7 feet thick, upon which was laid the outer shell to prevent the dome collapsing inwards. This had both aesthetic and structural advantages which would be advanced by later generations. The Duomo was a fifteenth-century miracle that marked Florence as the capital of the new classicism.

Yet Florence's Duomo would be superseded in the following century by St Peter's in Rome, designed by the masterful Michelangelo. Before the architect's arrival in 1546, St Peter's had been altered and designed by a series of leading architects such as Bramante, Raphael and San Gallo, yet while his predecessors went in search of the classical ideal, Michelangelo went farther and envisioned the cathedral anew. In 1561, as he turned his focus to the dome, he adopted many of the structural features of Brunelleschi's cupola, but also reimagined it as a modern expression. Michelangelo searched for the soul of the building and designed an elongated dome. The effect was a homage to the ancients but also a radical rupture from the past.

He lifted Bramante's single masonry dome upon a drum that raised it 452 feet above the Roman pavement. This dramatic gesture, however, created a problem, and Michelangelo was forced to experiment with the double-dome structure of the Duomo to find a solution. The two domes became dislocated, the inner dome used as a means to complement the interior space of the basilica, thus allowing the outer dome to rise into the air without affecting the internal dynamics of the building. Unfortunately, Michelangelo died as the drum was being built, so the final designs for the cupola were overseen by Della Porte, who made a few modifications but remained true to the maestro's vision. The cupola was finished in heavy masonry with a series of windows, and capped by a distinctive columned lantern.

This balance between reason and learning made the dome the symbol of the Counter-Reformation, the resurgence of humanist Catholicism in the early seventeenth century that had such a powerful effect on the skyline of Paris. Finally, England would have its dome at the heart of the nation, and it would be unlike anything seen in Rome or Constantinople; and a Protestant one at that. Wren would learn from history and adapt features from both the ancient East and West, the Renaissance as well as the Moderns. To this he would also add his own understanding of architecture and the New Philosophy.

THE CURATOR AND THE VIRTUOSO

Many of the attributes associated with the Victorians – industry, seriousness, thrift – should be used to describe the generation that sowed the seeds of modernity in London's fertile soil following the fire of 1666. They can particularly be seen in the figures of John Evelyn and Robert Hooke. When, in the 1810s, John Evelyn's diaries were first discovered in a basket at Wotton House and published, he was hailed as 'the First Victorian' for his sober, pious view of the world. Yet if ever there was a man who deserved an accolade for sheer industry, it was Robert Hooke.

Both men kept a journal; Evelyn's diary covered the whole of his life while only fragments remain of Hooke's. Hooke, the Baconian man, used his as a laboratory notebook, dating and marking results, meetings, discoveries and events as if they were experimental data, while Evelyn edited his life as the record of a public man as well as a pious portrait of a Christian family. In his diaries Evelyn recorded both the old and the new in equal measure. He was committed to the Royal Society and the pursuit of the New Philosophy, and was one of the most assiduous attendees, often bringing questions or ideas to the debating chamber.

By 1670, in his fiftieth year, John Evelyn was busier than ever. As commissioner for the sick and wounded he was in constant demand, and his rise within the court was fixed with his elevation to the Council of Plantations and Trade, presided over by the Earl of Shaftesbury. Nonetheless, Evelyn still hoped to spend more time developing his garden at Sayes Court and writing, telling a friend that he would prefer to spend his life 'plant[ing] cabbages, or blotting paper'.[7]

Hooke, in contrast, was unquestionably a public man. The coffee house was a daily forum for his life. It was here that Hooke enjoyed the company of his real friends and it was the small universe where he felt most convivial. Hooke's diary named 134 separate coffee houses in all quarters of the city. By 1672, he was thirty-seven years old, and at the height of his powers. His role as City Surveyor was at the heart of the redevelopment of London. In addition to his work alongside Wren he oversaw the rebuilding of the Navy Office in Seething Lane and city projects at New Thames Quay, Bridewell Hospital, Newgate and Moorgate, as well as working for the Mercers' Company, the Royal College of Physicians and the Merchant Taylors' School. In 1674 he had begun work on the Bethlem Hospital and had taken on private clients, for whom he negotiated and designed a house in St James's Square as well as drawing up plans for Montagu House in Bloomsbury. In addition, Hooke also had obligations as Professor of Geometry at Gresham College, where he lectured weekly during term time.

In the previous decade science was claimed to be for the benefit of all mankind, and the Royal Society was founded with a mission statement that promoted collaborative exploration and pragmatic solutions. But by the 1670s, the scientific domain had become increasingly commercial. 'Useful knowledge' was pursued in the hope of patents and scientific speculation offered possibilities of profit for the inventor. Thus, amid the social, courtly atmosphere of the club, there emerged the spectre of professionalisation. Hooke was in the eye of the debate.

Evelyn, on the other hand, was the epitome of the ingenious amateur. Throughout the decade, he continued with his great work of horticultural science, the *Elysium Britannicum*, which he had begun in the last years of the 1650s. But by the middle of the 1670s his survey of useful knowledge was still no nearer to completion. From the beginning, he seemed to have a better idea of the audience for his book than of its content, and within the pages of his commonplace book he struggled with his own lifelong contradictions as he tried to define his philosophy.

The First Book of the *Elysium* was a perfect example of the New Philosophy, as the author set out his scheme of the Hortulan Arts. He broke his sections down into 'heads' – first principles – under which he set out his argument, and thus the book began with the question 'What is a garden?' followed by 'What is a gardener?' He then set out to investigate the four elements, the influence of the sun and the moon, the climate, soil, composts and how plants grow, the right tools to use and the correct timing for planting, pruning and watering, the best way to obtain perspectives and features, essays on hydraulics for fountains, and even the joys of birdsong within the grove.

Thus far, he was a modern, but interwoven with these discourses was Evelyn's attempt to draw up a complete history of horticulture. He made accounts of a number of modern gardens, sites he visited himself or had reported to him by friends from across Europe, and amassed a huge knowledge of ancient gardens from sources ranging from classical literature, the Bible and myth to the *Natural History* of Pliny the Elder and Virgil's *Georgics*. This accumulation of material had a disastrous impact on the writing of the *Elysium*, and he found himself forced to account for the complete world rather than finding a focus for his argument. In particular he was struck down by a paradox: that most of the ancient wonders had been lost and remained only in literature, including the most perfect garden of all, Eden.

In 1679, he vented his exasperation at failing to complete his masterpiece:

When againe I consider into what an ocean I am plung'd, how much I
have written and collected for above these 20 years upon this fruitful
and inexhaustible subject. (I mean Horticulture) not yet fully digested
to my mind, and what insuperable pains it will require to insert the
(dayly increasing) particulars into what I have already in some measure
prepared, and which must of necessitie be don by my owne hand, I am
almost out of hope that I shall ever have strength and leisure to bring
it.[8]

In contrast, Hooke, the professional research scientist, was expected to
make experiments and the society showed their disgruntlement on the few
occasions when he failed to dazzle them or, rarer still, turn up. In addition,
the society wanted results so that they could promote their name throughout the European community of savants. Results also raised the glimmering
possibilities of patents in which intellectual capital was converted into cash
for the club's bare coffers. The pressure upon the curator was great, and
he maintained a voracious work rate and throughout the 1670s turned his
mind to a number of new areas of discovery that attracted his jackdaw eye.

Following a trip home to the Isle of Wight in 1667, he began to think
about natural history, offering the notion that the Earth itself had a past:
'a great Part of the surface of the Earth has been since the creation transform'd'.[9] This led to an exploration of fossils and earthquakes and would
place Hooke at the forefront of seventeenth-century geology. Continuing
his experiments in Oxford with Boyle and Willis, Locke and Lower, Hooke
searched for the key to respiration, combustion and the qualities of air,
hoping to discover what it was in the atmosphere that gave life. In experiments with the pneumatic pump and live dogs, in which he was forced to
put aside his distaste for dissection, Hooke came closer to an understanding
of the nature of air. He also contributed to the knowledge of congruity, the
reason why two chemicals combined.

From the records of his diary alone, it is apparent that Hooke's appetite
for knowledge was omnivorous; yet despite the diversity of his studies,
Hooke was increasingly interested in the theoretical foundations of the
New Philosophy. In particular he campaigned for the reorganisation of the
discipline, promoting specialisation and professionalisation: 'there ought to
be some End and Aim, some predesigned Module and theory, some
Purpose in our Experiments'.[10] This stood in stark contrast to the original
plans for the Philosophical Club in the 1650s and ensured that Hooke

would come up against repeated opposition and conflict. This widening gap between the virtuoso and the professional scientist would have an impact on the foundations of modern science.

THE HEDGEHOG AND THE FOX

The growing atmosphere of mistrust between the club and its curator was unhealthy and brought out an unattractive aspect of Hooke's personality that was not seen in any of his other dealings during the period. Where he was generous with friends and architectural clients, he became jealous and desperate over his claims for scientific discovery. Partly this can be explained by the souring of certain key relationships within the society. There can also be seen in Hooke's more combative stance an increased professionalisation in the role of research scientist which rubbed awkwardly against the amateur virtuosity of the society.

Embattled in disputes and slights, Hooke was traditionally coloured as the instigator, radiating arrogant aggression. But in all cases Hooke would have called himself the victim, defending his precedent and honour. As in so many squabbles, nobody emerged with much credit. This antagonism, the race to establish the claim as inventor of a new discovery, would become the method by which the modern scientific market developed. It was the professional scientist's role to make new discoveries and Hooke struggled to present himself as more than a paid performer for virtuosi and courtiers who dabbled for entertainment. For his fellow members of the Royal Society, however, his willingness to lock antlers gave the appearance of a disturbing inflation of the curator's ego.

Hooke did not help his cause by his choice of battles and often made a noise only after a rival had made their announcement. Too often he found himself defending many of the ideas he had left on the shelf half completed. Earlier in his career he had found himself defending his claims for discoveries in lens-grinding against Wren's Parisian friend Adrien Auzout. He would later have a similar spat with the Dutch microscopist Antony van Leeuwenhoek, as well as attacking the 'naked eye' astronomer Hevelius with proofs that were less than complete. He was discovering, to his cost, the difference between the fox and the hedgehog in Aesop's Fables: the fox knew many things but the hedgehog knew one great thing. The future of modern science would more often celebrate the professional hedgehog than the virtuoso fox.

At the end of 1671, Isaac Newton, the young Lucasian Professor of Mathematics at the University of Cambridge, sent his ideas for a telescope to the Royal Society. The new instrument, alongside instructions written in Latin, was passed to a committee including Wren and Hooke to test the invention's claims. The machine was ingenious, containing a series of mirrors, and was able to magnify distant objects better than a standard refracting tube as commonly used by astronomers. In January the following year, the telescope was presented to the society and its maker, Isaac Newton, was elected a fellow of the club. Until then, little had been known about the mathematician among the London members of the Royal Society. It was only at Cambridge, where Newton encountered Isaac Barrow, one of the founding members of the society, that his work started to be discussed among the virtuosi.

Newton's reflecting telescope had evolved out of the professor's fascination with the nature of light, and its introduction into the debating room of the Royal Society was a striking entrance. It also put Hooke and the inventor on a collision course, for neither man could contemplate being wrong. Hooke, the senior man, was unwilling to be upstaged by an unknown from the provinces, while Newton was equally, if not more, bull-headed. Initially Hooke was arrogant and churlish towards Newton. He laid claimed to having already invented a 'reflecting box' while also revealing that he had not had the time to complete the discovery, and he set about immediately constructing a model to his own designs. Yet Hooke had made the first error in thinking that the debate was about telescopes and the manufacture of instruments, rather than the nature of light itself.

Newton had read Hooke's *Micrographia*, in which the curator had included a series of experiments that confirmed his theory that light moved in waves. If light was motion then white light was pure, unhindered movement, while the colours were formed by the disturbance of this perfect wave. From the moment he read it, Newton felt that this was incorrect, and in the margin of his edition he noted, 'Though Descartes may be wrong so is Mr Hooke',[11] and over the following years he performed experiments to prove that light was not motion, a wave, but body, tiny particles. Thus colour was not the disturbance of white light but white light was the combination of all colours.

On 8 February 1672, Newton wrote down his theory of Opticks for the society. The theory was passed to Boyle, Ward and Hooke for analysis; Hooke was the only one to reply. In his response, Hooke attempted to browbeat the young scientist by both claiming to have discovered all before 'by many hundreds of trials', while also pouring scorn on Newton's findings: 'I do not therefore see any absolute necessity to believe his theory demonstrated'.[12] Finally, tempting fate, he promised that he would prove his own theory right. Hooke's attack was graceless, unnecessary and seriously underestimated his adversary. Throughout 1672 Hooke delivered a number of experiments in light to the society while an increasingly heated correspondence between the curator and his opponent was read out at meetings. Over the following years the *Philosophical Transactions* would be dotted with Hooke's objections to Newton's theory.

Hooke clearly believed that he was working for the good of the society, while many others saw a creeping arrogance and paranoia enter his working methods. In the end, Newton retreated from the arena, only to be drawn back into the ring in 1675 when, perhaps stirred up by the secretary, Oldenburg, who by this time was also at loggerheads with Hooke, he again raised his objections. Hooke once more set about attempting the demonstration of his own theory, claiming, 'I explain everything after a way so differing from him, that the experiments I ground my discourse on, destroy all he has said about them.'[13] On 27 April 1676, however, Oldenburg reported that the experiments were then conducted under Newton's instruction and found to be true.

This first gladiatorial challenge between Hooke and Newton had no victor. Hooke had defended his ground but Newton had been correct, yet the professor vowed not to publish his theory until after the curator's death, and his first great work, *Opticks*, would not be revealed until 1704. After this confrontation, Hooke would find himself making many more enemies in his pursuit to claim his precedent.

One of the great issues of the day was the longitude watch, a timepiece that could be used to tell the hour accurately at sea. At stake was not just engineering glory or the promise of vast wealth. As the third Anglo-Dutch War was raging, the ability to gauge longitude would give huge advantage to whichever navy possessed the watch. Hooke had been fascinated by the longitude watch since the 1650s when, alongside Wren, he first sought a mechanical solution. In 1663, he had again made advances on his pocket watch, including his newly designed spring balance, in a patent that he presented to the grandees of the Royal Society. On that occasion, negotiations had broken down as Hooke feared that any improvements to the mechanism would threaten forfeiture of the patent.

In 1674 the Dutch virtuoso Christiaan Huygens had announced in his book *On Pendulum Clocks* that he had completed the designs for a pocket watch that could accurately tell the hour in all conditions. Huygens' claim forced Hooke back to his project, and in a subsequent lecture at Gresham College he trashed the Dutchman's claims to have discovered anything and made counterclaims of his own.

On this occasion, Oldenburg, the Royal Society secretary, was happy to stir up the brewing conflict, for he had a personal interest in the contest. In January 1675, Huygens had sent Oldenburg the secret of the balance spring of his watch and offered the secretary the income from the English patent. Oldenburg published the findings and thus established Huygens' priority. When Hooke complained to the society that he had presented a similar design the previous decade, no record could be found, and Oldenburg steered the meeting to accept the Dutch claim. Hooke soon became aware of Oldenburg's ruse and accused him of subterfuge.

The race then took on a further dimension when the claims for priority rested not on who designed the first spring balance on paper but who could build the first working example. Hooke worked tirelessly alongside the master clockmaker Thomas Tompion to complete the task. On 7 April 1675, a meeting was arranged for Hooke and Tompion to present the new contraption to Charles II himself. As Hooke recorded in his diary: 'shewd him my new spring watch ... The King most graciously pleasd with it and commended it far beyond Zulichem's [Huygens']. He promised me a patent'.[14]

The watch was tested over the following months and corrections and repairs made. In the meantime Huygens' watch arrived in June and was examined by Lord Brouncker, the President of the society, but was found wanting. Hooke's watch had won, but it was still not accurate enough to help sailors measure the difference in time across the globe, and in the end Hooke did not earn a patent but a rebuke from the Royal Society for his behaviour. The longitude problem, which he had grappled with throughout his career, still stood beyond Hooke's grasp; his invention worked on paper but the precise technology did not exist that could bring his ideas to fruition.

The failure placed Hooke in a difficult predicament. He still had not found the invention by which he could make his name, and in the process he had damaged his relationship with the Royal Society. He could no longer depend on the club's support, and in Oldenburg he found a fellow who was actively campaigning against him.

In a recently discovered collection of Hooke's notes, the extent of Old-enburg and Hooke's falling out is revealed. The papers include a series of annotations that Hooke made of Oldenburg's *Philosophical Transactions*, which were sent out to all his correspondents around Europe. On occasion, there were meetings that had been, in Hooke's opinion, left unrecorded; in particular, notes on Hooke's timepiece had been purposely omitted. In addition, in transcribing Oldenburg's *Transactions*, Hooke could not stop himself adding notes of frustration in parentheses. On 3 July 1672, when Nehemiah Grew showed the meeting a particular characteristic of trees, Hooke added: '[NB I had shown them long before as appears by this booke vii.]' More worrying was Hooke's note of 13 November that same year, which read: '[NB this Report is noe where els mentioned. Which was a common with Olden[burg]].'[15] The curator's paranoia would quickly supply the reason why: Oldenburg had cooked the society's books to his own advantage and to belittle Hooke.

By 1675, Hooke had had enough. He saw that reform of the society could not be achieved from the inside. This was further confirmed that autumn while the curator was bringing together a number of his experi-ments and designs for publication in *A Description of Helioscopes and some other Instruments*. While the script was at the printers, Hooke added a postscript that laid out in full his own version of recent events, including a vociferous personal attack on Oldenburg. When news circulated about the content of the inflammatory chapter, Brouncker and others on the council of the Royal Society debated whether to eject Hooke. He was given a reprieve; but he had not finished. The following year he published *Lampas*, a collection of lectures on the improvement of lamps, as well as a series of speculations on gravitation and light. Again, he used the postscript as a forum to berate his colleagues.

In January 1676, Hooke attempted to set up his own Philosophical Club, dedicated to a new seriousness of debate and experimentation that was not afraid of speculation and discovery. The plot was first hatched on 10 December 1675, unsurprisingly including a number of Hooke's coffee-house crowd of grandees, merchants and City men. The club was set to meet weekly at Wren's house in secret, and meetings were initially well attended by Hooke's inner circle, including William Holder, Abraham Hill and Sir Jonas Moore.

The private rift between the New Philosophers was brought into public debate in May 1676 when the Duke's Company performed a new play in their theatre behind St Bride's Church, currently being rebuilt according to Wren's design. The author, Thomas Shadwell, was famed for his quick wit. The year before he had reinvented the Don Juan story in *The Libertine*, to huge acclaim, and now had set about looking for new victims of his barbs. *The Virtuoso*, first performed in front of a packed house including the king and his favourites, told the story of Sir Nicholas Gimcrack, a New Philosopher. It was plainly clear on whom the character was based. In his fascination for the new science Gimcrack looked painfully similar to the Royal Society curator as he explored the gamut of useless knowledge from the weight of air to the magnification of lice.

Shadwell had clearly studied Hooke's *Micrographia* as part of his research, and he showed no mercy to its author. At one point Gimcrack was found on the stage trying to read the Geneva Bible by the light of a leg of pork. He was also lampooned as 'one who has spent two thousand pounds in microscopes to find out the nature of eels in vinegar, mites in a cheese and the blue of plums'.[16] After Hooke went to see the debacle himself, he spat: 'damned dogs. Vindica me deus. people almost pointed,'[17] and he must have shuddered as the final lines were spoken: 'we virtuosi never find out anything of use, 'tis not our way'.[18] Having struggled to gain prominence within the scientific community and having offered so many new ideas and observations to the New Philosophy, Hooke found himself humiliated by the sly conjectures of Shadwell's venomed pen.

Hooke did not feel the spite alone. Evelyn also felt the dramatist's barbs, for the character of Sir Formal Trifle fitted the description of the virtuoso almost too well, and he sought to defend the society both publicly and in private. The public humiliation for Hooke, however, could not have occurred at a worse time, and it would affect both his public and personal life.

He had never married and he rarely engaged in the company of women. Instead he gathered around him an alternative family who all lived together in his rooms on the north-east corner of Gresham College. In 1672, two girls from the Isle of Wight came to live with him. One was Grace Hooke, his twelve-year-old niece, daughter of his brother John, the other Nell Young, a maid. Grace was in London in preparation for her betrothal to the son of Sir Thomas Bludworth. Under Hooke's supervision she was schooled and made ready for marriage, but by the summer of 1673 the union had been called off, and Grace returned to her father.

Nell stayed and managed the house for Hooke, cooking and sewing for

£4 a year. She also became intimate with her employer. From September 1672 until she left to get married in August 1673 the diary recorded Hooke's every orgasm with the symbol of the astronomical sign for Pisces. After Nell's departure, Hooke remained friends with his maid and would visit her at her new home by Fleet Ditch, where she continued to do small jobs and sewing for him. She was replaced by a series of incompetent housekeepers who lasted only a short time and inspired Hooke's anger. Even so, he had sexual relations with two of them, despite their faults.

In 1675, Hooke took on a distant island relation, Tom Gyles, as an apprentice at the same time as Grace Hooke returned to London. Hooke tutored both these young charges in preparation for their going out into the world, and they in turn kept him up to date with news from the Isle of Wight. His brother, John, had gained status in Newport as a grocer and would twice be named Lord Mayor, but everything was not what it appeared. There were frequent requests for loans, including £4,000 in August 1675, when John wished to purchase an estate in Avington. But John's debts continued to mount. That same year, Robert began a sexual relationship with his niece. The following year, he tried to send her away to the Isle of Wight but she came back to London and relations resumed.

This all had a terrible effect on Hooke's health. He had always been a frail man, yet throughout the decade, in a rising tide of experimentation with every form of purgative, digestive and painkiller, Hooke became addicted to a regimen of dangerous medicine. He dosed himself to sleep, being a victim of insomnia, and then self-medicated to keep his mind alert. His diaries were soon transformed from a record of meteorology to an exploration of the pharmacopeia as he did battle with ailments, giddiness, sweats, palpitations, poor vision, headaches and fits that could have been blamed as much on the effects of the medicine as on his own frailty. He became an avid collector of advice and medical remedies, from sources ranging from the physician to the quack and the tavern know-all.

Everything came to a head in 1677. In September, Tom Gyles died of smallpox. The death was long and drawn out and left Hooke devastated. In the same month Secretary Oldenburg also died from malaria. On 13 September, the day of Tom's funeral, Hooke took temporary control of the secretaryship until elections were organised. But opposition to Hooke did not end with Oldenburg's passing. The curator had gone out of his way to annoy other members of the club's hierarchy in his rants and animadversions. Elections were delayed until the end of November, which gave time for the society members to fall into factions and infighting over its future.

Christopher Wren backed his friend in finding a new regimen, although he was in two minds as to whether the busy curator had time in his schedule to take on the role of secretary. In October Hooke tried to persuade Wren to take on the presidency, but that came to nothing. Throughout the month Hooke, Wren, Evelyn and Abraham Hill, the society treasurer, met at Man's Coffee House in Chancery Lane to search for ways to rescue the club. Eventually, on 14 November, together with John Evelyn and Sir John Hoskins and others, Hooke visited the Secretary of State, Sir Joseph Williamson, to persuade him to act as president of the society.

All the schemes, however, did not go to plan. Williamson gained the leading role but on 13 December Hooke was surprised to see that Nehemiah Grew had been given the temporary job of secretary. He released his frustrations in his diary: 'It seemed as if they would have me still curator, Grew secretary. I stayed not at the crown. I huffed at [Abraham] Hills at Jonathan's'.[19] In the meeting of 19 December, the matter came to a head: if Hooke was to remain curator, he had to be given more power over the direction of experiments and demonstrations; his work should not be interrupted by the whims of court virtuosi and amateurs.

While this was occurring in London, Grace had returned to Newport to avoid the sickness that had befallen Tom Gyles. Once there, she was courted by a local aristocrat and governor of the island, Sir Robert Holmes. In January 1678, Hooke's brother committed suicide. Whether John had taken his life because of financial difficulties is impossible to conclude. There were, however, more mysterious circumstances. The following month, Grace fell victim to the measles, which later raised speculation that her quarantine was the result not of a virus but pregnancy, and John Hooke had committed suicide in shame. Sir Robert Holmes later acknowledged an illegitimate daughter, although the identity of the mother was never known.

Robert heard the sad news from Nell Young, whom he visited the following day, and he plainly recorded in his diary: 'This Morning Brother John Hooke Died'.[20] Beyond the emotional devastation, the death of John also placed the Hooke family in financial jeopardy. Suicide was unconscionable by law and the family feared that the whole estate would be lost to the king. His friends, Wren, Hoskins and Boyle, gathered around him to defend his case before the Crown, and in the end the family honour was saved. Yet the long-term effects on Hooke himself – an accumulation of a decade of brilliant exploration, rivalry, dedicated work on behalf of the city, a dangerous self-medication regime and his own feelings of guilt – may have been more than the frail man could bear.

Raised in Extremes

As the builders swarmed through the churchyard, Ludgate Hill would have appeared more like a ship than a building site. Scaffolding rose high into the city air, lashed together with ropes and struts, like rigging. Everywhere one looked vast stones were being raised by some pulley system or tackle. There were capstan-houses that raised the stone high on a crane; sheers were built for larger blocks that dangled on ropes in midair between two tall masts braced together by a lintel of strong timber. Carvers busied themselves in front of vast blocks of white Portland before the stones were put into place or, more dangerously, balanced on planks strung between scaffolding poles. A permanent sawmill was placed within the churchyard of the nearby St Gregory's.

No architect in England had ever attempted a construction of such vast proportions, yet Wren's experience within the Architect's Office for the city churches project would prove the best grounding available. By 1675, twenty-four parish churches were already in hand, and the office had developed a tested system of work and organisation which was transposed to St Paul's. Competition to work with the surveyor was heated, but many of the mason teams and partnerships that had been formed for the smaller projects gained contracts and Wren surrounded himself with men he could trust. In addition, the efficient methods of payment by work or measure were extended.

During the building season, from earliest spring until cold winter, a routine began to emerge on-site. At 6 a.m., 1 p.m. and 6 p.m. each day a bell rang for the workers to muster and be counted by the Clerk of Cheques for a head count. At night, two watchmen protected the precious stores from thieves. Every Thursday and Saturday Wren visited the site, weaving through the workmen to give directions or make enquiries. He met with his master masons at the office in the Convocation House Yard to peruse drawings and designs, as well as discuss issues with Hooke, who was always on hand to give advice. Often they would retire to Child's Coffee House, near to Hooke's new Royal College of Physicians, to discuss the issues of the day. Child's offered a mixed clientele of medical and ecclesiastical drinkers, and it was also here that Hooke and Wren intrigued over the Royal Society.

Soon, the citizens crossing the bustling churchyard were able to see signs of the cathedral beginning to return to the capital. As the poet James Wright announced in 1677:

> Once more from nothing Paul's shall pierce the Skie!
> And if a paradox like this can be,
> The immaterial Church in time may move
> Out of confusion into conformity . . .[1]

THE KING'S BROTHER

Yet political conformity remained elusive. Since 1675, Shaftesbury had become the most troublesome fly in the royal ointment. He had been thrown out of the court yet remained powerful as an agitator, despite numerous attempts to silence him with threats as well as bribes. In particular he had set his sights on the question of succession, haranguing Parliament with lurid scenarios of what would happen if the Catholic James, Duke of York, were to gain the throne. He was not a lone voice, and soon a powerful faction of grandees and city officials began to buzz with discontent. In exasperation, Charles first banned Shaftesbury from London, and when that didn't work finally called for his imprisonment in the Tower of London, where he was forced to remain until he apologised.

Imprisonment did little to dent the noble's fervour, and in fact gave him time to organise his opposition to the king. Finally released in February 1678, he continued his attack. In Parliament, he stoked the coals of Exclusion and in the streets and coffee houses, printing presses and pulpits developed what became known as the Whig Party. The emergence of the Whigs has often been seen as the first formation of a political party in English history; the truth, however, was not so clear cut. The Whigs of 1678 were never a single party but a fluid collection of interest groups, led by various peers rather than Shaftesbury alone. It is often assumed that the Whigs united under a single policy of Exclusion, yet the arena of discontent ranged far wider than who would next sit on the English throne. The rivalry between Whigs and the establishment Tories who rose up in defence of the court and the king's interests split London. The Whigs, in the most general terms, were anti-Catholic, anti-France and fearful of the influence of both upon Charles II. Within that concern, however, ranged a panoply of proposed alternatives, proving that while the Whigs knew what they disliked they shared little agreement on a solution.

Coffee houses became the new debating chambers and a number of Whig clubs – the Swan Inn, the Salutation Tavern, the Green Ribbon Club – became the nerve centres for the evolving opposition. Shaftesbury masterminded a print campaign through a series of stationery offices that flooded the London streets with tracts and broadsides. In addition, a number of highly visual events were organised to send a chill through the city, demonstrations were organised and the dramatic annual Pope-Burning procession in November was funded from Whig coffers. During these events the word 'mob', derived from the Latin *mobile vulgaris*, was first used to describe the organised rabble. The Whigs agitated the City to the point of giddiness.

By the autumn of 1678, Charles was on the back foot, and there were fears that he might use the standing army to regain control. And then Charles was told of a plot, cooked up by Jesuits, to have him murdered, and England delivered up to James, Duke of York, manipulated by his Catholic puppet master Louis XIV. In the distrustful atmosphere of the capital the conspiracy sounded too convincing not to be true. Furthermore, the rumours did not come from just one witness, but were first substantiated by an addle-headed clergyman, Israel Tonge, and then by a third, Titus Oates. They were fuelled further on 17 October, when the body of Edmundbury Godfrey, the Westminster magistrate who had taken Oates' and Tonge's depositions, was found in a ditch by Primrose Hill to the north of the City. He had been run through with his own sword and dumped on the pastureland. His clothes were clean and showed no signs of struggle; all his possessions remained in his pockets. As rumours circulated, Godfrey became the man murdered because he knew too much.

The Popish Plot, called by one historian 'one of the most remarkable outbreaks of mass hysteria in English history',[2] centred on one man – Titus

Oates. Oates had been born a Baptist in the early years of the Civil Wars, yet later joined the Anglican Church until he was expelled as a thief, drunk, sodomist and blasphemer. After a short stint in the navy he travelled to Spain and Flanders, infiltrating the Jesuit colleges, which had been set up with the purpose of converting England. Inevitably he was expelled from these as well, and he returned to London to exact his revenge. He found an eager audience in the eccentric and weak-minded cleric Israel Tonge, who lapped up his fanciful tales of espionage and skul-duggery. Tonge was absolutely convinced of their veracity and presented them to the king, who showed little concern. Nonetheless, there were some at court who were more willing to be gulled and the rumours began to catch fire.

As Oates began to talk, making accusations and spinning himself into contradictions, inaccuracies and paradoxes, his growing audience became increasingly eager to believe the words of this discredited priest. In the end Oates made so many accusations that some of them were bound to be accurate, and the discovery of Catholic plots within the court allowed many to believe that everything Oates said had a pinch of truth. Torture loosened the tongues of the accused and widened the net of suspicion.

Women began to hide firearms in their mufflers in case they were attacked on the streets, while rabid anti-Catholicism informed every debate. The Pope-Burning procession in November attracted a vast crowd of 200,000, which wound its way through London to a ceremonial pyre at Temple Bar. In St Paul's churchyard, among the work stalls and stones, a letter was discovered that threatened popish insurrection, promising a riot as devastating as the fire of September 1666. Christopher Wren was ordered to make a complete survey of the cellars of the Houses of Parliament when rumours of a new gunpowder plot circulated. There was even news that Louis XIV was mustering his forces for an invasion.

In the winter of 1678, Shaftesbury's loose coalition of exclusionists scented blood and saw the Oates' plot as the ideal wooden horse in which to drive through their ambitions. Shaftesbury himself would have no truck with Oates' accusations, he was too astute for that, but he was happy to harness the nervous energy of fear, pointing a finger at the 'Catholic' court and the Tory faction within Parliament, to further his policies, and he began to prepare an assault in his campaign for Exclusion. To protect himself from further insult, Charles had dissolved Parliament in December

1678 for the first time since his restoration, and called a general election the following year with a new selection of MPs. Writing to his secretary, John Locke, who had been in France since 1675, Shaftesbury demanded he make haste back to England and be by his side at his home, Thanet House, to plan the Whig strategy. Locke arrived back on 30 April and immediately made his way to his patron.

The election was called in January, and James was sent away from London to defuse the heat of the gathering, yet as soon as Parliament opened it was clear that Shaftesbury and his fellows would place Exclusion at the top of the political agenda. They attacked the king's chief minister, Lord Danby, and by the end of April began to debate Exclusion, stoked by the botched Metal Tub Plot, cooked up by court Catholics who claimed to have uncovered a Whig conspiracy to kill the king. On 21 May, the House of Commons passed the second reading of the Exclusion Bill by a majority of 207 to 128. The following week, rather than allowing the Bill to be read in the House of Lords and risk it becoming law, Charles prorogued Parliament and later dissolved it.

The King had reached an impasse. He could not rule by cabal or council without giving credence to the accusations that he wished for arbitrary government, neither could he call Parliament without the fear of Exclusion. The failures of the Restoration Settlement to define the limits of royal powers were threatening to topple the entire machinery of government.

Shaftesbury was not above manipulating every eventuality to his advantage, and without a parliament he became adept at stirring the popular masses on the streets. In 1679, distracted by the confusions of Exclusion, Parliament forgot to renew the Licensing Act, which provided for censorship of all printed materials, and swiftly the newly free press began to inform, stir and goad the reading public. In addition, a concerted policy of petitioning was organised to force the king to recall Parliament. In January 1680, 16,000 names were delivered to the king from the City of London alone. In the meantime Shaftesbury manoeuvred Charles II's bastard son, the Duke of Monmouth, into the limelight as the potential Protestant candidate for the throne, parading him through London and provincial cities as a hero for the people.

The tumult within London was not without ramifications and St Paul's was thrown into the heat of the turmoil. The cathedral's Rebuilding Commission had been based on a coalition between Church, court, Parliament and City. The Popish Plot and ensuing Exclusion Crisis sowed distrust between each member. The question that was first raised by the Second Rebuilding Act now began to haunt Ludgate Hill: who owned St Paul's? The City was resolutely Whig and anti-Catholic and in 1681 the Lord Mayor rewrote the history of the recent past when he commissioned a new plaque on the base of the Monument, commemorating the Great Fire, linking the conflagration with the popular suspicion that it was a Catholic plot, 'begun and carried on by the treachery and malice of the Popish faction ... for the extirpating the Protestant religion and English Liberties, and to introduce Popery and Slavery'. The Anglican Church was predominantly Tory but was growing suspicious of Charles's promise to be the Defender of the Faith while the king and Parliament were at loggerheads. If the cathedral were to be rebuilt it would have to be part of the process that redrew the ancient relationships of the capital.

John Evelyn watched this debate with growing anxiety and found that he too was in two minds. His brother, George, would sit in Parliament as a Whig, and John made little effort to distance himself from his Whig friends. He had even formed something of a friendship with Shaftesbury himself, both being members of the Royal Society and keen gardeners, as well as the Whiggist Earl of Essex and the future Mayor of London, Sir Robert Clayton. In addition he had become friends with John Locke since they had sat on the Council of Trade and Plantations together in 1674. So although an instinctive Anglican, he could not give his complete support to the Tory faction, and in 1679 he wrote: 'Unless we alter the entire scheme of our late politics, and go upon another hypothesis, we shall run into sudden and inevitable conclusion.'[3]

In the meantime, John Locke kept out of the heart of the tempest, spending much of his time outside London: yet he was always at Shaftesbury's call when the aristocrat needed his advice, riding to Thanet House or to the country, where Shaftesbury plotted far from the gaze of government agents. While Locke's movements suggested that during this period he was remarkably unengaged with the heated events in London, he was doing exactly what a politically engaged philosopher does when events force men to extremes: he was thinking, reading, visiting, talking to friends and formulating ideas.

Using his private journal to think through some of his notions, Locke was actively engaged with the debates of the moment. To question the foundations of faith was to examine the anatomy of power. His essay *The*

Idea We Have of God questioned the basis of original sin, while *Inspiration* explored the centrality of reason to understanding faith. In *Credit, Disgrace*, jotted down in December 1678, he took a measure of the times and the dangers of power: 'where power, and not the good exercise of it, gives reputation, all the injustice, falsehood, violence and injustice and oppression that attains that goes for wisdom and ability'.[4]

Locke was not alone in examining the architecture of authority. In the absence of Parliament the debate thrived in the coffee houses, printing presses and clubs. Here, one question began to emerge above all others: on what power was kingship based? The Whigs were adamant that political power came not from God but from the assent of the people, coordinated between the king, Commons and Lords; while the Tories saw the king's power as divinely ordained and administered through the Anglican Church. Among the sheets and broadsides that began to flood London were a number of pamphlets from the Civil Wars, reheated to stoke the fire. Philip Hunton's 1643 *Treatise of Monarchy* was republished to question the limitations of monarchical power. In response, the dean of St Paul's, Wren's friend William Sancroft, sponsored the publication of *Patriarchia* by the royalist philosopher Robert Filmer, written but never published in the late 1630s, which proposed that kingship was divine and man could not limit the God-given powers of the Crown. The pamphlet was only later published through the patronage of Sancroft, in the 1670s.

Patriarchia spoke of a world as yet untouched by the horrors of civil war, Hobbes's *Leviathan* or the execution of Charles I. Filmer returned to the biblical record and the story of Adam and Eve in the garden of Eden to prove his theory of the Divine Right of Kings by making three powerful observations on why the king had absolute political power over the nation. Man was not born free, he proposed. Instead, Adam was the first patriarch, granted lordship by God over all he surveyed. Secondly, all kings took their descent from him and, thus, all power evolved from God's original grant and remained in perpetuity.

Finally, Filmer applied this notion to the historical narrative of the English constitution, the development of state apparatus and politics. Despite the steady erosion of royal power over the centuries, the king remained beyond common law, for 'as Kingly power is by the law of God, so it hath no inferior law to limit it'.[5] Parliament, Magna Carta and the extension of the governmental machine remained a historical convenience rather than a natural right, which could be withdrawn by the king at any moment he chose. The king had allowed his powers to be shared as a practical necessity rather than as a diminution of his authority. In the end, the Crown remained answerable to God alone, not to the nation.

On 3 February 1680, Locke bought a copy of *Patriarchia* for 4s 6d, along with another work by Filmer, *The Freeholder's Grand Inquest*, before setting out on a journey from Oxford to visit friends in the West Country. This casual purchase would be the starting point for his most powerful and lasting philosophical ideas thus far: *The Two Treatises of Government*, which were published in 1688. A rebuttal of Filmer's proposals gave Locke the ideal opportunity not just to sketch out his ideas in full but also to issue a powerful rallying cry in the call for a new parliament. The *First Treatise* was forged in the heated debate of 1680/81 as Shaftesbury and the Whiggist faction were desperately pushing their policies forward.

As Locke began his *First Treatise of Government*, 'The False Principles and Foundations of Sir Robert Filmer', he took issue with *Patriarchia* and returned to the Book of Genesis to counter Filmer's claims. In particular, he re-examined God's grant of government to Adam at the creation of Eve: 'And thy desire shall be to thy husband, and he shall rule over thee.' To Locke this was a definition not of innate power but of property. He also examined God's curse to Adam: 'In the sweat of thy face, shalt thou eat thy bread,' in which man was cursed with the punishment of labour. Neither of these texts, Locke asserted, contained the presumption of governance: 'God sets him to work of his living, and seems rather to give him a spade into his hand, to subdue the earth, than a sceptre, to rule over its inhabitants.'[6]

Filmer's biblical source offered no foundations for divine rule. Locke insisted that authority and property existed on the basis of 'reason', which came not from God's grant but from the act of creation itself: 'For the desire, strong desire of preserving his life and having been planted in him as a principle of action by God himself, reason, which was the voice of God in him ... and thus man's property in the creatures was founded upon the right he had to make use of those things that were necessary or useful to his being.'[7] The reasonable pursuit of the preservation of the individual, not divine ordination, was the foundation of inheritance and the family. As a result, natural law, not the authority of the Bible, commanded politics. Government was not a blessing bestowed upon the chosen but was born out of the universal desire for security, for the benefit of all men.

If power was not a divine gift, who, then, had the right to rule? On this occasion, however, Locke, having asked the right question, fumbled his response. As Parliament was to be recalled, it was the task of the MPs and Lords to find the correct constitutional solution, not the musing of a philosopher who could not contemplate the consequences. Events, however, would force Locke to make his own mind up, and it would only be a matter of months before he found his answer.

In the autumn of 1680, Parliament met again and once more the Whigs attempted to drive an Exclusion Bill through the House. The Bill was passed by the Commons but was halted in the Lords, which was skilfully manipulated by the king's party. Shaftesbury tried another tack and proposed that Charles divorce his barren queen, remarry and father a Protestant heir. This cat-and-mouse game soon began to pall and Parliament was again prorogued in January 1681 and told to reconvene once more, far from London, in the royalist stronghold of Oxford. If Charles could not get the MPs he wanted in Parliament, he could at least hold Parliament in a place where he held the upper hand.

The Oxford Parliament would be the endgame of the Exclusion Crisis, and both sides came well prepared. In the build-up to March 1681, Shaftesbury and Locke wrote 'instructions to the Knights of the County ... for their conduct in Parliament', giving advice on how the Whig MPs should prepare for the confrontation. Locke was also set the task of organising accommodation for his patron and his team, which he found at Balliol College and in the house of the mathematician John Wallis. His own college, Christ Church, was requisitioned by the king. The MPs arrived in February in a blaze of pomp and spectacle. The king entered with an army of guards while the Whigs walked through the city shouting, 'No Popery, No Slavery', wearing ribbons in their hats. The London hacks and pamphleteers also moved to Oxford to follow the story and stoke the fire of debate.

The parliament finally sat on 21 March and the king promised to hear the appeals of his people, and to find a way of protecting Protestantism, if James took the throne. Shaftesbury, in the makeshift House of Lords located in the University Geometry School, raised Exclusion once more, and the issue was swiftly adopted by the Commons. The king, rather than ending the debate, allowed it to run its course, knowing that while the issue united the Whigs, any possible attempt to find a solution would only split the loose coalition. The Whigs did not want James on the throne but they could not agree on who they would prefer to replace him. The king's illegitimate son, Monmouth, was offered by one faction, while another favoured James's daughter, Mary. Others were bold enough to favour a republic. After six days, divisions began to appear and there was 'a general despair that nothing will be done for the protestant settlement and security'.[8] Two days later Charles dissolved both houses and sent them packing. He had won the debate by doing nothing at all.

Events following the Oxford Parliament were swift and effective, turning England into a nation of extremes. Charles II had made certain that he could rule without Parliament. His dues from the customs and excise, the money pouring into the Port of London from the colonies, steadied his coffers and were supplemented by a new pension from France which delivered 4,300,000 livres between 1681 and 1685. The Whigs could no longer rely on the king to call Parliament for the raising of taxes, and therefore lost the one forum where they could effect any legitimate changes.

Charles went on a counteroffensive, not only carrying a stick to beat the ringleaders of the Whigs but also learning from their methods. Opposition was driven underground or raised high on the gibbet. Spies infiltrated the Whig Party and even Locke was shadowed by one false friend, the Reverend Humphrey Prideux, the librarian at Christ Church (who also happened to be a friend of John Evelyn's), who reported back on the philosopher's movements. The king deployed his own propaganda machine and 'counter writers' to appeal to the mob, Roger L'Estrange became the Crown's chief spin doctor, with a commission to marry the mob to the king's cause, for, as he observed: 'Tis the press that made 'um mad, and the press must set 'um right again.'[9] The printing presses began to sing a new tune. The Tories presented themselves as defenders of the nation in opposition to the sedition of the Whigs, who wished to revive the Civil Wars. The Tories gained the high ground with the rallying cry of 'No return to 41'.

In July, the constables finally came for Shaftesbury. He was found at Thanet House, where he was arrested. The authorities confiscated his papers and he was sent once again to the Tower on charges of high treason.

London, however, remained the sorest thorn in Charles's side and the Crown dealt with the City with ruthless efficiency. The City's obstinacy was confirmed when Shaftesbury stood in the London Courts on 24 November

1681. The Grand Jury had been packed by sympathisers who judged the case unproven and Shaftesbury was released. In response, Charles issued a writ of *Quo Warranto* to the Corporation. The writ questioned on what authority the Corporation Charter rested, claiming that the City had broken its agreement with the Crown, and should therefore lose its status and its political power be reduced to that of a small village.

A hearing of the King's Bench was arranged for February 1683, and this time the king had packed the judges with his own men. The City was found guilty of breaking its charter, forcing the Corporation to plea for a pardon. Charles's agreement was swift but came with strings attached: no Lord Mayor, aldermen, sheriff, recorder, common sergeant or coroner could be elected without the king's approval. The king could veto Lord Mayors and even appoint his own if needed. Also, the Council of Aldermen should be able to veto appointments and JPs were to be appointed by the king. The City had been defanged and would cause the king no further concern.

The Whigs responded to this Tory rampage with caution. One of the most peculiar documents seized by the authorities from Shaftesbury's house in July 1681 was *De Morbu Gallicus*, 'The French Disease', a book on syphilis by John Locke, but no such document remains among the philosopher's papers. The real identity of this work was, in fact, far more infectious, for hidden behind a vulgar pun on the pathology of Gallic absolutism was writing that, if discovered, would have sent both Locke and Shaftesbury to the gallows: the *Second Treatise of Government*, later entitled *An Essay Concerning the True Original, Extent, and End of Civil Government*.

The *Second Treatise* goes farther than the first in answering the question Locke had fudged: who should we obey? After Oxford, the Whigs recognised that Charles was not about to recall a parliament and new methods of seeking change had to be found. The one thing Locke had tried all his life to avoid – rebellion – seemed the only resort to save the cause. Locke's tract was not just an argument for the rights of civil government over monarchy, but also a declaration of revolution.

At the dawn of time, Locke proposed, man was born equal in a state of Nature, in a world where property and inheritance did not exist. This right to freedom remained inalienable. As the population grew and the demands upon the land increased, money was accumulated and a commercial society evolved. Only with the rise of commerce was there a necessity for a government formed by consent and the agreement of the majority to be ruled by the few to protect property. The power of the governors, therefore, was a grant donated by the people as long as the government remained within the laws of the land. Tyrannical behaviour broke the bonds of government, and once the constitution had been broken, Locke defended the right of individuals, or society as a whole, to change the government by unconstitutional means:

> Whensoever therefore the legislative shall transgress this fundamental rule of society: and either by ambition, fear, folly, or corruption, endeavour to grasp themselves, or put into the hands of any other, an absolute power over the lives, liberties, and estates of the people; by this breach of trust they forfeit the power the people had put into their hand for quite contrary ends, and it devolves to the people, who have a right to resume their original liberty, and, by the establishment of a new legislative, (such as they shall think fit) provide for their own safety and security.[10]

In a final battle cry, Locke asked: who shall be the judge of tyrants? He answered, 'To this I reply: the people shall be judge.'[11]

By 1682, Locke was immersed in the subversive underground campaign against Charles II. In October the previous year, Prideux had reported to his spymaster: 'The Pamphlet entitled *No Protestant Plot* is with us, and John Locke is said to be the author of it.' In the meantime, Locke tried to give the impression of avoiding all involvement, as his shadow reported: 'not a word of politics comes from him, nothing of news or anything else concerning our present affairs, as if he were not at all concerned in them'. But Prideux was not convinced: 'I fancy there are projects afoot.'[12]

Locke was, in fact, slowly spiralling into plots of revolution, and even regicide. In the summer of 1682, Shaftesbury planned an uprising to be led by Monmouth, but when the plans fell apart the noble fled to the West Country. At the same time, another group of aristocratic conspirators were plotting the assassination of both Charles and James on their return from the races at Newmarket. Again the plot failed. On 28 November 1682, dressed as a Presbyterian minister, the disgraced Shaftesbury was forced to flee for his life to Holland. Within weeks, he had died from the still-extant liver complaint that Locke had first treated in 1667.

The plotting continued after Shaftesbury's death, yet the degree of

Locke's complicity is uncertain. In the first months of 1683 the 'Council of Six', a group of Whigs, concocted a rebellion, while another group led by Robert Wise devised the Rye House Plot, an assassination attempt which also came to nothing. The Council of Six planned a coup while also drawing up a new manifesto, which may have drawn strongly on Locke's arguments for rebellion in the *Second Treatise*. But the workings of the Council were soon betrayed and the plotters arrested.

It suddenly became clear to Locke that his life was in jeopardy. His first reaction was to dispose of his work and he destroyed many papers, including Shaftesbury's autobiography. As Sergeant Richard Holloway, a government informer, reported: 'in a clandestine way several handbaskets of papers are carried to Mr James Tyreell's house at Oakley ... or to Mr Pawling's, the mercer's, house in Oxford'.[13] As the plotters were being investigated in London and one by one being led to the gallows, Locke left Oxford, where he was being closely watched, withdrew to the West Country, and then fled to Holland. He arrived in Rotterdam on 7 September 1683, carrying an unfinished copy of his *Two Treatise*.

THE TWILIGHT OF THE KING

The failure of the Whiggish movement during the Exclusion Crisis gave Charles II the opportunity to be what he had always wanted to be: a Baroque Prince. No longer tied to the whims of Parliament and with enough money flowing in from excise and customs as well as the French, Charles could finally create an image of the English Crown that would rival that of the French Sun King, Louis XIV. At court a new rigid code of conduct was enforced and access to the king became increasingly regimented. Having fallen out of love with London and exhausted by the threats of assassination, he altered the terms of his kingship; where once he strolled through the newly sculpted St James's Park beside the huddled mess of Whitehall, showing himself to his public, he now retreated from the rabble, demanded distance, evoking power in his inaccessibility.

In the winter of 1683, the Surveyor-General, Christopher Wren, was commissioned to build a splendid baroque palace to rival Versailles. Wren set out to purchase enough land for the purpose in the Hampshire city of Winchester, once the capital of Alfred the Great's Wessex. By the beginning of the building season an army of London masons and builders had decamped to the countryside and work was started. Speed was everything, for the sickening king reported, 'if it be possible to be done in one year, I wil have it so, for a year is a great deal in my life'.[14]

Wren's palace was to be as French as an English palace could be, surrounded by sumptuous gardens. The building stood on top of a hill looking down towards the ancient city, surrounding three sides of a broad courtyard. Like Versailles, the palace would be not just a quiet retreat for the royal family but a seat of government far from – perhaps in opposition to – the bustle of London. There would be sixty rooms with the king's apartments in the south-eastern corner, comprising chamber, privy chamber, drawing room, bedchamber and cabinet, clustered around an inner courtyard. In the corresponding north-western corner were the apartments for the queen, the Duke of York and the king's current French mistress. In front of the palace was elegant housing for the courtiers and ministers. The front of the building was designed to reflect robust majesty and distance, with none of the elaborate frippery of Versailles.

Between 1683 and 1685, Wren visited the site on numerous occasions, his expense account claiming for seventy-eight days on-site. For such a busy man this showed his dedication to the project but also the need to rely on clear designs and plans, and he had a scale model produced to show his intentions. The surveyor was also fortunate to have hired within his Architect's Office a young draughtsman, Nicholas Hawksmoor, whose drawings set out Wren's hopes on paper for the builders while the architect was absent. The assistant would become increasingly important within the surveyor's team. After the foundations were laid throughout 1683, work on raising the walls began early the next year. By March 1685, although the project was seriously over budget, progress had been so rapid that the lead was being readied for the roof. All that remained was for the king himself to move in for this to become the powerhouse of the Stuarts to rival London itself.

Despite all the distractions in Winchester, by 1685 there were definite signs of progress on St Paul's Cathedral. The upheavals of the Popish Plot and the Exclusion Crisis had put St Paul's in a difficult situation. The grant of the coal tax from the 1675 Act was starting to look paltry in comparison to the real costs of the project – offering only £4,000 to £5,000 a year when Wren was easily spending more than £13,000 – and Wren was in desperate need of more cash. The surveyor could not go to his newly prosperous patron, Charles II, without fear of the City. The Church was just as unforthcoming – it could not trust the king, or his brother the future monarch, for fear of delivering up the cathedral to France. After the debacle of the Oxford Parliament in 1681, there was no house to grant any more money.

Wren became increasingly dependent on private subscriptions and gifts to maintain the smooth running of the rebuilding. In a meeting called in 1677, the extent of private giving was made public and shown to be sorely lacking. But who would give money to such a project? It was then decided to appeal to the nation at large to dip into their pockets, and the Bishop of London, Henry Compton, wrote to all the churches and councils to ask for help. Compton attempted to promote a new image of St Paul's outside the disturbances of the times, placing the city cathedral at the centre of the nation, and in opposition to Rome. It was a smart piece of rebranding with which many could agree, but the cathedral would not be drawn away from the political turmoils for long.

This would find particular focus in the case of Stephen College, a master joiner and known pamphleteer, who had worked with Wren at St Stephen's Walbrook and who had many companions on Ludgate Hill. College had travelled to Oxford in 1680 to be part of the jamboree surrounding the parliament. He had gained a reputation as 'an active and hot man',[15] for reading his satires and poems in coffee houses and taverns. At Oxford he was particularly proud of his newest broadside, *A Ra-Ree Show*, which became a favourite among the Whigs, and pictured Charles II as a fairground act, out to rob the citizenry of their liberty. After the failures at Oxford, College returned to London, and it did not take long for the authorities to exact their revenge. He was arrested in July 1681 and tried before the City Bench, who judged the case *ignoramus*. Dissatisfied by the verdict, the authorities decided that as his crime had been perpetrated in both London and Oxford, and seeing that they could not get a conviction in the capital, they would rerun the trial in loyalist Oxford.

The case became a cause célèbre, and many journeyed up to Oxford to offer their support and defend the Whiggish cause. The trial, however, was rigged, and College was convicted of treason, and executed two weeks later on 31 August at Oxford Castle. He almost instantly became a martyr for the cause – 'the Protestant joiner'. On Ludgate Hill, this personal attack on one of their own coincided with the king's attempts to reduce the powers of the City with the writ of *Quo Warranto* in 1683. Interest in progress on

The scene on Ludgate Hill in the 1680s

the cathedral began to dim, and there was even growing resentment against the building that represented the powers of the Crown within the city walls.

Work at St Paul's was also hampered by the weather. In the midst of a small 'Ice Age', each winter froze the City solid so that work became impossible during the bitterest months. Evelyn would record the joys of the frost fairs that congregated upon the solid Thames, while also bemoaning how the cold damaged his garden at Sayes Court. The winter of 1683/84 was particularly hard: the flow of the river was slowed down by the arches of London Bridge and to the west fields of ice began to form that could support 'some thousands of people'. In the New Year, booths and stalls were placed on the river by the watermen, who were missing out on valuable income while the coachmen drove their carriages over the ice as if still on the road. Soon a whole town had gathered on the ice, leading from the Temple Stairs to the south bank. As Evelyn reported on 24 January: 'Coaches plied from Westminster to the Temple, and from several other stairs to and fro, as in the streets, sleds, sliding with skates, a bull-baiting, horse and coach-races, puppet plays and interludes, cooks, tippling, and other lewd places, so that it seemed to be a bacchanalian triumph, or carnival on the water'.[16] The fair lasted until the second week of February.

Throughout the winter the whole St Paul's work site had to be boarded up to protect the structure as the rain would freeze and drive cracks through the stone. When swirling snow found its way into the interior it had to be quickly brushed away before it melted and attacked the brick vaulting below. Already some of the brickwork had had to be replaced because of such damage. One Edisbury of Deptford proposed an ingenious solution, offering his own invention, Glacis, which sealed the floor of the choir. There were also problems with drainage. The rain would collect on Ludgate Hill and bring silt and debris down the hillside and the local streets. With only a basic sewerage system in place, the locals found their homes flooded and their newly paved streets a mud-strewn mess. Thus Wren was forced to negotiate with the community to find new methods of sewerage and drainage, which also had to be paid for out of the Rebuilding Fund.

Yet with each spring the churchyard filled again with industry, and behind Inigo Jones's old portico the new cathedral was beginning to emerge. In fear that the cash-strapped commission would call a halt at any moment, Wren directed operations on all points of the structure. Rather than follow the recommendations of the commission by focusing on the construction bit by bit, he was attempting to raise the whole building in one go. The walls of the nave that would connect Jones's façade with the crossing point of the dome now reached ground level; the choir walls at the east end of the site rose over thirty feet into the air, while the carvers had begun to give the exterior its distinctive form. The eight strong pillars on which the dome would rest were almost near completion. In addition, he had deviated far from his approved Warrant Design. The transepts on the north and south sides of the building were now curved rather than flat, perhaps to mirror the curve of the dome, which had yet to rise above the building. More importantly, the walls of the east end were very different to Wren's original approved plans.

By 1685, the choir walls rose two storeys high. Inside, the side aisle walls had been completed, and Wren was ready to issue a contract for the carving of the elaborate, curved cornice at the east end of the choir. From the outside it was clear that Wren's designs for the surface of the wall had been inspired by the Banqueting Hall at Whitehall, Inigo Jones's masterpiece celebrating the majesty of the Stuart dynasty. The choice of details was deliberate: there was no better model to represent the relationship between the role of the king as a Defender of the Faith and the first Anglican cathedral to be built since the Reformation. But this was not the only meaning that Wren hoped to present. For St Paul's did not belong to the Crown alone.

The walls of the east end held another secret. Seen from the outside, the first storey contained a bank of windows that allowed light into the body of the choir. On the second storey, however, the four windows, divided by double pilasters, were blank, carved stone rather than glass. The wall was, in fact, a screen that hid another of Wren's features which would inform the identity of St Paul's. From the exterior, the east end of the cathedral appeared like a basilica, a single-height, two-storey building such as the Temple of Peace in Rome. From the interior, however, the cathedral offered a different experience – recreating a traditional Gothic form, with a high central choir with flanking aisles. With a deft hand, Wren had been able to design a Gothic choir hidden within the casing of a Roman temple.

Thus the surveyor was able to accommodate both the ancient and the modern at the same time. From the outside the cathedral was a thoroughly modern building; from inside it conformed to the traditional demands of the Anglican hierarchy; and in one design Wren was able to express the three different identities of St Paul's. Second, the false screen added downward thrust which would later support the dome. Third, the design created a well between the screen and the actual wall of the choir. Within this gap Wren constructed a series of windows.

Throughout his life, Wren had been fascinated by ways of seeing and the science of light. His experiments with telescopes and microscopes as a young man had educated him in the New Philosophy. For Wren, light not only illuminated the perfection of geometry, 'but also itself represented the gift of Reason'.[17] St Paul's would be a cathedral flooded with light, and unlike the tenebral Gothic spaces with their long shadows and stained glass, it would remind the worshipper that 'the gift of reason' came from God.

As the walls of the east end were rising on Ludgate Hill, John Locke was making his way to Rotterdam, and then Amsterdam, protective of his seditious writings, which would certainly have led him to the gallows if uncovered. Locke had proposed that all authority derived not from divine ordination but from the gift of reason, the voice of God within each individual. Although in 1685 they appeared at opposite ends of the political spectrum, this was the same voice that Wren wished to embody in the choir of his new temple. Both Wren and Locke were in the process of questioning the authority of the past and were painstakingly rebuilding a new settlement.

In the first week of February 1685, Charles II suffered an injury to his ankle. That night he slept fitfully, but in the morning was pale and spoke with a croaky voice. As he was being shaved he suffered convulsions. It was decided to bleed him while his Lord Chamberlain, Ailesbury, rushed to fetch James, Duke of York, who, in his haste, arrived at the scene wearing one slipper and one shoe. Charles knew that he was dying, yet over the next six days was bled, prescribed draughts and medicines, potions to make him sneeze, and plasters to draw out the poison from his feet. Yet the medicine of the day probably did as much harm to the patient as good. He also had to suffer a stream of visitors to Whitehall, who came with false concern to make their last homage. The Establishment prayed for the survival of the king but also made the right moves towards his successor; the Lord Mayor of London enquired after the state of the king and also promised obedience to James, Duke of York.

The question of succession swiftly became a violent whisper. On Thursday, the French ambassador visited the king and, shocked by what he saw, encouraged James to take the reins of power to ensure that he and not Charles's illegitimate son, the Duke of Monmouth, or the Protestant Dutch ruler, William, Duke of Orange, the husband of Princess Mary, took the throne. Yet the French ambassador had not finished his work. Talking to the king's mistress, the Duchess of Portsmouth, the ambassador elicited the confession that Charles might convert to Catholicism on his deathbed. The duke then asked his brother whether he wanted a priest. 'Yes,' the king whispered, 'with all my heart,'[18] and a plot was hatched to slip the Scotch cleric, John Hudleston, disguised in wig and cassock, into the king's chamber, where he would hear the patient's confession and administer the Eucharist. Through the night, Charles made his farewells to family and friends, and in the morning he fell into a coma and then died before noon.

Everything the Whigs had fought for – the hiatus of the Exclusion Crisis and the hysteria of the Popish Plot – had come to nothing: Charles named his brother as his natural successor. James was swift to take hold of the reins of power, but he was a very different man to his elder brother. James promised to work within the law; he made promises to France to uphold the alliance and took measures to ensure that the depleted Whigs would not rise up once more in the first hours of the new reign. He also uttered the right noises towards the Church of England and promised to defend and support it. He kept the Privy Council almost as he had inherited it and hoped to give the impression of continuity with his brother's reign.

Yet all was not quite as it seemed. Within a week James was openly worshipping at the Catholic chapel at St James's Palace, and at his coronation on St George's Day, 23 April, there was no sacrament. Rumours also began to circulate that popish priests and recusants were being released from prisons.

Following his coronation, James called back Parliament after four years in the wilderness. The house sat on 22 May, with great celebration, which Evelyn watched, listening to the king's speech, which was interrupted at every pause by cries of support. The new monarch took the opportunity to ask for a fixed annual income, and the revenue was granted immediately. One could hardly have imagined a more compliant group of politicians. The house had been packed by Tories, who, although as fervently anti-Catholic as the Whigs, were for the continuation of the monarchy at the head of the Anglican Church. Even the few remaining Whigs within the house cheered the king. Needless to say, James prorogued Parliament only six weeks after he had so courteously opened it. The king had his money, so he had no need for politicians.

One excuse for the suspension was the arrival of the Duke of Monmouth at Lyme Regis, leading an army of rebels who called the illegitimate prince the true King of England. Monmouth was living in a dream that had grown ragged since the days of Shaftesbury's plotting in 1682, but the image of his forces marching through the West Country, attracting new recruits as they entered every new town, only showed how shaky were the foundations of James's rule. The uprising was short-lived and the punishment of the rebels brutal. At Sedgemoor, on 5 July, 200 of Monmouth's men were killed, while nearly a thousand were cut down as they retreated; 100 were summarily executed by the army on capture.

In the following Bloody Assizes sent to suppress the region, presided over by the dreaded Judge George Jeffreys, all 1,500 prisoners were found guilty, 250 were executed and 850 were sentenced to ten years' imprisonment working as slaves in the West Indies. Monmouth, once he was captured, was given a show trial. He was executed with spectacular brutality, the executioner taking five strokes of the axe to sever the head from the shoulders. The horrified crowd had to be held back by the guards as they threatened to lynch the executioner for his cruelty. Evelyn hoped that this would be the end of the tumult: 'Blessed be God, the knot was happily broken, and a fair prospect of tranquillity for the future, if we reform, be thankful, and make a right use of this mercy!'[19] He was proved to be woefully wrong.

Looks Like a Revolution

N ineteen years after the fire of 1666, London had been reborn. As John Woodward, Gresham Lecturer in Physics, reported to Wren:

> the medieval plan had been substantially transformed into an elegant modern city of red brick and white stone. So many thousand houses, of even private citizens, built in such a manner as to render them not only more convenient ... but even superior in design and architecture to the palaces of princes ... By means of the enlargements of streets, of the great plenty of good water conveyed to all parts, of the common sewers and other like contrivances, such provision is made for free access and passage of air, of sweetness, for cleanliness and for salubrity, this not only the finest but the most healthy city in the world.[1]

Yet the transformation was as much the work of speculators such as Nicholas Barbon as it was of the Surveyor-General.

By the 1680s Barbon and his associates had their fingers in developments all over the metropolis and were turning the city into something never seen before. At Piccadilly, where Clarendon House and Berkeley House stood, the work of the refined aristocrats was being transformed. In 1675, Clarendon House had been sold off to the second Duke of Albemarle following the fall of the Chancellor, and after a disastrous fire, the land finally fell into the hands of a syndicate of speculators including Barbon's associate, the goldsmith John Hinde, and Sir Thomas Bond.

In a similar fashion, following Lord Berkeley's death, the aristocrat's wife was forced to develop the land. Evelyn was particularly struck by the loss of such noble houses: 'I could not but deplore that sweet place (by far the most noble gardens, courts, and accommodations, stately porticoes etc. anywhere about the town) should be so much straitened & turned into tenements.' But he was also clear as to the reason for doing so: 'my lady Berkeley's resolution for letting out her ground also for so excessive a price as was offered, advancing near 1000 pounds per Ann: in mere ground rents; to such a mad intemperance was the age come of building about a city'.[2]

The two great houses that had signalled the rebirth of London as a European capital were demolished and plans were afoot to convert the prime real estate into tenements and profit. Yet crisis struck. The land had been bought for too much and the syndicate was forced to mortgage it off. Hinde was particularly unlucky and soon found himself in prison for his debts. His failure was proof that in a competitive market, speculation could bring tremendous gains, but also ruin. There were, however, plenty of other candidates who would step into his shoes and take their chances in the volatile economy, and from the plot where these houses once stood was developed Bond Street, Dover Street, Albemarle Street and the first estates of Mayfair.

Development was not restricted to the west of the city. Close to the eastern gates, leading towards the port, the open fields of the old Spital Hospital and Henry VIII's Artillery Ground were being churned up to house the burgeoning merchants and traders. By the 1680s development had gone so far that it reached the hamlet of Bethnal Green, a mile to the east. This region was particularly popular with nonconformists, Jews and Huguenots, as it was outside the City's jurisdiction yet close enough to the heart of the trading capital for business. Soon there was a noisy call for the creation of a market in Spitalfields.

The previous decade Wren had tried his best to stop the eastward spread of the city, but the potential of profit was too strong. Barbon could not refuse an opportunity like this. He bought the lease on the house of the Duke of Devonshire in 1675. Devonshire Square was a handsome development, but Barbon's sights would reach farther, and in 1681, when the Crown decided to sell off the adjacent Old Artillery Field, Barbon secured the land, partly under his own name and partly in association with George Bradbury and Edward Noell, two lawyers who acted with Barbon on a number of deals. Barbon was characteristically slow in paying the purchase money and had to be chased twice by the Treasury. In the meantime he made sure to lease out the plots as quickly as possible for development, to a staggering seventeen different builders, all with separate contracts and terms.

The builders, who had completed the redevelopment of the city within the walls, now had turned into speculators, and were no longer seen as the saviours of the capital but accused of wreaking havoc, and by their selfish endeavours delivering the metropolis to the faceless mob. In Parliament, there were debates on whether a tax should be levied on all new building to restrict the rates of expansion. Nicholas Barbon was so concerned that he decided to tackle these questions in one of his rare writings, *An Apology for the Builder*, which he published in 1685.

An Apology was the opposite of an architectural tract, as the author made plain in his introduction: 'To write of architecture and its several parts, of situation, platforms of buildings, and the quality of materials, with their dimensions and ornaments: to discourse of the several orders of Columns … were to transcribe a Folio from Vitruvius, and others: and but mispend the reader and writer's time'.[3] His previous work had plainly shown that he displayed little interest in the debates on ornament and form; for him, building was concerned with money and profit.

The growth of the city was natural, Barbon proposed, and it expanded in response to demand. London was growing, as apprentices and young married couples entered the metropolis to find work and needed to be housed. The life of the city, he argued, was to be found in the continued influx of youth into the labour market. Building constituted one of the main industries of the city and fed and employed large sections of the community, and as new houses were created on the edge of the city, this increased the rents of the dwellings within the centre.

An Apology for the Builder also proposed that this development aided the nation as a whole: for the rural communities it provided a market for goods and a valve to release the pressure of the local population surplus. For the king it offered more revenue in the form of taxes, while creating labour for the restless citizenry. For trade it opened up new markets. Thus the burgeoning metropolis benefited all and promised a capital, built from private rather than royal coffers, that would become the envy of all nations: 'the artists of the Age have already made the City of London the metropolis of Europe, and if it be compared for the number of good Houses, for its many and large Piazzas, for its richness of inhabitants, it must be allowed the largest, best built, and richest City in the world'.[4]

The metropolis found ample space to grow to the north. By the 1680s, development had reached as far as Holborn, where in the 1640s the earth defences of the Civil War, the lines of communication, created a natural barrier to expansion. Much of the conversion of Bloomsbury Fields had been orchestrated by Lady Russell, whose husband had been executed following his involvement in the exclusionist Rye House Plot of 1683. Following her husband's death, Lady Russell had abandoned the court and vowed to 'converse with none but lawyers and accountants',[5] as she revived the family's fortunes. Where once, in the words of one visitor, 'The fields bordering on this place are very pleasant and dry grounds for walking and improving of health',[6] the Bloomsbury estate, leading up to Holborn, now became a building site.

No earthworks would halt the progress of the appetites of speculation for ever, and in 1683 Barbon negotiated for the plot north of High Holborn, Red Lion Fields. A no man's land famous for its inn, the Red Lion, it was believed to be the site where Cromwell and his generals had been buried after their posthumous humiliations. It is also beside these fields that the blind poet John Milton spent a few months after the Restoration. Barbon hoped to convert the fields into a splendid piazza that would be the pride of the speculator's portfolio.

By 1684, he had already started preparing the ground for building before he leased out the plots to subcontractors or lease-holding builders. The operation immediately caused a stir. The land cut across the royal thoroughfare that went from Whitehall to Newmarket, therefore instantly gaining the attention of Wren as Surveyor-General. The speculator showed his contempt for the usual niceties by using the king's ditch for his refuse tip, and even threatening to break down the King's Gate. The legal process was slow in combating Barbon's rapacious work and the Surveyor-General found himself powerless to censure the speculator.

Barbon also went out of his way to intimidate the local populace – the lawyers of Gray's Inn Field – who had complained about the disturbance and, in particular, he discarded 'severall laystalls there of garbage and offalls from severall marketts, sufficient to endanger the bringing of a plague into the neighbourhood'.[7] In addition, as the contemporary writer Narcissus Luttrell reported, on 10 June there was a scuffle between the lawyers and Barbon's workforce: 'the workmen assaulted the gentlemen and threw bricks at them again; so sharp engagement ensued, but the gentlemen routed them at the last and brought away one or two of the workmen to Graie's Inn; in this skirmish one or two of the gentlemen and servants of the House were hurt, and several of the workmen'.[8]

The case inevitably ended in court but as soon as judgement was passed on Barbon, the local magistrate and constable found themselves counter-sued by the speculator, and had to be indemnified by the Treasury. The case went all the way to the Attorney-General in an attempt to produce warrants to enforce 'the suppression of Dr Barbon and his men from committing any insolence in their late riotous meetings in Red Lyon Fields and to prevent from annoying his Majesty's subjects'.[9] But the warrants were never produced and little seemed to suppress Barbon.

Once the utilities – water, sewerage, roads – had been provided for, Barbon set about leasing out his plots to other builders. From the corners of the main square, roads led off in a star formation, leading to the secondary streets of the development. He split the streets into uniform frontages and leased them out on terms of forty, fifty, sixty and sixty-one years. Between 1686 and 1688, he leased out every plot in the scheme. In many cases, the transactions were mind-bogglingly complex.

In 1687, there were further complaints from nearby Christchurch Hospital concerning the effect the building had upon the supply of water that ran down nearby Lamb's Conduit Street. A survey was called for and a report drawn up. The report was not good and had to be passed over to the king's authorities, the royal attorney and the Solicitor-General. Barbon then claimed that the hospital did not own the conduit and therefore the supply could be shared. To prove this he built a large house and a wall to encase the stream. The stand-off evolved into a convoluted argument about ancient grants that lasted until 1690, and involved everyone from the Lord Chancellor to the Commissioners of Sewers. In the meantime Barbon went right ahead with his development. He eventually offered to pay for new sewer pipes for the hospital, for far less than he gained for the privilege of building.

Unlike St James's or Bloomsbury Square, Barbon's piazza was aimed not at aristocrats but at the better sort of City businessman, in particular the local professionals, lawyers and doctors. Inside the houses, Barbon provided everything for the emerging middle classes. He standardised even these interiors down to the smallest detail, but had clearly found his market. The room plan did not deviate from his previous template: each house had three floors and a basement, following the scheme of the First Rebuilding Act of 1667.

Barbon had, however, learnt his lesson concerning interior design. The attention to detail in interior decoration showed that the speculator made efforts to accommodate the tastes of polite society, who wished to show their new status in conspicuous consumption. There was panelling in the major rooms and the balustrades of the principal staircase were restrained and classical, prefiguring the elegant simplicity of the Georgian town house. Every detail of his buildings reflected the rise of a consumer culture, as Roger North observed: 'his talent lay more in economising ground for advantage and the little contrivances of a family than the more noble aims of architecture'.[10]

In 1686 Barbon's eye for profit went even farther when he negotiated with a Mr Thompson, who had bought the lease to land north of Gray's Inn Road, originally belonging to the Bedford Corporation. Thompson had hoped to develop new housing along Theobalds Road but had hit a spot of bother: the land interfered with the water supply to the new neighbourhoods of Holborn. Through serpentine negotiations Barbon gained this estate as well as others near by belonging to Rugby School. As ever Barbon soon found himself in arrears, unable to pay rent to the Corporation, but on this occasion they would not be fobbed off with his promises. Barbon offered some land in exchange to cover his costs, but the Corporation was wary of Barbon's reputation and demanded cash. The speculator had over-speculated, his assets were sunk in investments and he found that he did not have enough liquid cash. At the height of the building boom of the 1680s, he was stretched to his limits.

THE KING AND THE CITY

Meanwhile, the unfinished St Paul's was a mass of scaffold and ropes, and was falling victim to the uncertainties of James II's reign. On the king's succession Parliament was called and one of the least likely people to stand for the House of Commons was Christopher Wren. Thus far, the Surveyor-General had assiduously kept out of politics. On the succession, however, he had been encouraged by the king, who knew that the architect would support the Crown, to stand as MP for Plympton St Maurice, Devon (a place Wren never visited). Wren would also enter Parliament in the hope of rescuing his cathedral.

By the terms of the 1675 2nd Rebuilding Act, the grant of coal tax was to expire in 1687, and if Wren could not get Parliament to vote for an extension or an increase in the tax, St Paul's would never be completed. In Parliament Wren was joined by two peers in the House of Lords: the Archbishop of Canterbury, his old patron and friend, William Sancroft, and the Bishop of London, Henry Compton, with whom Wren had travelled in 1665, viewing the chateaux of France. All three took advantage of the voting of the royal revenue to push their demands forward. Wren, however, was also called to sit on a number of parliamentary commissions, none concerned with architecture, including investigations on the import of candle tallow, and the regulation of hackney cabs.

It was fortunate that the St Paul's team were able to gain quick support and the duty on coal tax was extended until 1700, before Parliament was prorogued after six weeks. In addition, they gained permission to borrow on the duty's security. This meant that by 1687 the commission could expect an annual income of £18,500. For the short term, the money problems of the cathedral could be allayed and work on Ludgate Hill could progress.

The Act allowed the cathedral to borrow money but attracting sponsors or negotiating loans was not an easy task, and it became increasingly difficult as James's reign progressed. St Paul's could hardly be considered a good investment. The stop on the Exchequer made all loans to the Crown, even if only a royal commission, a dangerous speculation, and especially when offering an interest rate of only 6 per cent. Wren hoped that he could raise £4,000 but the response was weak and he even had to open his own purse, passing £1,000 to the fund under the name of his housekeeper, Miss Mary Dominick.

In addition, London was growing suspicious of the king. Following the suppression of the Monmouth Rebellion, rather than disbanding his standing army, James increased the number of troops, and by the end of 1685 had nearly twenty thousand soldiers, armed and garrisoned about the country. James claimed that the failures of the local militia during the uprising proved the necessity of a permanent force, but others saw a more insidious cause. The king had also begun to distribute personal dispensations to his co-religionists, circumventing the strictures of the Test Act, and he placed them throughout the army so that by stealth the feared standing army was becoming riven with Catholicism. In the English imagination, Catholicism bred absolutism, and with Parliament prorogued between July and November of that year, it was difficult not to feel haunted by the spectre of martial law.

Things came to a head when Parliament was briefly recalled in November and James asked for more money to fund his army. The Bill passed the Commons, which had been packed and selected to ensure support for the king's cause, but as it was read in the House of Lords it came up against strong opposition. The Bishop of London, Henry Compton, who had welcomed the accession of James II, spoke for all the Anglican bishops when he condemned the issue of dispensations to Catholics and the infiltration of papists within the offices of government. Compton was not alone in his fears, and the previously compliant Earl of Halifax added his concerns: 'If the king, might by his authority, supersede such a law … it is vain to think of law anymore. The government would become arbitrary and absolute'.[11] This was a Conservative revolution in the making, and within ten months of taking the throne, James had begun to alienate the Anglican Tory establishment which had once defended his right to the throne against the exclusionists.

Elsewhere in London, similar signs of revolt were to be found. On the day that James prorogued Parliament the Anglican cleric, Samuel Johnson, faced a sham trial in which he was deprived of his living in punishment for his seditious tract 'An Humble and Hartie Address to all Protestants in the Present Army'. The pamphlet was a rallying cry for the protection of Anglicanism and had been distributed throughout the city and the army. At his show trial, Johnson had defended himself, saying, 'It is strange that I must be whipt for maintaininge the laws, and the protestant religion, when dayly are printed books and published books conteininge treason.'[12] Following his reduction to the laity, Johnson was taken to the pillory, where he was greeted by a cheering crowd. Following his public sentencing he was whipped, receiving 317 lashes (it was said) without crying out once.

An atmosphere of unease began to filter through the city. John Evelyn had also welcomed the accession of the king, hoping that James would be the nation's protector. He was even rewarded with the position of Commissioner to the Privy Seal. Yet his unease in the first years of the reign, especially after the cruel suppression of Monmouth's army, only increased. The rise in dispensations disturbed the sober Anglican, who feared that the threat of Catholicism would tear the nation apart once more. In particular, his dislike of the French monarchy escalated throughout the 1680s, and he abhorred both Charles II and James II's 'pseudopolitical adherence to the French interest'.[13] He watched as Louis XIV gained strength on the Continent while England did nothing, and by the end of the year he had chosen to absent himself from his court position. It was this change of political opinion, and retreat to his garden at Sayes Court, perhaps, which found its expression in the Deptford soil.

Following the bitter winters of 1683 and 1684, his English Eden had been devastated: 'many of the greene and rare plants utterly destroyed: the oranges and Myrtles very sick, the Rosemary and Lawrell dead to all appearance, but the Cypresse like to induce it out'.[14] He had reported the state of his *Trunculum*, an allusion to Pliny's villa, to the Royal Society. Many of his trees – oaks, cork, chestnut, cedars and pine especially – had been hit hard by the frost, as had the shrubs and other bedding plants. The more exotic plants had been brought indoors for the winter and had survived. Woefully he added: 'My Tortoise ... happening to be obstructed by a vine root, from mining to the depth, he was unusually wont to interr, is found stark dead.'[15]

To him the land had always been a place for the ordering of Art and Nature, a manifestation of God's power and his perfect society, and at Sayes Court, in the words of eighteenth-century horticulturist Stephen Switzer, Evelyn learnt how 'Gardening can speak proper English'.[16] Since the 1650s he had cultivated his vision of the ideal Stuart polity, combining native and exotic plants, integrating Continental ideas and traditional English forms to promote a vision of harmony. Perhaps he had got it all wrong.

Evelyn then returned to his original plans and decided on a radical reshape, and in February 1685, Morin's oval parterre was grubbed up, and the central ornament, modelled so precisely on the Parisian garden, was replaced by a very English lawn, a bowling green, which was then bordered by a box hedge. The complexity of Continental design was superseded by English simplicity. He also added a number of fruit trees, cherries, pears, apples, to replace the foreign cypresses. The roughing-up of the damaged parterre may have been a political comment, in response to the increasing dissatisfaction with the rule of the Stuarts. It could also be interpreted as a precursor to the Whiggist fashion for rational landscape that would become the signature of the next century.

THE REASONABLE REVOLUTION

The stirrings of revolution were felt not just in the gardens of Deptford or the streets of London. While the metropolis was fearful of political atrophy, the question of change was also being discussed among the small group of philosophers and virtuosi of the Royal Society. The club itself staggered into the 1680s, hampered by internal feuds, a constant need for money and still without a permanent home. Debates on building a permanent college for the society were often mooted but always fell short. Yet while the club stumbled the New Philosophy blossomed.

As James II's reign progressed, there was another revolution in the air, which would have a profound effect on the formation of the modern world. Out of the social upheaval of the times, in very different circumstances, two extraordinary visions of the world would emerge. The first was formulated a long way from London, in Holland, where the philosopher-in-exile, John Locke, was in hiding. The second was closer to home, and emerged from the long-standing rivalry between Isaac Newton and the society curator, Robert Hooke.

When Locke arrived in Rotterdam in 1683, he immediately made his way to Amsterdam. He purposely distanced himself from his recent past and did not wish to stay too long at the port known as a hotbed for exiles and anti-Stuart plotters. On arriving at the capital he took lodgings and began to write. Over the winter, despite the bitter cold, he would tell his friends back home how the clean air had improved his health, claiming that he did not 'cough once in a whole day'.[17] He was also fortunate to make acquaintance with Philip van Limborch, a professor of theology, and the microscopist Antony van Leeuwenhoek. As both Barbon and Evelyn had noted before, Amsterdam was an impressive city of trade, toleration and diversity which suited Locke well. The following spring, however, he took off on his travels again with his servant to tour the cities and towns of the Dutch Republic, where he found much to warm his own passions for a modern, tolerant society.

Yet the fear of persecution was not far away. In November 1684, Locke was informed of important news from Christ Church, Oxford, where the dean, John Fell, had been commanded by the king that 'one Mr Locke, who belonged to the late Earl of Shaftesbury, and has on several occasions behaved himself very factiously and undutifully to the government',[18] be expelled from the faculty. The dean made a plea for due process and for Locke to be allowed to defend himself, but the king would have none of it and Locke was to be cut off from the one place where he had been safe.

In desperation Locke sought the patronage of a Tory grandee, Lord Pembroke, and in a letter to the aristocrat outlined his version of the story. He attempted to claim that his relationship with Shaftesbury was circumstantial: 'chance, and not my own seeking ... threw me into my Lord Shaftesburys acquaintance and family, I challenge any one to say my behaviour was otherwise'. He had been the family doctor and no more, was no member of 'any suspected club or cabal', and was not the author of any seditious pamphlets. Thus far, he was economical with the truth. He also gave a good impression of his life in Amsterdam as a defence against any attacks. He presented himself as a bookish scribbler, who was averse to the society of political plotting, or seditious pamphlets: 'I write a good deal, I think I may say, more than ever I did in soe much time in my life, but noe libells, unless perhaps it may be a libell against all mankinde to give some account of the weaknesse and shortnesse of human under-standing, for upon that my old theme *de Intellectu Humano* (on which your lordship knows I have been a good while hammering), has my head been beating, and my pen scribbling all the time I have been here.'[19]

He was working on an idea that had fascinated him for many years, and in Holland he had found the freedom to focus his thoughts. Since the 1660s, working alongside Boyle and Hooke in Oxford, he had been intrigued by the questions of the mind and the idea that true knowledge could be found only in 'sense-experience'. Within the laboratory this had meant the primacy of experimentation and demonstration, but Locke had wanted to push these ideas farther. As he settled in Exeter House in London he had continued the debate with a number of philosophical and political acquaintances and had even penned a few of his first notions in what would later be called Draft A and Draft B of *An Essay on Human Understanding*. At the heart of his quest was how to establish the rightness of God's Law by intellect alone, without recourse to authority.

An Essay on Human Understanding was unlike any philosophy book before it. Rather than attempting to uncover the nature of all things, the book set out only to chart the waters that informed the way men act or, as he modestly claimed, 'truth as far as my shortsightedness could reach it'. He proposed to search for an explanation of how the mind worked, concerned not with measurement but a 'plain, historical method',[20] asking not what do we know but rather how do we gain the ability to know it.

Just as the *Two Treatise* grappled with the hiatus of the political times and the failure of the Restoration Settlement, Locke's *Essay Concerning Human Understanding* tried to combat the enthusiasms of the Quakers and Ranters, by placing reason at the heart of knowledge. In addition, he would propose that it was experience of the world, not the dusty commentaries of classical texts, the enthusiasms of fanatics or the persecuting powers of sovereigns, which provided the path to truth.

The *Essay* raises the image of the newborn child; what did this baby know? For many, the child already had a wealth of knowledge at birth: 'there are in the understanding certain innate principles; some primary Notions . . . characters, as it were, stamped upon the minds of men'.[21] These innate principles commanded the moral aspects of how one behaved, the self-evident truths of life, and could be seen at all times and in all societies around the world. For Locke, however, this accepted opinion was wrong. There could be no certainty that a child was born with any such notions and characters; rather the newborn was 'white paper, void of all characters, without any ideas,'[22] a blank slate (a term first used in Draft B in 1671) who must learn the world in stages. If it appeared that the newborn child brought ideas with her into the world – hunger, thirst and pain – she must have experienced these sensations in the womb.

In challenging the notion of innate knowledge, Locke needed to for-mulate a new method of acquiring it. If man was not born with the basic building blocks of knowledge, how would one then learn the world? Experience was the encounter with the world which provided the raw material of understanding, but did not constitute knowledge itself. The combination of reason and experience developed a cumulative picture of things through 'ideas'. For Locke, ideas were the abstraction of these memories in the mind.

In addition, there was a hierarchy of 'ideas', a panoply of intertwining notions from the simple sensations of pleasure and pain to the complex idea of infinity. Thus, once in the world the child began by learning sensations: 'the senses at first let in particular ideas, and furnish this yet empty cabinet, and the mind by degrees growing familiar with some of them, they are lodged in the memory, and names got to them'.[23] These first ideas were simple, yet as experience accumulated they became more complex, combining with other ideas: 'and that they get no more, nor no other, than what experience, and the observation of things, that come in their way, furnish them with'.[24]

Thus, as the newborn widened her experience, the breadth of her ideas expanded and the keener her perception of the physical world became. As the child began to learn the world, another level of understanding offered itself. 'Perception', which Locke described as 'the first step and degree towards knowledge, and the inlet of all material of it,'[25] allowed the child to build up complex notions of objects into a number of 'qualities'. An oak seen on a summer's day expressed ideas of trees in general, the oak in particular, size, season, colour, age, etc., all of which had been formed from previous experiences. The child also grew to develop reflective ideas, 'the internal operations of our minds, perceived and reflected on by ourselves,'[26] which worked not from external stimuli but upon the ideas already accumulated within the mind.

Despite the attempts to maintain a philosopher's life in Holland, Locke was never far from danger. He worked on the manuscript over the winter of 1684/85 and attempted as best he could to avoid the gatherings of English radicals and exiles who had fled to Holland, while also fearful that he was being watched by the king's spies. But on the announcement of Charles II's death, Locke found himself associated with a number of the plotters who had sailed with the Duke of Monmouth against the newly crowned James II. After the rebels had been defeated at Sedgemoor the king also went after the conspirators who had remained abroad, writing to his son-in-law, William of Orange, commanding: 'Pray consider of this, and how important it is to me, to have those people destroyed'.[27]

A paper trail soon led to Locke, who was once again forced to go underground. When a warrant was put out for his arrest, Locke hid in the house of an Amsterdam medic, Dr Egbertus Veen, and later that autumn he travelled to Cleves under an assumed name, Dr van der Linden. He did not emerge from hiding until May 1686, and would later write how this 'discontinued way of writing' affected his ability to concentrate, forcing him to construct the book in 'incoherent parcels'. Nonetheless he was determined to continue with the *Essay*.

In September 1686, he sent his friend Edward Clarke a version of Book III, which looked at the relationship between ideas and language. The ancients had believed in the nominal 'essence' of language – that there was a connection between the object and the word – but Locke threw out this idea and stated that words had no meaning except that dictated by convention. Language was a tool, on occasion not a very good one, of perception, the invention of understanding, not understanding in itself, used to improve the communal pursuit of reason.

In November, as he worked on the fourth and final book of the *Essay*, Locke was informed that he was to be expelled from Utrecht as a 'dangerous alien', and he was sent on his travels again. He could not find lodgings in Amsterdam and had to stay with friends. Yet nothing would interfere with the completion of the work. The fourth book of the *Essay*, 'Of Knowledge and Opinion', brought together the many aspects of his philosophy into a single theory of knowledge where reason, experience, perception and ideas form the basic blocks of understanding which could then be built up into ever more complex notions. Together they combined into a method by which man can understand the world and, through it, come closer to God.

Just as the New Philosophers had attempted to show the variety of God's creation through measurement, so Locke's aim was to place reason at the heart of the search for truth. It was a bold reminder that the birth of modern science was not the death of God but the attempt to see His work more clearly. In his later introductory 'epistle to the reader', Locke made this connection between the New Philosophy and his work explicit: 'The commonwealth of learning, is not at this time without master-builders, whose mighty designs, in advancing the sciences, will leave lasting monuments to the admiration of posterity: But everyone must not hope to be a Boyle, or a Sydenham, and in an age that produces such masters as the Great Huygenius, and the incomparable Mr Newton.'[28]

Locke's choice of Isaac Newton as an exemplar of the age was not without complications. On 21 April 1686, four months after Locke completed the *Essay*, the clerk of the Royal Society, Edmund Halley, read out a letter from Cambridge at the meeting acclaiming the conclusions of the work that had absorbed the Lucasian Professor for the last two years. When Newton's manuscript was sent to Halley the following week, 28 April, the chairman, Sir John Hoskins, announced the society's approval, claiming that the book, the *Principia Mathematica*, should be printed immediately and that Newton should be praised as both inventor and perfecter of the new theory of the laws of orbital motion – Why did the moon circle the planet in this peculiar orbit? Was this a magnetic attraction? If so, why did the planets not collapse into each other? There must be an attractive force that drew planets together as well as a balancing force that kept them apart.

Hooke, who had sat quietly through the meeting, was incensed. After the club had adjourned, he took off with his fellows to Jonathan's Coffee House, where his tongue was loosened. Inventor? Perfecter? Hooke was certain that he was partly to be credited for Newton's new ideas and he was determined that his coffee-house audience should know that it was he who had given Newton 'the first notions of this invention'.[29]

By the 1680s Hooke was a shadow of his former self. He had remained busy with a continual round of experiments and ideas but each lacked the inspiration and spark that drove his former work. His self-medication continued but offered infrequent succour, yet he remained a prominent architect within the capital, completing a number of projects he had started in the 1670s on behalf of leading aristocrats. He developed a number of country-house projects such as Escot House in Devon, as well as a chapel for his old mentor and friend, the headmaster of Westminster, Dr Busby. The architectural historian Giles Worsley makes a strong case for Hooke also redesigning Montagu House after an unexpected fire in 1687. If this is true it is then probable that Hooke also worked for the same family at Petworth, Kent.

His fortunes within the Royal Society, however, had risen and fallen. After a brief stint as secretary, he remained curator, but was now no longer the sole demonstrator of experiments. His presentations began to look tired and repetitive, his adherence to the mechanical philosophy dogmatic and slightly old fashioned. Hooke's explorations, which had once seemed thrilling in their omnivorous diversity, now lacked cohesion, and he was soon commanded by the society to register his demonstrations a week in advance so that the committee could ensure that they fitted their agenda.

As early as 1666 Hooke's demonstrations showed that gravitation was a force that acted on all bodies, yet he had not been able to find the physical property of 'gravity' itself. This was partly due to the instruments he was using, which were useless for recording such minute measurements, but also he was looking in the wrong place for his answers. In a 1670 lecture, 'An Attempt to Prove the Motion of the Earth by Observations' (which would later be self-published, rather than under the imprimatur of the Royal Society), he proposed a series of important suppositions that he held to be true: all bodies move in a straight line unless their path is deflected by a force placed upon them; all bodies possess gravity, which works not just on the surface of the body but on other bodies at a distance; and finally, the distance between bodies has an inverse impact on the strength of their attraction.

This last supposition, the inverse square law, was particularly important and proposed that gravity worked in proportion to the distance between two bodies: the farther apart the objects, the weaker the gravitational pull. Hooke could not, however, find the experiment to physically show his thinking. Nonetheless, he pronounced that whoever found the unifying system that held the planets together would possess mastery of astronomy.

It was this desire for useful experimentation which drove Hooke to write to Newton in 1679 and in a brief exchange, which began in politeness and descended into poorly concealed vitriol, the question was recast anew. Hooke's letter pricked Newton's inquisitiveness and while he denied any interest in the matter he proposed an experiment to measure the daily turning of the Earth. It was a mistake that drew Newton into headlong confrontation once more. By dropping a large object in a straight line from a height, Newton suggested, the object would fall to the east of the perpendicular point from which it was dropped. His supposition was deemed correct by everyone, but his explanation of the motion of the falling body was questionable. It was an honest mistake, but Hooke set about devising a series of experiments to disprove his rival's theory. In a barrage of increasingly heated letters, the two batted diagrams and well-guarded insults at each other while also unexpectedly getting to the heart of the question.

Both soon came to reduce their dispute to a choice of axioms on which to base their explorations, and form the building blocks of any theory. First, they agreed that a moving body would not change direction without a counter-force. They both accepted the veracity of the shape of the curve, an ellipse, that a body would adopt as it orbited. Therefore, the body following a straight line must be influenced by a counter-force for its path to bend in such a shape. Third, they agreed that the inverse square law described the relationship between bodies at a distance, suggesting that this counter-force could be an influence at a distance.

After this point, however, neither man could work out what this counter-force was, and both supposed that some form of centrifugal force, a flinging outwards, counterbalanced the attractive quality of gravity. They knew this was wrong but could not say why until a chance deletion occurred in Hooke's letter of 6 January. In his original draft he refers to *'Conatus Recedendi'*,[30] the centrifugal force in relation to gravity, but in the finished letter he struck this out and attempted to find another term; in the end, he left out the description altogether. The centrifugal force would no longer be needed to describe the motion of the planets. The slate had been wiped clean and calculations could start afresh.

The trail went temporarily cold and was revived only four years later. In January 1684, Wren, Hooke and Edmund Halley were sitting in a coffee house. As Halley wrote in his diary, Wren offered: 'Mr Hook or me 2 months time to bring him a convincing demonstration thereof, and besides the honour, he of us that did it, should have from him a present of a book of 40s.' Hooke claimed to have already devised his theory, bluffing, that 'he would conceal it for some time that others triing and failing might know how to value it, when he should make it public', but Wren was not so convinced and let the challenge stand. Six months later, Halley travelled to Cambridge and told the same story to Newton, who, like Hooke, claimed to have already found the answer, but when asked to show his proof he stalled for time: 'Sr Isaac looked among his papers but could not find it, but he promised to renew it, and send it him.'[31]

Newton immediately stopped everything he was doing to find the proof, while Hooke continued his many tasks, safe in the knowledge that he had done enough to gain recognition. He had got as close as he could to demonstrating the correctness of his supposition. He was, however, to be proved woefully wrong. While the curator maintained that the answer would be found in experiments, Newton sought his answers beyond the laboratory, in pure mathematics. Thus far, the Royal Society had made its creed in demonstrable knowledge, the revelation of useful experiments through the theatre of the society meetings. Gravity, however, could not be shown to a room of grandees and virtuosi; its nature was not to be uncovered in the sketchy measurement of weights dropping down a shaft or the imprecise motions of a pendulum. It could emerge only in ideas, proved by the cold logic of equation. While Hooke provided at least some of the inspiration for the solution, Newton provided the proof.

On the evening of 28 April 1686, Newton's manuscript revealed his workings and his equations atomised the mathematic principles that underpinned the workings of the whole universe. Hooke's ire that evening, however, was justified, even if he would never have been able to have achieved such a feat himself.

Initially Newton was happy to be reminded of Hooke's contribution, but his mood turned sour on further reflection, and he later responded that if Hooke had indeed found the 'inverse square rule' it had been at best a guess. Newton deserved the sole credit because he alone found the proof. Spurred on by other reports of Hooke's conduct in London, Newton plunged the dagger in farther: Hooke's demonstrable experiments were mere speculation, science was found in mathematical proof: 'Now is this not very fine? Mathematicians that find out, settle & do all the business must content themselves with being nothing but dry calculators & drudges & another that does nothing but pretend & grasp at all things must carry all the invention'.[32] Returning to his correspondence, Newton picked holes in Hooke's argument and only grudgingly offered the curator a crumb of acknowledgement. As the manuscript was being prepared, Newton took the opportunity for a last edit. In the script for Book III, Hooke was originally named *Cl*[arissimus] *Hookius*, 'the most distinguished Hooke'; in the finished book he was named only '*Hookius*'.

Newton's fame was not instantaneous, however. The Royal Society was fearful of the expense of such a large publication, and while they were happy to offer the club's imprimatur, all the printing costs were met by Halley. *Principia* was finally printed in June 1687, and on publication would famously be one of the least-read bestsellers of the age; as one Cambridge student pointed out as he spied Newton in the street: 'There goes the man that writ a book that neither he nor anyone else understands'.[33]

John Locke reviewed the book (only four reviews appeared in total) in the journal *Bibliothèque Universelle* in 1688. He hailed it, although the mathematics were beyond him, as was the model of methodological knowledge. The *Bibliothèque Universelle* was also home to the first publication of an abridged version of Locke's *Essay Concerning Human Understanding*, in January that same year. Together, the *Principia* and the *Essay Concerning Human Understanding* would change the world and initiate a new era, the Enlightenment. While one book found order in the physical world the other offered a map of the human mind. Both books placed reason at the heart of all knowledge, beyond the authority of received wisdom, government or Church. Their achievement laid the foundation for a new system of thought. None of this, however, was considered of prime importance in the middle of the 1680s as England unsteadily headed towards another civil war.

PRELUDE TO A REVOLUTION

In January 1686 James II named his new Commission for the Rebuilding of St Paul's. The commission included the usual mix of grandees, experts and professionals. Sir Christopher Wren was renamed the surveyor while John Oliver, the city commissioner who had staked out the streets alongside Hooke, became his deputy, replacing the late Edward Woodroffe. As Bishop of London, for whom the cathedral was his parish church, Henry Compton was a necessary member, as was the Lord Mayor, Sir Robert Jeffrey. For Wren the new commission confirmed a team that he could work with, and who shared his ideas. William Holder, his brother-in-law, had been named residentiary of the chapter and also given a seat on the commission, and Dr John Tillotson, a fellow member of the Royal Society and son-in-law to Wren's Oxford patron, John Wilkins.

The new commission combined to give the deanery and chapter a more modern face. Unlike the highly conservative Anglican hierarchy of the Restoration, this group of men had seen the Troubles of the Civil Wars in a different light, and while the Clarendon Code of the 1660s had sought to bury nonconformism and dissent, the new generation – later to gain the name latitudinarian or Low Churchmen – went in search of means to incorporate and understand the diversity of faiths in the capital. Their cathedral would not be a single beacon of stern orthodoxy but one of comprehension, seeking a new universalism that bound the faithful together beyond matters of doctrine and ritual.

The remaining members of the committee, however, would make this a difficult task: the Lord High Chancellor, George Jeffreys, had already gained a bloody reputation in suppressing the Monmouth rebellion. Before attaining high office he had made his name as the Recorder of London, in particular persecuting the Catholic traitors in the Popish Plot; nonetheless, he caught James II's eye and was the king's representative on the commission. At the first meeting, on 22 February 1686, at Jeffreys' house, Compton, who had already made his stand in the House of Lords against the king, made his excuses and stayed away. In all subsequent meetings, held at the chapter house in the churchyard, Jeffreys refrained from attending. The commission soon found it impossible to represent the many different demands of its members.

In March James II issued a directive to stop political sermonising in response to the large number of London preachers who used their pulpits to warn against the Catholic tide rising up the Thames. When in May John Sharp, rector of St Giles-in-the-Fields in Holborn, ignored the ruling and continued to caution his flock, the king commanded Sharp's bishop, Compton, to punish his wayward cleric. Compton refused. If the bishops would not do the king's bidding James himself would have to put his house in order, and he set up a Commission for Ecclesiastical Causes, led by Chancellor Jeffreys, to weed out dissent from within the established clergy. The commission's first judgement was to suspend Bishop Compton for failing in his duties. London was now without a bishop, St Paul's without its priest.

As Surveyor-General, Wren remained at the beck and call of the king.

When James commanded alterations to his palace at Whitehall, Wren was pulled away from his work at St Paul's to devise new designs for the jumble of houses and buildings in Westminster. James had decided that the half-completed palace at Winchester was not suitable, and so the spare material was sold and the palace boarded up. Instead, James wished to express his power within London with new apartments, a council chamber and a Catholic chapel where he could worship in public. The leading Anglican architect was therefore forced to serve Rome. By Christmas 1686, the chapel was completed and held its first service.

While Wren was quiet about his feelings concerning the chapel, John Evelyn was less so. He was impressed by the elegance of the designs; the exterior was simple stone and brick with few adornments but the interior was a blaze of gilt and carving, a complete study of European baroque, but he could not disguise his distaste: 'I could not have believ'd I should ever have seen such things in the King of England's Palace, after it had pleas'd God to enlighten this Nation.'[34] There was further alteration to the chapel almost as soon as it was completed to make it more 'Roman' when a Lady's Chapel and a chancel were added. The king was now not even attempting to disguise his Catholicism in the belief that if the nation saw the truth of his faith, they would follow. It was a major miscalculation regarding the deep-seated English hatred of Catholicism that had been incubating for over a century.

The king's move towards Rome would reflect upon the rebuilding of St Paul's. In the growing atmosphere of mistrust James now felt he had lost the support of the Tory Anglicans, the very establishment that had preserved his brother's reign. Rather than courting what he had lost, the king went in pursuit of a new establishment among the factions and dissenting sects that had been his brother's enemies, and throughout 1686 he began to court the nonconformists. On 4 April 1687 he issued a Declaration of Indulgence (using the legal precedent developed by Locke in 1672) that offered religious freedom to Baptists, Quakers and Catholics. This allowed James to fill his Privy Council with his co-religionists, even including his confessor, the Jesuit Edward Petrie. He also attempted to introduce Catholics into key positions at Oxford and Cambridge universities, and a month after completing his *Principia*, Isaac Newton was dragged into the conflict as he stood against the king's attempts to pack the university hierarchy with papists.

The response to the Declaration was muted. In London, dissenters preferred to continue to visit their Anglican parishes rather than reveal themselves. They were unsure of the cost of this particular liberty, conscious that this freedom of conscience had come from arbitrary government. As James Tyrrell wrote to John Locke: 'More are displeased at the manner of doing it than at the thing itself'.[35] The Catholics were less guarded and began to set up chapels within the city. The first was built under diplomatic privilege on Lime Street, but was fitted out to hold a congregation far outnumbering the members of the embassy. By the end of 1688 there was a monastery in Clerkenwell, eighteen chapels and two Jesuit schools within the city and Catholic presses were given licence to print their rallying sheets. The open practice of the papists made the city bristle.

James had hoped that his call for toleration would bring together a strong power base of grateful dissenter, and during the summer of 1687 he expected to receive the official thanks of his subjects. Gratitude, however, was thin on the ground. A small number of addresses of thanks came from nonconformist congregations, yet by August only forty-three had arrived from around the kingdom. Responses from the established Church were even more mealy mouthed. The Archbishop of Canterbury, William San-croft, composed a lengthy 'Reasons against Subscription' and gave his support to a policy of passive obedience, which acknowledged James's position as defender of the faith but not his religious policies. This was endorsed by the anonymous pamphlet *A Letter to a Dissenter*, which warned the nonconformist to be wary of the king's generosity: 'you are therefore to be hugged now, only that you may be squeezed at another time'.[36]

Despite these upheavals, work at St Paul's continued as the walls of the east end were completed and Wren began to set the roof of the choir. In his original Warrant plans Wren had projected a system of cross-vaulting for the east end, but this was now unsatisfactory. Inspired by the church of Hagia Sophia, the cathedral in Constantinople, Wren devised a series of ingenious shallow saucer domes that crossed the span of the choir covering, as different to St Peter's in Rome as imaginable. The effect gave the impression of harmony and lightness. It was also structurally innovative, for rather than exerting an outward thrust upon the choir walls, the saucer domes accentuated the vertical pressure.

While the east end was nearing completion, Wren began to concentrate on the west front. So far he had avoided the inevitable moment when he had to decide what to do with Inigo Jones's Tuscan portico, which stood stark within the churchyard, a hymn to Laudian orthodoxy and the Stuart dynasty. Wren considered Jones's work to be exemplary and had hoped to integrate the simple frontage into his new cathedral, but in the 1680s he changed his mind. He had now built the nave foundations to ground level within a short distance of the front but had refrained from connecting the old work with the new. According to his 1675 Warrant Design, Jones's front would connect with the domed crossing by means of a long single-width nave. Wren had always feared that this would not work, creating a structure that gave the impression of a tapering body, overpowered by the bulk of the dome above. Something needed to be done to the west end to give it a grandeur to counterbalance the as yet unbuilt cupola. As a result, he finally decided that Jones's Tuscan portico had to be demolished, and in 1686 he gave the command to remove the last remains of the old St Paul's. The architect, however, did not want to do away with one of the nation's masterpieces and he hoped at least to preserve part of the portico, damaged but victorious over both the Civil War and the Great Fire. In February 1687, he proposed the sale of one of the towers to his other project, the Chelsea hospital, to the west of the capital, but was denied by the terms of the commission's warrant, which stated that materials could not be sold from St Paul's unless they went to help the rebuilding of the city churches. In the end, Wren was forced to abandon the idea and the west front was cleared by September 1687.

He needed to give weight to the 'face' of the cathedral, which would stand boldly above London. This alteration needed to work on three different viewpoints: from the west, from the perspective of a visitor entering the churchyard; from the south, looking from the Thames; and third, from within the interior. In the Warrant Design the nave had moved from the dome to the front in a sequence of five equal bays, yet while this design allowed space for processions, it lacked ceremony as the bishop and the chapter made their transition through the various stages of the church.

In his search for a solution, Wren took away the final two west bays and replaced them with a single space, a vestibule, which would be the width of the front rather than of the narrower nave. This broke up the repetitive order of the nave and offered a large, open room at the front of the church which could be used for assembly. It also had the effect of shortening the nave from the side, thus redressing the balance between the dome and the west front. Most significantly of all, this allowed a grander gesture to be added to the frontage. On either side of the vestibule, Wren added two chapels which stood out 25 feet beyond the wall of the nave, one to be used for the morning prayer, while there had also been plans to add a library, a consistory and accommodation for the Bishop of London. This would have the effect of broadening out the west front by over fifty feet.

Many believed that Wren added the chapel by direct command of James II. There were rumours that in this form James would be able to deliver the building to the Pope almost complete. It was a powerful murmur, but also false. In fact Wren had been thinking through these issues before 1685, and in the year before James's accession, Wren and Evelyn had discussed the addition of a library as Evelyn had recently heard the complaint that the clergy had become too fond of the local taverns and had nowhere to find alternative nourishment from good books. But through rumour and association the cathedral was becoming the symbol of a disliked monarchy within the city. The Anglican Church, however, would soon find itself at loggerheads with the Crown over its own survival. Meanwhile, Wren could only hope that he would soon see his vision completed and pressed on regardless.

THE LAST INVASION OF ENGLAND

In the autumn of 1687, James II decided to recall Parliament. Throughout the year he had conducted a series of purges of local and civic institutions in the hope that he could place his own men in power, and had instructed his officials to make a poll of every office holder, MP and civic dignitary in the land to test their allegiance. The survey included twelve questions, such as whether they would accept the Declaration of Indulgence if elected to Parliament, whether they would ensure the election of an MP who held such views, and whether they would live peacefully under religious toleration. The results were far from encouraging, for as the Imperial Ambassador commented: 'before this inquiry everyone suspected his neighbour of being a partisan of the King and people suppressed their disaffection, which now they express without fear'.[37]

Rather than bolstering the king's position, the poll encouraged the opposition. Without regard for the facts, James continued to wade into disaster, and by the spring of 1688 he had purged over 1,200 officials from their positions in the hope of restoring a complicit establishment. His influence was particularly felt in London, where in November 1687 he set up a commission to regulate the corporations and through threats and censures gained a compliant Lord Mayor; but he dealt with the livery companies with a heavy hand for which he would not be forgiven. James, having lost the support of the very people who had once protected him, had recast himself in the role of an absolute monarch.

A further crisis erupted in January 1688, when it was announced that the queen, Mary of Modena, was pregnant, which sent a shudder of fear through the nation. This was exacerbated in April 1688 when the king reissued his Declaration of Indulgence and commanded the clergy to read it out from the pulpits for two Sundays in a row. James had underestimated the strength of Anglican feeling, however, and in the run-up to the order the leaders of the Church in London held a number of meetings. With the Bishop of London, William Compton, still suspended, this committee included the dean of St Paul's, Edward Stillingfleet, John Tillotson, dean of Canterbury, Simon Patrick, dean of Peterborough, and William Sherlock, Master of the Temple, and after consulting with both high-ranking nobles and bishops, they announced their refusal to read out the Bill, claiming that to preach the Declaration went against their consciences and parliamentary law.

The refusal turned the Church's passive obedience into active resistance, and the established Church now politely squared up to the king. Following the declaration of the London divines, seven bishops, led by Archbishop William Sancroft, also refused, and decided to present a petition to James himself at Whitehall. The petition was delicately worded, ensuring that it did not attack the Crown's powers or the sensibilities of the dissenters, but plainly rejected the Declaration itself. When James heard their complaints, he burst into fury, and claimed that the bishops were threatening rebellion. The divines stood fast, and on that Sunday only seven congregations in London read the Declaration, and in three the congregation showed their disgust and left the churches during the announcement.

The devout Anglican John Evelyn watched the proceedings with dread. He was by no means a natural revolutionary but could no longer offer the king or the government his support. On 25 May, he reported the city's reaction to the failures of the clergy to do the king's bidding: 'The action of the Bishops was universally applauded, and reconciled many adverse parties, Papists only excepted, who were now exceedingly perplexed, and violent courses were every moment expected'.[38] The king's reaction, however, was swift, and on 8 June, he ordered the bishops to Whitehall to explain themselves. They refused, claiming that 'no subject was bound to accuse himselfe'.[39] The king then asked the bishops for bail and to present themselves to the King's Bench for judgement, but they refused once more. James, exasperated, had all seven bishops indicted for seditious libel and taken to the Tower. As their barge glided past, a crowd gathered along the banks of the Thames to offer their support.

In the meantime, on 10 June, news emerged from Whitehall that the queen had given birth to a son. Rather than celebrate, the City descended into panic: the king had an heir and England was to be condemned to Catholicism. As one report noted: 'The birth of the Prince [gave] the greatest joy to the King and Queen, and to all those who wished them well ... [but] gave the greatest agonys immaginable to the generality of the Kingdom.'⁴⁰ Almost immediately rumours began to spread that the prince was no such thing, and had been smuggled into the queen's chambers in a bedpan. In the churches, when prayers were commanded for the celebration of the Prince of Wales' birth, there was only silence. At St Giles-in-the-Fields, the congregation showed their displeasure: 'very many very rudely and indecently laughed, or smiled upon each other or talked with one another'.⁴¹ Rumour or not, the existence of the prince condemned England to Rome.

Five days later the bishops returned to Westminster, where they stood before the Judges' Bench. As Evelyn reported: 'when the indictment was read, and they were called on to plead; their Counsel objected that the warrant was illegal'.⁴² This was ignored, and they were forced to plead. By this time they had gained formidable support throughout the country from both Anglicans and dissenters, who saw the attack on the bishops as an assault on Protestantism itself. One Somerset Quaker even put up the £100 bail for the Bishop of Bath and Wells. The accused men then had to wait two weeks for their trial.

On that day, Westminster Hall was filled from nine in the morning to dusk, while a crowd gathered outside. The mob crowed their support for the bishops and jeered the king's men as they filed into the court. The prosecution built their case around the fact that the bishops had deliberately undermined the prerogative of the king by issuing their petition, while the defence pointed out that the bishops had not published their petition but had delivered it in person to the king, and their claim was nothing more than a reminder to the king that the Declaration had been repealed in 1673, and therefore was illegal. The four judges made their conclusions, the jury then retired and the court adjourned until the next morning.

Throughout the night the jury deliberated, and at nine o'clock the next morning recorded their verdict. Two of the members, Arnold, the King's Brewer, and Mr Done, the King's mace bearer, unsurprisingly considered the libel true; the other ten, however, unanimously acquitted the bishops. The room erupted in joy, while outside, Evelyn watched the city explode in celebration: 'there was great rejoicing; and there was a lane of people from the King's Bench to the [Thames] waterside, on their knees, as the Bishops passed and repassed, to beg their blessing. Bonfires were made that night, and bells rung, which was taken very ill at Court, and an appearance of nearly sixty Earls and Lords &c. on the bench, did not a little comfort them; but indeed they were all along full of comfort and cheerful'.[43]

The bishops' victory was a turning point for England. That night, as the celebrations continued, a group of nobles, including the suspended Bishop of London, set about launching a coup. They wrote to the leader of the Dutch Republic, William of Orange, the husband of James II's eldest daughter from his first marriage, inviting him to involve himself in English politics. In secret William began to plan his next step. An army was raised during the summer in preparation for the foreign invasion of England.

In the meantime, James II tried his best to contain the nation, which had begun to seethe beneath him. He had shown his displeasure in the celebrations following the collapse of the bishops' trial by arresting a number of revellers, but when they were brought in front of the magistrate, they were acquitted, forcing him to deal harshly with two of the judges who had dared to defy him. Elsewhere, government seemed to be crumbling: at St Paul's, while building continued, the last meeting of the commission was held on 28 June; anti-Catholic riots began to fill the streets, the chapel on Lime Street was ransacked on three occasions, and the monastery in Clerkenwell was turned over. On the traditional day for Pope-Burning ceremonies, the apprentices gathered forces and had to be held back by the militia as they attempted to pillage the houses of known papists.

News of William of Orange's impending invasion became an open secret. When Evelyn visited Whitehall on 18 September, he found 'the Court in the utmost consternation on report of the Prince of Orange's landing; which put Whitehall into so panic a fear, that I could hardly believe it possible to find such a change'.[44] Evelyn had clearly made up his mind on which side he stood. He wrote to the Archbishop of Canterbury to warn him of a plot, concocted by the Jesuits, to stir up division between the divines and force the bishops to condemn the Dutch invasion. He looked on with mixed feelings of dread and salvation, and wrote: 'it looks like a revolution'.[45]

PART FIVE

London Reborn

Melting It Down and Making It Anew

O n 27 January 1689, in the midst of the troubles, John Evelyn went to dine at the Admiralty with his friend Samuel Pepys, where he met the son of a certain Dr Clench, not yet twelve years old, who was being promoted as some kind of prodigy. Evelyn and Pepys decided to test the child and asked him a panoply of questions concerning 'chronology, history, geography, the several systems of astronomy, courses of the stars, longitude, latitude, doctrine of the spheres, courses and sources of rivers, creeks, harbours, eminent cities, boundaries and bearings of countries not just in Europe, but in any other part of the earth'. The examination then embraced the whole history of the ancient world, classical texts, common law and philosophy. In time Evelyn found himself exhausted and summoned a last question: 'if, in all he had read or heard of, he had ever met with anything which was like the expedition of the Prince of Orange, with so small a force to obtain three great kingdoms without any contest'.[1] The boy had to pause and search his mind. Not since the fourth century, when Constantine the Great marched from England to Rome, had such an event occurred.

On 5 November 1688, William, Prince of Orange, arrived in Brixham, South Devon, upon the 'Protestant' easterly wind. Tramping the rain-sodden road was wearisome and William's international brigade of over fifteen thousand English, Scottish, German, Greek, Dutch, Swiss and Huguenot soldiers hauled '21 good brass field pieces, some needing 16 horses to pull them',[2] supplies of collapsible boats, 10,000 spare boots, muskets and tents. After getting used to being on dry land once more they marched into the county city of Exeter on 9 November, promising 'to have a free and lawfull Parliament assembled as soon as possible'.[3] As they entered the city the civic reception was mixed: the Anglican clergy were equivocal, the civic officers, packed after James II's purges, were absent, but the local citizenry crowded the streets to spy the arriving prince.

Having played his opening gambit, William waited to see how James would react. In London, the king was in a frenzy. A gathering of peers and bishops pressed the need for a free parliament, but James, once a courageous military leader, only made promises that it would be called 'as soon as the present troubles were appeas'd'.[4] As William waited in Devon, prominent nobles began to cross the lines to offer their support: Lord Cornbury, the son of the Earl of Clarendon, was the first on 14 November, while in the north, other peers were rallying to the prince's colours.

James rode out to his troops stationed in Salisbury, where in his panic he began to suffer nosebleeds. It was only this bleeding, however, which saved him, for at Salisbury one of his previously most faithful generals, John Churchill, had devised an outrageous plan to abduct the king while he was reviewing his troops and take him to Exeter. It was only the erratic royal nose which thwarted the plot. Instead, on 23 November, James commanded that his troops retreat to behind the Thames at Reading to wait for the prince, while he scarpered back to London.

When the king arrived in the capital he found that more of his court had fled. In particular his second daughter, Anne, Princess of Denmark, had been escorted from London by the Bishop of London, Henry Compton: 'My own children have forsaken me,'[5] James bemoaned. In an attempt to deflect his imminent defeat, he took the call for a free parliament more seriously, although he would later confess that this was a ruse to give him time to get his wife and the Prince of Wales out of the country. It did not work, for as December began William commenced his advance towards London, reaching Salisbury on the fourth and engaging the remains of the standing army at Reading on the seventh.

As William's army began to march across the south of England towards London, the capital descended into panic. With his blessing Evelyn's son rode to join the prince's army, while Evelyn noted with a certain relish: 'The great favourites at Court, Priests and Jesuits, fly or abscond. Every thing, till now concealed, flies abroad in public print, and is cried about the streets. Expectations of the Prince coming to Oxford. The Prince of Wales and great treasure sent privily to Portsmouth ... Address from the Fleet not grateful to his Majesty. The Papists in offices lay down their commissions, and fly. Universal consternation amongst them'.[6] It was only a matter of time before William entered London.

Yet the prince had a problem: he had promised that he came not as conqueror but as guardian of the liberties of the nation. How could he claim to be a liberator if James was still in the city? Would he have to jail the king? Or even bring him to trial? It would be far easier if James just disappeared, and on 12 December James took the hint, lamenting: 'my children hath abandoned me ... my army hath deserted me, those that I raised from nothing hath done the same, what can I expect from those I have done little or nothing for?'[7] He burned the call to Parliament he had prepared, and took to a boat on the Thames. Disguised as a servant, he threw the Great Seal – the symbol of legitimacy needed to warrant every law – into the river and headed towards Kent, hoping to find a ship to France.

In the Swale, off the Isle of Sheppey, the boat came across a number of smaller vessels that were anchored, hoping for a quick profit. They waited not for fish but Jesuits who were making good their escape to the Continent. James's boat was boarded and one of the passengers, the Kent gentryman Sir Edward Hales, was recognised. The fugitives were then towed to Faversham and the human booty transported to the Queen's Arms, where they were searched, the king stripped 'even to his privities'. The spectacle soon attracted a leering mob, but it was not until the mayor arrived that the quality of the prize was known: 'The rabble (who stood all the while at the door) seeing the mayor kneel to him & remembering Marsh's report, cried out The King, the King'.[8]

James's flight had failed and it set the nation on edge. In London, the mob rose up and, without a government, set about rampaging through the streets. In a spate of organised chaos, the remnants of James's Catholic rule were torn down: prayer houses, printing presses and chapels were destroyed, known papists were hunted and their homes demolished. Not even the Catholic diplomats of foreign nations were spared, and in the heady brew of mob rule, rumours began to circulate that James's disbanded Irish army were moving towards London, reviving terrible memories of the Catholic revolt of 1641. When the Lord Chancellor, George Jeffreys, dressed as a sailor, was caught in Wapping attempting to escape, he pleaded that he be taken to the Tower as the only safe haven in the city. As he waited his fate, the mob circled his window, waving a noose.

In the hope of bringing peace to the city, a caretaker administration of peers, bishops and city officers was set up in the Guildhall. Their calls to William to enter London were desperate, but when news arrived from

Kent that the king had not fled, it sent all plans to settle the nation into the abyss. William had clearly won the military contest, but James, as he re-entered London on 16 December, had failed to leave the field. He was a powerless opponent, a straw king, but by law and divine ordination, still the rightful owner of the crown. Would James remain as king with William the power behind the throne? Could William depose his father-in-law?

On 17 December James asked to meet with William in Windsor to sue for peace but, instead, William arrested the king's messenger and sent a guard to patrol the royal palaces, making James a virtual prisoner. James became haunted by the image of his own father, and feared he might suffer a similar fate. Eventually, William gave the king the option to slip away before his own victorious entry into London, and James found ample opportunity to make his way to Rochester. There he waited, as news arrived that William had been greeted by the city with open arms, crowds flocking to the marching soldiers with oranges on pikes, women calling to the entering heroes, 'welcome, welcome, God Blesse you, you come to redeeme our Religion, lawes, Liberties and lives, God reward you'.[9] William travelled to St James's Palace yet remained powerless to rule until James had actually left the country. On 23 December, the king found the back door of his house unguarded and finally made his way to France.

The throne was empty. William was advised by some that he should assume his place on it without debate, seeking precedent in the conquest of Henry VII after the Battle of Bosworth Field, which ended the Wars of the Roses and initiated the Tudor dynasty. Yet the prince had claimed to have entered England not to take the throne but to deliver liberty, promising a free parliament, not conquest. William accepted the role as de facto ruler and decided that a new government needed to be called to decide the outcome of what many considered a family feud.

Two days after James's flight, William called the remaining members of the last free parliament, along with the peers and bishops, to form a Convention to debate the new settlement. The Convention was not a parliament, as only a king could call such a meeting, but as in 1660, before the restoration of Charles II, it could decide on the terms of the next government. Elections were swift and returned a balanced meeting with an even number of Tories and Whigs in the lower house and a small Tory majority in the Lords. In Windsor, Christopher Wren stood as a Tory, but his election was sent for appeal and found void. His Whig opponent took the seat.

Between the call for a Convention and the first sitting on 22 January, there was plenty of time for the terms of the debate to be digested and contested, and divisions to appear. The uncensored printing presses began to belch out numerous tracts and broadsides that set out both sides of the debate. The coffee houses hummed with the discussion of contractual kingship, natural law and the sanctity of oaths. As Evelyn reported:

> Sorry I was to find there was as yet no accord in the judgements of those of the Lords and Commons who were to convene; some would have the Princess [Mary] made Queen without any more dispute, others were for a Regency; there was a Tory party (then so called) who were for inviting [James] again under conditions; and there were Republicans who would make the Prince of Orange like a Stadtholder. The Romanists were busy amongst these several parties to bring them into confusion: most for ambition or other interest, few for conscience and moderate resolutions.[10]

On 15 January, a group of bishops and Tories met at the home of the Archbishop of Canterbury, William Sancroft. The Lambeth Palace meeting set out the Tory position in the forthcoming Convention. As ever Evelyn watched from the sidelines, yet even in this debate he showed himself to be more the rebel than he is traditionally painted. He could not agree with the bishops: 'they were all for a Regency, thereby to salve their oaths, and so all public matters to proceed in [James's] name, by that to facilitate the calling of a Parliament, according to the laws in being'. Instead, he saw the desperate need for the nation to find a new settlement, 'a new-creation amongst us',[11] before the revolution reawakened the spectre of civil war.

The one person noticeably absent from the debate was John Locke, who remained in Holland throughout the winter. In January 1689, Lady Masham, the wife of a noted Whig, wrote to him: 'by this Convention [there is] an occasion not of amending the government but of melting it down and make it all new, which makes me wish you there to give them a right scheme of government'.[12] But radical renewal of the nation was not the purpose of the convocation. The goal was to determine succession, the replacement of one king with another. The transition of power into the hands of William was inevitable, and his impatience at the debates over words and terms made this ever more so. Yet the terms of succession, and the clarification of the constitution into a Bill of Rights, were essential to the settlement. On 22 January, the Convention met, warmed by William's words of encouragement to get a move on, and began to debate four days later.

The first task of the meeting was to define the end of James's reign, for the throne of England could never be vacant. Everyone could agree that James had left but the true meaning of 'abdication', 'demise' and 'the vacant throne' became vital for settling the future. The debate raged between the Commons and the Lords, and it was only after some pressure from William that a Declaration was fixed. The choice of words was a minor Whiggish victory but the achievement was collective; the transition of power was neither favourable nor owned by one party, but by the whole Convention: 'That King James the Second, having endeavoured to subvert the Constitution of the Kingdom, by breaking the Original Contract between King and People; and by the advice of Jesuits, and other wicked Persons, having violated the fundamental Laws; and having withdrawn himself out of the Kingdom; has abdicated the Government; and that the Throne is thereby vacant.'[13]

The past had been defined but the Convention had to sort out who was to take the throne in James's place. Was William to be regent? Could Mary, James's eldest daughter, rule on her own? Was the Prince of Wales ever to wear the crown? If William was to rule, would he be '*de facto*' by power of conquest, '*de iure*' by the ordination of the law, or '*de divino*', God's anointed lieutenant? As in 1641, the mob flooded Westminster Yard to hear their future debated while some members feared that the power of the rabble would force an unwise conclusion.

By February, William, a leader more accustomed to the swift justice of the sword than the debating chamber, was close to losing his patience with the Convention and made his feelings clear to a few well-placed courtiers. He would not be his wife's consort: 'he was so made, that he could not think of holding anything by apron strings'.[14] Neither would he contemplate being regent, and he threatened to 'go back to Holland and meddle no more in their affairs'. The Convention needed to make its mind up. Thus, on 6 February, in the Painted Hall in Westminster, behind closed doors, while the mob's cries resounded through the yard, it was concluded that the throne was to be shared between William III and Mary II. The poet, John Dryden, would be more curt and describe it as 'A Curtail'd Mungril monarchy, half Commonwealth'.[15]

If William and Mary were to be 'their majesties' the terms of succession were to be laid down for the future. No Catholic could ever sit upon England's throne, and neither could a monarch marry a Catholic. This ruled out James's return, or the accession of the Prince of Wales, the infant now exiled in Paris. If William and Mary both died without issue, the crown went to Princess Anne, the younger sister of Mary, who was married to George, Prince of Denmark. If Anne had no children, then the throne would be given to the next Protestant relative. Thus, the rules of succession were taken out of the hands of God and put into parliamentary statute. At their coronation on 11 April, both monarchs swore to uphold the Crown not by the weight of inheritance but according to the gift and laws of Parliament.

While these debates were being conducted another issue needed resolution. If there was to be a new sovereign, then how was he to rule, and on what foundation rested the Crown's power? The Convention, not God, had played kingmaker, and there was an opportunity to define in law the powers of the throne. This, more than the other debates, was rich soil for division between the Whigs and Tories, for this was not the urgent issue of filling the throne but the debate on the limitations of the king once in power. There could be no union between Tories and Whigs in the creation of new laws to define the parameters of kingship, and William would refuse any such limitations. It was exactly this issue which had heated Parliament in 1641/42 and drove England to civil war.

The debate struck at the heart of Locke's ideas on government, for the *Second Treatise* had been emphatic about the rights of the people to depose the sovereign if the political contract had been broken, as it had in 1688. The philosopher, still in Rotterdam, was shocked, however, that the Convention now wanted to rewrite the contract between king and subjects. Locke's letter to an English friend complained that there was no need to change the constitution, but rather a need to safeguard against the abuses that the nation had suffered in his lifetime. The problem was not the powers of the Crown, which had been defined by natural law, but their misuse by a succession of Stuart kings. The Convention should not initiate a constitutional revolution of new laws but should instead offer a clarification and consolidation of ancient rights.

The Convention agreed and set up a committee of twenty-eight Whigs and twelve Tories to consider the issue. The Declaration of Rights that emerged from these debates, and which was read out to William and Mary on 13 February, was not a new set of rules placed before the king before he was allowed to take the throne, but a reminder of the laws as they stood.

In the final version, the document began with a list of abuses perpetrated by James II and his brother: the royal power to suspend laws, the prerogative of dispensations, the creation of a standing army and the formation of the Ecclesiastical Commission. The document was less a contract of employment for William and Mary to sign than a warning that if they were to step out of line, James II's fate would also befall them.

For many, this stating of the old rules was radical enough to signal a new type of monarchy, a mixed and limited Crown working alongside a strong parliament. The fact that the Declaration was read in front of the king at all was again a victory not for a party but for the Convention as a whole. Both sides of the political divide had experienced the horrors of civil war, and the memory of the 1640s was not exclusively Tory or Whig. Both were determined never to allow chaos to ransack England again. The Declaration plainly annunciated, to the best of their memory, what both parties considered to be the rights of Parliament and kings already stated.

Locke returned to England the day before the Declaration was announced. Since the invasion he had been back in contact with many of his friends who were now close to the victorious prince, and thus he was given the privilege of travelling back alongside Princess Mary, who had remained in Holland until called for by her husband. As Mary entered London, there was jubilation. On the day after her arrival she was crowned queen.

Locke was immediately welcomed into the new king's circle. Unlike many that crowded the new court, however, he was not in search of position or influence, although he found that he was 'more generally esteemed and respected than ever before',[16] and his opinion was often asked on all manner of public affairs. By 21 February, he had already been offered the prestigious job of ambassador to Frederick III, Elector of Brandenburg, which he turned down owing to his health. William then offered him Vienna, and subsequently a third post, both of which he refused, settling for the minor role of Commissioner of Appeals, which offered £200 a year for very little work. He took rooms in Westminster, although, like the king, his health suffered from the pollution and he would half-heartedly complain he was so busy 'that I am hardly able to touch a book now'.[17]

Nonetheless, the new reign gave the philosopher an opportunity to declare his ideas, which had previously been considered too subversive to see the light of day, and he set about organising the publication of his works. His boxes of goods had been sent from Rotterdam to the Whiggish printer Awnsham Churchill, who agreed to print the politically charged *Two Treatise on Government*. Although Locke had written it in the heat of the Exclusion Crisis at the beginning of the 1680s, his views on natural law, contractual kingship and the right of the people to usurp their king were still highly controversial.

Locke decided to publish anonymously and wrote in the new preface in support of the new regime, 'to make good his Title, in the Consent of the People, which being the only one of all lawful Governments, he had more fully and clearly that any Prince in christendom; and to justify to the world, the People of England, whose love for their Just and Natural Rights, with their resolution to preserve them, saved the Nation when it was on the very brink of Slavery and Rome'.[18] Yet the *Two Treatise* was not a rationalisation of the revolution, or a common Whiggish tract. Locke declared himself a staunch Williamite, yet the publication in August 1689 remained a warning to the new monarchy, just as the original purpose of writing the tracts had been a warning to Charles II.

While Locke refused to enter the political stage he continued to advise and direct friends and prominent Whigs who were on the front line of the debate – for following the settlement of 1689 things did not quieten down, but became more divided. In the first moments of the development of political parties, as the Whigs and Tories formed a permanent opposition, there were dangers and threats. In the winter of that year, Locke began to write a pamphlet in the hope of avoiding a fractured nation:

> Complaints are every where soe loud and the apprehensions that people droope under are so visible, that they cannot but be taken notice of. Tis not the want of courage in our Nation nor the distrust of our forces that makes any body despair. They are our divisions which throw a dread amongst us, and every one sees and says unless we are better united we cannot stand ... I desire every protestant, every Englishman amongst us to lay his hands upon his heart and seriously consider with himself what mortal quarrell he has to any of his country men to that degree that rather than live on any tolerable terms with them he would venture the religion, liberty, safety of himself and his country, for all these are at stake and will be lost if we hold not now together.[19]

If 1688 really was a revolution, it was not one that brought peace to the nation. In fact, it did the opposite, and yet it found a way to institutionalise difference and change.

AN ENGLISH VERSAILLES

The change in the political regime introduced a number of new faces to the government. William and Mary needed to reward their supporters, just as Charles II had distributed his favours following the Restoration of 1660. The choice of favourites was not an easy task, and while the Whigs expected a central role in the new government as they had done so much to bring William and Mary to the throne, the king remained suspicious of their intentions; after all, they had deposed one king already. The Tories, in turn, were suspicious of a king who had gained the throne by law rather than divine right. To bolster his own team, William placed a number of Dutchmen in prominent positions: the newly elevated Earl of Portland, Hans Willem Bentinck, became the most important man in William's court and gained the contemptuous nickname 'The Wooden Man', while Christiaan Huygens, Hooke's rival clockmaker, was named the king's secretary.

There was no knowing whether the change of regime would affect the position of the Surveyor-General. Both William and Mary had a passion for design and architecture, and in 1684 William had started work on the summer palace of Het Loo, in Holland. It would become one of the finest houses in Europe, and stood in stylistic opposition to the Gallic swagger of Paris. Who was to say that a Dutch architect would not arrive from Holland as soon as the Crown decided to set their reign in stone?

It had not taken the monarchs long to realise that London, and the court, was not to their liking. William, although a gallant military leader, was an asthmatic, and the fumes of the capital were already beginning to affect his health. The naturally reticent man disliked the display and rambunctious goings-on of English society and the fancy of the court, where the Crown was on public display at all times. The new monarchs needed a palace to signal the intent of their reign as well as to accommodate William's needs, a house that would rival Versailles. Ten days after the coronation, the two monarchs took themselves out of London towards Hampton Court, a Tudor palace a few hours' ride west of the capital.

William and Mary arrived at Hampton Court on 23 February 1689 and found that the palace had barely been used for royal occasions since Charles II's honeymoon in 1662. It had subsequently been the country house of one of the king's mistresses, and an occasional summer retreat for the court, where the Privy Council sat while the king stayed at Windsor near by. A few repairs were made in the 1680s when the house was made over to James II's second daughter, Anne, yet by 1689 the place was decidedly down at heel. William and Mary decided immediately, however, that Hampton Court would be the ideal site for an English Versailles. Two days later they commanded the Surveyor-General to make a survey. On 2 March the royal bed was sent by barge to the palace and ten days later it was declared that Hampton Court would be the new home for the whole court, which had to be transported up the Thames from Whitehall.

Wren, despite all his other commitments, set about his plans with alacrity. He was the perfect choice of architect because he was the finest in England, and because he desired to build a palace that would stand for ever and articulate the supremacy of the English throne. He had to come up with the ideas fast, however, as William and Mary were impatient to move in as soon as possible.

Parliament did not like the fact that the court would be so far from London, and already the absence of the Crown was commented on, as Lord Halifax observed: 'the King's inaccessibility and liveing soe at Hampton Court altogether, and at soe active a time ruined all the business'.[20] In acknowledgement that the Crown could not retire from the capital entirely, a compromise was found on the far fringes of Westminster, at the western edge of Hyde Park, which would become a winter residence for the royal couple, and Wren was commanded to make alterations to another royal house, renamed Kensington Palace, formerly the home of the Earl of Nottingham. The house was not to be splendidly replanned but made a comfortable accommodation, 'a very sweet villa', as Evelyn would later comment.

With the continuing frustrations of St Paul's, Wren was facing pressure on every front to accommodate his new patrons. William and Mary wanted building to start at Hampton Court that year and Wren's office swiftly came up with three schemes for them in rapid succession, hoping to identify and meet the monarchs' taste and temperament. Both Charles II and James II had adopted the French fashion of the bedchamber, where the closest nobles were bound into a system of ritual revolving around attendance to the Crown's most intimate daily routines. Both William and Mary were more private than previous monarchs, and while the palace needed grand rooms for audiences and celebration, the privy chambers were of the utmost importance.

Their Majesties were very involved at the early design stage. Wren's first scheme was a complete demolition of the Tudor palace, apart from the central Great Hall built by Henry VIII. The inspiration was French, but unlike at Versailles the whole scheme would work around a vast quadrangle, and the palace would face away from the river and look out over an extensive landscaped garden. Inevitably, like so many of Wren's plans, this scheme fell on the rocky ground of cost; it would be too expensive and take too long to complete. The surveyor was forced to return to his drawing board at Scotland Yard and start again. He did not, however, throw away all the ideas of the first palace, and in the second scheme the quadrangle was smaller and there was still to be a grand portico, above which reigned a dome. Again this was rejected as it would take too long to complete.

Rather than totally demolishing the Tudor palace, Wren then decided that he would work his designs around it; the old palace would remain and be extensively renovated. Wren therefore was seriously constrained in what he could achieve by how the building was set within the landscape. The old building would be covered by a vibrant classical surface of pedimented windows, recesses and a single balustrade that ran along the roof. It was a dramatic façade that would hide the problems of the old palace beneath. As ever, Wren found the invention that could unite and improve where money and time placed impossible burdens upon his designs.

Building started in April 1689, coinciding with the campaign season, which saw William increasingly absent from the nation, leading England's army abroad first in Ireland and then in what would become known as the Nine Years War, while the government and the administration of the two palaces were left in the hands of Mary, who felt uncomfortable in the role. The palace became a demolition zone as the roofs were stripped of their lead, the wooden wainscots that lined the interiors were ripped out and much of the stone was removed. The stone would be stored, or spread about the land to level ditches and moats, while some was transported to London to build a flood barrier for Wren's own garden at Scotland Yard. A series of workshops were built in readiness. The Thames Gallery, a Tudor gatehouse on the Thames, was converted for the queen.

One of the key problems for Wren, however, was the supply of new stone. At St Paul's he already had problems with the supply from the

Portland quarry, and with the commencement of the war with France, the threat to shipping from piracy only increased. Wren therefore had to look for quarries, preferably inland, that could supply the palace by road, and in the rush to get started he was even willing to salvage the original stone from the old palace. That winter the haste to complete the new palaces would have a disastrous effect.

In early November there was an accident at Kensington. The foundations had been laid over a vault and part of the walling collapsed. Five week later a more serious accident occurred at Hampton Court, where internal walls in the south range, the long side of the palace, fell, bringing down the roof, chimneys and parts of the third floor. Even worse, the collapse killed two carpenters and injured eleven others; the mortar that had been used in that section was later found to be poorly prepared. Wren was distraught, while Queen Mary blamed herself for her selfish urging of the work. Two weeks later there was a hurricane, yet no further damage was sustained.

Wren set about the repairs, but the occasion could not pass without official notice, and he was requested to raise a report on the matter. It also gave the comptroller of the Office of Works, William Talman, the opportunity to undermine his boss. Talman was one of a new generation of architects; he had designed the south front of Chatsworth House, home of the Duke of Devonshire, one of the finest examples of English baroque. Talman presented the Treasury Board with a catalogue of Wren's errors and the two men were then requested to present their cases. Talman brought with him testimonies from two master masons who held grudges against Wren because of lost contracts at St Paul's. The meeting degenerated into accusations and counter-attacks. The committee sided with Wren and the surveyor was commanded to continue his work, but the occasion was a reminder of the dangers surrounding Wren's position.

Wren was now fifty-eight years old, and never busier at work, yet as he noted in the *Architectural Tracts*, building was politics in stone, and he would need to ensure that he did not become trapped by the shifting ground about him. The old Surveyor-General could not deny his proximity to the old regime, while Talman was of the new generation that rose on the coat-tails of the Glorious Revolution. The surveyor would now have to be wary of his competitors as the new regime added to the complex relationships that pervaded his architectural practice.

THE MORAL REVOLUTION

The events of 1688 were a revolution for the definition of monarchy – the role of Parliament, the Convention and the Bill of Rights changed for ever the great institutions of the country. This was further enforced by a series of parliamentary Acts which confirmed the centrality of Parliament within government; when the house refused to grant the Crown a revenue for life, William also became financially dependent upon Parliament.

From the moment of his coronation William was eager to fight on all fronts and would lead his army in Ireland against James II, who had landed with French troops to whip up support among the Catholics in an attempt to regain the crown. In addition, in May 1689 William declared war on France, leading his European coalition of Protestant forces on the Continent, in opposition to Louis XIV's absolutist ambitions. The king's ability to wage war was dependent on being able to convince Parliament to share his enemies. This was made concrete with the 1694 Triennial Act, which ensured that a new parliament was elected every three years. In addition, William made the Crown more reliant on Parliament through his foreign policy, constantly requesting that Parliament pay for his ventures abroad.

The religious question following 1688 remained unresolved, however. While the Convention had settled the rights and laws of succession and government, the events of the Glorious Revolution had made the need to seek a religious settlement ever more urgent. The confusion of the last fifty years, in which faith and citizenship had become such fractious bedfellows, needed resolution.

William had come from Holland, where a culture of toleration had been the mainstay of their constitution, if not enshrined in law. He was a Calvinist by temperament, not an Anglican, yet his new role demanded that he act as 'Defender of the Faith'. Mary, on the other hand, was a devout Anglican, who saw the preservation of the established Church as the holy warrant for the events of 1688. God's providence, not just the Convention, had delivered her to the throne. Their Majesties found, however, not just that religion was divided between the established Church and nonconformists, but that the political settlement itself had caused ructions within the Anglican Church.

For men like the Archbishop of Canterbury, William Sancroft, the sacred oath he had made in naming James II King of England was an oath before God and could not be broken, even though the archbishop himself was a victim of James's persecution. Sancroft could not recognise the succession of William and Mary as monarchs *de iure* while James remained alive. He refused to officiate at the coronation and took no part in government, and also to leave his palace at Lambeth, on the south bank of the Thames. He was joined by a number of High Anglican preachers and worshippers who by their refusal to take oaths of allegiance to the Crown would come to be called 'non-jurors'. The number of such refusals was small, around 4 per cent of the total clergy, but their impact would be far-reaching. A schism formed within the established Church which would reverberate for some time and come to highlight the role of religion within government and the nation at large.

To counter the non-jurors the Crown courted a more tolerant clergy, such as the so-called 'latitude men', who included John Tillotson, dean of St Paul's. Influenced by the New Philosopher and Wren's early patron John Wilkins, Tillotson had developed a strong 'latitudinarian' liturgy which sought a rational Christianity and toleration of other faiths and espoused a hatred of the persecution of dissenters enshrined in the Clarendon Code.

The schism between the non-jurors and the 'latitude men' would find a dangerous focus in the attempts to find a religious settlement in 1689. In that year, Locke published *A Letter Concerning Toleration*, which he had penned while in exile in Holland. The *Letter* was a stark warning against intolerance and the question of authority over an individual's choice to believe what he wanted. He asked why the sovereign should have power over the religious beliefs of his subjects. Belief, unlike actions, was not something that could be imposed from above as the freedom to think for oneself was inalienable.

The *Letter* focused particularly on the problems of persecution, the enforcing of orthodoxy through threat and punishment. If the state forced its subjects into religious practice that went against individual belief, it would most likely fail. The record of the last fifty years offered enough proof for any magistrate to agree. Therefore, Locke asked, should the state be in the business of regimenting religion at all? Each individual should be allowed to choose his or her form of belief (except unbelief), but the state should be careful if ever it considered a policy of persecution. What the modern state needed was an established Church that was broad enough to include a number of the most moderate sects. In addition, there should be no persecution of the congregations that did not come under such 'comprehension'.

In 1689, this was put to the test. During that summer the Whiggish Earl of Nottingham introduced a twinned set of Bills into Parliament: the Act of Toleration and the Act of Comprehension, offering the absorption into Anglicanism of moderates who could uphold a number of the thirty-nine Articles of Faith and profess a belief in the Trinity, as well as a limited toleration of other faiths. There was a strong chance of success for both Bills until William encouraged the additional repeal of the Corporation and the Test Acts. This appeared to the parliamentary Tories like a frontal attack launched against the Church. As a result, only a reduced 'comprehension' survived in the highly amended 1689 Act of Toleration. As Locke wrote to a friend in Holland, the Act was a glimmer of hope and was 'not perhaps so wide in scope as might be wished for by you and those like you who are true Christians and free from ambition or envy. Still, it is something to have progressed so far. I hope that with these beginnings the foundations have been laid of that liberty and peace in which the Church of Christ is one day established'.[21]

No side was satisfied. The Whigs had not gained enough, and the Tories thought they had given away too much, fearing that any form of toleration undermined the uniformity of the Anglican Church and that England would sink once again into tumult. William was so dissatisfied with the conclusion that he called a convocation, a gathering of all clergy, to set their own purpose straight. The dean of St Paul's, Tillotson, was assiduous in planning the strategy of the 'latitude men', hoping to push wider the boundaries of comprehension, developing a new liturgy that could encompass many sects. He was thwarted, and the convocation returned a staunchly conservative message of entrenchment. William then attempted to rid the Church of the non-jurors, and some four hundred clerics, including William Sancroft, were removed, and Tillotson was named Archbishop of Canterbury to lead his 'moral revolution' from the head of the Church.

The two sides of the unresolved argument would trade blows for many years to come. One particular example of this was a series of punches between the supposedly anonymous author of *A Letter Concerning Toleration*, John Locke, and the chaplain of All Souls' College, Oxford, Jonas Proast. Proast was a skilled polemicist who forced Locke to make concessions and clarifications at every step. In a series of pamphlets the public exchange soon became nasty, yet Locke began to articulate a strong vision for the new role of the established Church within a nation that allowed many faiths. In the 1691 *A Third Letter for Toleration*, which stretched to over two hundred pages, Locke imagined a new Church that established its predominance not by law and persecution but by reason and persuasion. The Anglican Church would show its true character by pastoral work and comprehension, a centre for national commemoration, rather than ritual and obedience, which Locke claimed had more to do with Catholic absolutism than the true religion.

The 'moral revolution' of 1688 oversaw the rise to prominence of the 'latitude men', and gained the approval of the queen. As a result she also became interested in the work at Ludgate Hill and would often peruse the designs. Every autumn, Mary would show her affection for the work at the cathedral by sending a buck from Windsor forest, so that Wren and his workmen could toast the queen over venison at the annual 'passing of the books' at the end of the building season when all accounts were collated.

In the first years of the new reign, work at St Paul's continued despite the upheavals. After Dean Tillotson was elevated to the see at Canterbury, the deanery was then taken by William Sherlock. In addition to the disturbances caused by the change of regime, financial problems continued to hamper progress. Wren found that taking loans against the coal tax was a risky business, as the minutes of February 1689 showed: 'due to severall persons of whom money was borrowed on the credit of the Act of Parliament £5,150, and that there is also due to ye workmen for materials & workmanship til Xmas last, which is already stated and measured, £5,575. And also for Mason's Work, not yet stated and Measured, by estimate £3,500. In all £14,225'.[22] In 1692, there was a salary freeze on all works to try to stem the flow of funds.

There were also recurring problems at the Portland quarries, and the progress of the cathedral was made even more desperate by the new regime's taste for war, which drew money away from the City and cast all shipping into disarray. The transportation of stone from the quarries became perilous, while the fleets in the Channel made the delivery of coal to the capital haphazard. In 1691, the Cathedral Commission reported that a boat carrying 158 tons of Portland stone, trying to keep up with the convoy 'for fear of being taken by the French Privateer, foundered and sunk at sea.'[23] By the end of the building season of 1694, however, the cathedral had reached a milestone with the completion of the stonework of the choir. A large timber screen was erected to shield the east end from the rest of the cathedral and work would continue beyond the gaze of inquisitive London.

The choir was traditionally the holiest place, divided from the rest of the church, where the clerics and dignitaries sat encased within a sanctum. Wren professed that he wished a 'free and airy prospect of the whole of the church',[24] yet his cathedral would be a single building of many parts: the length of the nave was a place for ceremony and processions; the as yet unbuilt dome would offer a Protestant rebuttal to Rome, a temple to peace and light. Yet most importantly of all, the cathedral space was devised for the performance of Anglican religious services, which combined sacramental rituals and preaching. At the choir these functions came together.

The Clarendon Code of the 1660s had enforced Anglican communion as a sign of allegiance while Puritanism had been hounded from the pulpit. In Wren's first plans, he had placed importance on the role of the Word within the English sacred space, writing: 'In our reformed religion, it should seem vain to make a parish church larger than that all who are present can both hear and see.'[25] This was further enforced by the latitudinarian desire to persuade rather than persecute. St Paul's would be the pulpit of London, and in his original plans Wren seemed to suggest a division between the choir and the auditory. The religious service would be held in the choir while the pulpit would be elsewhere, perhaps under the dome.

But by 1694 Wren had decided on a single space where liturgy and sermonising combined. Thus he needed to create a space within the east end, beyond the great crossing where the dome would reign, which could function as both pulpit and altar. In all his experience of rebuilding the fifty-one city churches he knew precisely how big this space should be: 'I can hardly think it is practicable to make a single room so capacious, with pews and galleries, as to hold above 2,000 persons, and all to hear the service, and both to hear distinctly, and see the preacher'.[26]

Approaching the choir from the west end, Wren planned a screen to cover the entire width of the eastern edge of the crossing. It was to be impressive, without setting the choir apart from the rest of the cathedral, offering a more intimate room rather than an enclave within the vast cathedral space. Above the screen the elegant carved boxes that contained the great organ rose 22 feet into the air. As one entered through the wooden portico of four Corinthian columns into the body of the choir, there were to be elegantly carved wooden stalls on either side in which the established order of Church and City was organised in ritual and decoration, symbolically restoring the shared ownership of the cathedral. There was seating for 116 in two rows on either side, where the various levels within the cathedral hierarchy, from the bishop to the ten singing choristers, sat. There was also seating for the City dignitaries, Lord Mayor and aldermen who often shared in worship. Thrones for the bishop and the Lord Mayor were prepared close to the altar and opposite each other.

Along the reverse of the stalls that backed on to the aisles were a series of galleries and stairs which offered more space for ordinary worshippers. A banked row of seats with windows ran along both stalls, like theatre boxes, offering more seating, while steps led up to the top of the stalls, where seating was arranged as a balcony along the full range. These innovations allowed a congregation of at least three hundred to participate within the intimate space of the choir. In addition, Wren also designed a series of retractable benches on wheels which, on particular occasions of celebration, could be pulled out from under the stalls with steel handles and assembled within the open central space of the choir. Finally, to ensure that the space worked as a perfect auditory, Wren designed a simple hexagonal pulpit on wheels.

The choir was also a place of liturgical ritual. So, for the acts of communion, Wren devised a new symbolic space. Since the Civil War, the position of altars, communion tables and railings had become less controversial, yet there were still debates to be had about the positioning and ordering of the signs of the Church. The apse at the east end of the cathedral, under the large clear window, was to be the focal point of all ritual. Wren first devised an impressive reredos, 'consisting of four pillars wreathed, of the richest Greek marbles, supporting a canopy hemispherical, with proper Decorations of Architecture and Sculpture'.[27] He wished to place his altar at St Paul's in direct correspondence to St Peter's, Rome, and Bernini's baldachin, but Wren's ideas were on the table at the same time as another important shift in the identity of St Paul's. In 1696, Bishop Compton published a series of statutes on how the London clergy should conduct services in order to ensure that the cathedral was a shrine to the latitudinarian doctrine.

In response, Wren developed a more economical plan: there was to be no ornate 'architecture and sculpture' but a simple carved, movable communion table. Wren suggested that this modest approach was temporary, yet there was no attempt later to revive any long-forgotten plans for embellishment. The walls of the apse were not to be encased in marble but, as reported by Wren: 'first twice soaked with oyle, then primed and painted with fflake White and v[e]ined',[28] to appear like marble. Crimson velvet was ordered to give the apse some sense of decoration. Instead of an elaborate balustrade, as devised in a series of designs by Nicholas Hawksmoor, a simple marble-topped low railing was commissioned. Wren's choir perfectly reflected the new demands of the new Anglican Church.

The London Revolution

While many historians have often argued about the impact of the Civil War and the Glorious Revolution as the great turning points of the seventeenth century in the nation's story, few have wondered aloud whether in fact the true 'English Revolution' was seen not in the 1640s, or in 1688, but in the 1690s.

Looking back, the London of fifty years before would have seemed a different place, a different country even, as within the soil of the city the first seedlings of a new era were beginning to flower. The fledgling modern metropolis was now bigger than could ever have been imagined. As Thomas Brown noted in 1702: 'London is a world by itself. We daily discover in it more new countries, and surprising singularities, than in all the universe besides. There are among the Londoners so many nations differing in manners, customs, and religions, that the inhabitants themselves don't know a quarter of them.'[1] London's residential population lived in over 57,000 houses spread out over 740 hectares (1,830 acres), four times the size of the area destroyed by the fire.[2]

This vast expansion had shattered the traditional urban space into enclaves and modern neighbourhoods. The city at large became a fluid mixture of anonymous and closely knit communities formed by new relationships dependent on work, status, religion and gender, so that *The Spectator* would joke: 'the inhabitants of St James's ... are a distinct people from those of Cheapside, who are likewise removed from those of the Temple on one side, and those of Smithfield on the other by several Climates and Degrees in their way of thinking and conversing together'.[3]

By 1700, London had become the largest city in Europe. Although historians cannot be completely accurate, the accepted population figure is between 525,000 and 575,000, in comparison to its main European rivals –

Amsterdam (200,000) and Paris (510,000). It was more than twice the size of either Rome or Madrid. In an age when the size of the population was a nation's strength, London was the powerhouse of Europe. It also constituted 10 per cent of England's total population and 60 per cent of its urban population. The capital had become a magnet, or for some the principal drain, for the rest of the nation. Most of all it attracted the young, who came to chance their hand at the centre of commerce or to take up an apprenticeship in one of the many guilds, and in 1700 there were between 27,000 and 30,000 apprentices in the city. There was also the hope of higher wages which drew the surplus population from the outlying regions. This young workforce – without ties to land or family and mostly unmarried – would make up the faceless mass of London street life, and feed the fear of the mob.

This rapid growth also had a dark side. London remained a dangerous place to live; the majority of arrivals were poor and had little hope of finding their fortune. Even though the rebuilding had improved streets and housing, more people died in London every year than were born there. The metropolis would become a place of economic extremes without the traditional structures to protect the poor or sick from deprivation.

In addition to internal migration, London had become a centre for international immigrants. In the previous century a stream of Protestant Walloons and Dutch had sought out the city as a refuge from religious persecution. In the 1650s, Oliver Cromwell had welcomed a congregation of Dutch Jews, and in the 1690s work had been completed on the City's first synagogue, Bevis Marks, on the eastern edges of the wall. By 1695, the Jewish community numbered approximately one thousand.

Most significant was the flood of Huguenots that entered England following the Revocation of the Edict of Nantes by Louis XIV in 1685. By 1700 nearly fifty thousand French Protestants had fled to England, and had developed communities in the capital at Spitalfields to the east and in Soho to the west of the walled city. They brought with them skills and international contacts that benefited the home markets, particularly in such luxuries as silk weaving and international banking.

As the writer Daniel Defoe would make clear in his satire *A True Born Englishman* (1700), this foreign flood had an instant effect on the national character. To be English was to be a man of the world, bound by outlook rather than blood:

A true born Englishman's a Contradiction
In speech an irony, in fact a Fiction
A bander made to be a test of fools
Which those that use it justly ridicules.
A metaphore invented to express
a man a-kin to all the Universe.[4]

This flow of strangers nevertheless caused unease in the nation. The arrival of the poor and homeless foreigners inspired unprecedented levels of charity, and it is estimated that £200,000 was raised to help the refugees, yet it also brought disquiet. Throughout the 1690s the Common Council of the London Corporation was inundated with petitions against the aliens, charging them with undercutting the guild rates.

The influx of foreign skills also had an impact on St Paul's. Throughout the rebuilding Wren had commonly used builders, masons and carpenters who had come from the City guilds or teams from outside London. While the stone hulk of the cathedral had been completed by English hands, Wren's decorative craftsmen came from Europe.

The cathedral organ was designed by Bernard Schmicht, sometimes called Father Smith, a German. Smith arrived in England from Holland, where he had gained a reputation for building the organ at the Grote Kirk in Horn. Within three years of his arrival in England in 1668, he had risen to the position of king's organ maker, had built the organ at Wren's Sheldonian Theatre, and was organist at St Margaret's, Westminster. He soon became a recognisable face among the virtuosi of London. He was the ideal candidate for the task at St Paul's, and the commission ordered an organ far larger than any Smith had attempted before. It was supposed to be finished for Lady Day, 1696, but took a further seven years to complete.

Wren selected the Huguenot Jean Tijou to execute the elaborate iron-work within the cathedral. Wrought-iron decoration had become increasingly popular since the 1660s and within the city churches there had been great demand for new work, much of it taken in hand by master craftsmen of the Guild of Blacksmiths. The arrival of Tijou in England saw a leap in innovation: his ability to twist and turn wrought iron into natural forms was unlike anything seen in the country hitherto. In 1690 he was commissioned to build gates at Hampton Court and was immediately in demand to decorate the country houses of the nobles.

In 1691, he began work at St Paul's by building the huge window frames for the choir. The window was a fundamental aspect of Wren's design as a means of filling the interior of the church with a flood of natural light. The frames were simple and undecorated, apart from a fashioned fastener: the thinness of the leading was deceptively strong, to hold the transparent panes of glass together. He completed the windows in his workshop at Hampton Court, then moved them by barge down the Thames to London. It was the screens at the east end of the cathedral, to the north and south of the altar, however, which defined Tijou's work. He worked at St Paul's on the intricate gates for over seventeen years.

For the choir, Wren was determined to use the finest craftsmen he could afford. Grinling Gibbons had already gained a reputation as the master woodcarver of his generation. Gibbons had first come to the attention of Wren in the 1670s after the artist had been discovered by John Evelyn in Deptford. His extravagant talents were first utilised on royal projects by Hugh May as he redecorated the palace at Windsor for Charles II, and in 1682 he was named the king's surveyor and repairer of carved wood. He was commissioned to carve for the privately funded St James Piccadilly, the parish church of Henry Jermyn's St James's. Gibbons' work was also used in the sumptuous Italianate decoration of James II's Catholic chapel at Whitehall.

At St Paul's the stalls of the choir had been erected in oak imported from northern Germany, and then built by the master craftsman Charles Hopson. German oak was used as it had better grain and was less knotty than the native variety. Wren and Gibbons then finalised decorative designs, which the carver would make in pale limewood. Within the Anglican auditory the decision on what to carve was critical: Catholic statues were to be eschewed; overtly symbolic or esoteric decoration was also to be shunned. Instead, Gibbons developed a scheme of decorations that he had learnt while gaining his trade in Holland, where paintings of still life and natural scenes had been popular, and the carver proposed to recreate ordered and abundant nature from the unyielding wood.

Wren commanded that each feature throughout the cathedral be unique, and so Gibbons reduced his palette of figures to a selection of peaches, tulip blossoms, crocuses, wheat ears, forget-me-nots, acanthus leaves and, most famously, bursting pods offering up their peas. Gibbons then intermingled this finite selection of elements, offering an infinite combination of pieces, festoons and cornucopias throughout the cathedral.

Wren also commissioned Gibbons to design and carve sixty-six cherub heads and wings to rise above the seats of the prebendaries within the stalls. Each cherub was unique, with its own expression, carved in his workshop in Bow Lane and then brought to the cathedral complete. Gibbons also designed seraphims, some holding trumpets, to stand on the organ case facing westward towards the nave. Another set of eight angels rested on the summit of the case, high within the eastern arch of the dome space, to give an elegant silhouette to the choir screen which divided the east and west ends of the cathedral. Thus through Gibbons's designs Wren created his choir not as a reliquary or the resting place of saints and idols, but a home for angels.

On 5 October 1694, John Evelyn made his first visit to St Paul's. The visit would inspire him to consider a new edition of his *Parallel*, which would later play a role in promoting the cathedral and his old friend, Wren. Studying the new choir, he would conclude that the building was 'a piece of architecture without reproach'.[5]

BOOM AND CHANGE

Building to supply the demands of the burgeoning population continued into the 1690s, pushing out the boundaries of the city ever farther. North of Red Lion Square, Nicholas Barbon worked on transforming farmland belonging to the Bedford Corporation into streets of terraced houses for the rising middling sort. By the 1690s, however, both schemes had reached an impasse. He defaulted on the annual rents to the Bedford Corporation because he had overstretched himself; too much money was tied into long-term projects without enough ready cash to hand.

This and other financial woes affected his other schemes. In 1684 he had bought the former country house of Thomas Gresham, Osterley Park, to the west of London, for £9,500. Although the house had been purchased as a rural retreat for the successful metropolitan investor, Barbon could not help but use it as an investment, mortgaging it on the Exchange for £12,000. He then began to alter the house. In the inevitable court proceedings, brought to the Exchequer Court in 1690, the two empty-handed investors, one of whom was the representative of Sir Josiah Childs, the leading merchant, attempted to get their money back. They soon found themselves outfoxed by Barbon, who had purchased a seat in Parliament. His new position preserved him from prosecution, and the case was allowed to drop.

It would also offer him new opportunities in the changing economy of the city.

In the last fifty years England had moved from being an agricultural economy to a manufacturing centre, yet it would take some time for government policy to acknowledge the transformation. James II's economic policies during 1685–8 had typified the old-fashioned idea that the basis of all wealth came from the land, which should be lightly taxed, while the burden fell on imports and manufacturing. Hearth tax punished the urban dwellers rather than the rural farmers. For the last twenty years Barbon had thrived under this easy regime but it was to change.

Many merchants in the capital resented the impositions placed on their trade by the Stuart regime. It was one reason among many why the City had remained far from the court. In 1688 they found a new monarchy, well-versed in the enlightened economic policies of the Dutch Republic, which would happily endorse their view of the economy: the heavy taxes on manufacturing were lifted, the low taxes placed upon building were raised, and the monopolies of the trading companies were broken to allow the financial markets to blossom.

Between 1660 and 1700 imports from the colonies to London doubled, and in all categories the volume of goods increased. In 1686 the Americas exported £900,000 into London alone; in the same year the West Indies delivered £675,000. The rise in imports did not only supply the home market, creating new industries to finish and manufacture goods with the new materials, but also allowed a surplus to be exported either back to the plantations (by 1700 India took 15 per cent of all England's exports) or to Europe (England supplying 40 per cent of Europe's sugar).

The rise of trade since the 1650s had remained the preserve of the few, but in the 1690s the fashion for speculation and profiteering became feverish. The old-fashioned system of granting exclusive trade agreements to certain companies was soon condemned as monopolistic, while the capital was becoming a bustle of private stockers and investors. The coffee houses that once rumbled with gossip and politicking now ran with news of the latest ships in the port and the burbling chatter of stockjobbers. This new class of businessman was investing in everything from Barbon's schemes to overseas adventures.

As the merchant classes began to grow, there were calls for these restricted markets to be opened up to all. Before 1690, there were about

fourteen companies with a collective worth of £0.9 million; by the middle
of the 1690s a number of these monolithic joint stock companies had been
floated on the emerging stock exchange, while other ventures were offered,
and by 1695 there were nearly 140 trading companies with a valuation of
over £4.5 million. As in the Internet boom of 1999–2000, investors, giddy
with caffeine, blindly threw their money after the promises of swift profit.
It was a market fit for a skilled speculator such as Nicholas Barbon. Soon
the catchphrase 'How bare-bon'd they are'[6] was bandied around for any
stock that looked less than a sure bet, and the speculator also gained the
moniker Damn'd Barbon.

Much of the business of business was conducted in coffee houses, and
by 1700 there were estimated to be over two thousand of these within the
city. Two of Hooke's favourite coffee houses swiftly became the centres of
the new stockjobbing, as Gresham College rested so close to the Royal
Exchange, highlighting the relationship between the New Philosophy and
the organised chaos of the trading floor. The stock market, it seemed, was
born in the marriage of mathematics, hope and caffeine.

There were successive attempts to stop the rise of stockjobbers, and in a
1697 Act the number was restricted to one hundred, who were licensed
and regulated. The following year they were forced out of the Royal
Exchange and had to do their dealing outside. Coffee houses soon began
to specialise in their markets, and thus Exchange Alley became the home
of an emerging stock exchange. In Jonathan's there was a list displayed for
shares in the various joint stock companies. The earliest marine list, which
charted the locations of ships and their cargo, was established by Edward
Lloyd, who gained all his information from his own coffee house in
Lombard Street. A financial press emerged to deliver the news of all kinds
of transactions which one would pick up over a coffee. Speculation fever
grew, shrugging off any attempts at regulation.

Yet while William III oversaw the economic dawn of the modern
market, his policies also drove the nation into conflict, and Barbon, like
many speculators, would be hit by a downturn that no negotiation or
subterfuge could assuage: war. In May 1689, William III declared war on
France and would be absent from England every year leading his troops
in Europe. The king's passion for war would alter the shape of the metropolis, for his army in Europe marched on bullion alone, which needed to
be found by any means necessary, and London would suffer the greatest
burden of keeping the Protestant army in the field. After initial gains a

war of attrition would rage on land and sea for nine years, and the funding for it could be raised only in two ways – tax or borrowing.

The changes in the market in the 1690s would force Barbon away from housing and draw him into the major debates of the age. John Locke would also be drawn into the exchange of ideas. A strong economy could fund wars, but what did this mean? Everyone could agree that the market needed to be regulated, but how?

In 1692, a widespread land tax was initiated which immediately brought in more income than customs. In 1694 another barrage of taxes were imposed on marriages and deaths and there were new forms of assessment of non-land-based wealth such as stocks and trade goods. In addition, excise taxes were extended to almost every commodity, including salt, hops, malt and spirits. The organisation of lotteries and 'tontines' satisfied the speculative spirit of the age with promises of cash prizes and dividends and helped to prop up the government's funds. John Evelyn's coachman won £40 on one occasion.

Efficient methods of collecting the new taxes were inaugurated; mathematical systems of accounting and auditing were introduced to calculate the tax burden. It was during this decade that one Treasury official, William Lowndes, famously advised: 'look after the pennies and the pounds will look after themselves'.[7] Increasingly the study of trade resorted to the New Philosophy, its methods of measurement and data collection, to find its solution. A nation's wealth was judged by the size of its population and this needed to be estimated. One of the founder members of the Royal Society, Sir William Petty, was the first to study demography, a system that would come to be called 'political arithmetic'.

In 1696, Gregory King, who was also a member of the society and had worked alongside Wren and Hooke on a number of committees, followed Petty's lead and produced *Natural and Political Observations upon the State and Condition of England*, which attempted to analyse the demography of the nation in its various stations, from temporal lords to vagrants, calculated from a number of sources in 1688.

The need to regulate and oversee government, in particular the collection of taxes, had seen a rise in the number of state officials. As the need to find revenue resulted in the excise of levy on taxable consumable goods, so the number of officers to oversee and record each transaction grew. A series of new departments and offices – the Board of Trade, Inspector-

General of the Customs, the Register of Shipping – were established to further enforce a scientific system of accounting and measurement. The mixed mathematics of the New Philosophy would be used to squeeze the nation for money.

By November 1693, however, the government coffers were empty. These short-term measures could not disguise the poor planning of a government that had thought that the war would be short and cheap. The continuing conflict hampered the flow of gold and silver on to the market, so there was an additional scarcity of available bullion. This raised the thorny issue of borrowing, and in particular the question of interest rates. Parliament debated lowering the rates, yet opinion was divided over the best way to regulate borrowing – would a standard rate encourage or stifle the market?

To the master merchant Josiah Childs, a reduction of the rate was a guarantee of wealth accumulation as it would encourage borrowing and investment. This had obvious advantages for the government, which wanted to borrow heavily to fund the war. Nicholas Barbon agreed with this position in his own *Discourse on Trade*, which was published in the same year.

John Locke, however, had different ideas. He believed that interest rates should be deregulated and find their 'natural' level dependent on the supply and circulation of money at any given time; the state should not involve itself in the private barter of two individuals. In *Some Consideration of the Consequences of the Lowering of Interest, and raising the Value of Money*, published in 1691, Locke proposed that the relationship between supply and demand was in constant flux. He was determined to influence the parliamentary Bill of January 1692 but failed. The interest rate was reduced to 5 per cent rather than left to the whims of the moneylenders and market forces of the urban financial markets.

William III would attempt to fund his war by borrowing, but it was clear that running to the City cap in hand was not the best way to defeat Louis XIV. When, in 1689, the king approached the City to ask for money, the response was mute, as the writer Roger Morrice observed: '£100,000 will be raised but not very readily and in little parcels'.[8] This was hardly an ideal manner of funding an international campaign. By 1695, the costs of government were audited at the staggering sum of nearly £5.5 million a year, and a new means of borrowing had to be found.

In *A Discourse on Trade*, Barbon had written:

In Cities of Great Trade, there are publick Banks of Credit, as at Amsterdam and Venice: they are of great advantage to Trade, for they make payments easie, by preventing the continual trouble of telling over mony and cause great dispatch in Business: publick Banks are of so great a Concern in London that the merchants of London, for want of such a bank have been forced to carry their cash to Goldsmiths, and have thereby raised such a credit upon Goldsmiths Notes.[9]

By the 1690s, the use of credit and goldsmiths' notes issued by private banks was becoming common. In the 1670s, Charles Hoare had begun his own credit house in Cheapside; in 1690, he moved to Fleet Street. In the 1680s, Child's Bank also started on Fleet Street and became so popular that in 1698 the founder, Francis Child, was named Lord Mayor of London. In 1692, the Scot John Campbell arrived in London and set up business in the Strand, offering loans, taking deposits and issuing notes, and gave birth to Coutts Bank. The explosive rise of private credit, however, did not necessarily make paying for the war effort any easier. Private investment went in search of private profit, but the state needed a public bank to manage the national debt.

There was no one better than Nicholas Barbon at seeing a gap in the market and exploiting it. Being a Member of Parliament allowed him to drive forward his plans for a land bank. Working alongside the lawyer and religious writer John Asgill, he set up the 'Government' Land Bank, hoping to raise money from investment in land. It was an instant hit with the Tory faction, who lived up to their moniker, the Country Party. The bank was an unlikely pairing of entrepreneurs, but by 1695 the venture was said to be successful with holdings of £350,000 and an office above the stamp office in Lincoln's Inn.

The Government Land Bank was not the only such scheme, as similar projects emerged throughout London. But while other land banks hoped to make their interest in the collection of future rents, Barbon planned his future on mortgages, launching the very first building society. It offered money at 3.5 per cent, far lower than other lenders, and promised that it could advance from its reserves up to £300,000. On this wave of hubris, the bank merged with John Briscoe's National Land Bank, and seemed even to challenge for the role of the safest house in the nation. The amalgamated banks then pushed for recognition by Parliament, and received royal assent in 1696. This was, however, dependent on the operation being able to raise

£2.5 million for the government. Nothing went right; the City did not trust Barbon, whose reputation as a speculator preceded him. In the end they were able to raise only £2,100.

Elsewhere, however, a more secure means of managing the national debt was being discussed. A National Bank was proposed among a group of speculators and traders in 1693, similar to ones that had been developed in Holland. The group was a decidedly Whiggish outfit, including William Paterson, who had spent time trading in the Netherlands and had an eye for profit equal to Barbon's. In 1691, he had been among a first group of speculators to suggest a 'Dutch' bank of credit. The plan was initially rejected, but in 1694 Paterson and his team presented their ideas again to a Parliamentary committee. It would be a bank to manage debt, not speculation.

On this occasion, Parliament leapt at the opportunity dangled in front of them to raise £1.2 million, made immediately available to the government at a mere 8 per cent. At that rate, buoyed with a sense of patriotism, everybody was keen to lend to the state, and the bank would be left to manage the debt. The bank was formed as 'a perpetual fund of interest' and was not allowed to loan money to the Crown, without parliamentary permission, or to deal in goods and merchandise. It was strictly controlled to oversee the exchange of bills in the form of legal-tender banknotes. Within ten days of business, beginning on 21 June 1694, the coffers were filled, as Evelyn recorded: 'The first great Bank for a fund of money, being now established by Act of Parliament was filled and completed to the sum of 120,000 pounds.'[10] As bullion gold and silver was deposited and replaced with paper notes, so the precious metal could be shipped over to the Continent to pay for William's army.

There were obvious teething problems from the start. These were made all the more desperate after only a year, as the nation plunged into a serious cash crisis. By the mid-1690s much of the silver within the nation had been shipped to Europe to pay for the war, and trade had become so disrupted that the supply of bullion overseas to pay for imports was low and there was a scarcity of coinage within the home market. This had a disastrous effect on the National Bank, for on 6 May 1696 there was a run on the bank.

In recognition of his economics writing John Locke had been named as one of the commissioners on a new Board of Trade to oversee colonial policy and trade practice, which was suffering under the pressures of the international war. Once again, after nearly twenty years outside government, Locke was placed at the heart of the state. He was a dedicated commissioner and was soon seen as the dominant voice in the chamber, able to push forward his ideas on trade and currency.

Locke believed in the 'natural law' of economics, the vision of a regulated market, fuelled by the dynamic circulation of currency. Yet there were moments when intervention was necessary. Since the beginning of the war, Locke had noticed how silver was becoming scarce, while speculation on the gold guinea was on the rise. Since 1691, there had been calls from Parliament to counter the problem, but between 1689 and 1695 £938,000 of bullion had been sent to the Continent, and as a result prices had risen at home. By 1696 England was suffering its worst economic crisis of the century.

The lack of money threatened the country's position in foreign markets, while heavy taxation and poor harvests had devastated agriculture at home. There was literally no money left to borrow. For speculators like Barbon the situation was a disaster; he could not find investors in his land bank and no buyers for his building project, and very swiftly he found creditors who needed their money back knocking down his door.

A variety of methods were employed to preserve silver stocks: the government annually debated whether to devalue the coins, depressing prices by forcing merchants to reduce the cost of the wares. For the consumer, clipping or milling, whereby bits of the minted coin were cut off, had become commonplace. Locke considered this destruction of the king's coin a crime, yet the state seemed paralysed by uncertainty about how to combat the crisis.

Throughout 1695/96 numerous debates and schemes rose and fell, and the printers produced a plethora of pamphlets on every possible project to save the nation's currency. At the centre of the debate was the question of what money was. The debate would bring the speculator Barbon and the philosopher Locke into direct challenge. In Locke's view a coin had 'intrinsic value', its exchange value determined by its silver content. The worth of the coin was to be found in the value of the metal. As stocks of silver became scarce, however, this value was rising. The opposing faction saw money in a different light. Value was not to be found in its weight or bullion content but was to be defined by law. Barbon became one of the most vocal advocates of this view. Anything could be called money, he proposed, if it held the legitimate authorisation: 'It is not absolutely necessary money should be made of gold or silver; for having its sole value from the law, it is not material upon what metal the stamp be set.'[11]

When in 1695 Locke published *Further Considerations of the Consequences of the Lowering of interest, and raising the value of money*, Barbon retaliated with *A Discourse concerning coining the new money lighter*. In desperation, the government collected the opinions of a random group of thinkers, most of them long-term members of the Royal Society: 'Mr Locke, Mr D'Avenant, Sir Christopher Wren, Dr Wallis, Dr Newton, Mr Heatcote [a goldsmith], Sir Josiah Child, and Mr Asgill, a lawyer [and Barbon's partner]'.[12] The group was pretty evenly balanced between those who agreed with Locke and those who agreed with Barbon. Wren offered his own opinion: 'Money is nothing but a Common Measure, for the More ready Exchange of all Commodities, prescrib'd and Fix'd by the Government; the Material of this Common measure may be any thing Enact'ed and stamp'd by the government'.[13] He also offered a decimal system of coinage, which was rejected. Newton, too, threw in his opinion, which was against recoining.

Locke worked assiduously through 1695/96 to present his views as the most reasonable approach to the question of money, and in a series of pamphlets including *For Encouraging the Coining of Silver Money in England* he again argued that value was intrinsically linked to the worth of the coin. If his opinion was to be adopted by government, there would need to be a complete recoinage. In the end, the Chancellor of the Exchequer, Charles Montagu, agreed with Locke, who was invited to Parliament (even though Barbon was currently an MP) to make his views known. Government fell for his solution and it was decided that the whole currency needed to be recoined. Throughout 1695/96, a series of parliamentary debates took place and Acts were passed to prepare for the operation. It was ordered that from 1 January 1696, no clipped or milled coins should be allowed to circulate in the marketplace.

In the spring of 1696 the new Master of the Mint was named – Isaac Newton, who did not agree with the recoinage but was forced to fall into line with his friend's scheme. His gift for mathematics made all accounting a simple task, and it also allowed him to systematically organise the process. In London, the mint at the Tower was opened at four every morning and remained open until midnight, where 300 workmen and fifty horses turned the mints and fires to melt and press the nation's silver, surrounded by a cordon of armed militia to keep the gawping crowds at bay. The recoinage continued until 1698.

The transformation of England into a 'military fiscal state' had a profound impact on the city of speculation. War had raised a number of essential questions about the regulation of interest rates, the nature of money and the growth of the state. What was trade? How could profit be encouraged? What emerged from this time of economic uncertainty and transformation would be the first seedlings of the modern market.

'IMPORTANT AND LASTING CONSEQUENCES'

There was another war that fomented during the 1690s, the Battle of the Books, in which the conflict between the ancients and the moderns was played out. Since the Restoration the New Philosophy had been making a claim for itself as the driving force behind London's transformation. The achievements of the moderns were already apparent. Yet they did not necessarily toll the death of *ancienneté*.

As the New Philosophers demanded that the slate of human understanding be wiped clean and the foundations of knowledge be rebuilt, the cry for the preservation of the past became ever stronger. In 1692, the retired minister and courtier William Temple published *An Essay upon Ancient and Modern Learning*, in response to a number of recent publications, including Bishop Burnet's *Sacred Theory of the Earth*, and the French *Digression sur les anciens et les modernes*. Temple criticised the idea that the modern world could add anything new to the achievements of the ancient world.

Three years after Temple's *Essay* appeared, a new era in the intellectual struggle erupted. In 1695, Parliament was set to debate the repeal of the Licensing Act, which had regulated and censored all publications. The freedom of the press was a dangerous concept which had haunted each moment of national crisis. To many a free press encouraged anarchy, yet once again Locke could be found as the voice of reason near the epicentre of the debate. His argument was subtle – he judged the expression of ideas in the same way as he saw the toleration of worship: government persecution would neither deliver unity nor abolish sedition. In addition, Locke saw in the free publication of ideas a reflection of the free traffic of trade.

His argument was persuasive, and the relaxation of the law heralded an explosion in publishing. London became a rash of newsprint, and by the end of the year there were three tri-weekly papers, *The Post Boy, Post Man* and the *Flying Post*, to compete with the government organ, the *London Gazette*. The coffee houses, which had long stood as debating chambers and talking shops, soon gained the appearance of libraries. A literary culture was born which some considered the symbol of liberty, and others the sewer of libel. Emerging from this swarm of ink and paper came Daniel Defoe, and *The Spectator*, edited by Addison and Steele. Between 1689 and 1714 some five to six thousand political polemics and a swirl of satires as well as economics tracts were published. The Commonwealth of Ideas, first prophesied by John Milton in the 1640s, had become a reality. In these very first moments of liberty, Grub Street, the scoop, the novel, the sensation, the laws of spin and the public outcry were invented.

John Locke was no bystander, and in the 1690s he produced more work than ever before on a bewildering assortment of subjects. He remained in conflict with Proast over *A Letter Concerning Toleration*, and produced replies in 1690 and 1692, and his writing on economics continued throughout 1692–96. In 1693 he completed *Some Thoughts Concerning Education*, an attack on scholasticism which placed him firmly on the side of the moderns and crystallised his long-held feelings about the New Philosophy and his own childhood. Education, Locke proposed, made the man. A strict education taught virtue through reason and brought the child towards morality. Most important of all, education was not the acceptance of authority but the discipline of the mind.

Two years later, he brought his many ideas together into a single statement of intent: *The Reasonableness of Christianity*. Locke preferred to publish anonymously, although his cover was thin and he soon gained the attention of the disapproving Oxford scholars. He had argued all his life that reason, not revelation, was the path to morality, but in this essay he proposed that the scriptures themselves could offer a rational path to morality. The essay brilliantly articulated his aversion to the enthusiasms of his childhood, when the scriptures had been used by the fanatics of Cromwell's Commonwealth to demand a theocracy. Rather than bringing the Second Coming, Locke argued, the scriptures were an aid to understanding natural law.

Yet many read in Locke's work the opposite of faith, in particular taking offence when Locke restated his aversion to the idea of original sin, which he had first promoted in the *Essay*. The book's reception had initially been slow. Ironically, the work gained its reputation only once it began to be attacked by those who considered that he was knocking down the pillars of belief and replacing them with liberty and unfeeling reason. In their eyes Locke's God was a distant and mathematical deity who took no part in the world, and it was even suggested that Locke had rejected the idea of the Holy Trinity and the divinity of Christ.

In 1696 Locke received an unexpected attack from a one-time friend, Edward Stillingfleet, until recently the dean of St Paul's and now Bishop of Worcester, which pitched him into the centre of the public debate between the ancient and the modern and forced him to defend his ideas on human understanding in print in a series of pamphlets, and to edit and reprint the *Essay*. By the following year the *Essay* had taken its place at the centre of the religious and philosophical debate as other commentators, spurred on by Stillingfleet's objections, attempted to undermine Locke's view of the world. As he confessed to a friend: 'My book crept into the world about six or seven years ago, without any opposition, and has since passed among some for useful and, the least favorable, for innocent. But as it seems to me, it is agreed by some men that it should no longer do so.'[14]

He may not have enjoyed the attention but Locke's legacy would be established by these objections and he would rarely stray from the centre of intellectual controversy for the next century. In 1704, Oxford University decided to bestow on him the highest praise and proposed to ban publication. Locke did his best to avoid responding to every insult and query, observing, 'the world now has my book, such as it is: if any one finds, that there be too many questions that my principles will not resolve, he will do the world more service to lay down such principles as will resolve them, than to quarrel with my ignorance'.[15]

PEACE

When the City suffered in the war, so did its cathedral. As money began to disappear from the streets, and as the interest rates were debated in Parliament, this had a direct impact on the ability of Wren to rebuild St Paul's. By 1697 the roof of the nave had yet to be built and the west front still lacked a face, while a gaping hole sat at the centre of the bulk high above the crossing where the dome was intended. The interruptions to trade caused by the conflict at sea had affected the ability of the City to raise the coal tax levy, while the absence of coin due to the shortage made the raising of loans more haphazard. By 1692, the project was already £23,000 in debt. In May 1694, the workmen petitioned the commission to receive payment to cover their costs, and the only thing Wren could do was convert the arrears into a loan and promise to pay interest until such time as the money was available.

The lack of funds also caused disturbance to the supply of materials to the churchyard itself. To roof the aisles, 42-foot-long wooden beams were needed. The Duke of Newcastle had promised timber from his own forest at Welbeck, yet this had not been sufficient. There were still insufficient stocks of the native timber to span the whole building, and Wren struggled to import suitable lengths of oak from Germany. It was almost impossible to find native timber of the right size, and the Welbeck oaks had to be transported from Yorkshire to London. This was first attempted by road, but when the load arrived at the village of Bawley, the immense trunks could not be driven through the main street and had to be barged back to the capital and then dragged by horse up Ludgate Hill.

Wren was also being drawn away from his master project by other royal projects that developed out of the war. In October 1694, two years after Wren's hospital for soldiers at Chelsea had opened, Their Majesties gave permission for the building of a hospital for seamen at Greenwich. A committee of trustees was created, and it named John Evelyn as treasurer. The project was particularly close to Queen Mary's heart, but she soon became sick and died on 20 December 1694. Her passing was a blow to many, including Wren, who had been a close ally. It also had devastating effects on Wren's work at Hampton Court, as William III, unable to visit the palace he had built without his wife, allowed the project to wither for three years. Wren was allowed, however, to throw his energies into the hospital at Greenwich and produced one of his most spectacular designs.

Thus Wren was busier than ever: in 1694 he was sixty-four years old and still working to the fullest of his capacities. He was dedicated to the work at Greenwich. He was stretched at St Paul's. In 1698 work began again at Hampton Court. And on 4 January, a further burden was added to his roster when Whitehall Palace burned down in a freak fire started by a laundry woman. Wren was forced to evacuate his own house in Scotland Yard, carrying all the books he could manage. When he saw the flames attack the Banqueting Hall he commanded his servant to drop the books and 'For God's sake let all things alone here and try to save the fabric.'[16]

The hall was the only building to survive, and Wren was immediately charged with finding new grand plans for the palace.

As at Hampton Court, Wren worked on Greenwich with his deputy, Nicholas Hawksmoor. Since 1689, Hawksmoor had earned the right to be called an architect on his own merits. In 1690 he designed Broadfield Hall, near Buntingford. Two years later, Wren allowed his apprentice to take control of the designs for the Writing School of Christ's Hospital school in London. His work at Kensington Palace continued and his influence can be strongly felt in the King's Gallery, begun in 1695, on the south front of the building. Hawksmoor had learnt much from his mentor but he was developing his own voice. At Greenwich he worked alongside Wren and prepared all the drawn plans for the project.

In time, Evelyn introduced another young architect, the clerk of the Treasury Chamber, John Vanbrugh, to the project. Born in 1664, he had already made a name for himself as a dramatist, specialising in the adaptation and translation of classics of French, English and ancient plays, as well as sparky, original works such as *The Relapse* (1696) and *The Provok'd Wife* (1697). By the new century, however, his focus had changed, noted in a pun by Jonathan Swift: 'Van's genius without thought or lectures, /Is hugely turned to architecture'. And in 1702 he was named Comptroller of the King's Works within Wren's office.

By the new century Vanbrugh and Hawksmoor (who had been named Clerk of the Works in 1698) had become a close unit, working together on the Duke of Carlisle's country house at Castle Howard in Yorkshire, which would be one of the first examples of a new English baroque, and later at Greenwich. This collaboration was perfected in the first decade of the new century at Blenheim, built by the state for the Duke of Marlborough, John Churchill, in gratitude for the general's valour in battle.

It would be fitting that these two innovators should be brought together by Wren, and that his influence should be felt well into the next generation. It would be these two men who took on Wren's mantle but never allowed it to define them. They would be the progenitors of English baroque, and the finished hospital at Greenwich would, while based on Wren's original designs, also reflect the innovations of his immediate successors.

Peace came to England in September 1697 with the Treaty of Ryswick and a victory for the Grand Alliance of Protestant nations which had ground France down to a stalemate. The peace, however fragile, offered a respite for England after nine long years, in which the demands of maintaining a warfare state had altered the nation. This was a time to rejoice, and St Paul's Cathedral was chosen as the location for the elaborate celebratory mass to give thanks for England's success and the triumph of Protestantism.

Once 2 December was announced as the day of thanksgiving, work on Ludgate Hill accelerated at a hectic pace in order to get the cathedral ready for its official opening. Work on the choir was still incomplete and the master painter William Thompson had to oil and paint the stone apse to make it appear like marble with gold and lapis lazuli veins; it was then swagged with luxurious crimson velvet drapes. Furnishings were selected to add lustre to the choir; velvet cushions were prepared for the benches of the stalls; an altar table was placed at the east end, resting upon a Persian carpet and then draped (again) in crimson velvet, fringed with gold; upon it were two gold candlesticks and two cushions on top of which rested fine chased gold editions of the Bible and the Book of Common Prayer.

The night before the thanksgiving service, the choristers stayed late, practising the new anthem as final checks were made to 'Father' Smith's organ, which was being pressed into service before it had been completed. A team of women were employed to polish the marble pavement.

On the day itself, the city was filled with jubilant crowds that lined the streets to watch the formal procession of the Lord Mayor's carriage and the aldermen, the marching companies of the City with their flags and drums, as well as the grandees who made their way from Westminster. Everybody was present, apart from William III himself, who disliked such public display and stayed in his palace. As the principal men and women of the nation entered the cathedral and made their way to the stalls, the cathedral organist, Dr John Blow, played his anthem, especially composed for the occasion, as well as music by Henry Purcell.

The public stalls were full and vergers were employed to allow only the invited into the choir as a crowd gathered inside under the crossing. The scrum was so thick that Evelyn was forced to join the crowds outside. At the high point of the service, the Bishop of London, Henry Compton, climbed up to the top of the new pulpit and preached a sermon on the psalm. 'I was glad when they said unto me: We will go into the house of the Lord'.

As the poet James Wright exulted, when he first saw the choir decked in splendour:

Without, within, below, above, the eye
Is fill'd with equal wonder and delight;
Beauty appears in all variety,
Yet in every different dress, 'tis exquisite.[17]

14

The Phoenix Is Risen

The celebration in December 1697 for the peace of Ryswick hid a jumble of ongoing and minute problems at St Paul's. The supply of Portland stone to Ludgate Hill had been interrupted in February 1696 when a section of Dorset cliff that rose above the South Pier, where the boats were loaded with stone for London, had collapsed, ruining the pontoon, the cranes below and a stretch of road that had followed the cliff path. All supply of stone to London was halted, and in the meantime the vast blocks would either have to be hauled to Chesil Beach down the coast or carried overland to the capital.

When the news reached London, the commission commanded Wren to send a team of experts to assess the damage and to see whether any stone could still be freighted. Two masons, a carpenter and a measuring clerk visited and reported back. The South Pier was beyond repair but a minimal supply could be restored if stone were carried to the north side of the island, where an old jetty still stood, covered in shingle. For the short term at least it would have to do, but as the quarrymen tried their best to work their way to the north jetty it soon became clear that the location had been abandoned for good reason.

The plan worked during the summer of 1696 but as winter drew on and the seas began to rise, loading the barges became increasingly dangerous. In May 1697, Wren was forced to go down to Dorset himself, taking Hawksmoor along with him, to survey the situation. He found little hope in the new organisation of the quarry, yet could not find an expedient solution. The water was too shallow and rocky near the old castle to build a new wharf. The north jetty was 'extremely choaked up by a driving Beach'.[1] The quarry master, Thomas Gilbert, suggested that a new road and quay be built, but this would cost over £1,000 and would take time.

Wren considered whether it was possible for the quarrymen to deliver the stone to a repaired south quay by toppling it over the cliff side.

This cheaper but more dangerous option was discussed when Wren returned to London and was agreed upon. It was a measure that had short-term gains – preparations could be quickly accomplished and for little expense – but it had one particular disadvantage. The process of toppling the stone over the cliff, dragging it to the pier and then loading the boats allowed the supply of smaller blocks to recommence, but it ended the prospect of any large stones ever reaching Ludgate Hill.

Wren's latest plans for the façade of the cathedral had envisioned a grand portico standing emphatically at the west end of the cathedral. A long, broad flight of steps would lead up to the portico, where vast columns, 90 feet high, would rise into the air, capped with an impressive entablature and pediment. With the disasters at Portland, the prospect of not receiving stone large enough to create such effects forced Wren to rethink.

As a compromise, he returned to his Definitive Plans and created a new façade to face the metropolis. Rather than a single grand order of vast pillars, the architect broke the front into two rows of columns, following the line of the building, below a large pediment. On the first level twelve coupled 40-foot Corinthian pillars rose from the wide black marble stairs, offering a recessed portico before the main west entrance with its white marble door case. On the second storey of the portico sat another series of eight coupled pillars lifting up a highly carved entablature that raised the face of the cathedral to the height of the roof, above which reigned the pediment, which would later be carved, with statues placed upon the parapet.

The result would be less dramatic than he had originally hoped, and he attracted some criticism. In response to comments by Roger North who considered himself something of a connoisseur, Wren was forced to admit: 'They could not have materialls to make good single columns, not to project the entablatures so farr as to range strait over the heads of the columnes.' Later, *Parentalia* would offer a further excuse – historic pre-cedent: 'In the Temple of Peace, the most magnificent in old Rome, the Columns were very properly and necessarily doubled to make wider Openings ... Bramante used double Openings without scruples, as did Michel Angelo within and without the Cupola of St Peter's in the Vatican ... The French architects have practised the same to good effect, especially in the beautiful façade of the Louvre.'[2] Yet it was Wren's

The west front of St Paul's Cathedral

aspiration not just to replicate history but to surpass it, despite all the problems on the ground.

The slow supply of stone from Dorset caused numerous problems on the work site. When there was no stone in the churchyard the masons were forced to find other employment, and this often soured relations with the surveyor. In defiance, Wren decided to push ahead with his dome. The interior crossing now rose to the level of the roof, and Wren had already been forced to reorganise his designs for the heart of the cathedral. Because of the way he had organised the arches, the four openings leading into the aisles were lower than those that opened into the nave, choir and two transepts. These had to be raised to offer a more perfect balance, and upon this he ran an entablature around the whole circumference of the opening, which would act like a carved rim at the base of the dome.

The Danish sculptor Caius Gabriel Cibber, with whom Wren had worked on the reliefs on the base of the Monument, was then commissioned to begin carving the eight bold keystones at the summit of the piers. Wren had ordered a sculptor to do a mason's job with good reason. Cibber had travelled to Italy and studied the work of Michelangelo and Bernini, and was able to bring a grandeur to the crossing, each featuring a carving of an angel holding an emblem of the cathedral, the crossed swords. Wren then set his masons to work on building the base of the dome. Thus far the masons had built up to the height of the roof. He wanted his creation to reign high over London and designed a circular entablature to divide the dome from the interior of the building, upon which he planned a drum of windows and alcoves.

Fortunately, the drum could be achieved without Portland stone, although the exterior and the pillars were added later, and the masons began to work in readily available freestone. The project, however, was complex, as it had to fulfil both structural and aesthetic standards. The drum itself needed to be sturdy enough to hold the dome above with a series of buttresses to support the downward thrust while also pushing the dome into the London sky. The walls were designed to incline inwards, so that the light from the windows was aimed at the cathedral floor, as Michelangelo had done at St Peter's.

But the cathedral was not just stone but also a living place of worship. The previous year, on 16 July 1696, Bishop Henry Compton had served a formal notice to the cathedral's chapter and dean to resolve how the cathedral was to work. He wished the incomplete cathedral to begin to play its part in the life of the metropolis once more. This was a crucial issue for, as the new city cathedral was emerging, what would be the role of the Church within modern London?

Compton demanded a spiritual renovation for the cathedral alongside the rebuilding programme. Working alongside the dean, William Sherlock, the chapter devised a liturgy and a daily pattern of services, psalms and prayers, as well as a scheme to organise how the surrounding parishes performed, and how the estate lands were managed. There would be morning and evening prayers in the side chapel at 6 a.m. and 6 p.m.; public prayers were to be said in the choir at 9 a.m. and 3 p.m. The work of each member of the chapter hierarchy was defined, and a system of fines established for those who were late or absent from daily psalms or failed to preach, and for bad behaviour among the choristers. Following the service to celebrate the peace of Ryswick, the cathedral was encouraged to play its role within the city, and in 1698 twenty-five weddings were conducted amid the bustle of the work site, and the following year daily services were held in the newly completed morning chapel.

Compton hoped the cathedral would become the centre for preaching at the heart of the nation. Sermons that aimed to unite the people in rational Christianity began to be delivered from the pulpit. In particular, it was from here that the many ceremonies of remembrance, the feasts and festivals of the City, Crown and Church – the martyrdom of Charles I, the double deliverance of 5 November, Guy Fawkes' Day, and the arrival of William III, the Great Fire services of 3 September, and St Paul's Day on 5 January – were orchestrated, binding the congregation in faith and memory.

For the work to be finally completed, however, the commission needed still more money. The terms of the parliamentary grant of 1685 meant that the coal tax levy would run out in 1700. The commission was forced to go back to Westminster, cap in hand once more, begging for the levy to be extended. In preparation, the commission asked Wren to draw up a document to outline what remained to be done. Wren tried to put a positive spin on the situation: 'The work west of the Choire is advanced in several places to the upper Cornice, and together with the great Portico must so remaine for want of large blocks till the peers and Cranes in the Isle of Portland be restored.'[3]

Yet the surveyor also expressed a hint of doubt in his plans. He sensed that the patience of the commissioners was running out and he feared the loss of his dome: 'If this Work of the Dome be not now set upon while there is considerable supply for 3 1/2 years to come, it cannot in reason be thought a fit Enterprise for a smaller revenue.' He needed to persuade the commission to hold firm: 'The Cupola, were it to be finished, would be so remarkable an ornament to this mighty City, which is yet inferior in Publick Buildings to many Cities of lesse note and wealth, that all persons native or fforigners will be extreamly satisfied.' And if forced into a choice between completing the west front or the dome, Wren's preference was clear: 'It will cost much more to finish the Body and Great West front with the Porticos and belfreys, than the whole Cupola to the Top.'4

This outline was taken to Parliament, where the petition did not receive a welcome. Wren's plea inspired the jibes of wits and Whigs, who saw the grandiose pile as a Tory behemoth and its architect as an anachronism who was slowing down progress in order to collect his annual salary of £200. Now no longer an MP, Wren could not protect his project once it passed the door to the House of Commons, and inside a Bill was grudgingly drawn up and a parliamentary committee called to consider the matter.

In Wren's estimate, £178,285 was needed to complete the work, and a further £25,000 to complete the city churches. As these figures were scrutinised, other institutions – Westminster Abbey and St Thomas's Hospital in Southwark – saw an opportunity to gain funding and made claims as to why they deserved a proportion of the coal tax levy. Some of the MPs visited the site and were led around the cathedral and tempted by wine and biscuits, yet they still reported back their dissatisfaction at the slow rate of progress.

Wren's method of working on all sections of the building at once rather than following the strictures of the warrant and raising the structure in parts meant that it was impossible to halt the project and make do. This riled the committee, who passed the Bill but only with an amendment to show their chagrin towards the surveyor. The cathedral would get the money if Wren's salary were halved to £100 a year. In the hope of incentivising him, however, the committee promised that he would receive his full remittance six months after the completion of the whole cathedral.

Humiliated, the architect was forced to accept and remained silent in the face of the mealy-mouthed slight. This was not easy as he had invested much of his own money in the stock market, and following the recoinage of 1696 his portfolio was looking decidedly shaky. He knew, however, that he would now be able to complete his cathedral, and found comfort in the generosity of others who came to his cause. His old friend Thomas Spratt, now dean of Westminster Abbey, offered him the role of Surveyor of the Abbey, with an annual income of £100. In the same year, John Evelyn published a new edition of his translation of Fréart's *Parallel* with an ancillary *Account of Architects and Architecture*, which he dedicated to his long-time companion. In the preface, he lauded Wren's genius:

> I have named St Paul's, and truly, not without Admiration, as oft as I recall to mind (as frequently I do) the sad and deplorable condition it was in when (after it had been made a stable of horses, and a den of thieves) You, (with other gentlemen, and my self) were by the late King Charles, nam'd Commissioners to survey the Dilapidations, and to make Report to his majesty, in order to a speedy Reparation: you will not, I am sure forget, the strugle we had with some, who were for patching it up any how, (so the steeple might stand instead of New Building, which it altogether needed) ... Out of the ashes this Phoenix is risen and by Providence Design'd by you.[5]

THE NEW CENTURY

In 1700 the rakish English writer Ned Ward published the first edition of his scurrilous guidebook to London, *The London Spy*, in which he lampooned the recent fashion for foreign travellers to the capital and was intent on showing the real face of the metropolis. On one of his peregrinations he recounts a visit to St Paul's. Outside, the churchyard was a vast, industrious workshop covered in piles of stones and heaped with timber, but the workmen seemed to be doing as little as possible, under the shade of the building: 'instead of using their hankerchiefs to wipe the sweat of their faces, they were most of them blowing their nails'. Inside the cathedral work seemed to be going at a similar pace, and Ward observed 'ten men in a corner very busy about two men's work'. Yet even the cynical Ward couldn't fail to be impressed by what he saw inside: 'We were gazing with great satisfaction at the wondrous effects of human industry, raising our thoughts by degrees to the marvellous works of Omnipotence from those of His creatures'.[6]

Yet Ward's account also reminded the reader of the origins of Wren's new temple, almost at the same time as they were being forgotten. As the new century dawned the memories of the old conflicts were passing;

London was once again a young city and the old was swiftly being discarded. Even the Rebuilding Commission itself was changing. In 1698, the
death of Wren's brother-in-law, William Holder, created a division within
the group. Holder was replaced by Dr Younger, an ambitious cleric, who
had none of the bitter memories of the Civil War and sided with the
younger members of the team, Dr Godolphin and Dr Stanley. The commission would now be split between the generations, and while for the
moment all things were in balance, this would not always be the case.

The new commission showed little sympathy for Wren in his treatment
by Parliament and did little to defend its architect. Instead, it urged that
'the work of the Dome be now set upon and carried on as fast as conveniently may be'.[7] Wren, however, was determined to set the record
straight, and in 1698 sought a licence to produce a series of prints of St
Paul's. The images showed the inquisitive Londoners what their future
cathedral would soon look like. It was a deft piece of advertising as well as
a canny insurance policy, for it ensured that if any further changes were to
be forced upon him, they would not go unnoticed. A further three prints
were produced in the following four years, showing both the exterior and
the interior from various angles.

The first print showed a cross-section of the cathedral, and in particular
the structure of the dome as it had been envisioned in 1675. In 1702, the
second print, engraved by the Huguenot printer Simon Gribelin, showed
the west front with its double portico, the two towers rising either side
and, high above, London's dome. The cupola sat above the cathedral, an
almost exact copy of St Peter's in Rome. Both these images were elegant
articulations of Wren's dreams, but both would prove inaccurate. As Wren
entered the eighteenth century it was clear that the final form of St Paul's
Cathedral had still not been fixed.

In the first decade of the new century, the great symbol of the turmoil
of the last century would gather pace towards completion. While the bulk
of the work had been finished, the most important features of the cathedral
had not yet been finalised. The new grant of money from Parliament had
come with strings attached for the surveyor, but it nonetheless allowed him
to accelerate work on Ludgate Hill – yet it was still not enough. This
situation was exacerbated by unexpected news from abroad, and again the
cathedral was caught up in the political events of the day.

By 1701, Wren had become used to planning for most unexpected
eventualities but he had failed to predict the death of the exiled James II

in Paris that September. Few had foreseen that following the death Louis XIV would instantly acknowledge the birthright of the young prince, James II's son, whose birth in 1689 had accompanied the Glorious Revolution. Parliament was thrown into panic and William took the opportunity to close it down and call a new house, one that would clamour for war and be willing to give him as much money as he wanted.

Wren stood as an MP for the Dorset constituency of Melcombe Regis, and was elected, hoping to get an increase on the coal tax to complete the cathedral, yet his pleas would be drowned out by the debates on the next military campaign. His hopes were dashed for good when, on 21 February the following year, while hunting in Richmond Park, King William III stumbled over a molehill, fell and broke his collarbone. Initially the injury did not seem serious and the king was taken to Kensington Palace to recuperate, but by the beginning of March his condition had deteriorated, exacerbated by long-standing problems with tuberculosis. On 8 March he died and Anne, the youngest daughter of James II and sister of Mary, was named queen.

Anne was a very different character from her brother-in-law. She inherited a state of war as the conflict over the Spanish succession drew English forces into the Protestant alliance against the ailing Louis XIV. In Parliament, however, she favoured the Tory faction, which brought relief to Wren, who was now one of the last representatives of the old regime. Anne had visited St Paul's once before in 1697, just before the first ceremonial opening to mark the peace of Ryswick, and had shown her appreciation. Under the new reign Wren was confident he would find the support he had been hoping for, and although she was a woman of few words her appreciation of her surveyor was tangible. He began his work again in earnest, determined to see the cathedral finished.

Upon the west front, work had already begun on the façade, but the final decision on how the towers would rise into the London sky still remained unresolved. The 1702 Gribelin prints showed Wren's original plans based on the designs of the Roman master Bramante, with simple domed *tempietti*, like whips of ice cream upon rectangular cones. But within months, Wren had changed his mind. The towers had risen to the level of the roof and the time had come to finalise how the face of the cathedral would be framed. Wren had noted in his *Tracts*: 'Fronts ought to be ... rather projecting forward in the middle, than hollow,'[8] and the design of the twin towers brought a slow music to the impressive face of the cathedral and framed the dome that was emerging above. The west towers would be Wren's most articulate example of the baroque.

The towers offered an aesthetic as well as a mathematical conundrum – how does the sturdy square body of the tower rise and taper towards a circle?[2] Through his city churches Wren had been inspired to experiment, and nowhere was this more clear than in the variety of steeples and towers. In *Parentalia*, he noted the importance of constructing modern spires to echo the old pre-fire Gothic buildings: 'together with handsome spires or lanterns, rising in good proportion above the neighbouring houses, may be of sufficient ornament to the town without a great expense'.[9]

Yet Wren's new steeples, which were begun in the 1680s and would continue into the 1710s, were something more than plainly sufficient. In the new century the London skyline was pricked by an extraordinary array of designs, as if Wren were back in the laboratory again. There were Gothic towers, Dutch spires, old English square towers, baroque studies in geometry, stone needles, cylindrical cones and wooden, leaded spikes that still give the city its most elegant punctuation today. In 1753, the Italian visitor Count Algarotti would comment that he knew of only one steeple in Italy worthy of comparison.

This appetite for playful novelty was something new for Wren, as opposed to his usual experiments in function and common sense. For the Surveyor-General, the baroque had expressed flexibility of gesture and design on an intellectual level, rarely giving way to swagger or flourish, and he would never have described himself as a baroque architect. The two towers of St Paul's, however, were the result of Wren's rare excursions into 'fancy'. Each tower was to be made of four sections, musically twisting and mutating upwards.

The designs consisted of sixteen coupled pillars upon a sturdy cornice with richly carved wreaths around them, and four pairs of coupled columns at each corner to add to the sense of dynamism, on top of which was laid a further level rising to a flat dome, ending in a tapered finial. The towers finally rose to two golden pineapples designed by the London-born sculptor Francis Bird, and around the edge, small urns of fire in gilt glinted in the London sky, the flames ruffled as if blown by the westerly winds.

The first level of the south tower would hold a clock, while the cathedral bells were hidden in the north tower. Wren had been fortunate in 1698 to obtain the great bell of Westminster Hall from the old clock tower in New Palace Yard, which had been allowed to decline to ruin. As the property of the Crown, the bell had been offered by William III to the local parish, St Margaret's, Westminster, which then sold it to Wren for the price of the metal. On New Year's Day 1699, the bell that had rung since the reign of Edward III was lowered on to a cart and driven through the city towards Ludgate Hill. There it was repaired in the workshop of Christopher Hodson, who provided a new clapper. Unfortunately, the new addition was too powerful, and within a week the bell had cracked and needed to be recast. It was finally placed in the tower in 1706.

That same year Wren signed contracts for the clock, which had been a feature of many of his city churches as they had been before the fire. In many cases these timepieces were elaborately designed, standing out from the church tower on brackets or frames. Yet the cathedral timepiece would be bigger than any before. In the early stages, there were designs in Hawksmoor's hand of a highly elaborate timepiece with hands like scurrying clouds, reminding the people below, '*Tempus Fugit*'. The finished clock was completed, however, by Langley Bradley, a clockmaker on Fenchurch Street who had completed some of the parish clocks and would work at Hampton Court and Blenheim Palace. The clock, with its plain face, was installed in 1708, but had a very short life, and was replaced in 1719.

More intriguingly, the south-western tower was designed to contain a library and triforium. These two rooms were connected by a geometric staircase, a stone spiral similar to that at the Monument. The library itself was rushed into action when the vicar of Islington, Walter Gery, bequeathed his collection to the chapter, and it would be an important symbol of the new Latitudinarian Church, a place of preaching and learning rather than persecution and orthodoxy. The books arrived at Ludgate Hill by a wagon and five horses, which took two and a half days to deliver the full collection. As Humphrey Wanley, librarian to the Earl of Oxford, later wrote: 'I look upon this library, not only as a Library belonging to the Dean & Chapter of a Cathedral Church, but as the Chiefest Public Library in the Metropolis.'[10]

As the towers were rising, the carving on the portico that spanned the two was also in hand. In 1705, Wren commissioned Francis Bird to carve the relief on the pediment above the cathedral's entrance. Bird, a Catholic, was perhaps a strange choice, but he had trained alongside both Gibbons and Cibber, had travelled in Flanders and studied in Rome. Bird's relief, 62 feet in span, was a dramatic portrait of St Paul's conversion. The completed frieze is almost Bernini-esque in its drama, as horses rear and fall in the sight of the divine, the moment of revelation on the road to Damascus, the voice of God transformed into the voice of reason. The frieze was dramatically revealed at the end of 1706, as the scaffolding was dismantled from the west front on the occasion of the thanksgiving mass for victories in the European wars. Elsewhere on the exterior, along the west side of the door, Bird continued St Paul's story.

Wren's other pre-eminent carvers were also changing the surface of the building. Grinling Gibbons mirrored his interior designs of cherubs, festoons and cornucopias on the face of the two towers and above the north transept. He was also commissioned to design the pediment above the north transept, where he carved the royal crest supported by angels in Portland stone. Although Caius Cibber had been disappointed not to have been awarded the prize of carving the portico pediment, he gained another, more personal, mark from the architect. Above the south transept, Wren commissioned a phoenix rising from the flames above a tablet that harked back to 1675, the very first moment that the ground was broken to rebuild the cathedral. The tablet held one word: RESURGAM.

THE CATHEDRAL OF GREAT BRITAIN

The cathedral was now regularly the place for Sunday worship, marriages and municipal events, and was regaining its position in the political life of the city and the nation beyond. Under Queen Anne, who was a devoted Anglican and took a personal interest in the final years of progress on Ludgate Hill, the cathedral came to stand for traditional Tory Anglicanism, accentuating the building's Stuart legacy. It stood not just as a meeting place between the many aspects of the city but also as a place of memory, to bind the collective sense of the whole nation in the celebration of the past, as well as the hopes for the future. The modern cathedral was not just a religious institution that shepherded the souls of the faithful or symbolised the power of the Establishment but also a repository of nationhood in which every citizen could share.

Queen Anne would be the fourth monarch under whose rule the rebuilding of St Paul's had been projected, and the cathedral had been transformed in the last thirty years just as the identity of kingship itself had changed. Within Wren's lifetime the king had gone to war with his own people over the question of the Crown's role in the religious life of the nation. Charles I had been executed in the belief that he alone was God's lieutenant on earth and that his subjects could approach the Creator only through him. Sixty years later the world had changed and the Crown was now in contract with the people through Parliament. Anne remained Defender of the Faith but the Church now represented a policy of reason and comprehension.

St Paul's would have to persuade rather than persecute, convince the faithful rather than instil awe in the subdued. The loss of one identity meant the cathedral could become the symbol for others. The choice of St Paul's as the site of celebration for England's foreign victories allowed it to become a reflection of the nation's growing international status and symbolically placed St Paul's at the centre of the emerging empire.

In 1702, the celebration to commemorate the victory at Vigo Bay began at St James's Palace and processed through the city to the cathedral. Inside, the queen sat on her throne with her two ladies-in-waiting beside her; the choir was filled with members of the Houses of Lords and Commons, the Lord Mayor, aldermen and all the members of the cathedral chapter; the powers of the nation – temporal, ecclesiastical, military and economic – all under one roof. There was also room for well-chosen guests such as foreign dignitaries and their families to be shown the omnipotence of England. The cathedral choristers were supplemented from the choirs of Westminster Abbey and the Chapel Royal, while the Bishop of Exeter preached a sermon on 'For the Lord hath driven out from before you great nations and strong: but as for you, no man hath been able to stand before you unto this day'. There were also celebrations for victories at Blenheim in 1704, Tirlemont in 1705 and Ramillies in 1706. Each was more spectacular than the last, and on every visit the queen would have an opportunity to see the slow progress of her cathedral as it approached completion.

St Paul's was the setting for another celebration in 1707 – the birth of a new nation: Great Britain. On 1 May the cathedral was filled to give thanks for the Union of Scotland and England. Although the two nations had shared a monarch since 1603, when the Scottish James VI had travelled to London and was crowned James I, England and Scotland had remained separate political nations with individual parliaments and established churches until the 1706 'Treaty of Union of the Two Kingdoms of Scotland and England' founded a new era in British politics.

The Union created a new state, and a new future for both sides of the border, as the first article pronounced: 'The two kingdoms of Scotland and England shall ... forever after be United into One Kingdom by the name of Great Britain.'[11] Scottish politicians were to come to Westminster to have their say, creating forty-five new seats for MPs, and sixteen elected peers in the Lords. The borders were open to trade and English coinage was to be used. The Scottish legal system, however, would remain intact and separate from the English, while the Church of Scotland would remain as distinct as it had always been.

On 1 May, as the bells of the cathedral of Edinburgh, St Giles, pealed the song 'Why should I feel sad on my wedding day', the nobles of both nations were gathered in London under the crossing of St Paul's. As the Bishop of Oxford, William Talbot, preached on that day, London's cathedral was now at the heart of the new united nation.

THE DOME

By the time of the celebration, the structure of the cathedral was almost finished, apart from the dome. Inside, the transepts and vaults of the nave were being coated with plaster, later to be whitewashed, and the stones were being painted with a coat of coloured oil paint. The choir was completed and Tijou's iron grilles installed, while the intricate paving on the floor was also in hand: in the east end and the morning chapel, white marble was used to signify areas of worship while the rest of the cathedral space was finished in black-and-white diamond patterns. At the heart of the building the concentric patterning in the space below the crossing mirrored in two dimensions the dome rising above.

Wren's vision of St Paul's had been born with the desire to deliver a cupola to London. By 1700, work on the inside of the drum had commenced in simple freestone while on the exterior more complex designs were initiated. Thrusting the dome high above the skyline, the drum needed formal decoration, and Wren planned a peristyle, a continuous circle of columns, in Portland stone, rising to a heavy stone balcony 172 feet in the air. Wren devised this series of columns with an eye to both aesthetics and structure: the peristyle gave an ornate balance to the dome, a harmonious, ordered link between the body of the church and the cupola above.

He was determined, however, to improve on Michelangelo's designs at St Peter's which he had so assiduously studied for decades. He chose thirty-two pillars, slightly larger than in Rome, and rather than a continuous round of columns he filled in the space between every third and fourth column as a niche. This was reflected on the interior – an alcove was embedded into the drum wall between each third and fourth window and later filled with eight statues of Old Testament saints.

This design had a very practical application, for Wren was always conscious that when the dome was completed the outward thrust of the weight needed to be counterbalanced with a downward force. It was necessary for the whole building to push the weight 'inwards' and 'down', while the force of the dome wanted to push 'down' and 'outwards'. In structural terms, this was the complex equation between 'compression', the force that attempted to push or shorten, and 'tension', the energy that pulled or stretched. Wren needed to create a system in which all the various energies of the building balanced and channelled its weight towards the earth. Although nearly impossible to see from the churchyard, each column in the peristyle was linked by an arch to the wall of the drum, and each filled niche acted as a balance against the downward push of the structure.

It had become increasingly necessary to take such precautions. Rumours from Rome had reported that cracks were already appearing in Michelangelo's cupola, and Wren was determined that his dome would be built for eternity. In addition, the surveyor had known for some years that his work was showing faults. Deep in the basement of the crypt, below the level of the church floor, there were already signs of stress and fractures as the weight of the massive piers that would hold the dome up exerted impossible pressure on the foundations below. In 1675 he had begun rebuilding the crypt piers by filling the lower-level columns with rubble to create a solid core on which the body of the cathedral rested. This, it appeared, had not been done properly. In some places the rubble core had shrunk, forcing the whole weight of the cathedral upon the marble rims of piers; in others the marble was coming away and fracturing. He would be able to repair these foundations only after the dome had been completed, not before, and therefore he would have to find a solution that did not thrust the whole weight of the building upon these faulty piers.

He also wanted to find a way to disperse the compression throughout the building without causing too much tension. At the top of the peristyle he laid a stone entablature to sweep around the whole exterior base of the dome. Here, Wren took extra precautions in balancing the forces by circling the top of the drum with a continuous chain of iron, and a sophisticated system of cramps and hangers which were used to prevent the stones moving in the heat and during the initial stages of the building process. It was said that Wren was so confident of his mathematics that before this chain was cemented into the stone he cut a link to prove to himself that his dome was perfect. In fact, the opposite was true. As he launched the final stage of rebuilding, he was desperately concerned that his vision would fail.

The architect-mathematician had begun his thinking with a problem – the creation of the drum to raise the dome caused an internal anomaly. The peristyle added a dramatic and powerful silhouette to the exterior of the cathedral but would make the interior of the crossing seem cavernous, breaking the harmony of the central space. Michelangelo had encountered similar problems at St Peter's, and Wren would have been familiar with the view that the crossing of St Peter's was unsatisfactory.

To satisfy the difficulties of height, Wren had often included a double dome within his designs, which had been common practice as far back as Brunelleschi's Duomo in Florence and had been used by Michelangelo at St Peter's. The outer dome seen from the exterior would be an elegant hemisphere, and in the Definitive Design he had imagined this in stone, material strong enough to support the heavy lantern above. The interior dome, however, would be lower to give a sense of harmony to the internal crossing. The curve of the inner dome would begin at the height of the windows of the drum, while outside Wren wished to begin his exterior dome above the level of the peristyle's entablature, and also to include an attic floor with windows. How were these two domes to be related? Wren, the New Philosopher, would have to deal with all these issues.

Wren was not the genius of structural engineering that many former biographers and historians have presented. He did not know theories before his time and certainly did not instinctively know the right systems of load-bearing and stress to allow the dome to stand as if by a miracle. By 1705 he had spent a lifetime thinking and studying this problem, yet had not found an answer. Only the experience of building the dome itself would provide that. Nonetheless, his lifetime of enquiry in considering both the rules of architecture and the science of mechanics informed everything he did. In addition, he would have had ample opportunity to discuss his ideas on arches with his friend Robert Hooke, who had first announced a theory of statics in 1670/71. In 1675, Hooke reported in his diary that Wren had used his ideas on his paper designs for the Definitive Design.

Hooke's ideas, demonstrated in a number of experiments, proposed that the ideal shape for an arch followed the 'line of thrust', curving in such a way that the balance of compression passed through from the top to the bottom with as little tension as possible. This 'line' would naturally take the shape of a chain hung between two points, and 'as it hangs in a continuous flexible form, so it will stand contiguously rigid when invert-ed.'[12] In 1695, Hooke's ideas were presented again within the Royal Society by David Gregory (proving, on this occasion at least, that Hooke had a right to fear his ideas being stolen by others) in a paper called 'The Ca-tenaria'. While Hooke's arch worked in the laboratory, however, Wren needed to imagine the same mechanics working on a massive scale.

In 1705, as he looked at the relationship between the interior and exterior domes, Wren began to realise a further solution: rather than trying to link the two domes together, he could join them by a third structure, a brick cone that rose from the base of the interior dome and met the outer dome at the summit. This idea had further innovations: the cone, rather than the exterior dome, could be used to raise the lantern aloft and would follow the line of Hooke's catenary arch exactly, allowing the outer dome to be made as light as possible in timber and metal. Wren had used experiments, theories and equations to develop his ideas thus far but above all he was a practical man, and the proof would be found in the final construction.

In April 1705 Wren gave orders for his workmen to begin the inner dome. He also invented a timber frame and scaffold, a series of circular ledges, that would support both the work and the masons without needing to be held up from below – and without disturbing the daily work on the cathedral floor. The whole surface of the inner dome would later be covered with a plaster made from cockleshells. A central eye, high above the crossing, was left open, and was later circled by a balcony, called the Golden Gallery. The workmen then painstakingly began to build the elongated hemisphere (called by Hooke a 'cubico-parabolic-cuboid') of bricks which tapered imperceptibly upwards. The cone was made as light as possible, 18 inches or two bricks thick, and then strengthened every 5 feet by a ring made from longer, 18-inch bricks, so that it would support nothing but itself. Work would continue through 1705 and into the next year, despite the city being attacked by a plague of flies, so that walking upon the streets left footprints as if walking in snow.

The cone would continue to rise, layer by layer, its steep incline describ-ing the perfect angle, built by the master craftsman Billinghurst and three dozen workers. Wren was keen that every precaution be taken in the final stages of the construction, and rather than paying by measure, which encouraged haste, he commanded his comptroller to account for work 'by the day'. Wren was so pleased by progress that by the end of 1706 he

The completed cathedral in cross section showing the structure of the
dome

rewarded the mason, Richard Jennings, and his men with a bonus of 50 guineas.

Throughout 1707, work began to pick up pace. By the spring the brick cone was almost finished and the mason Edward Strong, son of Wren's first master mason, was fixing the top on which the lantern would sit, while below, the churchyard was filled with carpenters. The master carpenter, Jennings, had already made his visits to Kent to survey the timber that would be used to create the ribs of the outer dome, which were then cut, planed and prepared on the ground until ready for placing high above, where a wooden frame began to spring up around the brick cone. On occasion, the cranes would be used not to carry timber but the seventy-four-year-old surveyor, who wished to check on progress at the summit. By summer Wren was ready to consider the covering of the outer dome. In addition, he was also thinking of designs for the lantern. But even at this late stage the work on the fabric of the cathedral could not be divorced from the events that circled Ludgate Hill.

On 23 August, St Paul's became the unexpected setting for political intrigue for very different reasons, and proved that controversy concerning the cathedral would not disappear. On that day, Queen Anne arrived in her carriage to celebrate the victory of Oudenarde, escorted by her favourite, Sarah Churchill, wife of the army's finest general, the Duke of Marlborough. The two had been squabbling in the carriage because Anne had forgotten to wear the jewels put out for her and Churchill considered this oversight a deliberate snub of her husband's valour. The argument continued as they reached the cathedral door, and as they entered, Anne curtly silenced her lady-in-waiting. The insult would cause an irreconcilable rift between the two.

Yet the occasion was more intriguing than a tiff between friends, for it was also the scene for the Screw Plot, in which it was insinuated that Whig conspirators had devised the unscrewing of certain roof joists that would fall on the queen as she passed up the nave. Of course, the whole debacle was a fantasy, but it reminded all of the place of the cathedral within the Stuart polity. The political standing of the cathedral was crucial for, two days after the plot, the Rebuilding Commission met to discuss what metal should cover the outer dome. A person representing the copper industry had approached the committee to suggest that the dome be covered in copper. This was discussed, and it was decided to follow Wren's recommendation that while copper was durable it tarnished quickly, turning first black and then green. Wren wished his dome to be coated in lead and with the committee's permission contracted the plumber Roberts to line the dome with 'the best Derbyshire lead', for £2,500, while he was also 'willing to encourage the English Copper Works'[13] by promising to include some of the metal in the west towers and the lantern.

The episode did not end there, however, for as Parliament returned to Westminster for its winter session, the copper industry began lobbying the MPs. Soon the question of whether St Paul's should be domed in copper or lead came to the attention of the parliamentary committee and finally to a vote in February 1708. Although the estimate for the copper was £550 more than Roberts', the MPs voted in favour. Sent up to the House of Lords, the Bill was rejected, and an impasse reached. The fate of the dome was now in Parliament's hands. Nothing could be done until both houses were dissolved in April. Once Westminster was emptied, however, the commission took the bold step of vaulting over any parliamentary hurdle and voted to urge Roberts to resume his work, and as quickly as possible. Throughout the summer, tarpaulins and waxed sheets were spread over the frame of the dome as the plumbers nailed and soldered the heavy sheets of lead together. Wren was especially particular about ensuring that no corrosion be allowed in.

In his original designs, Wren studded the dome with windows, but as the lead was being placed he changed his mind once more. The space between the outer dome and the brick cone needed to be lit, and from below the windows in the attic wall allowed a certain amount of light. Yet Wren decided that, rather than follow Michelangelo's St Peter's, the lead would be unbroken by windows, vertically divided into thirty-two arching ribs to echo the pilasters around the attic wall. This gave the impression of greater robustness, an unbroken verticality that emphasised the rising up of the dome. Instead, he set a number of windows at the summit of the outer dome, unseen from anywhere but above, which allowed light into the space without ruining the face of the cupola.

Wren was determined to finish his cathedral by the end of the year, and attention was focused on the lantern that would sit on the top of the brick cone and rise above the outer dome. On 14 May 1708 final designs were agreed with Francis Bird, the sculptor of the relief on the portico pediment, for the great copper cross and ball that would stand on top of the lantern. The stone lantern itself would weigh 850 tons, and all of it was carved on the churchyard floor and then hoisted above during that summer. The circular base had been prepared the summer before and a fence was added.

The lantern echoed the two west towers, with a plinth rising to four long open windows facing to the four corners of London flanked by columns, rising to a miniature cupola. It also related to the interior of the cathedral, for from the centre of the crossing looking up through the aperture of the inner dome, the base of the lantern provided another light-filled hemisphere at the summit of the dome. The light from the windows flooded through the inner dome's aperture, adding luminescence to the crossing below and proving that Wren's dome was as much an instrument of seeing as it was designed to inspire awe.

By October, the building season was coming to a close and the work had almost been completed. The armourer Andrew Nibbet was nearly ready to deliver the copper cross and ball to be raised to the top of the lantern. On such occasions, as one would expect, a pinch of mythologising enters the account. On 26 October 1708, we are told, a group of workers gathered in St Paul's churchyard six days after the surveyor's seventy-sixth birthday. It was a small gathering – no dignitaries, no regalia, and no official historian to record the moment. Christopher Wren was there with his son, Young Christopher, who had been born in 1675, the year when the first stone of the new cathedral had been laid, and was now thirty-three years old. The son left his father in the churchyard and rose to the top of the dome by crane alongside Edward Strong, the son of Wren's first master mason.

For those few left who could remember, the cathedral had been through war and devastation; it had been shunned by the city during the Commonwealth and had become a symbol of mockery. Following the Restoration, it had been left to decay until it was too late, and perhaps the fire had saved it from a more ignoble fate. The road to completion since 1666 had been arduous, and despite the fact that it would become the first English cathedral to be completed in the lifetime of the architect, Wren had become the victim of numerous attacks and allegations of tardiness. St Paul's had fallen and been reborn within one lifetime; the childhood memories of Inigo Jones's Tuscan basilica, harking back to classical times, replaced by Wren's modern reinterpretation of the sacred space, promoting reason and the Word. Thirty-three years after the first stone was laid, Wren's son, Christopher, was preparing to lay the final section of the cathedral.

Parentalia remains the sole record of that day when the copper cross, 12 feet 10 inches high and 10 feet 6 inches across, and the ball, 6 feet in diameter, were raised to the top of the lantern and fixed in place. There is no record of the weather, although it can be guaranteed that the London air would have been filled with smoke, just as it had been in the 1660s when Wren's friend, John Evelyn, wrote *Fumifugium*. Wren would complain that the raising of a dome in such conditions seemed pointless when it could not be seen through the fog: 'our air being frequently hazy prevents those distant views, except when the sun shines out, after a shower of rain has wash'd down the clouds of sea-coal smoke that hang over the city from so many thousand fires kindled every morning'. But he nonetheless estimated that his dome would be seen 'at sea eastwards and at Windsor westwards'.[14]

The placing of the lantern would complete his vision of London's dome, and as *Parentalia* records: 'The Highest or last stone on the top of the lantern was laid by the hands of the Surveyor's son, Christopher Wren, deputed by his father, in the presence of that excellent artificer Mr Strong, his Son, and other free and accepted Masons, chiefly employed in the execution of the work.'[15]

The building of St Paul's had been completed, the final stone had been laid, although the finished cathedral was some way off, and another three years of work would be needed to see the official end of the decorating. As the tarpaulin and scaffolds were slowly broken and removed from the body of the cathedral, London was able to see its mother church for the first time in over forty years. The nation had changed in that time, the city had been transformed into a world capital, and it would take time for the metropolis to become acquainted with its cathedral. Yet for the poet James Wright, the resurrected St Paul's was a miracle:

> How shall I fitly name this matchless pile?
> What equal epithet can fancy give?
> Glory of London, Glory of the Isle!
> Best of the best! Double Superlative
> . . .
> The Cupola, that mightly Orb of stone,
> Piercing the clouds in figure of a crown,
> A diadem that crowns not Paul's alone
> But the whole Isle, placed on her head-town.[16]

At last, England had a cathedral to rival St Peter's. The Crown claimed the church for its own as a symbol of the continuation of the Stuart monarchy and the Tory establishment, while the Whigs of the city also laid claim to it as their place of worship. The cathedral would be a temple to reason as well as a place of unity, the centre of the nation where divisions were healed, and where God's grace would descend upon His people.

15

Endings

Eighteenth-century London was a paradoxical place which professed improvement and enlightenment, while offering the majority of its inhabitants misery and a fast track to the grave. The seeds of the new metropolis, sown by Locke, Barbon, Wren, Evelyn and Hooke, produced unexpected flowers. It was the century in which the English language itself was systematically catalogued in the most scientific manner by the least scientific mind, that of Samuel Johnson. It was also an age of revolution, in the new settlements in America as well as in France, inspired by John Locke's ideas of government. Speculation would result in the debacle of the South Sea Bubble but also produce Adam Smith's *The Wealth of Nations*. London became the capital of the world in all its paradoxes and extremes.

Nicholas Barbon did not live to see in the new century. Having come so close to establishing the Government Land Bank as the leading credit house in England, the failure to gain enough subscriptions to fulfil the promises made to the government hit the organisation hard. The land bank was demerged and wound down. He retired to his country house in Osterley, to the west of the city, and on 18 May 1698, Barbon made his final will, naming Asgill as his executor. He died two months later on the verge of bankruptcy. Apart from the expense of his wife's funeral he commanded that none of his debts be paid.

While few of Barbon's original houses remain – most had been demolished by the 1750s – his influence can be found on almost every street, for he set the pattern for the archetypal terraced row. There are no monuments – Barbon Court, a small opening off Great Ormond Street in Holborn, is little more than a car park, while Barbon Alley near Devonshire Square is a blind pathway between two modern office blocks. His most long-lasting venture in fire insurance, however, was more of a success. In 1710 the Fire

Office would merge with Phenix Office and become Sun Fire Office, which today is known as the Royal and SunAlliance Company, the oldest insurance office in the world.

In 1705, a poem was published which may have best summed up Barbon's participation in the formation of modern London. Bernard Mandeville's 'The Grumbling Hive: or Knaves Turn'd Honest' was a seditious and libellous attack on Britain which announced that the nation was a swarm of bees, in which industry and profit were driven forward by self-interest and vice, rather than virtue and morality. It was the most scurrilous but prescient vision of the birth of capitalism:

> As Sharpers, Parasites, Pimps, Players,
> Pick-Pockets, Coiners, Quacks, Sooth-Sayers,
> And all those, that, in Enmity
> With down-right Working, cunningly
> Convert to their own Use the Labour
> Of their good-natur'd heedless Neighbour.
> These were called Knaves; but, bar the Name,
> The grave Industrious were the Same.
> All Trades and Places knew some Cheat,
> No Calling was without Deceit.[1]

Having risen so high in the 1670s, pushing the boundaries of knowledge and understanding, Robert Hooke experienced a slow and painful decline. He continued to attend every meeting of the Royal Society, delivering demonstrations and experiments, and he still proclaimed to anyone willing to listen that Newton owed him a debt. Even in 1690 he argued for his name to be joined to the 'Discovery of the cause of the celestiall motions to which neither Mr Newtone nor any other has any right to lay claime'.[2]

While his powers may have waned, Hooke's passion for science and debate continued. Nor did he lose any of his bite; he was still willing to challenge anyone who dared claim his inventions. He remained on the society's council for most of the 1690s but became an increasingly peripheral figure, despite the fact that the club continued to meet at his rooms at Gresham College. In time, Edmund Halley, Hooke's friend, assumed the role of energetic cheerleader for the New Philosophy. This sense of being passed over enraged Hooke.

If Hooke's scientific career was on a steady decline, there was no indication that his role as architect suffered in a similar fashion. In 1690 he was commissioned to build a school and a series of almshouses for the Haberdashers' Aske's Company in Hoxton, to the east of the city. As a designer of country houses, Hooke was still in demand, and according to architectural historian Giles Worsley, his signature can be found at Stenfield Place, near Brentwood, which was built for Richard Vaughn, an Essex landowner, as well as Kiveton Park in Yorkshire, for the Duke of Leeds. When Hooke therefore resigned from Wren's Architect's Office in 1693 it may have been a result of too much work rather than too little energy.

Hooke's body, however, was weak, and as the new century approached, his eyesight began to fade, even if his mind remained alert. In 1697, it was reported, 'he began to complain of the swelling and soreness of his legs, and was much over-run with the scurvy, and about the same time being taken with a giddiness he fell down the stairs and cut his head, bruis'd his shoulder, and hurt his ribbs, of which he complain'd often to the last'.[3] He began to contemplate his end and set out to write his autobiography, a catalogue of every invention and event in his life, warning that it would include 'the time when, the manner how, and the means by which, with the success and effect of them, together with the state of my health, my employments and studies, my good and bad fortune, my friends and enemies'.[4] Yet he did not get very far.

He grew concerned about his fortune, which remained locked in a chest in his rooms, and began to let his lodgings decline into squalor, so that his friend Captain Knox would bemoan that he 'lived miserably as if he had not sufficient to afford him foode and rayment'.[5] He had promised his fortune to the Royal Society, but at the last moment would change his mind, and died intestate. After his death the chest would reveal a personal fortune of over £8,000. He died on 3 March 1703, and was buried three days later in a solemn ceremony.

Hooke's passing had an effect on the future of the Royal Society. Three weeks after the funeral the Mercers' Company, which owned Gresham College, demanded the keys of Hooke's lodgings, where he had lived for nearly forty years, and commanded that the society find new housing. The place that the club would eventually call home was in Crane Court, the house built by Nicholas Barbon, presumably made available to pay the late speculator's debts. The man who announced the location to the meeting was the new president of the society, Isaac Newton.

Hooke's death had liberated Newton. In 1704, he published his *Opticks*, having vowed to keep it private until his rival's death. No mention of Hooke's contribution to the study of light made it into the printing. Newton would reign over the Royal Society for the next twenty years and ensure that Hooke's name was erased from the record on every possible occasion. Yet as his biographer Richard Waller complained, a proper account of Hooke's life would show that 'all his errors and Blemishes were more than made amends for, by the Greatness and extent of his natural and acquired parts, and more than common, if not wonderful sagacity ... For these his happy qualifications, he was much respected by the most learned philosophers both at home and abroad: and as with all his failures, he may be reckon'd among the greatest Men of the last age'.[6]

John Locke finally retired from the Commission for Trade in May 1700, and his resignation was accepted unwillingly by William III. He attempted to avoid London, yet his health did not seem to improve, his legs began to swell and he spent much time in bed, reading the latest news from the Royal Society and about London life. Although his body was telling him to slow down he baulked at rural retirement, as he wrote to one friend: 'I think myself on the brink of another world ... Do not think now I am grown either a stoic or a mystic. I can laugh as heartily as ever, and be in pain for the public as much as you. I am not grown into a sullenness that puts off humanity – no, nor mirth neither.'[7]

Nonetheless, his mind did rest more often on religious matters than before. He began rereading the Epistles of St Paul and made a commentary on the text, which would be published after his death. Rather than going to London he began to receive guests at Oates, in Essex, the house of his friends Sir Francis and Lady Masham, where he had moved to get out of the fug of the capital. From here he continued his vast correspondence, kept up with the news at court and Parliament. He was also forced, on occasion, to do battle in defence of his work.

There was another reprint in hand of the *Essay*, with extensive corrections in response to Bishop Stillingfleet's criticisms. In 1703, with the Tory party ascendant under the newly crowned Queen Anne, Oxford University again went on the attack. Proast reignited his assaults on the anonymous author of *Letters of Toleration* and the heads of college discussed whether to ban the *Essay Concerning Human Understanding* altogether. Locke took the assault with a pinch of salt and, rather than launch a riposte, remained stoical, knowing that in the end the storm would blow over.

The case did, however, raise the question of Locke's legacy. In February 1703 the head librarian of the Bodleian Library at Oxford wrote to the philosopher to request that a copy of every book he had written be sent to the collection. Locke was more than happy to comply and had the *Essay*, *Some Thoughts on Education* and his many pamphlets on money and interest forwarded by his printer. In his letter of thanks, the librarian checked that these were all of Locke's works, writing: 'I shall presume not to enquire, whether these be all you intended us.'[8] Absent from the cache that arrived at Oxford were the *Two Treatise* and the *Letter of Toleration*. Locke would guard the anonymity of both books to his deathbed.

Yet the request would make him think about his work, and in a codicil to his will that he added on 14 September 1704 he wrote:

> The Reverend Dr Hudson ... writt to me some time since desireing of me for the said Library the books whereof I was the author I did in return to the honour done me therein present to the said library all the books that were published under my name which though accepted with honourable mention of me yet were not understood fully to answer the request made me ... I do hereby further give to the publick library ... all the books whereof I am the author which have been published without my name to them[9]

and he listed three: *Letters Concerning Toleration, Two Treatise of Government* and the *Reasonableness of Christianity*. Locke would finally accept at his death authorship of the books that set the foundation stones for the Enlightenment.

In October 1704 his body had begun to decline and he could no longer stand. On the night of the 27th, his family around him for prayers, he said: 'My work is almost at an end, and thank God for it. I may perhaps die tonight; but I cannot live above three or four days. Remember me in your evening prayers'.[10] He rose the next morning, but at about three in the afternoon he passed away, sitting in his chair, his hand in front of his face.

Lady Masham, Locke's long-term hostess at Oates and one of the first published female philosophers, and perhaps the woman he loved throughout his later life, would later write a letter to Jean le Clerc, who wished to write a eulogy to the philosopher:

> He was a true Lover of his Country; and faithfully discharged his Duty to it not only to the satisfaction of his Conscience, but to the real Benefit

of the publick perhaps beyond what most men in such a Station as he was in, have ever done ... He was always in the Greatest, and in the smallest affairs of Humane life, as well as in Speculative Opinions, dispos'd to follow reason, whosoever it were that Suggested it; he being a faithful Servant (I had almost said a Slave) to truth; never abandoning her for any thing else; and following Her for her own sake purely.'[11]

John Evelyn also sought retirement in the new century. Since the 1680s he had begun to editorialise his legacy by rewriting his diary for posterity, and he was also keen to make sure that his family was provided for after his death. For Evelyn, retirement was a return to his roots and the attempt to ensure that his children made advantageous marriages.

In 1691, Evelyn's nephew died, making him, at the age of seventy-one, heir to his brother George's estate at Wotton. George encouraged John and Mary to move to the estate, but it was not easy because the couple had lived at Sayes Court for over forty years and the accumulation of books and objects had become a burden. They were also increasingly poor – a gentleman's income came to very little in the new economic markets and, like many, Evelyn had played the stock market and lost an unhealthy sum.

Of their many children, only two had survived. The daughter, Susanna, had married and was attempting to start a family. In 1692 Evelyn's son and heir, John, was given an official post in Ireland. In his absence the parents temporally decamped to his apartments in Dover Street, near fashionable Piccadilly. Where once he had surveyed the elegant Clarendon House and Berkeley House, the land before him was now divided into plots and tenements. In 1694, John and Mary finally left for Wotton, where they lived with the brother, George, until his death in 1699.

The memories of his family home had haunted Evelyn throughout his life, and now he had returned. He had worked on the gardens in the 1650s, turning the thick woods into a vision of Italian fancy with a grotto and pond, and now there was time for more alterations. In 1700, he described his new life to Samuel Pepys: 'I pass the day in the fields among horses and oxen, sheep, cows, bulls and sows etc. ... We have I thank God finished our hay harvest prosperously ... Never was any matron more busy than my wife.'[12]

Yet he had not fully forgotten the thrills of London, telling his old friend: 'Is Philosophy, Gr[esham] Coll[ege] and the example of Mr Pepys and agreeable conversation at Yorke buildings quite forgotten and abandoned[?] No!'[13] He would often return to the meetings of the Royal Society

to catch up on the news, and remained treasurer at the Greenwich Hospital.
Yet the 'wood-born' Evelyn would also dedicate himself to reviving
Wotton, and he dreamt of redesigning the house as a Palladian villa, and
improving the gardens.

Sayes Court was given over to his son-in-law, William Draper. By now
Deptford and the suburbs engulfed the gardens, as wharfs and warehouses
clung to the riverbank from London Bridge to Greenwich. The marshes
behind the house had been drained, ridding the area of the malarial mos-
quitoes which may have killed at least one of his sons, making more room
for London's omnivorous sprawl. Evelyn's Elysium, his villa away from
the bustle of the city, had become consumed by the metropolis.

In 1696, the house was let to Admiral Benbow, who in turn sublet to an
unusual visitor in 1698, when Peter the Great, Tsar of Russia, came to visit
London to observe the ports, lessons from which he would later translate
to his new capital, St Petersburg. When Evelyn came to inspect the damage
with Christopher Wren a few months later, he was shocked to find that
the holly bush that he had planted forty years before, which had grown to
'four hundred foot in length, nine feet high and five in diameter',[14] had
been ruined by the tsar running through it with a wheelbarrow.

There was also time for writing, and he published his great book on
medals, *Numismata*, in 1697. There was unfinished work on manuscripts
and planned essays on 'The Dignity of Man', 'Of Stones', 'Of Reason in
Brute Animals', a work attacking the atheistic philosophy of Spinoza, and
various mathematical papers. More importantly, however, the *Elysium
Britannicum* remained incomplete, and the last dated correction to the text
was in 1702. Rather than aiming to complete the whole, Evelyn published
a discrete extract, *Acetaria*, a discourse on salads, in 1699. In the preface he
obliquely refers to his defeat in the grand project: 'you will not wonder,
that a person of my acquaintance, should have spent almost forty [years]
in gathering and amassing materials for a Hortulan design, to so enormous
an Heap, as to fill some Thousand pages ... This man began to build but
was not able to finish; this has been the fate of this undertaking.'[15]

In the same year Evelyn's son John died, leaving only a grandson, also
John, nicknamed Jack. Evelyn devoted himself to the settlement of his last
male descendant: the boy went to Oxford and the grandfather began
to plan his future; travels around England were organised and he was
encouraged in languages, learnt the flute and attended fencing school.
Evelyn wrote a notebook to pass over at the appropriate time, *Memoirs for*

my Grandson, exhorting him to a pious life, dedication to the gardens at Wotton, which he would inherit, an avoidance of too many friends, and the joys of an extensive library. As a final directive, Jack was forewarned about London life: 'Unless you have an office to support the charge, . . . [it] will be exceedingly expensive. It will alienate your wife and daughter from domestical things more necessary and virtuous.'[16] Evelyn also set about finding his grandson a wife, and in 1706 the young John married Anne Boscawen, a relative of the influential Godolphin family. The future of the family was ensured.

Evelyn died in London in his sleep on 27 February 1707, and was buried at the family plot in Wotton. On his epitaph was written: 'living in an age of extraordinary events, and revolutions he learnt (as himself asserted) this truth which pursuant to his intention is here declared. That all is vanity which is not honest and that there's no solid Wisdom but in real piety'.

THE ARCHITECT AND HIS CATHEDRAL

The raising of the final stone of St Paul's in October 1708 had been a private affair. There was no fanfare, for although the stonework of the cathedral had been completed the project had not ended. It took another two years before the building was officially declared ready for service.

One particular turn of events worked against Wren, for as the dome was being prepared in 1707, the dean, William Sherlock, died and was replaced by the young Henry Godolphin. The fissures that had begun to emerge within the committee between the two generations began to widen over the question of who had the final say on the form of the cathedral. The dean wished to thank the surveyor for all his work and reclaim the cathedral for the chapter, but Wren, having worked on St Paul's for over forty years, would not, and perhaps could not, let go of his masterpiece. He was determined that he would see the cathedral to its completion, and in his own way. A power struggle erupted, which Wren could only lose.

In 1708 there was discussion on how to ornament the interior of the dome. Wren's plans for a mosaic 'with a most magnificent and splendid appearance'[17] were overruled, and he then offered the suggestion that a painter might be used to highlight the architectural detail of the dome, but was commanded instead to find a history painter and develop designs. His dome, it seemed, would become the canvas for the work of others. Wren hoped that if he did nothing until the chapter saw the dome in the final form they would finally allow him the mosaic, but this was not to be. Five painters were requested to submit plans and the commission rather than the surveyor would select one.

In the same meeting there was discussion about a railing to encircle the whole cathedral. A fence was needed to guard it from the nearby passing traffic – it also allowed for a piazza in front of the cathedral on which Wren proposed a statue of Queen Anne. He expressed a preference for wrought iron while Godolphin saw value in cast iron. The exercise seemed to be little more than the chapter proving to the architect that the client had the final say, but Wren reacted badly and refused to sign the contract for the new work, kicking up enough of a fuss that soon it was the talk of the town. One sympathetic pamphlet observed: 'it was thought strange by most people, that after Sr Chr had compleated so noble a Fabrick with universal applause, the Direction of so small a Circumstance as a fence to encompass it, should be peremptorily and obstinately denied him'.[18] This petty spat about railings caused untold bitterness.

In March 1709, as the scaffolding was coming down from the exterior of the building to reveal the glories of the dome to London for the first time, the commission met to decide on the final decoration of the fabric. The animosity between the Architect's Office and the chapter soon began to spill out beyond the churchyard. The division was as political as it was personal: Godolphin was the brother of the Lord Treasurer, the first earl, Sidney Godolphin. Wren now represented everything that was old, as well as Tory, and he had few contemporaries to defend him. Queen Anne herself could not protect her surveyor from every attack. Meanwhile, plasterers completed the whitewashing of the interior of the cathedral and the marble flooring was laid.

The official date for the completion of the project was long after the final stone of the dome was placed. The reason for this was officious and confused. By January 1710, Wren had reached his breaking point, and in a letter to the archbishop he claimed that it had been made impossible for him to complete the cathedral. In addition he demanded that his salary, which had been frozen since 1697, should be paid. The request was passed to the Attorney-General, who claimed that as St Paul's was still incomplete, the surveyor had to wait. The following year Wren took his complaint to Parliament, which agreed that St Paul's was complete enough for Wren to be paid. The money finally arrived at the end of that year, and as if by default, the cathedral was proclaimed finished.

There was to be no celebration or thanksgiving mass, but the cathedral's popularity itself would be testament to Wren's great work. Soon the print shops of the churchyard were doing a roaring trade in prints, and the cathedral became a permanent fixture in the many 'stranger guides' for visitors to London. As Zacharias Conrad von Uffenbach wrote in his diary while travelling in June 1710, he climbed to the lantern 'right at the top of the tower [where] we found countless names written in chalk, or scratched on stone, so we had ours done also by our man'.[19] Overwhelmed by the experience he left, having bought a full series of drawings and engravings as a memento. Yet there were also growing murmurs of discontent.

The surveyor was not satisfied, and by no means finished. In the face of opposition from the commission he took his complaint to the queen, telling her that 'Tis well known, what sort of person and way [the Chapter] are included to'.[20] He wanted her to dismiss the commission altogether and allow him to complete the task without further pestering. In particular, he wanted the queen to know that Godolphin was interfering in his plans for an elegant balustrade around her own statue. Wren's petition was read out to a meeting of the commission in April 1711, and despite the faux-innocent protestations of Godolphin, the commission was dissolved in October. Wren would be allowed to get on with his work without meddling from the deanery. Jean Tijou completed his wrought-iron fence around the royal statue in front of the west end of the cathedral, and all discussions on how to decorate the interior of the dome were put to one side.

Without the committee room in which to air their differences, the confrontation between the dean and the surveyor resorted to the printing press, and in April 1712 *Frauds and Abuses at St Paul's*, a damning indictment of Wren, was published. He was accused of every sleight of hand. It did not matter that St Paul's was the first Anglican cathedral to be built for centuries and undoubtedly the first that had been designed and completed within a single lifetime – to Wren's enemies, it had taken too long. The surveyor was accused of taking bribes, he gave jobs to his friends, the accounting process was leaky, the cathedral itself was not what anyone hoped. There were rebuttals and counter-rebuttals, which did not end until the death of Queen Anne in 1714.

The arrival of the new king, George I, demanded a new commission. George assumed the throne, barely hiding his lack of interest in the old Stuart dynasty and openly committed to establishing the legitimacy of his own shaky claims to the throne. He had gained the crown because Anne had died heirless and, according to the laws of succession devised to ensure that James II or his son could not regain the crown, the next in line was the grandson of Charles I's sister. On his accession he rewarded his Whig supporters, and thus there was little chance that Wren was in line for favours. He was named Surveyor-General once more but was effectively silenced by those around him. He would attend the first two meetings of the new cathedral commission but after 15 July 1715 he stopped going. He had been defeated and saw no point in watching the opposition take his cathedral away.

Without the surveyor, the commission was able to go ahead with its scheme for the dome, selecting the English painter James Thornhill. Forty years old, the same age as Wren's cathedral, Thornhill had come to London to live in the household of his great-uncle, Sir Thomas Sydenham, the physician who had worked with John Locke in the 1670s. He had quickly made a reputation for himself and had already worked on royal projects at Hampton Court as well as having begun, in 1707, the great painted hall at Wren's Greenwich Hospital, one of the finest examples of English baroque art in the country.

Thornhill started on the dome in June 1715. For his designs he focused on the life of St Paul and divided the dome into eight panels, set within the frame of an arcade. Carpenters constructed a system of 'treadways' around the dome, on which Thornhill and his assistants could move and work. Within four months the arcade had been completed and work began on the panels. By 1717, the dome was completed with eight scenes from St Paul's life.

That year also saw Wren's last involvement in the cathedral. It was decided that the outside of the dome needed a balustrade. Dean Godolphin preferred a cast-iron railing but the commission felt it necessary to consult Wren. He was given a week to produce his response. His reply was curt: 'Persons of little skill in architecture did expect, I believe, to see something they had been used to in Gothic structures; and ladies think nothing well without edging ...' The balustrade would 'break into the harmony of the whole machine'.[21] Nonetheless, it was added.

By 1717 Wren was eighty-five years old and still showing an enviable vitality. There is no doubt, however, that he carried on working for too long. In the same year the city church project was finally wound up, but he remained the Surveyor-General of the King's Works for another three years. His final departure was inevitably unpleasant and he was rudely ousted by a sustained campaign of slander. He was also attacked for no longer being a modern architect. In the passing decades, Wren's experimentation in baroque, liberating architecture from the classical orders, had been superseded by a new generation of Palladians, who relished the restrictive confines of ancient tradition. Wren's buildings, once criticised for not being traditional, were now not classically severe enough. To revive a national architecture, the neoclassical Young Turks looked not to Wren but to 'the famous Inigo Jones' for inspiration.

Wren retired to his house in Hampton Court, where he seemed to brood on his legacy: if history would not celebrate him as an architect, he cursed Charles II for drawing him away from the laboratory to 'spend all his time in rubbish'.[22] He also returned to his first passion of the New Philosophy. A few years before, Isaac Newton, as president of the Royal Society, had raised £20,000 for the man who could break the intractable problem of longitude. Wren worked on finding a way of discovering location through astronomical observation, but the prize eluded him. It would later be claimed by the horologist John Harrison, who followed Robert Hooke's prediction that the enigma of longitude would be unravelled by a well-made clock that could accurately tell the time at sea.

Time soon took its toll on Wren. His son, Christopher Jr, would comment that although it 'enfeebled his limbs, (which was his chief ailment) yet had it little influence upon the vigour of his mind, which continued, with a vivacity rarely found at that age'. Even in his retirement the attacks on his service continued, and in 1719 he was forced to complain: 'after serving the crown and Publick above fifty years, and at this great age … I hope it will be allow'd me to Die in Peace'.[23] Yet peace would not come for another four years.

On 23 February 1723, Wren travelled once more up to London – it was said to visit his cathedral – where he caught a cold. He was too ill to return to Hampton Court and stayed at the house that he had leased in St James's. On the afternoon of 25 February, his servant came into his room to wake him from his sleep but could not.

Eight days later, on 5 March, the funeral cortège, including fifteen carriages and the coffin, left from the house in St James's Street and wound its way from the West End that ninety years earlier had been open fields, towards the east. In his lifetime Wren had seen this whole area of London transformed: the Strand had once been lined with the elegant Tudor palaces of the nobility but they had been knocked down by the likes of Barbon and turned into leased housing for the well-to-do. It was here in 1670 that John Locke had lived at Shaftesbury's Exeter House, and had first begun his discussion of human understanding.

The cortège passed by the Temple Bar, which Wren himself had designed in the 1670s. The houses on both sides of Fleet Street would have been legacy enough for the architect and his contemporaries, for fifty-six years earlier this whole area had been ashes and charred debris. His friend, Robert Hooke, had measured and staked this very stretch of ground and recorded each new house to be rebuilt. They passed Crane Court on the north side of the road, the new home of the Royal Society which Wren himself had helped found. Descending Fleet Street, they would soon encounter St Bride's parish church, one of Wren's own triumphs of the city church project, the telescopic spire rising in Portland stone into the city sky. Finally, as they crossed over the Fleet river and then ascended Ludgate Hill, the glistening façade of St Paul's began to emerge from the winding street.

Wren was buried in the south-eastern corner of the crypt. His son wrote the epitaph that still remains upon the tomb:

Lector si Monumentum Requiris Circumspice

'Reader, if you seek his monument, look about you.'

NOTES

INTRODUCTION

1. J. Evelyn, *A Character of England*, from W. Upcott (ed.), *Evelyn's Miscellaneous Writings* (1825), pp. 141–67.
2. W. Lilly, *Observations on the death of Charles I*, from Francis Maseres and R. Wilkes (eds), *Select Tracts relating to the Civil Wars in England* (1815), p. 141.
3. Evelyn, *Diaries*, vol. II, p. 11.
4. Ibid.
5. Wren, *Parentalia*, p. 293.

CHAPTER I

1. Lilly, *Observations on the death of Charles I*, p. 141.
2. Peacham (1962), p. 243.
3. Wren, *Parentalia*, p. 42.
4. V. Smith and P. Kelsey, 'The lines of communication: civil war defences of London', from Porter (1996), p. 118.
5. Evelyn, *A Character of England*, pp. 141–67.
6. Quoted in Tinniswood (2001), p. 14.

7. Quoted in Purkiss (2006), p. 392.
8. R. Waller, *The Life of Dr Robert Hooke*, from R. T. Gunther (ed.), *Early Science in Oxford*, vol. iv, (1930), p. 3.
9. Evelyn, *Diaries*, vol. I, p. 14.
10. Ibid., vol. I, p. 13.
11. Ibid., vol. I, p. 14.
12. From Milton (1974), p. 237.
13. From Scriba (1970), p. 40.
14. Wren, *Parentalia*, p. 203.
15. Oughtred (1653), Preface.
16. J. Evelyn, *The State of France*, from ed. Upcott (1825), pp. 39–95.
17. Evelyn, *Diaries*, vol. I, p. 45.
18. Quoted in Horne (2002), p. 99.
19. Evelyn, *Diaries*, vol. I, pp. 45–6.
20. Evelyn, *The State of France*, pp. 39–95.
21. Evelyn, *Diaries*, vol. I, p. 102.
22. Ibid., vol. I, pp. 118–24.
23. From 'The Legend of Philastres and the Pearle', quoted in Harris (2002), p. 41.
24. J. Evelyn, *Servitude and Liberty* from ed. Upcott (1825), pp. 1–38.
25. Evelyn, *Diaries*, vol. I, p. 248.

CHAPTER 2

1. Quoted in Zimmer (2004), p. 63.
2. R. Hooke. ed. Gunther, vol. iv, (1930), p. 8.
3. From Peacham (1962).
4. Wren, *Parentalia*, p. 222.
5. Ibid., pp. 198–9.
6. Ibid., p. 227.
7. Scriba (1970), p. 40.
8. Evelyn, *Diaries*, vol. I, p. 276.
9. Ibid., p. 276.
10. Quoted in Harris (2002), p. 29.
11. Quoted in Darley (2006), p. 111.
12. Quoted in Harris (2002), p. 45.
13. Evelyn, *A Character of England*, pp. 141–67.
14. Evelyn, *Diaries*, vol. I, p. 117.
15. Ibid., vol. I, p. 284.
16. Quoted in P. Leith-Ross, 'The gardens of John Evelyn at Deptford', *Garden History*, 25(2), *passim*.
17. See Evelyn (1679).
18. Aubrey (1996), p. 164.
19. Locke's Correspondence, ed. E. de Beer, vol. 1, L. 14.
20. Quoted in M. Feingold, 'Mathematical Sciences and New Philosophies', in Tyacke (1997), p. 359.
21. R. Woolhouse, 'Lady Masham's Account of Locke', *Locke Studies*, vol. 3, p. 173.
22. Aubrey (1996), p. 165.
23. Evelyn, *Diaries*, vol. I, p. 293.
24. Quoted in Dixon Hunt and Willis (1975), pp. 57–8.
25. Evelyn, *Diaries*, vol III, p. 92.
26. Wren, *Parentalia*, pp. 200–6.

CHAPTER 3

1. J. Evelyn, *The Golden Book of St John Chrysostom*, 1659, from ed. Upcott (1825), Preface.
2. Evelyn, *Diaries*, vol. I, p. 330.
3. Quoted in Harris (1987), p. 45.
4. J. Evelyn, *An Apology for the Royal Party*, 1659, from ed. Upcott (1825), pp. 169–92.
5. Quoted in Harris (2002), p. 49.
6. Evelyn, *Diaries*, vol. II, p. 336.
7. Locke's Correspondence, vol. 1, L. 81.
8. Ibid.
9. From Hunt (2003).
10. The pamphlets were not discovered until 1954. See Locke (2002).
11. Quoted in Harris (2005), p. 48.
12. Quoted in Purver (1967), p. 129.
13. Wren, *Parentalia*, p. 197.
14. Quoted in Purver (1967), p. 131.
15. From Oldenburg's letter to Christiaan Huygens, 7 September 1661. Quoted in Jardine (2002), pp. 180–81.
16. Evelyn, *Diaries*, vol. I, p. 344.
17. Evelyn (1961), *passim*.
18. Wren, *Parentalia*, p. 260.
19. Quoted in Purver (1967), p. 76.
20. Quoted in Hunter (1995), p. 153.
21. Quoted in Birch (1968), vol. II, p. 142.
22. From Samuel Butler's satirical poem *Hudibras* (1665).
23. Quoted in R. Hooke, ed. Gunther (1930), p.122.
24. From R. Hooke, *An Attempt to Prove the Motion of the Earth from Observation* (1674), published a

decade after his Gresham lecture and included in Gunther (1930).

25. R. Hooke, *Micrographia* (1664), Preface.
26. Ibid.

CHAPTER 4

1. From Alexander Pope's poem *The Dunciad*, 1743.
2. From N. Hanson (2001), p. 43.
3. Quoted in Tinniswood (2003), p. 32.
4. Evelyn, *Diaries*, vol. I, p. 355.
5. Quoted in Colvin (1976), p. 5.
6. Evelyn (1664), p. 2.
7. Ibid., p. 2.
8. Evelyn, *Diaries*, vol. I, p. 382.
9. Quoted in Thorgood (2000), p. 35.
10. Quoted in Keane et al. (2004), p. 66.
11. Wren Society, vol. XIII, p. 13.
12. Ibid.
13. Ibid., p. 14.
14. Wren, *Parentalia*, p. 335.
15. Evelyn, *Diaries*, vol. II, p. 39.
16. Quoted in Champion (1995), p. 2.
17. Quoted in Cowie (1970), p. 15.
18. Leasor (1962), p. 42.
19. Hodges (1720), p. 2.
20. Boghurst (1894), p. 13.
21. Quoted in Moote and Moote (2004), p. 54.
22. Quoted in Leasor (1962), p. 51.
23. Vincent (1667), p. 30.
24. Quoted in Hanson (2001), p. 45.
25. Evelyn, *Diaries*, vol. I, p. 396.
26. Quoted in Moote and Moote (2004), pp. 115–16.
27. C. Wilcox, *The Case of Charles Wilcox*, BL 816. m.9. (28).

28. Vincent (1667), p. 30.
29. The physician Simon Patrick quoted in Champion (1995), p. 4.
30. Boghurst (1894), p. 30.
31. Vincent (1667), *passim*.
32. Evelyn, *Diaries*, vol. I, p. 397.
33. Vincent (1667), p. 50.
34. Evelyn, *Diaries*, vol. I, p. 399.
35. Vincent (1667), p. 53.
36. Locke's Correspondence, ed. E. de Beer, vol. I, L. 163.
37. Ibid., vol. I, L. 175.
38. Wren Society, vol. XIII, p. 40.
39. From a letter by Henry Oldenburg to Robert Boyle, August 1665. Ibid., vol. XIII, p. 43.
40. Quote from Ranum (2002), p. 337.
41. Letter from CW to (probably) John Evelyn, *Parentalia*, p. 261.
42. Quoted in Gould (1981), pp. 33–4.
43. Wren, *Parentalia*, p. 262.
44. Ibid., p. 261.
45. Ibid.
46. Wren Society, vol. XIII, p. 44.
47. Ibid., p. 44.
48. Ibid., p. 17.
49. Ibid.
50. Ibid.

CHAPTER 5

1. S. Pepys, *Diaries*, ed. R. Latham (1985), p. 567.
2. Wren Society, vol. XIII, p. 18.
3. Evelyn, *Diaries*, vol. II, p. 9.
4. Waterhouse (1667), p. 2.
5. Ibid.
6. Rege Sincera (1809), p. 292.
7. Taswell (1853), p. 11.

8. Quoted in Tinniswood (2003), p. 46.
9. Evelyn, *Diaries*, vol II, p. 10.
10. S. Pepys, *Diaries*, ed. R. Latham (1985), p. 660.
11. Vincent (1667), p. 63.
12. Ibid., p. 62.
13. From a letter by William Sandys quoted in Bell (1923), p. 316.
14. S. Pepys, *Diaries*, ed. R. Latham (1985), p. 663.
15. Corsellis (1941/42), p. 132.
16. Vincent (1667), p. 63.
17. Bell (1923), p. 314.
18. Vincent (1667), p. 61.
19. Taswell (1853), p. 13.
20. Quoted in Tinniswood (2003), p. 83.
21. Evelyn, *Diaries*, vol. II, p. 11.
22. Ibid.
23. Quoted in Bedford (1966), p. 82.
24. Ibid, p. 24.
25. Quoted in ibid., p. 92.
26. Stow (1908), p. 345.
27. Taswell (1853), p. 14.
28. S. Pepys, *Diaries*. ed. R. Latham. (1985), p. 669.
29. Evelyn, *Diaries*, vol. II, p. 11.
30. Vincent (1667), p. 69.
31. Evelyn, *Diaries*, vol. II, p. 14.
32. Quoted in Bedford (1966), p. 135.
33. Evelyn, *Diaries*, vol. II, pp. 13–14.
34. Ibid, p. 12.
35. Ibid.
36. From letter by William Sandys quoted in Bell (1923), p. 318.
37. Ibid.
38. Evelyn, J., ed. de la Bédoyère, (1997), p. 337.
39. Ibid., p. 338.
40. Ibid., p. 339.
41. Ibid., p. 340.
42. Ibid.
43. Ibid., p. 341.
44. Quoted in Reddaway (1940), p. 55.
45. Birch (1968), vol. II, p. 115.
46. Evelyn, *Diaries*, vol. II, p. 16.

CHAPTER 6

1. Published in the *London Gazette*, 17 September 1666.
2. Ibid.
3. Ibid.
4. Quoted in Reddaway (1940), p. 29.
5. Ibid., p. 49.
6. Quoted in Tinniswood (2003), p. 190.
7. J. Evelyn, *Public Employment*, 1667, from ed. Upcott (1825), pp. 501–50.
8. Description of Jerman originally by Pratt, quoted in Tinniswood (2001), p. 156.
9. Wren, *Parentalia*, p. 263.
10. Quoted in Tinniswood (2003), pp. 224–5.
11. Evelyn, *Diaries*, vol. II, p. 18.
12. Quoted in Cooper (2003), p. 127.
13. From the First Rebuilding Act of February 1667, 19 Caroli, II.
14. Ibid.
15. Ibid.
16. Evelyn, *Diaries*, vol. II, p. 22.
17. Quoted in Cooper (2003), p. 133.
18. From R. Hooke, ed. Gunther R. vol. VI. (1930), p. 32.
19. Locke's Correspondence, ed. E. de Beer, vol. I., pp. 284–5.
20. Dewhurst (1963), p. 35.
21. Quoted in Cranston (1957), p. 91.
22. Quoted in Dewhurst (1963), p. 36.

23. Locke (1997), Preface.
24. Locke (1936), p. xiii.
25. Quoted in Bell (1923), p. 253.
26. Evelyn, *Diaries*, vol. II, p. 24.
27. First Rebuilding Act of February 1667, 19 Caroli, II.
28. Ibid.
29. P. Mills, ed. P. E. Jones and T. F. Reddaway, *Mills Survey*, London Topographical Society, vol. II, p. 29.
30. Anon. (1966), vol. II, p. 85.
31. From T. Tyndell Daniells, *The Lawyers*, www.online-law.co.uk/bar/middle–temple/history.html.

CHAPTER 7

1. Wren Society, vol. XIII, pp. 20–21.
2. Ibid., p. 45.
3. Ibid., p. 46.
4. Ibid., p. 45.
5. Ibid., p. 46.
6. Ibid.
7. Quoted in A. Saunders. (ed.), *The Royal Exchange* (1997), p. 138.
8. J. Collins, *Edward Jerman 1605–1668* (2004), p. 144.
9. Wren Society, vol. XIII, p. 46.
10. Wren Society, vol. XVIII, p. 156.
11. Evelyn, *Diaries*, vol. I, p. 357.
12. Colvin (1976), p. 11.
13. Wren, *Parentalia*, p. 194 (insert section no. 9).
14. Ibid., p. 285.
15. Second Rebuilding Act of 1 May 1670, 22 Caroli, II, cap. 11.
16. Description of the Royal College of Physicians.
17. Quoted in Cooper (2003), p. 165.
18. Wren Society, vol. V, p. 47.

19. Guildhall Ms 25540, f. 3, 13 June 1670.
20. Wren Society, vol. XIII, account books, 1675–84, pp. 69–202 *passim*.
21. Quoted in Tinniswood (2001), p. 206.
22. Soo (1998), p. 115.
23. Ibid., p. 113.
24. Ibid., p. 153.
25. Ibid., p. 154.
26. Ibid., p. 159.
27. Ibid., p. 157.
28. Ibid.
29. Ibid., p. 158.
30. Ibid., p. 178.
31. Wren Society, vol. XIII, p. 26.
32. Ibid.
33. Ibid.
34. Wren, *Parentalia*, p. 282.
35. Wren Society, vol. XIII, p. 26.
36. Ibid., p. 27.
37. Ibid., p. 320.
38. Hooke (1935), 3 October 1675.
39. Wren Society, vol. XIII, p. 28.
40. Ibid., p. 31.
41. Wren, *Parentalia*, p. 282.
42. Ibid., p. 283.

CHAPTER 8

1. Quoted in Arneil (1996), p. 130.
2. Quoted in McKellar (1999), p. 25.
3. North (1890), p. 53.
4. Ibid., p. 55.
5. Ibid.
6. Ibid., p. 53.
7. Quoted in Brett-James (1935), p. 326.
8. McKellar (1999), p. 25.

9. *Survey of London*, vol. 29, 1960, p. 88.
10. North (1890), p. 56.
11. Ibid., p. 54.
12. *Survey of London*, vol. 33, p. 30.
13. Ibid., p. 379.
14. Ibid.
15. Ibid.
16. From Barbon (1678).
17. Evelyn, *Diaries*, vol. II, p. 70.
18. *A Letter from a Person of Quality to his Friend in the Countryside*, from W. Cobbett, MP, *Cobbett's Parliamentary History of England*, vol. 4, 1806.

CHAPTER 9

1. Wren, *Parentalia*, p. 292.
2. Soo (1998), p. 31.
3. Ibid., p. 32.
4. Wren Society, vol. XIII, pp. 57–9.
5. Wren, *Parentalia*, p. 194.
6. Quoted in *Helioscopes*, from Hooke (1969).
7. Quoted in Darley (2006), p. 136.
8. Evelyn (2001), Introduction.
9. Hooke (1969), pp. 320–22.
10. From *A General Scheme or Idea of the Present State of Natural Philosophy*, in Hooke (1969), p. 15.
11. Quoted in Gleick (2003), p. 86.
12. Quoted in Inwood (2002), p. 164.
13. Ibid., p. 168.
14. Hooke (1935), p. 157.
15. From the New Hooke Papers, Royal Society, *passim*.
16. From T. Shadwell, *The Virtuoso* (1676).
17. Hooke (1935), p. 243.

18. From Shadwell, *The Virtuoso*.
19. Hooke (1935), p. 333.
20. Ibid., p. 346.

CHAPTER 10

1. From James Wright's *Ecclesia Restaurata*, in Aubin (1943), p. 275.
2. Kenyon (1972), Preface.
3. Quoted in S. Pincus, 'John Evelyn: Revolutionary', in eds. Harris and Hunter (2003), p. 189.
4. Quoted in Locke (2003), p. 236.
5. Filmer (1991), p. 35.
6. Locke (2003), p. 31.
7. Ibid., p. 56.
8. Quoted in Cranston (1957), p. 200.
9. Quoted in T. Harris (2005), p. 211.
10. Locke (2003), p. 197.
11. Ibid., p. 208.
12. Quoted in Cranston (1957), p. 202.
13. Ibid., p. 228.
14. Quoted in Jardine (2002), p. 336.
15. DNB (2004), vol. XII, p. 616.
16. Evelyn, *Diaries*, vol. II, p. 192–3.
17. Downes (1982), p. 67.
18. Quoted in Fraser (1979), p. 591.
19. Evelyn, *Diaries*, vol. II, pp. 229–30.

CHAPTER 11

1. Quoted in Milne (1986), p. 88.
2. Evelyn, *Diaries*, vol. II, pp. 197–8.
3. Barbon (1685).
4. Ibid.
5. Thorgood (2000), p. 49.
6. Ibid., p. 48.

7. Quoted in Brett-James (1935), p. 330.
8. Ibid.
9. Ibid.
10. North (1981), p. 54.
11. Harris (2006), p. 100.
12. Vallance (2006), p. 78.
13. Quoted in S. Pincus, 'John Evelyn: Revolutionary', in Harris and Hunter eds. (2003), p. 196.
14. *Phil. Trans.*, vol. 14, p. 562.
15. Ibid.
16. Quoted in Darley (2006), p. xiii.
17. Quoted in Cranston (1957), p. 232.
18. Ibid., p. 246.
19. Locke (1976), vol II, pp. 661–66.
20. Locke (1997), p. 56.
21. Ibid., p. 59.
22. Ibid., p. 109.
23. Ibid., p. 65.
24. Ibid., p. 66.
25. Ibid., p. 147.
26. Ibid., p. 110.
27. Cranston (1957), p. 253.
28. Locke (1997), pp. 10–11.
29. Halley's letter to Newton, in Newton, *Correspondence*, vol. 2 29 June 1686.
30. Ibid., Hooke to Newton, 6 January 1679 (p.260).
31. Ibid., 29 June 1686.
32. Ibid., 20 June 1686.
33. Quoted in Gleick (2003), p. 135.
34. Evelyn, *Diaries*, vol. II, p. 261.
35. Dillon (2006), p. 84.
36. *A Letter to a Dissenter* is presumed to have been written by Lord Halifax, 1687.
37. Harris (2006), p. 231.
38. Evelyn, *Diaries*, vol. II, p. 274.
39. Harris (2006), p. 264.
40. Dillon (2006), p. 117.
41. Ibid.
42. Evelyn, *Diaries*, vol. II, p. 275.
43. Ibid., p. 276.
44. Ibid., p. 280.
45. Ibid., p. 285.

CHAPTER 12

1. Evelyn, *Diaries*, vol. II, pp. 288–9.
2. Quoted in Dillon (2006), p. 154.
3. Ibid., p. 162.
4. Harris (2006), p. 286.
5. Quoted in Vallance (2006), p. 140.
6. Evelyn, *Diaries*, vol. II, p. 285.
7. Vallance (2006), p. 140.
8. Dillon (2006), p. 178.
9. Ibid., p. 198.
10. Evelyn, *Diaries*, vol. II, p. 287.
11. Ibid.
12. Quoted in Dillon (2006), p. 214.
13. Quoted in Harris (2006), p. 324.
14. Quoted in Vallance (2006), p. 173.
15. From John Dryden's poem, quoted in Schwoerer (1992), p. 99.
16. R. Woolhouse (ed.), *Locke Studies*, vol. 3 (2003), p. 183.
17. Locke's Correspondence, ed. E. de Beer, vol II, L. 1127.
18. Locke (2003), vol. I, p. 3.
19. Quoted in Farr and Roberts (1985).
20. Quoted in Colvin (1976), p. 155.
21. Locke's Correspondence, ed. E. de Beer, vol II, L. 1147.
22. Wren Society, vol. XVI, p. 62.
23. Ibid.
24. Quoted in Tinniswood (2001), p. 313.
25. Soo (1998), p. 115.

26. Wren, *Parentalia*, p. 292.
27. Ibid.
28. Ibid.

CHAPTER 13

1. Quoted in Shoemaker (2004), p. 20.
2. See Spence (2000).
3. Quoted in ed. Merritt, J. F. (2001), p. 122.
4. From Defoe (1997).
5. Evelyn, *Diaries*, vol. II, p. 332.
6. Quoted in Dillon (2006), p. 340.
7. Quoted in Hoppitt (2000), p. 125–6.
8. Quoted in Dillon (2006), p. 318.
9. Barbon (1905), p. 19.
10. Evelyn, *Diaries*, vol. II, p. 331.
11. Barbon (1905), p. 16.
12. Locke (1991), vol. 1, p. 25.
13. Li (1963), p. 70.
14. Locke's Correspondence, ed. E. de Beer, vol. IV, L. 2202.
15. Cranston (1957), p. 469.
16. Quoted in Tinniswood (2001), p. 321.
17. From James Wright's 'The Choire', in Aubin (1943), pp. 278–83.

CHAPTER 14

1. Wren Society, vol. XVI, p. 88.
2. Wren, *Parentalia*, p. 288.
3. Wren Society, vol. XVI, p. 85.
4. Ibid.
5. Evelyn (1707), Preface.
6. Ward (1955), p. 78.
7. Wren Society, vol. XVI, p. 82.
8. Soo (1998), p. 155.
9. Ibid., p. 113.

10. Keane et al. (2004), p. 421.
11. Act of Union, 1707.
12. Hooke (1931), p. 151.
13. Wren Society, vol. XIII, p. 37.
14. Wren, *Parentalia*, p. 292.
15. Ibid., p. 293.
16. From 'The Cupola' by James Wright, in Aubin (1943), pp. 298–304.

CHAPTER 15

1. Quote from Mandeville (1970).
2. R. Hooke, ed. Gunther, vol. IV (1930), p. 189.
3. R. Hooke, ed. Gunther, vol. VI (1930), p. 63.
4. Quoted in Jardine (2003), p. 21.
5. Ibid., p. 305.
6. R. Hooke, ed. Gunther, vol. VI (1930), p. 66.
7. Locke's Correspondence, ed. E. de Beer, vol. VII, L. 3199.
8. Ibid., vol. VIII, L. 3569.
9. Locke's Will, in ibid., vol. VIII, p. 425.
10. Quoted in Cranston (1957), p. 480.
11. Quoted in R. Woolhouse, 'Lady Masham's Account of Locke', *Locke Studies*, vol. 3, p. 185.
12. Quoted in de la Bédoyère (1997), p. 279.
13. Ibid., p. 276.
14. Evelyn, *Diaries*, vol. II, p. 349.
15. From *Aceteria*, in J. Evelyn, ed. Upcott (1825), pp. 721–812.
16. Evelyn (1926), p. 4.
17. Wren, *Parentalia*, p. 292.
18. Quoted in the pamphlet *An Answer to the Pamphlet entitul'd Frauds and Abuses at St Paul's etc.* (1713), *passim*.

19. Quoted in Keane et al. (2004), p. 317.
20. Quoted in Tinniswood (2001), p. 354.
21. Wren Society, vol. XVI, p. 131.
22. Quoted in Tinniswood (2001), p. 365.
23. Wren, *Parentalia*, p. 347.

BIBLIOGRAPHY

PRIMARY SOURCES

Anon., Tracts concerning banks, coinage, insurance etc., BL 816. m.10, vol. K, no. 65–74.
———, Administrative documents, Christchurch Hospital, GL Ms 22536.
———, *The Fire Court* ... , ed. P. E. Jones, Corporation of London, 1966.
———, *Bank of England, Selected tracts 1694–1804*, Gregg Press, 1968.
Arundel, T., *Arundel's Remembrances*, ed. J. M. Robinson, Roxborough Club, 1987.
Aubrey, J., *Brief Lives*, ed. D. Lawson, 1996.
Barbon, N., *Apology for the Builder*, BL 8245.a5, 1685.
———, *A Discourse shewing the great Advantages that New Buildings, and the Enlarging of Towns and Cities Do Bring to a Nation*, 1678.
———, *A Letter to a Gentleman* ... , BL 816.m.10 (74).
———, *An Answer to A Letter from a Gentleman*, BL 816.m.10 (75).
———, *A Discourse on Trade*, ed. J. A. Hollander, Baltimore, MD, 1905.
———, *A Discourse concerning coining the new money lighter*, Gregg Press, 1971.
Birch, T., *The History of the Royal Society of London*, 4 vols (facsimile), Royal Society, 1968.
Boghurst, W., *Loimographia: An Account of the Great Plague in the Year 1665*, ed. J. F. Payne, Shaw, 1894.
Bohun, E., *The Diary and Autobiography of Edmund Bohun*, privately published, 1853.
Burnet, G., *History of his Own Times*, J. Brettell, 1813.
Butler, S., *Hudibras*, ed. J. Wilder, Clarendon Press, 1967.
Clarendon, *History of the Rebellion and Civil Wars of England*, ed. G. Huehns, Oxford University Press, 1955.
College, S., *Strange News from Newgate* ..., BL T.100 (164), 1683.

Corsellis, N., 'Experiences in the Great Fire of London', ed. L. C. Sier, *Essex Review*, vol. 50(1), 1941/42.

Defoe, D., *Tour through the Whole Island of Great Britain*, vols I, II, Peter Davies, 1927.

Defoe, D., *A Journal of the Plague Year*, Penguin, 1966.

Defoe, D., *A True Born Englishman and Other Writing*, ed. P. N. Furbank and W. R. Ownes, Penguin, 1997.

Dugdale, Sir W., *The History of St Paul's Cathedral in London from its foundations*, 1716.

Evelyn, J., Commonplace Books, BL Mss. 78328–78331.

———, *A Parallel of the Ancient Architecture with the Modern*, 1st edn, 1664.

———, *Sylva, A Discourse of Forest Trees, and the Propagation of Timber in His Majesties Dominions*, 1679.

———, *Acetaria, a Discourse of Sallets*, 1699.

———, *A Parallel of the Ancient Architecture with the Modern*, 2nd edn, 1707.

———, *Evelyn's Miscellaneous Writings*, ed. W. Upcott, Henry Colburn, 1825.

———, *The Diary of John Evelyn*, ed. W. Bray, 4 vols, Henry Colburn, 1850–52.

———, *Memoirs for my Grand-son*, ed. G. Keynes, Nonesuch Press, 1926.

———, *Directions for the Gardiner at Sayes Court*, ed. G. Keynes, Nonesuch Press, 1932.

———, *Fumifugium: or the inconvenience of the aer and smoake of London dissipated*, National Society for Clean Air, 1961.

———, *Elysium Britannicum, Or the Royal Gardens*, ed. J. E. Ingram, University of Pennsylvania Press, 2001.

Fiennes, C., *The Journeys of Celia Fiennes*, ed. C. Morris, Cresset Press, 1947.

Filmer, R., *Patriarchia and other Political Writing*, ed. J. Summerville, Cambridge University Press, 1991.

Graunt, J., *Natural and Political Observations Upon the Bills of Mortality*, ed. P. Laslett, Gregg International, 1973.

Hartlib, S., *A description of the famous Kingdome of Macaria*, 1641.

———, *Designe for Plentie by a Universall Planting of Fruit Trees*, 1652.

Hodges, N., *Loimologia*, 1720.

Hooke, R., Classified Papers: Hooke Papers, Royal Society, 160(31).

———, New Hooke Papers, Royal Society, 166(7).

———, 'Life and Works of Robert Hooke', ed. R. T. Gunther, *Early Science in Oxford*, vol. VI, printed for subscribers, 1930.

———, 'Life and Works of Robert Hooke', ed. R. T. Gunther, *Early Science in Oxford*, vol. VII, printed for subscribers, 1930.

———, 'The Cutler Lectures', ed. R. T. Gunther, *Early Science in Oxford,* vol. VIII, printed for subscribers, 1931.

———, *The Diary of Robert Hooke, 1688–93*, ed. R. T. Gunther, printed for subscribers, 1935.

Hooke, R., *The Diary of Robert Hooke 1672–1680*, ed. H. W. Robinson and W. Adams, Taylor & Francis, 1935.

———, *Micrographia*, ed. R. T. Gunther, *Early Science in Oxford*, vol. XIII, printed for subscribers, 1938.

———, *Philosophical Experiments and Observations*, ed. W. Denman, Library of Science facsimile, 1967.

———, *Posthumous Works*, ed. R. Waller, Introduction by R. Westfall, Frank Cass & Co., 1969.

King, G., *Natural and Political Observations . . .*, ed. P. Laslett, Gregg International, 1973.

Locke, J., *An Early Draft of Locke's Essay*, ed. R. I. Aaron, Clarendon Press, 1936.

———, *Locke's Travels in France (1675–1679)*, ed. J. Lough, Cambridge University Press, 1953.

———, *The Correspondence of John Locke*, ed. E. de Beer, 7 vols, Clarendon Press, 1976–89.

———, *Locke on Money*, ed. P. H. Kelly, 2 vols, Clarendon Press, 1991.

———, *Political Writing*, ed. D. Wootton, Penguin, 1993.

———, *An Essay Concerning Human Understanding*, ed. R. Woolhouse, Penguin, 1997.

———, *The Essays on Natural Law*, ed. W. von Leyden, Clarendon Press, 2002.

———, *Two Treatise of Government*, ed. I. Shapiro, Yale University Press, 2003.

Luttrell, N. A., *Brief Historical Relations of State Affairs from September 1678 to April 1714*, 6 vols, 1857.

Mandeville, B., *A Fable of the Bees*, ed. P. Harth, Penguin, 1970.

Maseres, F. and R. Wilkes, *Select Tracts relating to the Civil Wars in England*, 1815.

Mills, P., 'A Survey of Building Sites after the Great Fire 1666', ed. P. E. Jones and T. F. Reddaway, *London Topographical Society*, 89, pp. 97–9.

Milton, J., *Selected Prose*, Penguin, 1974.

Newton, I., *Correspondence of Isaac Newton*, ed. H. W. Turnbull, vol. 2, Cambridge University Press, 1959–61.

North, R., 'Life of the Honorable Sir Dudley North', *Lives of the Norths*, G. Bell & Sons, 1890.

———, *Of Building: Roger North's Writings on Architecture*, ed. H. M. Colvin and J. Newman, Oxford University Press, 1981.

Oughtred, W., *Mathematical Recreations (Clavis Mathematicae)*, 1653.

Peacham, H., *The Complete Gentleman and Other Writings*, ed. V. Heltzel, Cornell University Press, 1962.

Pepys, S., *The Shorter Pepys*, ed. R. Latham, Bell & Hyman, 1985.

Pratt, R., *The Architecture of Sir Roger Pratt*, ed. R. T. Gunther, Oxford University Press, 1928.

Rege Sincera, 'Observations Both Historical and Moral upon the Burning of London', *Harleian Miscellany*, III, 1809.

Royal Society of London, *Philosophical Transactions*, vols I–XX, Royal Society facsimile, 1963.

Scriba, C. J., 'The Autobiography of John Wallis', *Notes and Records of the Royal Society*, 1970.

Spratt, T., *A History of the Royal Society*, Routledge and Kegan Paul, 1959.

Stow, J., *A Survey of London*, ed. C. L. Kingsford, 2 vols, 1908.

Stow, J. and J. Strype, *The History and Survey of the Cities of London and Westminster*, 2 vols, 1720.

Talbot, W., *A Sermon Preach'd before the Queen at the cathedral-church of St Paul's on May the first*, 1707.

Taswell, W., 'Autobiography and Anecdotes by William Taswell D.D.', ed. G. P. Elliott, *Camden Miscellany*, II, 1853.

Temple, Sir W., *Five Miscellaneous Essays by Sir William Temple*, ed. S. Holt Monk, Univeristy of Michigan Press, 1963.

Vincent, T., *God's Terrible Voice in the City*, 1667.

Wallington, N., Notebooks, BL Add. Ms 21935.

Ward, N., *The London Spy*, ed. K. Fenwick, 1955.

Waterhouse, E., *A short narrative of the late dreadful fire in London*, 1667.

Wilcox, C., *The Case of Charles Wilcox*, BL 816. m.9 (28)

Wren, S. (ed.), *Parentalia* . . . , Facsimile of Heirloom edn, 1965.

———, *Parentalia*, Royal Society of London, GB 117.

Wren Society, vols. 1–20.

SECONDARY SOURCES

Ackerman, J. S., *The Architecture of Michelangelo*, Penguin, 1970.

Ackroyd, P., *London: The Biography*, Chatto & Windus, 2000.

Andrews, J., A. Briggs, R. Porter, P. Tucker and K. Waddington, *The History of Bethlem*, Routledge, 1997.

Appleby, J. O., *Economic Thought and Ideology in Seventeenth-century England*, Princeton University Press, 1978.

Aries, P., *Centuries of Childhood*, Jonathan Cape, 1962.

Arneil, B., *John Locke and America: The Defence of English Colonialism*, Clarendon Press, 1996.

Ashcraft, R., *Revolutionary Politics and Locke's Two Treatise of Government*, Princeton University Press, 1986.

——— (ed.), *John Locke Critical Assessments*, 4 vols, Routledge, 1991.

Ashcraft, R. and M. Goldie, 'Locke, Revolution Principles, and the Formation of Whig Ideology', *Historical Journal*, 1983.

Ashley, M., *James II*, Dent, 1977.

Aubin, R. A., *London in Flames, London in Glory: Poems on the Fire and Rebuilding of London 1666–1709*, Rutgers Univeristy Studies in English, vol. 3, 1943.

Ballon, H., *The Paris of Henri IV: Architecture and Urbanism*, MIT Press, 1991.

Barker, F. and P. Jackson, *A History of London Maps*, Barrie & Jenkins, 1990.

Barker, T. C., *Three Hundred Years of Red Lion Square 1684–1984*, London Borough of Camden, Libraries Department, 1984.

Baron, X. (ed.), London 1066–1914, vol. 1, Helm Information, 1997.

Beard, G., *The Work of Christopher Wren*, Bartholemews, 1982.

———, *The Work of Grinling Gibbons*, John Murray, 1989.

Bedford, J., *London's Burning*, Abelard-Schuman, 1966.

Beier, A. L. and R. Finlay (eds), *London 1500–1700*, Longman, 1985.

Bell, W., *The Great Fire of London*, Bodley Head, 1923.

Ben-Chaim, M., *Experimental Philosophy and the Birth of Empirical Science: Boyle, Locke, Newton*, Ashgate, 2004.

Bennett, J. A., *The Mathematical Science of Christopher Wren*, Cambridge University Press, 1982.

Bennett, J. A., M. Cooper, M. Hunter and L. Jardine (eds), *London's Leonardo: Robert Hooke and the Seventeenth Century Scientific Revolution*, OUP, 2003.

Berlinski, D., *Newton's Gift: How Sir Isaac Newton Unlocked the System of the World*, Duckworth, 2001.

Black, J., *The British Seaborne Empire*, Yale Univeristy Press, 2004.

Blackstone, G. V., *A History of the British Fire Service*, Routledge & Kegan Paul, 1957.

Bold, J., *John Webb: Architectural Theory and Practice in the Seventeenth Century*, Clarendon Press, 1989.

———, *Greenwich: An architectural history of the Royal Hospital for Seamen and the Queen's House*, Yale University Press, 2000.

Borozdin-Bidnell, M., 'Interiors: Nicholas Barbon in Red Lion Square', *Georgian Group Journal*, Spring 2003.

Bowle, J. E., *John Evelyn and His World*, Routledge & Kegan Paul, 1981.

Brett-James, N. G., 'A Speculative London Builder of the Seventeenth Century, Dr Nicholas Barbon', *Lon. & Middlesex Arch. Soc.*, vol. VI, 1933.

———, *The Growth of Stuart London*, Allen & Unwin, 1935.

Burke, P., B. Harrison and P. Slack (eds), *Civil Histories: Essays presented to Sir Keith Thomas*, Oxford University Press, 2000.

Campbell-Culver, M. A., *A Passion for Trees: The Legacy of John Evelyn*, Eden Project Books, 2006.

Chamber, D., 'The Tomb in the Landscape: John Evelyn's Garden at Albury', *Journal of Garden History*, 1(1), 1981.

Chambers, J., *Christopher Wren*, Sutton, 1998.

Champion, J. A. I., *London's Dreadful Visitation: The Social Geography of the Great Plague of 1665*, University of London, Centre for Metropolitan Studies, 1995.

Chaney, E., *The Evolution of the Grand Tour*, Frank Cass & Co., 1998.

Chapman, A., *London's Leonardo: Robert Hooke and the Seventeenth Century Scientific Revolution*, Sutton, 2005.

Chappell, V. (ed.), *The Cambridge Companion to John Locke*, Cambridge University Press, 1994.

Charlesworth, M. (ed.), *The English Garden*, vol. 1: *Chronological Overview 1550–1730*, Helm Information, 1993.

Charlton, C., *Going to the Wars: The Experience of the British Civil Wars 1638–1651*, Routledge, 1992.

Clapham, J., *The Bank of England: A History*, 2 vols, Cambridge University Press, 1944.

Clark, Sir G., *A History of the Royal College of Physicians*, Clarendon Press, 1964.

Clark, P. (ed.), *The Cambridge Urban History of Britain*, vol II: *1540–1840*, Cambridge University Press, 2000.

Cobb, G., *The Old Churches of London*, Batsford, 1942.

Collins, H., *Edward Jerman 1605–1668: The metamorphosis of a master-craftsman*, Latterworth Press, 2004.

Colvin, H. M., *Biographical Dictionary of British Architects 1600–1840*, Yale University Press, 1971.

———, *History of Office of the King's Work*, vol. 5, HMSO, 1976.

———, *History of Office of the King's Work*, vol. 6, HMSO, 1977.

Cooper, M., *Robert Hooke and the Rebuilding of London*, Sutton, 2003.

Cooper, M. and M. Hunter (eds), *Hooke 2003: Papers presented at a conference*, Ashgate, 2006.

Cooper, N., *Houses of the Gentry 1480–1680*, Yale University Press, 1999.

Coote, S., *Royal Survivor: A Life of Charles II*, Sceptre, 1999.

Cottret, B., *The Huguenots in England, Immigration and Settlement c. 1550–1700*, Cambridge University Press, 1991.

Cowie, L., *Plague and Fire: 1665–6*, Wayland, 1970.

Cranston, M., *John Locke: A Biography*, Longmans, 1957.

Crawfurd, R., *The Last Days of Charles II*, Clarendon Press, 1909.

Cruickshanks, E. (ed.), *The Revolution of 1688–9*, John Donald, 1989.

Darley, G., *John Evelyn, Living for Ingenuity*, Yale University Press, 2006.

De Krey, G., *A Fractured Society: The politics of London in the first age of party 1688–1715*, Clarendon Press, 1985.

———, *London and the Restoration 1659–1683*, Cambridge University Press, 2005.

De la Bédoyère, G., *Particular Friends. The Correspondence of Samuel Pepys and John Evelyn*, Boydell Press, 1997.

De Mare, E., *Wren's London*, Folio Society, 1975.

Dewhurst, K., *John Locke (1632–1704) Physician and Philosopher*, Wellcome Historical Library, 1963.

Dickson, P. G. M., *The Financial Revolution in England: A Study in the Development of Public Debt 1688–1756*, Macmillan, 1969.

Dillon, P., *The Last Revolution*, Jonathan Cape, 2006.

Dixon Hunt, J. and P. Willis (eds), *The Genius of Place: The English Landscape Garden 1620–1820*, Elek, 1975.

Dorn, M. and R. Mark, 'The Architecture of Christopher Wren', *Scientific American*, vol. 245, July 1981.

Downes, K., *English Baroque Architecture*, Zwemmer, 1966.

——, *Hawksmoor*, Thames & Hudson, 1969.

——, *Christopher Wren*, Whitechapel Gallery, 1971.

——, *The Architecture of Wren*, Granada, 1982.

——, *Sir Christopher Wren: The Design of St Paul's Cathedral*, Trefoil, 1988

——, 'St Paul's and Its Architecture', *London Topographical Record,* vol. XXVIII, 2005.

Dunn, J., *The Political Thought of John Locke*, Cambridge University Press, 1969.

——, *The British Empiricists*, Oxford University Press, 1992.

Du Prey, P. de la R., *Hawksmoor's London Churches*, University of Chicago Press, 2000.

Durston, C., *The Family in the English Revolution*, Blackwell, 1989.

Dutton, R., *The Age of Wren*, Batsford, 1951.

Earle, P., *The Making of the English Middle Class: Business, Society and Family Life in London 1660–1730*, Methuen, 1989.

——, *A City Full of People: Men and Women of London 1650–1750*, Methuen, 1994.

Elmes, J., *Memoirs of the Life and Work of Sir Christopher Wren*, Priestley and Weale, 1823.

Emberton, W., *Skippon's Brave Boys: The origins, development and Civil War service of London's trained bands*, Barracuda, 1984.

Esterly, D., *Grinling Gibbons and the Art of Carving*, Victoria and Albert Museum, 1998.

Fara, P., *Newton: The Making of Genius*, Macmillan, 2002.

Farr, J. and C. Roberts, 'John Locke on the Glorious Revolution: A Rediscovered Document', *Historical Journal*, 28(2), 1985.

Field, J., *The King's Nurseries: The Story of Westminster School*, James & James, 1987.

Fraser, A., *King Charles II*, Weidenfeld & Nicolson, 1979.

Gardner, J. S., *English Ironwork of the 17th and 18th Centuries*, Tiranti, 1911.

Gauci, P., *The Politics of Trade: Overseas merchants in state and society 1660–1720*, Oxford University Press, 2001.

——, *The Emporium of the World: The London Merchant*, Continuum, 2007.

Gherarty, A., 'Nicholas Hawksmoor and the Wren City Steeples', *Georgian Group Journal*, vol. X, 2000.

Gherarty, A., 'Robert Hooke's Collection of Architectural Books and Prints', *Architectural History*, vol. 47, 2004.

Gibson, W., *The Church of England, 1688–1832*, Routledge, 2001.

Gleick, J., *Isaac Newton*, 4th Estate, 2003.

Goldie, M., 'The revolution of 1689 and the structure of political argument', *Bulletin of Research in the Humanities*, 1980.

———— (ed.), *John Locke: Selected Correspondence*, Clarendon Press, 2002.

————, 'Roger Morrice and his Entr'ing Book', *History Today*, November 2001.

————, 'John Locke: Icon of Liberty', *History Today*, October 2004.

Gould, C., *Bernini in France*, Weidenfeld & Nicolson, 1981.

Gregg, E., *Queen Anne*, Routledge & Kegan Paul, 1980.

Grell, O. P., J. I. Israel and N. Tyacke (eds), *From Persecution to Toleration: The Glorious Revolution and Religion in England*, Clarendon Press, 1991.

Gribbin, J., *Science: A history 1543–2001*, Penguin, 2002.

Gwynne, R., *Huguenot Heritage*, Routledge & Kegan Paul, 1985.

Hamilton, S., 'The Place of Sir Christopher Wren in the History of Structural Engineering', *Newcomen Society Transactions*, vol. XIV, 1933–34.

Hampson, N., *The Enlightenment: An evaluation of its assumptions, attitudes and values*, Penguin, 1990.

Hanson, N., *The Dreadful Judgement: The True Story of the Great Fire of London*, Doubleday, 2001.

Harris, F., *Transformations of Love: The friendship of John Evelyn and Margaret Godolphin*, Oxford University Press, 2002.

Harris, F. and M. Hunter (eds), *John Evelyn and his Milieu*, British Library, 2003.

Harris, I., *The Mind of John Locke*, Cambridge University Press, 1994.

Harris, T., *London Crowds in the Reign of Charles II*, Cambridge University Press, 1987.

————, *Restoration: Charles II and his Kingdoms 1660–1685*, Penguin, 2005.

————, *Revolution: The Great Crisis of the British Monarchy, 1685–1720*, Penguin, 2006.

Hart, V., *St Paul's Cathedral*, Phaidon, 1995.

Hartley, Sir H. (ed.), *The Royal Society: Its Origins and Founders*, Royal Society, 1960.

Hennessy, E., *Coffee House to Cyber Market: 200 years of the London Stock Exchange*, Ebury Press, 2000.

Hill, C., *The World Turned Upside Down: Radical Ideas during the English Revolution*, Penguin, 1972.

————, *The Experience of Defeat: Milton and some contemporaries,* Faber & Faber, 1984.

Hiscock, W. G., *John Evelyn and His Family Circle*, Routledge & Kegan Paul, 1955.

Hobhouse, H. and A. Saunders (eds), *Good and Proper Materials: The Fabric of London since the Great Fire*, London Topographical Society, 1989.

Holme, T., *Chelsea*, Hamish Hamilton, 1972.

Hopkins, A., *Italian Architecture from Michelangelo to Borromini*, Thames & Hudson, 2002.

Hoppitt, J., *A Land of Liberty? England 1689–1729*, Oxford University Press, 2000.

Horne, A., *Seven Ages of Paris*, Weidenfeld & Nicolson, 2002.

Horsefield, J. K., *British Monetary Experiments 1650–1710*, G. Bell & Sons, 1960.

Houston, R. A. and W. W. Knox (eds), *The New Penguin History of Scotland*, Penguin, 2001.

Huizinga, J. H., *Dutch Civilization in the 17th Century*, Collins, 1968.

Hunt, C., 'A Forgotten Poem by Locke', *Locke Studies*, vol. 3, 2003.

Hunt, T., *The English Civil War at First Hand*, Weidenfeld & Nicolson, 2002.

Hunter, M., *Science and Society in Restoration England*, Cambridge University Press, 1981.

——, *The Royal Society and Its Fellows 1660–1700*, British Society for the History of Science, 1982.

—— (ed.), *Robert Boyle Reconsidered*, Cambridge University Press, 1994.

——, *Science and the Shape of Orthodoxy*, Boydell Press, 1995.

Hunter, M. and S. Schaffer (eds), *Robert Hooke: New Studies*, Boydell Press, 1989.

Hutton, R., *The Restoration: A political and religious history of England and Wales 1658–1667*, Clarendon Press, 1985.

Hylson-Smith, K., *The Church in England from Elizabeth I to Elizabeth II*, SCM Press, 1997.

Inwood, S., *A History of London*, Macmillan, 1998.

——, *The Man Who Knew Too Much: The Strange and Inventive Life of Robert Hooke 1635–1703*, Macmillan, 2002.

Israel, J. (ed.), *The Rise and Greatness of the Dutch Republic*, Clarendon Press, 1995.

——, *Radical Enlightenment: Philosophy and the Making of Modernity*, Oxford University Press, 2001.

——, *Enlightenment Contested: Philosophy, Modernity and the Emancipation of Man 1670–1752*, Oxford University Press, 2006.

Jardine, L., *On a Grander Scale: The Outstanding Career of Sir Christoper Wren*, HarperCollins, 2002.

——, *The Curious Life of Robert Hooke: The Man Who Measured London*, HarperCollins, 2003.

Jeffreys, M. V. C., *John Locke, Prophet of Common Sense*, Methuen, 1967.

Keane, D., A. Burns and A. Saint (eds), *St Paul's: Cathedral Church of London*, Yale University Press, 2004.

Kent, P. and A. Chapman (eds), *Robert Hooke and the English Renaissance*, Gracewing, 2005.

Kenyon, J., *The Popish Plot*, Phoenix, 1972.

———, *Revolution Principles*, Cambridge University Press, 1977.

Keynes, Sir G., *John Evelyn: A Study and a Bibliography*, Clarendon Press, 1968.

King, R., *Brunelleschi's Dome: The story of the great cathedral in Florence*, Pimlico, 2000.

Kishlansky, M., *A Monarchy Transformed: Britain 1603–1714*, Penguin, 1996.

Knights, M., *Politics and Opinion in Crisis, 1678–81*, Cambridge University Press, 1994.

———, *Representation and Misrepresentation in Later Stuart Politics*, Oxford University Press, 2005.

Lane, J., *Puritan, Rake and Squire*, Evans Brothers, 1950.

Lang, J., *Rebuilding St Paul's after the Great Fire of London*, Oxford University Press, 1956.

Leapman, M., *Inigo Jones*, Hodder Review, 2003.

Leasor, J., *The Plague and the Fire*, Allen & Unwin, 1962.

Lehmann, J. F., *Holborn*, Macmillan, 1970.

Leith-Ross, P., 'The Gardens of John Evelyn at Deptford', *Journal of Garden History*, 25(2), 2005.

———, 'A Seventeenth-Century Paris Garden', *Journal of Garden History*, 22(2), 2002.

———, 'Fruit planted around a new bowling green at John Evelyn's Garden at Sayes Court, Deptford, Kent'. *Journal of Garden History*, 2006.

Letwin, W., *The Origins of Scientific Economics*, Methuen, 1963.

Levin, J., *The Charter Controversy in the City of London 1660–1688, and Its Consequences*, Athlone Press, 1969.

Levine, J., *The Battle of the Books*, Cornell University Press, 1991.

———, *Between the Ancients and the Moderns: Baroque Culture in Restoration England*, Yale University Press, 1999.

Li, M.-H., *The Great Recoinage of 1696 to 1699*, Weidenfeld & Nicolson, 1963.

Lillywhite, B., *London Coffee Houses*, Allen & Unwin, 1963.

Lindley, K., *Popular Politics and Religion in Civil War London*, Scolar Press, 1997.

Lindsay, J., *The Monster City: Defoe's London 1688–1730*, Hart-Davis, MacGibbon, 1978.

Lindsey, J., *Wren: His Work and Times*, Rich & Cowan, 1951.

Lubbock, J., *The Tyranny of Taste: The Politics of Architecture and Design in Britain 1550–1969*, Yale University Press, 1995.

Luu, L. B., *Immigrants and the Industries of London, 1500–1700*, Sussex Academic Press, 2005.

MacCulloch, J. R. A. (ed.), *A Select Collection of Scarce and Valuable Tracts on Commerce*, London, 1850.

MacDonald Sinclair, W., *Memorials of St Paul's Cathedral*, Chapman & Hall, 1909.

McInnes, A., 'When was the English Revolution?', *History*, October 1982.

McKellar, E., *The Birth of Modern London: The development and design of the city 1660–1720*, Manchester University Press, 1999.

McMahon, D., *The Pursuit of Happiness: A History from the Greeks to the Present*, Allen Lane, 2006.

Magnusson, M., *Scotland, the Story of a Nation*, HarperCollins, 2000.

Matthews, W. R. and W. M. Atkins, *A History of St Paul's Cathedral and the Men Associated with It*, Phoenix House, 1957.

Maynard Smith, H., *The Early Life and Education of John Evelyn: 1620–41*, Clarendon Press, 1920.

Merritt, J. F. (ed.), *Imagining Early Modern London: Perspectives and Portrayals of the City from Stow to Strype 1598–1720*, Cambridge University Press, 2001.

Miller, J., *Seeds of Liberty: 1688 and the Shaping of Modern Britain*, Souvenir Press, 1988.

Milne, G., *The Great Fire of London*, Historical Publications, 1986.

Milton, J. R., 'John Locke and the Fundamental Constitutions of Carolina', *Locke Studies*, no. 21, 1990.

——, 'Locke's Pupils', *Locke Studies*, no. 26, 1995.

Mitchell, R. J. and M. D. R. Leys, *A History of London Life*, Longman, 1963.

Moote, A. and D. Moote, *The Great Plague: The Story of London's Most Deadly Year*, Johns Hopkins University Press, 2004.

Morrill, J. (ed.), *The Impact of the English Civil War*, Collins & Brown, 1991.

Mowl, T., *Gentlemen and Players: Gardeners of the English Landscape*, Sutton, 2000.

Nichols, R., *The Diaries of Robert Hooke, the Leonardo of London 1635–1703*, Book Guild, 1994.

Ochs, K., 'History of Trades', *Notes and Records of the Royal Society*, 39, 1984/85.

O'Malley, T. and J. Wolschke-Bulmahn (eds), *John Evelyn's Elysium Britannicum and European Gardening*, Dumbarton Oaks Research Library, 1998.

Pearce, D., *London's Mansions: The Palatial Houses of the Nobility*, Batsford, 1986.

Pearl, V., *London and the Outbreak of the Puritan Revolution 1625–43*, Oxford University Press, 1961.

Pevsner, N., *An Outline of European Architecture*, Penguin, 1960.

Pevsner, N. and S. Bradley, *London: The City Churches*, Yale University Press, 1998.

——, *London 1: The City of London*, Yale University Press, 1997.

Pevsner, N. and B. Cherry, *London 4: North*, Yale University Press, 1998.

Picard, L., *Restoration London*, Weidenfeld & Nicolson, 1997.

Pincus, S. C. A., *England's Glorious Revolution, 1688–89: A brief history with documents*, St Martin's Press, 2006.

Plumley, N. and A. Niland, *A History of the Organs in St Paul's Cathedral*, Positif, 2001.

Ponsonby, A., *John Evelyn*, Heinemann, 1933.

Porter, R., *London: A Social History*, Penguin, 1994.

———, *Enlightenment: Britain and the Creation of the Modern World*, Penguin, 2000.

Porter, S. (ed.), *London and the Civil War*, Macmillan, 1996.

Price, J. L., *Culture and Society: The Dutch Republic in the Seventeenth Century*, Batsford, 1974.

Purkiss, D., *The English Civil War*, HarperCollins, 2006.

Purver, M., *The Royal Society: Conception and Creation*, Routledge & Kegan Paul, 1967.

Quarrell, W. H. and M. Mare (eds), *London in 1710, from the Travels of Zacharias Conrad von Uffenbach*, Faber & Faber, 1934.

Quest-Ritson, R., *The English Garden: A Social History*, Viking, 2001.

Rabb, T., *The End of the Renaissance and the March of Modernity*, Basic Books, 2006.

Ranum, O., *Paris in the Age of Absolutism*, Pennsylvania University Press, 2002.

Rasmussen, S. E., *Experiencing Architecture*, Chapman & Hall, 1959.

———, *London: The Unique City* (revised edn), Penguin, 1982.

Reader, J., *Cities*, Heinemann, 2004.

Reddaway, T. F., *The Rebuilding of London after the Great Fire*, Jonathan Cape, 1940.

Royle, T., *Civil War: The Wars of the Three Kingdoms 1638–1660*, Little, Brown, 2004.

Saunders, A. (ed.), *The Royal Exchange*, London Topographical Society, 1997.

———, *St Paul's: The Story of the Cathedral*, Collins & Brown, 2001.

Schama, S., *The Embarrassment of Riches: An Interpretation of Dutch Culture in the Golden Age*, HarperCollins, 1987.

Schwoerer, L., *The Declaration of Rights, 1689*, Johns Hopkins University Press, 1981.

——— (ed.), *The Revolution of 1688–89: Changing Perspectives*, Cambridge University Press, 1992.

Scott, E., *The King in Exile: The wanderings of Charles II from June 1646 to July 1654*, Constable, 1904.

Scott, J., *England's Troubles: Seventeenth Century English Political Instability in European Context*, Cambridge University Press, 2000.

Scouloudi, I. (ed.), *Huguenots in Britain and Their French Background, 1550–1800*, Macmillan, 1987.

Seaver, P., *Wallington's World: A Puritan Artisan in Seventeenth Century London*, Methuen, 1985.

Sekler, E. F., *Wren and His Place in European Architecture*, Faber & Faber, 1956.

Sennett, R., *The Conscience of the Eye: The Design and Social Life of Cities*, Faber & Faber, 1990.

Sennett, R., *Flesh and Stone: The Body and the City in Western Civilization*, Faber & Faber, 1994.

Shapin, S., *A Social History of Truth*, University of Chicago Press, 1994.

——, *The Scientific Revolution*, University of Chicago Press, 1996.

Shapiro, B., *John Wilkins 1614–1672: An Intellectual Biography*, University of California Press, 1969.

Sheppard, F., *London: A History*, Oxford University Press, 1998.

Shoemaker, R., *The London Mob: Violence and Disorder in 18th Century England*, Hambledon & London, 2004.

Smith, G., *The Cavaliers in Exile, 1640–1660*, Palgrave Macmillan, 2003.

Soo, L., *Wren's Tracts on Architecture and Other Writings*, Cambridge University Press, 1998.

Spence, C., *London in the 1690s: A Social Atlas*, University of London, Centre for Metropolitan Research, 2000.

Spurr, J., *England in the 1670s: 'This Masquerading Age'*, Blackwells, 2000.

Stewart, L., *The Rise of Public Science: Rhetoric, Technology and Natural Philosophy in Newtonian Britain 1660–1750*, Cambridge University Press, 1992.

Stoye, J., *English Travellers Abroad: 1604–1667*, Yale University Press, 1989.

Stroud, A., *Stuart England*, Routledge, 1999.

Stuart, M. A., 'Locke's Professional Contacts with Robert Boyle', *Locke Newsletter*, no. 12, 1981.

Summerson, Sir J., *Architecture in Britain 1530 to 1830*, Penguin, 1963.

——, *The Classical Language of Architecture*, Yale University Press, 1964.

——, *Inigo Jones*, Penguin, 1966.

——, *Georgian London*, Yale University Press, 2003.

Survey of London, vol. 27: *Spitalfields*, University of London for London County Council, 1957.

——, vol. 29: *St James's, Westminster*, part 1, University of London for London County Council, 1960.

——, vol. 32: *St James's, Westminster*, part 2, University of London for London County Council, 1960.

——, vol. 33: *St Anne's, Soho*, part 1, University of London for London County Council. 1966.

——, vol. 34: *St Anne's, Soho*, part 2, University of London for London County Council, 1966.

Tames, R., *Bloomsbury Past*, Historical Publications, 1993.

Tarlton, C., 'The Rulers Now on Earth: Locke's "Two Treatise" and the Revolution of 1888', *Historical Journal*, 28(2), 1985.

Thorgood, P., *The London Rich: The Creation of a Great City from 1666 to the Present*, Penguin, 2000.

Thurley, S., *The Lost Palace of Whitehall*, RIBA, 1998.

Thurley, S., *Whitehall Palace: An Architectural History of the Royal Apartments*, Yale University Press, 1999.

———, *Hampton Court: A Social and Architectural History*, Yale University Press, 2003.

Tinniswood, A., *His Imagination So Fertile: A Life of Christopher Wren*, Jonathan Cape, 2001.

———, *By Permission of Heaven: The Story of the Great Fire of London*, Jonathan Cape, 2003.

Tomalin, C., *Samuel Pepys: An Unequal Self*, Penguin, 2002.

Trevor, M., *The Shadow of a Crown: The Life Story of James II of England and VII of Scotland*, Constable, 1988.

Turnbull, H. W. (ed.), *Isaac Newton's Correspondence*, vol. 2, Cambridge University Press, 1960.

Tyacke, N. (ed.), *The History of Oxford University*, vol. IV: *Seventeenth-century Oxford*, Clarendon Press, 1997.

Uglow, J., *A Little History of English Gardening*, Chatto & Windus, 2004.

Underdown, D., *Royalist Conspiracies in England 1649–1660*, Yale University Press, 1960.

———, *Somerset in the Civil War and Interregnum*, David & Charles, 1973.

Valliance, E., *The Glorious Revolution: 1688 – England's Battle for Liberty*, Little, Brown, 2006.

Van der Kiste, J., *William and Mary*, Sutton, 2003.

Van der Zee, H. and B., *William and Mary*, Macmillan, 1973.

———, *1688: Revolution in the Family*, Viking, 1988.

Vickers, D., *Studies in the Theory of Money 1690–1776*, Peter Owen, 1960.

Von Leyden, W. (ed.), *John Locke: Essays on the Law of Nature*, Clarendon Press, 1954.

Waldron, J., *God, Locke and Equality*, Cambridge University Press, 2002.

Waller, M., *1700: Scenes from London Life*, Sceptre, 2000.

———, *Ungrateful Daughters: The Stuart princesses who stole their father's crown*, Sceptre, 2002.

Walsh, J., C. Haydon and S. Taylor (eds), *The Church of England c.1689–c.1833*, Cambridge University Press, 1993.

Webster, C., *The Great Instauration: Science, medicine and reform 1626–1660*, Duckworth, 1975.

Weinstein, H., 'The Paper Wars of the 1640s', *BBC History*, February 2005.

Weiser, B., *Charles II and the Politics of Access*, Boydell Press, 2003.

Westfall, R., *Never at Rest: A Biography of Isaac Newton*, Cambridge University Press, 1980.

———, *The Life of Isaac Newton*, Cambridge University Press, 1993.

Whinney, M., *Wren*, Thames & Hudson, 1971.

Whitaker, K., *Mad Madge: Margaret Cavendish, Duchess of Newcastle, Royalist, Writer and Romantic*, Vintage, 2002.

Woolf, V., *The Common Reader*, Hogarth Press, 1925.

Woolhouse, R., 'Lady Masham's Account of Locke', *Locke Studies*, vol. 3, 2003.

Woolley, B., *The Herbalist: Nicholas Culpeper and the Fight for Medical Reform*, HarperCollins, 2004.

Worsley, G., *Classical Architecture in Britain: The Heroic Age*, Yale University Press, 1994.

———, 'Taking Hooke Seriously', *Georgian Group Journal*, vol. XIV, 2004.

———, *Inigo Jones and the Classical European Tradition*, Yale University Press, 2006.

Yolton, J., *Locke and the Way of Ideas*, Oxford University Press, 1956.

———, *A Locke Dictionary*, Blackwells, 1993.

Zimmer, C., *Soul Made Flesh: Thomas Willis, the English Civil War and the Mapping of the Mind*, Heinemann, 2004.

ACKNOWLEDGEMENTS

Many people may think that writing a book was a solitary pursuit, hunting down sources through dusty shelves and looking at the blank computer screen for hours on end. Nothing could be less true. The writing of *The Phoenix* has been a collaboration between many different people. There are many to thank as a result.

Firstly, the librarians and archivists who are the custodians of the nation's heritage and are too often underappreciated. As our public libraries are attacked by budget cuts and are forced to redevelop as 'idea centres', their role as repositories of our history is being sidelined. This book would not have been possible without the many archives around London, including the British Library, the London Library, the National Archives, the Royal Society and the Guildhall Library. Whether we will be forced to pay to continue to use these valuable resources, I don't know. What is important is that they must remain alive and accessible. The continued investment in our shared history will always produce a profit.

To all the people that have helped me with the writing and publication of the book, I owe a huge debt. From the very first idea to the finished book the advice and expertise of others have vastly improved the work: my agent, Patrick Walsh, at Conville & Walsh; Helen Garnons-Williams, Bea Hemming and Kelly Falconer at Weidenfeld & Nicolson; George Gibson and Jacqueline Jackson at Walker. Also, my copy editor, Ian Paten; Jessica Mead, Alan Samson, Katie Hambly and the sales team.

The book also became part of the family, and the support at home and of friends was invaluable. Rose, Louis and Theodora; Mum and Ed; Emma and Tim. The book is dedicated to Nigel and Michael, my father and my father-in-law, both of whom died too young. There is something of their loss within the telling of this story.

INDEX

Page numbers in *italic* indicate illustrations and captions